A Jackpo

Gambling is fun. Losin~~g~~ and expanded edition of *The Winner's Gambling*, you get more vital tactics, tips, and professional secrets to give you an even sharper winning edge at . . .

Blackjack—new card-counting principles to beat the odds

Craps—the best plays and bets to make

Roulette—how to avoid the "sure thing" system that's bound to lead you into bankruptcy

Baccarat—the mathematics and winning systems, including mini-baccarat, *chemin de fer*, and *baccarat en banque*

Let It Ride® and **Caribbean Stud Poker**—a full analysis of these exciting new games

The Slots—find out which machines are due for a jackpot

Video Poker—successful strategies and tips on which progressive machines to play

And much more!

THE WINNER'S GUIDE TO CASINO GAMBLING

THIRD EDITION

Edwin Silberstang

A SIGNET BOOK

*This book is dedicated
to the memory of
Louis Silberstang.
He was a gentle man,
but a tough player.*

SIGNET
Published by the Penguin Group
Penguin Putnam Inc., 375 Hudson Street, New York, New York 10014, U.S.A.
Penguin Books Ltd, 27 Wrights Lane, London W8 5TZ, England
Penguin Books Australia Ltd, Ringwood, Victoria, Australia
Penguin Books Canada Ltd, 10 Alcorn Avenue, Toronto, Ontario, Canada M4V 3B2
Penguin Books (N.Z.) Ltd, 182–190 Wairau Road, Auckland 10, New Zealand

Penguin Books Ltd, Registered Offices: Harmondsworth, Middlesex, England

Published by Signet, an imprint of Dutton NAL,
a member of Penguin Putnam Inc.
Also published in a Plume edition.

First Signet Printing, October, 1998
10 9 8 7

 REGISTERED TRADEMARK—MARCA REGISTRADA

Printed in the United States of America

Contents

Introduction

Since the last revision of this book, gambling has exploded as a growth industry in America. Nearly all the states have gambling in one form or another, and many states now permit gaming on riverboats and casinos. Gambling also is booming on Native American reservations. I cover this phenomenon in detail in my chapter entitled Gambling in America—An Overview.

With riverboat gaming, I go state by state in showing what is available, and in some states, county by county and town by town, so the reader has a full picture of what is happening, which boats sail and which stay docked. I discuss the games offered on the riverboats, the betting and loss limits, if any, and the boarding fees, if any. I also cover the laws that affect this type of gambling, state by state. In order to get this information, I spoke directly with the gaming commission representatives of a number of states.

With tribal land gaming, I give a broad overview of how this form of gambling began, and what it means for the future. The casinos and games offered vary from state to state, and the situation is quite dynamic, with more and more Native American casinos coming on line. I discuss what the giant Foxwoods Casino in Ledyard, Connecticut, offers, as well as the smaller casinos in states like Minnesota and Oklahoma.

I also have a special section on the new atmosphere in Las Vegas, which has become the family resort destination for many Americans. I describe the new casinos that have been built and the ones that are to be built, with a brief description of my own feelings about them.

The chapter entitled Keno—The Imported Game has been enlarged to include state keno games, which are rapidly growing in popularity. At the time of writing eight states have introduced the game, with others expected to follow. I point out the differences between the state game and the casino game, and list representative payouts. I also suggest which games to avoid playing.

I've not only enlarged and added chapters, I show you how the pros play, conducting interviews with gamblers who always are looking for that extra edge, and revealing how their minds work so that you can get that edge. In addition, I show how I've played in certain situations, for I believe a reader can learn a great deal from proper play. I never play hunches and I always try to make the right play. I want to be a winner, for winning is fun. It's the ultimate enjoyment one gets out of gambling. Let's all be winners.

In this book the reader will get a rundown of all the casino games worth playing, plus the odds inherent in these games —whether those odds are neutral, favor the house, or favor the bettor. Obviously, the casino sets up most of its games to get an edge over the player. However, this doesn't mean that the player can't work out an intelligent method of play so that the edge can be neutralized. We show how this can be done in craps, for example, where the best bets and best play can lead to awesome wins.

Again, I want the reader to be a winner. That's the main purpose of this book. And anyone who studies the strategies, theories of play, and winning approaches I suggest, and then plays according to these precepts, should be a winner.

Also included is a section on proper money management. This can be just as important as correct play. I have been very careful in formulating the way players should handle their money at the table. As a result, not only have my readers prospered, but I have been quoted as the ultimate authority on money management in other books. This is because my approach is always pragmatic. I've been there. I've put out my chips. And I have seen, through years of experience, just how treacherous a random approach to gambling can be, either in terms of play or money management.

I know there are other gambling books on the market, but I feel that they present only a narrow picture of the games themselves, and are defensive in tone. And more important, they don't really discuss the psychology of the gambler and the actual conditions he or she finds when betting with hard cash at a casino table.

Knowing the rules and strategies of the games themselves is not sufficient. To enable players to take advantage of everything a casino offers, this book gives them a complete picture of what the casino is all about, describing the men and women who run it—the people who staff and service the games and with whom players will come in contact. Sometimes the difference between being a winner and a loser is how the casino personnel are handled by the player. The price of the book can easily be recouped by following the hints on how to get free meals, drinks, and even shows out of those same casino personnel.

Most gamblers, I know from experience, bring cash to the casinos when it is unnecessary to do so. Therefore, I go into detail not only on how to play the games correctly, but on how to establish credit at casinos and use that credit in the most effective manner possible.

A full chapter is devoted to casino credit and another to preferred treatment of gamblers. I show how players are rated, and how they can qualify for everything from a free meal to full RFB; that is, room, food, and beverages. Players may also be eligible to get their air fare reimbursed if they play at a high enough level. I show the pros and cons of getting "comped," and the correct way to pick a hotel and casino. Most players don't realize that their play can be monitored just by asking a floorman, who will make sure they're eligible for a free meal, a show, or a reduced room rate. I discuss all these things at length.

I also discuss the use of casino membership cards offered by practically all casinos, and why these are valuable to the players of electronic games. I show how to get these cards and how to make the best use of them. These cards can be valuable tools in the player's hands, and may qualify a player for reduced room rates and other benefits.

I've also included two new games in this book. *Caribbean Poker* and *Let It Ride* have become popular in recent years, and are now available as table games in many casinos. I discuss the odds inherent in these games, the best playing strategies, and analyze the big payouts and when they are worth going after.

All of these new chapters and sections bring the book right up to date. They give an overview of the new look of gambling in America, and provide the reader with all the information he or she needs to deal with the new games. I've covered gaming from coast to coast, from the riverboats rolling down the great rivers of the USA to the small gaming towns in the Plains States, from the giant Native American casino in Ledyard, Connecticut, to the small tribal clubs in the Southwest. It's all here for the reader.

1

Gambling in America— An Overview

At one time, the only state in America where gambling was legal was Nevada. This situation remained in effect for many years, and although there was sporadic gambling in other jurisdictions, such as the draw poker clubs in California and lotteries in certain states, it wasn't until Atlantic City legalized gambling that Nevada had any competition in the way of full-fledged casinos offering games such as craps, blackjack, roulette and baccarat, as well as slot machines. One of the rationales for legalizing gambling in Atlantic City was to use the tax money engendered from gambling to improve the city.

But that didn't happen. The millions of dollars spent in the casinos, or should I say, billions, didn't improve the city one whit. While the number of pleasure palaces of gambling rose, Atlantic City remained a festering slum. As it is today. The tourists go to the casinos and occasionally walk on the boardwalk, but they don't venture into Atlantic City proper. Still, there were mighty revenues that could be taxed by the municipality, and other jurisdictions took note of the frantic pace of building and the millions of tourists who poured into the New Jersey resort.

After all, the leaders of these states and cities argued, everyone likes to gamble, and they do gamble illegally. So why not legalize it and cash in on these millions of dollars? The floodgate was opened, and gambling, which in puritan America had remained a hidden and illegal vice, was now thrust into the open in state after state. The money it poured into state and municipal coffers was used for a variety of causes, including education. With that rationalization, the state governments could pat themselves on their backs and overlook the fact that these millions of dollars were dollars lost to the casinos or to lotteries or whatever gambling was legalized. Someone was paying for all this, and it was the general public who patronized the casinos or bought lottery tickets. or sat down to a game of cards at a legalized card club.

Let us therefore divide this chapter into several sections dealing with the burgeoning world of American gambling. First, the status of gambling in general. Secondly, the state lotteries. Thirdly, the American Indian reservation gambling. Then riverboat gambling. Finally, the changing character of Las Vegas itself.

Gambling in General in America

At the present time, there is some form of gambling, whether it be lotteries, Indian reservation gaming, riverboats or card clubs, or straight casino gambling, in forty-eight of the fifty states. Perhaps all the states eventually will have gambling; all signs point to this happening. What at one time caused moral indignation is now a commonplace. People are willing to wager money on some form of gaming, and the states and municipalities, hungry and desperate for infusions of tax money, are willing to provide their citizens with the opportunity.

Nevada is still the leading state as far as gaming is concerned. You can wager on anything here, but the state doesn't have a lottery. It doesn't need one. Games such as Quartermania and Megabucks provide the players with opportunities to make millions by risking several coins or dollars.

Atlantic City, New Jersey, when it first legalized gambling, was thought of as a serious competitor to Nevada, especially Las Vegas, but since gambling has been introduced in the Garden State, Nevada has experienced an explosive growth in gaming. Atlantic City is an example of a community which hasn't benefited at all from gambling. The influx of customers has merely lined the pockets of the casino owners who put up sumptuous palaces to attract them. Still, more casinos are going up, and business continues to increase in A.C. A lot of jobs have been created, but the city is still a slum, and the tourists stay in the hotels or venture along the boardwalk, and that is it.

Mississippi, with its liberal riverboat laws, has moved into prominence in American gambling. It now ranks third in revenues, an amazing situation for a conservative, rural, and Bible Belt state. Other states along the Mississippi and Great Lakes have jumped into riverboat gaming with both feet—for example, Missouri, Iowa, Indiana, and Illinois. The heartland of America has embraced legalized gaming in a big way.

Washington State and Colorado haven't been shy about making various forms of gambling available. Montana has legalized certain table games. A backwater like Deadwood, South Dakota, has brought itself national attention by legalizing gambling, and in the process, pushed real estate values to the sky in that small, isolated community. Gambling does that. Towns magically rise up when gambling becomes big business. A good example of this is in Laughlin, Nevada, where Mr. Laughlin named a city after himself and built a casino on the Colorado River. In the space of a few years, this has become one of the meccas of gambling in Nevada.

Indian reservation gaming, emboldened by the Indian Gaming Regulatory Act of 1988, has been involved in an explosion of gaming, with more on the way. The Native Americans are pushing in all directions. A successful operation such as Foxwoods in Connecticut is spawning other casinos in the Nutmeg State, with Greenwich the next possibility. State legislatures are falling all over themselves to get on the gaming bandwagon.

Usually, a referendum is needed to promote gaming. It can be done statewide, as in Florida, or county by county, as in Mississippi. Even though an initiative failed a few years ago in Florida, the big money casinos can raise, along with their promise of future profits, mean that the push to legalize gaming will be on again in the Sunshine State. New York, which for years flirted with legalized gaming in Sullivan County, may now allow gaming in the empty shells of hotels in Monticello, New York, which once was a resort hub.

The big cities of America, such as Chicago and Miami, to name just a couple, are ripe for legalized gambling. The push is on all over the map to legalize gaming in major cities, which can easily support it with their huge population centers. I feel that this will happen in the next decade. The momentum is building, and the irresistible lure of gaming will win the hearts of legislators and citizens in more and more communities.

It is not only the casinos that benefit from legalized gaming. A whole support industry has sprung up to feed their insatiable needs. Riverboat design and manufacture, once a moribund industry that had seen its best days in the nineteenth century, is now alive and perking. Manufacturers of equipment such as electronic games are also benefitting, the two leaders being International Game Technology and Bally's Manufacturing.

Surveillance equipment manufacturers, change-maker manufacturers, interior designers, lighting and carpeting specialists, card manufacturers, dice and chip manufacturers, are all grabbing a piece of the pie. And let's not forget the makers of roulette wheels and craps and blackjack tables. At the gaming conventions in Las Vegas, we see a whole corporate structure offering its goods and services. They realize that this is an explosive growth industry just waiting to take off.

Whole industries have sprung up or been invented to feed the casinos. And then there are the employees of the casinos, thousands and thousands of them, getting jobs that previously didn't exist. Dealers, change persons, cocktail waitresses, waiters, busboys, floorpersons, pit bosses, hotel clerks, maids, and dozens of other job categories are there to service gamblers while they play or rest. The list goes on and on.

What is obvious is the fact that people want to gamble. No one has to throw a net out to pull in players—they are there clogging the casino aisles. When the first casino, Resorts International, opened in Atlantic City, there were huge lines of gamblers waiting to get in, then waits of an hour or more to get to the tables. Players came in droves and couldn't wait to get their money on the tables. As the riverboat operators have found out, their customers will pay for the right to gamble on a cruise. If there was no gambling on these riverboats, who would go on them but for a few tourists wishing to look at scenery on the Mississippi? It is the same question one can ask about racetracks. Who would pay admission to watch horses run ten races, if no betting was allowed? The crowd would probably number about a hundred, most of them owners of horses.

Legislators also realize that the taxes they take in from gaming is a hidden revenue. People who lose don't think of their money going towards taxes. They win or they lose. But tax these same individuals for purchases they make at the grocery store and there'd be hell to pay. After all, the solons state, the citizens want to gamble, and we're simply providing the means. Nobody gets hurt, and everybody benefits. And gambling fever spreads in America, and the crowds get bigger and bigger, and the casinos grander and grander. It's the new American growth industry, and it will continue to grow and grow.

What I suggest is that this new horde of unsophisticated gamblers learn to play correctly, that they not go into a casino figuring that they will lose money. We want them to go in and play with a winning attitude. Each game has certain odds built into it, and gamblers should learn the correct odds, which games to avoid and which to play, and how to make the best bets. Gambling, after all, is done with real money, and real money is lost. What I attempt to do in this book is protect players by showing them how to gamble in a sane and knowledgeable manner, so that they become winners. There is an enormous choice out there, and many temptations. I want my readers to end up as winners.

The Lotteries

At one time, in America, lotteries were rampant in all the big cities where the Mafia held sway. The lotteries were known as the "Italian Lottery" or given other names, such as the "numbers racket." They were particularly popular among the poorest sections of the population, African-Americans and the working poor, for the lottery promised a big jolt of money for a minuscule investment—as little as a nickel. The payoff for the lotteries was generally 500–1. In order to win, a player had to pick three numbers out of 999. If the number came up, you got paid 500–1. On any given day, you could play the lottery. Let's assume you picked 764. The odds against this number coming up were 999–1, because the number 000 was a live one as well. You got 500–1 if you won. This meant that the operator of the lottery was working close to a 50 percent profit margin.

How did you know if you had a winner? Many of the lotteries were tied to a series of numbers. For example, if there was a racetrack nearby whose total tote or complete betting revenue was listed in a newspaper, then the last three digits of that revenue was the number for the day. Let's assume that Belmont track in Elmont, New York, was in operation. And let's assume that at the end of the eight or nine races in those days the total tote shown after the last race was the complete monies bet that day and was $2,544,701. Then 701 was the number for that day, and anyone betting it would win 500–1.

These lotteries ran deep into the hearts of the various poorer communities. They not only gave the occasional winner some quick money, but supported a whole network of working poor—people who were runners, and those who worked in offices run by the local syndicate, which was eventually beholden to the Italian Mafia. It was a sweet deal for the Mafia. Their profit margin was immense, and as long as all kinds of numbers were bet, they stood to make a gigantic profit. They would sweat out certain days such as July 4, when a lot of people patriotically bet 776 as in 1776, but other than those situations, the money poured in. As talk in the state capitals turned to legalized lotteries, the Mafia saw their income threatened.

Eventually, the states began their own lottery systems. These weren't the nickel-and-dime operations of the illegal syndicates; no longer could you bet just five or ten cents as in the old days. Inflation and the very pragmatic considerations of income forbade that. The minimum bet was $1, and payoffs of more than 500–1 were promised. Now that dollar ticket could win a lucky holder millions of dollars. And no longer did he or she have to select just three numbers—the new norm was six numbers. Pick all six and win the big jackpot, which could be upwards of ten million dollars! Now we were talking big bucks.

To make sure that everyone could make a bet, the lottery commissions didn't limit the lottery to just a pick of six numbers out of 49 or more possibilities. They allowed pick 3s, with the old Mafia 500–1 payout. They also had pick 5s and all kinds of daily picks. Anything to fill the coffers and get the money out of the hands of the taxpayers, or perhaps the non-taxpayers, for these lotteries were attracting people who were willing to part with their money at horrendous odds in the hope of getting a big payout. The poor were once more heavily involved, and state government leaders told the public in self-aggrandizing ways that the new lotteries were there to promote education, because after all the expenses were deducted, the money left over would improve the schools in the state.

Not only was there a lottery involving three, four, five, or six numbers, with different payouts, some gigantic, some merely $500, but scratch-off tickets. And you didn't need to read the paper or watch television to see if you had won—you just scratched off the numbers and presto, you won or lost. You could win up to $10,000 on these scratch-offs instantly. Most of the time, you lost, or if you won, your win was $1 or a free ticket. But like all gambling, the sense of the unknown possibilities was enticing. The numbers or whatever you scratched off on your next ticket could be the big winner. I recall going to a party at a millionaire's house in the Malibu Colony of Los Angeles, and after the food and the wine and the music, he gave each of the hundred or so guests ten scratch-off tickets as a farewell gift. We all got busy scratching away to see what lay under the print and the paint, to see what we had won. I was one of the lucky ones. I won $1. Of the thousand tickets scratched by the guests, the total winnings were $180, including twelve tickets which gave the recipients a free ticket.

At that party there were people in the movie business, doctors, lawyers, and other professionals, and it was amazing to me to see the rapacity of their efforts to produce a winner by scratching the tickets. Yes, gambling has a hold on people. The possibility of a big score enticed them, though I'm sure that only one or two would ever bother to buy scratch-off tickets. But imagine all the poor laborers who buy five of these tickets daily. After a year, a lot of money that should have gone toward the rent, or toward food or clothing for their kids, has gone down the drain.

Lotteries, however, are here to stay. A great many states have them, and each year, more and more come on board. The states are starved for revenue, and lotteries are their quickest source of money. If legislators raise taxes, they run the risk of being voted out of office, but if they introduce a lottery and mumble something about improving education, they're heroes.

The following states now have lotteries: Arkansas, California, Colorado, Florida, Illinois, Indiana, Kansas, Minnesota, Missouri, Montana, New Jersey, New York, North Dakota, Ohio, Oklahoma, Rhode Island, South Carolina, South Dakota, Tennessee, Texas, Virginia, Washington, D.C., and West Virginia, and the roll call goes on. This isn't meant to be a complete list. It just shows that no region of the country is immune from this form of gambling.

Generally, for the super lotteries, where millions of dollars are payable to a single holder, six numbers have to be selected from 49 or more numbers. In California there are 51 numbers on the sheet, with odds upwards of 20 million to one against picking all six numbers. Again, the enticement is the huge payout. If a person picks all six numbers, the payout is in the millions; five numbers picked will pay only about $1,800 and it goes down rapidly from there, with someone who picks only three numbers getting a paltry $5.

In California, to continue the example, the lottery, called Super Lotto, is played twice a week, with the selections coming on Wednesday and Saturday evenings at 8 P.M. It starts at $3 million. If no one has the big winner, the next payout is about $7 million, then $12 million, then about $20 million. At this point the odds are still higher against winning than the payout, but if the $20 million jackpot isn't won, it escalates to the mid-$30 millions, and "lotto fever" overtakes the citizens of the Golden State.

Everybody gets involved, and people who wouldn't usually waste their money now start buying blocks of tickets. The poor can use up two weeks' salary praying and hoping for that big score—$30 million! Paid over twenty years, that comes to $1.5 million a year. This is cut down by federal taxes, but there are no state taxes on the winnings.

The really gigantic payouts are in the Midwest, where there is a "power ball" lottery tied to seven midwestern states. In addition to the six numbers, another number, the "powerball," must be selected. The odds against this happening are enormous, so the payouts escalate even more rapidly. They can come to more than $100 million, all to one lucky ticket holder!

Lotteries have become a part of the American landscape, and millions tune in to the results when they are announced on television. In California, some scratch-off prizes allow the winners to go to *The Big Spin*, where they spin a huge wheel to win prizes of a million dollars or more. This is a regular half-hour program on channels throughout California.

Should you play the lottery? The big prizes, running into the millions of dollars, look awfully enticing, and of course, there are winners. But for the millions who buy lottery tickets in the hope of becoming millionaires, only a few, a handful, ever win. As one wit said succinctly, "You have the same chance of winning a lottery whether you play or don't." That sums up my feeling about lotteries.

As to scratch-offs for smaller prizes, and the daily picks of three or five numbers, the house, in this case, the state, takes as its cut about 50 percent of the revenues. It's a losing proposition for any player. It's like being at a blackjack table and betting $10, only to get back $5 for each win, while you take the full $10 loss. How long could you last before going broke? My best advice is to avoid any kind of state-run enterprise in gambling, such as lotteries, scratch-off tickets, or whatever other gimmicks they come up with. The losses add up. If you bet $10 a week on these various tickets, that's well over $500 you're going to lose in a year. You might ask, what about the wins? Well, what about them? An occasional $5 payoff or free tickets, or, if you're really lucky, an $80 or $50 payout will still leave you a big loser at the end of whatever time period you decide to count as your lottery fiscal year. Be firm and avoid the temptations that these lotteries offer. Save your money for better things. If you want to play, then read the various sections and chapters in this book which tell you how to get an edge up on the casino, where you're the favorite, not the big underdog.

Tribal Reservation Gambling

As any casual student of American history knows, the Native Americans were given the shaft by the colonizers of the United States. The government broke practically every treaty it made with the tribes that had inhabited this land for centuries and kept it in its pristine condition. Finally, the Indians were shunted about, with whole nations, such as the Cherokees, being moved from North Carolina to Oklahoma and settled there against their will, dumped on inhospitable land.

The same thing happened to the western tribes, such as the Navajos and the Apaches. They were set down in wretched reservations where no one else wanted to live, in the arid plains and deserts of Western America. The Native Americans became second-class citizens, prone to disease, alcoholism, and extreme poverty. By the laws of the land, they were separate and apart from American society, with their own laws and police. In many ways they ruled themselves and were not subject to the laws of the state or nation in which they lived. For decades these rules worked against them; they were left to their own devices, scratching out an existence on the God-forsaken lands they occupied.

Then, in 1988, Congress passed the Indian Gaming Regulatory Act, which legalized gaming on Native American-owned land. Suddenly, Native Americans' apartness had a monetary value. They weren't subject to the gambling restrictions the states imposed on their ordinary citizens. They could have gambling on their lands and reservations and entice the same citizens who ordinarily avoided them into parting with their monies. All they had to do was open up their lands to gambling enterprises. And this the Native Americans have done with a vengeance.

Let's give a partial roll call of the states that have some form of Indian gaming: Alabama, Arizona, California, Connecticut, Florida, Idaho, Iowa, Kansas, Louisiana, Michigan, Minnesota, Mississippi, Missouri, Montana, New Mexico, New York, North Carolina, North Dakota, Oklahoma, Oregon, South Dakota, Washington, Wisconsin, and Wyoming. The tables have turned. Native Americans, once one of the most impoverished minorities in America, now have some of the most affluent citizens. To give an example—in Connecticut, a small tribe, once thought to be extinct, owns the most profitable casino in the world, the Foxwoods High Stakes Bingo and Casino. They are the Mashantucket Pequot Tribe.

This casino is located in Ledyard, Connecticut, and has more table games available to players than any other casino in America. It is constantly expanding its casino and adding hotel space for the thousands of visitors who come each year. The casino is about two hours from Boston, and has mostly a New England clientele, but gamblers also come from New York and other areas. It now has three hotels and 120,000 square feet of casino space. It is a monstrous operation, and a very profitable one. You can play craps, blackjack, video poker, roulette, slots, baccarat, keno, the big six wheel, chuck-a-luck, Caribbean poker and Pai Gow poker, as well as many forms of ordinary poker.

You can't do this legally anywhere else in New England except at other tribal reservations. It's illegal according to the state laws. But Native Americans can open gambling casinos on land they own, and invite the public. The public hungers for gambling action and they flock to these casinos, especially the one the tiny tribe of Mashantucket Pequot Indians own.

For those who want to visit this unique casino, the rules are as follows on some table games: Double odds on craps, the dealer stands on all 17s and adheres to Las Vegas rules in blackjack. Eight decks are used. Roulette has a double zero like all American wheels, keno is played, and baccarat has a $6,000 limit. The casino is open twenty-four hours a day.

Other Native American gaming establishments can be big or small, can offer table games as well as video and electronic machines, or merely bingo. It depends on the state and the location of the casino. For example, in Alabama, the one casino run by Native Americans is located in Atmore, and has bingo only. This casino is owned by the Poarch Creek Indians. Just because only bingo is offered, doesn't mean the games are played for peanuts. The Creek Bingo Palace has a $1 million jackpot on weekends.

A huge state like California has close to twenty tribal casinos in operation, running the length and breadth of the state. Most of them feature bingo, but some also offer poker, video poker, and table games. The Palace Indian Bingo Casino in Lemoore seats 1,300 players, while the San Manuel Indian Bingo Casino in Highland seats 2,700 players. These are big, profitable operations. In Colorado, the casinos run by Native Americans feature slot machines, video poker, blackjack and keno, among other games. Iowa has slot machines, blackjack, roulette, craps and big six available in its casinos in Onawa, Tama, and Sloan. These casinos are run by the Omaha, Mesquaki, and Winnebago Tribes of Iowa.

Minnesota is another hotbed of Native American gaming. There are more tribal casinos in this state than in California. Games offered in the various casinos include video poker, video blackjack, video craps, blackjack, slot machines, bingo, keno, and poker. One of the casinos, the Mystic Lake Casino, in Prior Lake, run by the Mdewakanton Dakota Tribe, has 2,300 slot machines and 125 blackjack tables. Slot machines are big business in tribal gaming in Minnesota. The Northern Lights Casino in Walker has 600 machines, while the Shooting Star Casino and Lodge in Mahnomen, owned by the White Earth Band of Chippewa Indians, has 900 slot machines, in addition to thirty-six blackjack tables. This casino is open twenty-four hours a day, seven days a week.

New York has a number of tribal gaming casinos, but they are limited to bingo operations. However, a couple of them are huge operations. The Mohawk Bingo Palace in Hogansburg seats 2,500 players and is owned by the St. Regis Mohawk Nation. The Seneca Bingo/Irving Casino in Irving seats 2,000 players. It is owned by the Seneca Nation of Indians.

North Dakota, a state in which several treaties were broken by the U.S. Government, has several casinos around the state.

They are rather small operations, with small limits, though the Turtle Mountain Casino, which consists of three separate enterprises in Belcourt, has a bingo room seating 700 players, as well as slot machines, poker and keno machines, and blackjack tables, and something called Indian dice games. It is owned and managed by the Turtle Mountain Tribe.

In Oklahoma, the transplanted Cherokee Nation owns and manages a casino in Catoosa. It is called the Cherokee Nation Bingo Outpost and seats 1,400 players for bingo alone. The Cherokees own and manage several other bingo operations in the state. Other tribes that own casinos featuring bingo include the Absentee Shawnee Tribe, the Checotah Nation, the Chickasaw Nation, the Choctaw Nation, the Comanche Tribe of Oklahoma, the Creek Nation, the Iowa Tribe of Oklahoma, the Kaw Nation of Oklahoma, the Kiowa Tribe, the Osage Tribe, the Otoe-Missouria Tribe, the Panca Tribe, the Pawnee Tribe, the Potowatomi Tribe of Oklahoma, the Quapaw Tribe of Oklahoma, the Seminole Nation of Oklahoma, and the Thlopthlocco Tribal Town.

I point out the various tribes involved in gaming to show just how many Native Americans have used this vehicle to bring in money and to lift their people out of dire poverty. Many of the bingo palaces are both owned and operated by Native Americans, but when more complex gambling is allowed, outside managers are often called in. The managers are generally given a limited contract of about five years, though time periods and terms vary widely.

What is the future of Native American gaming? It is bright, according to insiders in the industry. Interest in gaming is on the increase throughout America and many states where gambling is opposed by various organizations and churches will look the other way when it takes place on tribal land. In most states, they have no alternative, for the reservations are governed and ruled by laws different from those for the general population. For a people long mired in poverty, decimated by disease and hardship, gambling is a godsend, a way to bring in large sums of money.

To find out more about Indian gaming, a North American Tribal Gaming Directory is published out of Prior Lake, Minnesota. The toll free number is 1-800-665-0037. It is published twice yearly, and lists all the tribal gaming in the United States and Canada.

I suggest playing at the reservation casinos if they are convenient. Many are near interstate highways, and feature inexpensive food in good restaurants. They are generally well run and offer an honest game, whatever your game is. If you travel by car on long trips you're bound to see a sign advertising a nearby Native American casino.

For those of you who live near an Indian gaming establishment, you can call the casino and find out what games are offered, the hours of operation, and so forth. If there's a game that you'd like to play, the host will gladly tell you the betting limits and rules. Visit the casino and check it out. I'm sure you'll be pleasantly surprised. My feeling is that in the near future other megacasinos on the order of the Foxwoods Casino in Connecticut will spring up. Gambling has a bright future in America, and Native American gaming holds a key place in that future.

Riverboat Gambling

In the old black-and-white Hollywood movies, the riverboat gambler was a stock character. He sat, dressed to the nines, always with a fancy vest, smoking a cigar and keeping his cards close to that fancy vest. He was a legendary sort of gambler, often honest, at times not so honest, ready to start a fistfight or gunfight if crossed. These riverboat gamblers plied their trade on the Mississippi, the "father of waters," one of the few rivers in America able to accommodate the really big riverboats.

Today, riverboat gamblers are back. But they're not those fancy dudes all dressed up; they're ordinary people seeking some action on the riverboats along the Mississippi. Or on the Ohio or other great rivers of America. Riverboats now ply the Great Lakes and other large midwestern lakes. However, not all of these boats travel somewhere. A good number are permanently docked, glamorous vessels running in place.

They're like the *Queen Mary* at Long Beach, California, going nowhere, but looking very impressive all the same.

Riverboat design changes from state to state, depending on local laws, as does riverboat gaming itself. For example, in Mississippi, gaming is not permitted on a moving boat; therefore, the riverboats in that state must remain dockside if gambling is to be allowed. On the other hand, in Louisiana, gaming is not permitted dockside on riverboats, so the boats must be seaworthy. And so it goes from state to state.

The riverboat industry is a dynamic one, with boats constantly being put into service, while others are subject to losses and go out of business. Eventually, the riverboats will reach a point of no return, competing for a limited number of gamblers in a limited number of towns. Another factor that may slow their growth is the push for legalized gambling in various big cities in America. For example, if legalized gambling comes to Chicago, it will surely have a negative impact on the riverboats that ply their trade in that state. The same holds true for the other big cities that line the Mississippi River.

Let's now look at the riverboat scene along the mighty river and other great water regions of the Midwest. We'll start in the north and work our way down to the delta region of Louisiana, where the Mississippi empties into the Gulf of Mexico.

Illinois Riverboats

The first riverboat to open in Illinois waters was the *Alton Belle*, which began its existence in 1991. It was replaced a couple of years later by the *Alton Belle II*. The boat can accommodate 1,300 passengers, and has slot, video poker, and electronic keno machines. It also has a number of table games, including blackjack, craps, and roulette. The dockside facilities are at Alton and while they include some good restaurants, there are no sleeping quarters on the boat. Argosy Gaming owns the boat, and there is a $4 charge for the cruise.

Hollywood Casino runs two riverboat casinos, known as *City of Lights I* and *City of Lights II*, out of Aurora, which is located less than 40 miles west of Chicago. Each of the boats can hold 600 players, and offers table games in addition to slot and video games. Charges range from $2 to $15 for the weekend cruises.

This kind of charge is unique as far as gambling is concerned. No matter how ornate or splendid a casino may be in Nevada or Atlantic City, there is never an admission charge as on certain riverboats.

Other Illinois boats are docked at East Dubuque, East Aurora, Rock Island, East Peoria, Metropolis, Joliet, East St. Louis, and Elgin. On any of the boats in these towns and cities, expect to find slots and video games as well as table games. Also expect to pay an admission fee.

Iowa

Iowa was the first state to legalize riverboat gambling. The law was passed in 1989, and by 1991 the first boat was ready for its customers. With the law came restrictions on wagering. Bets were limited to $5, and a loss limit of $200 per player was imposed. The people of Iowa are conservative, and only recently have various laws been changed, including those restricting the size of bets and imposing loss limits.

The *President Riverboat Casino* is advertised as the biggest cruising riverboat casino in the world, but this claim has been made by other riverboat operators. It is stationed in Davenport, and the owners also run riverboats in Missouri and Mississippi. This riverboat offers the usual slot and video machines as well as table games and poker. Admission is free during the week, but there is a charge for the Friday night and weekend cruises. Other riverboat casinos are located in Dubuque, Clinton, and Sioux City.

Indiana

Indiana has approved riverboat gambling, with casinos opened in 1996. At the present time, two are in Gary, the *Trump Indiana* and the *Barden/PRC/Gary LLC*. Aztar Corporation will have one in Evansville, while the Indiana Gaming Company LP will feature a riverboat casino in Lawrenceburg. There will be an admission charge to all riverboats, which will cruise the waters of the various lakes and rivers in and surrounding Indiana, though none will be on the Mississippi, which does not run through the Hoosier State. Table games as well as slot and video machines will be featured on these riverboats. There will be no state-imposed limitations on betting or losses.

Missouri

The "Show Me" state first introduced gambling on riverboats in 1993, but soon after the Missouri Supreme Court differentiated between games of skill, such as poker and blackjack, and games of pure chance, such as roulette and craps. It decided that games of skill would be allowed, but games of chance were outlawed on the riverboats. Since then the matter has been resolved. Games of skill as well as games of chance are allowed on all riverboats operating in the state of Missouri at this time.

Two great rivers run through Missouri, the Mississippi and the Missouri, and all riverboats are on one or the other. The law permits a riverboat casino to operate either at dockside or while cruising, and some of them cruise while others remain stationary. All feature table games as well as slots and other electronic devices. The state imposes a tax on admissions; some riverboats charge a minimum of $2 while others charge a greater amount, and still others waive the fee and absorb the tax themselves. Check beforehand if an admissions charge is important to you.

One final note: While there is no betting limit on any of the riverboats, a $500 loss limit per excursion is enforced. An excursion means either a cruise or a simulated excursion on a boat that remains dockside.

In St. Louis, the President Casino operates the *Admiral* which is a dockside riverboat. It is huge, with five decks and more than 70,000 square feet available for gaming. At least 4,000 people can use the casino at one time. It is located under the famous arch that is the Gateway to the West, and is convenient to many of the facilities in the city of St. Louis.

The other riverboat docked on the Mississippi River is in

Carruthersville. This is operated by the Aztar Corporation and is a cruise ship.

In St. Charles, on the Missouri River, Station Casinos operates two riverboats, one dockside and one cruising. Also on the Missouri, in St. Joseph, the St. Joseph Riverboat Partners operate a cruise boat.

The Boyd group operates a dockside riverboat in Kansas City, which is on the Missouri River. In Riverside, there is another riverboat that cruises. Finally, in North Kansas City, a few miles from downtown Kansas City, Harrah's runs another huge riverboat operation. This boat stays dockside and contains well over a thousand slots and video poker and other electronic machines, in addition to more than fifty table games.

Mississippi

Of all the states permitting riverboat gaming, Mississippi would have to be considered the most liberal as far as its gaming laws are concerned. Whereas other states require a certain seaworthiness for riverboats, as well as certain designs, Mississippi will allow any boat, no matter what kind and what design—even a barge will do. All the boats, however, must stay dockside. In effect, what you have in Mississippi are huge casinos in the water, tethered to docks. To all intents and purposes, these casinos might just as well be built on the land. Why this restriction?

For one thing, Mississippi is a Bible Belt state, with a strong aversion to gambling. So, by having dockside gaming, the citizens can rest with clear consciences, knowing there is no gambling *per se* on the land itself. And Mississippi is a very poor state. Gambling brings in a ton of money, and probably at this time is responsible for a substantial part of the state's tourist industry.

There are two other restrictions. Riverboat gaming is allowed only in the eight counties that are along the Gulf Coast or the Mississippi River, and voters must approve a referendum in those counties before gambling will be permitted. Other states have been careful to limit the number of riverboats allowed in their waters, but Mississippi has no such restriction.

The eight counties that can have riverboat gaming include Tunica, the most northerly on the Mississippi, and closest to the large population center of Memphis, Tennessee. South of Tunica is Coahoma County, then Washington County, which includes the city of Greenville. Warren County is the home of Vicksburg, remembered by Civil War buffs for its siege by General Grant. The next Mississippi county is Adams, containing the city of Natchez. Neshoba County, somewhat rural even by Mississippi standards, is eligible for gaming, but no riverboats are presently situated in its confines.

Then there are two gulf coast counties. Harrison County holds two cities, Biloxi and Gulfport, while Hancock County has two smaller communities, Bay St. Louis and Lake Shore. Lake Shore is basically a name at the end of a road leading to coastal waters.

Tunica County

Let's start with Tunica in our look at riverboat gaming in Mississippi. Tunica County had the distinction, three years before gaming was introduced to Mississippi, of being the most impoverished county in the nation. It was basically a dirt-poor rural region. But not anymore. There are now seven riverboats in the county, some owned by the biggest names in gaming. When I speak of riverboats, I am using the term rather loosely. These boats aren't built to go anywhere. They are floating palaces meant for gambling alone. What they do primarily is feed the state of Mississippi 12 percent of the gross earnings they take in. They're open twenty-four hours a day, and they take in a fortune. In 1994 alone, 30 billion dollars were wagered on the riverboats in Mississippi, and the gross gaming win from October 1994 to September 1995 was well over a billion dollars—$1,666,600,000.

Within Tunica County, we have several areas with gaming casinos. In Buck Lake, there's the *Grand Casino*, which is putting the finishing touches on a huge casino. A little to the south is *Binion's Horseshoe*, *Circus Circus*, and the *Sheraton*

River Club Casino. The Polk's Landing holds *Fitzgeralds,* and Commerce Landing holds *Sam's Town Hotel and Casino.* Then there is the *Hollywood Casino,* and in Casino Center near Robinsonville, *Bally's* has moved its casino from Mhoon Landing, which no longer holds any casinos. Some of these are tremendous enterprises. *Circus Circus* alone has over 60,000 square feet of gaming space, including close to 1,500 slot machines and over fifty table games. All the casinos in Tunica County offer slots, video poker, and electronic games, as well as table games, and some have poker tables also. They are open twenty-four hours a day, 365 days a year, and have no admission charge.

Coahoma County

In the town of Lula, Lady Luck has built the *Lady Luck Rhythm and Blues,* which does a fabulous business, and Lady Luck claims that this casino is among Mississippi's highest producers in terms of win-per-position rates. So far, this is the only casino operating in Coahoma County.

Washington County

In the Greenville area, two casinos are in operation, the *Cotton Club* and the *Las Vegas,* both owned by small casino groups. Both are open twenty-four hours a day, 365 days a year. They have table games as well as the usual slots, video poker, and electronic games. The *Las Vegas Casino* is the larger of the two, and much of the business comes from neighboring states such as Arkansas as well as places as far away as Oklahoma.

Warren County

Vicksburg is the big attraction in Warren County; one of the sights to see there are the monuments erected by the states who lost their sons during the Civil War on the Vicksburg battlefield. Vicksburg has four casinos on the Mississippi River. The *Ameristar,* which is the largest, has top-notch entertainment in its 350-seat showroom. Other casinos are the *Rainbow,* the *Isle of Capri,* and *Harrah's.* All feature table games, as well as slots and electronic games such as video poker. All are open twenty-four hours a day, seven days a week, and as with all riverboats in Mississippi, there is no admission fee.

Adams County
Adams County's main city is Natchez, home of the *Lady Luck Natchez*, with close to 15,000 square feet of gaming space including over five hundred slots and close to forty gaming tables. It is open twenty-four hours a day, seven days a week.

Neshoba County
At the time of writing, there is no riverboat gaming in this county.

This ends our roundup of gaming along the Mississippi, and leaves us with the two Gulf Coast counties, Harrison and Hancock. All together, there are twelve riverboats in these coastal areas.

Harrison County
Biloxi and Gulfport are the two main cities in Harrison County on the Gulf waters. Grand Casinos owns two of the largest casinos in the Gulf Coast region, the *Grand Casino Biloxi*, which is the biggest, and the *Grand Casino Gulfport*, the second biggest. The *Biloxi* is a three-story building set upon moored and linked steel barges located twelve miles east of Gulfport. The *Grand Casino Gulfport* is located right in the Gulfport Harbor and is likewise a three-story structure. Other "floating" casinos include the *Copa Casino, Isle of Capri, President, Casino Magic, Lady Luck Biloxi, Palace Casino, Treasure Bay Casino*, and *Boomtown*.

As with all other casinos in Mississippi, these are open all the time, there is no admission charge, and the players can gamble at table games or electronic games, such as slots and video poker.

Hancock County
This is the other county on the Gulf Coast of the state of Mississippi that allows gambling. There are two smaller towns here, Bay St. Louis, which holds the *Casino Magic Bay St. Louis* riverboat, and Lake Shore, which has the *Bayou Caddy's Jubilee*.

The situation in Mississippi is quite dynamic, with many applications being made to open new casinos. Operators love the regulatory climate here—the casinos don't have to be sea-worthy, which saves the enormous cost of outfitting them. The money spent by gamblers in Mississippi is awesome, as I pointed out, with a huge net win from these eager and unso-phisticated gamblers. As of 1996, Mississippi ranks third in revenues from gambling operations, and second in square foot-age devoted to gaming, overtaking Atlantic City.

Louisiana

While Mississippi doesn't permit any of its casinos to cruise, Louisiana has taken the opposite tack. All of its riverboats must be seaworthy, and none can stay dockside for gaming purposes. The riverboats must be newly constructed rather than converted, must be paddlewheelers, must be at least 120 feet long, and must be able to carry a minimum of 600 people. And one other thing—they must be aesthetically pleasing, conforming to the historic designs of nineteenth-century riv-erboats. The laws relating to riverboats were passed by the state legislature in 1991. A separate law permitting a land-based casino in New Orleans was passed in 1992.

The Louisiana boats operate on a variety of waterways including lakes and rivers. There are no regulations concerning size of bets or loss limits, but the boats are limited to 30,000 square feet for gaming purposes. Table games, as well as slots, video poker, and other electronic games are offered to the play-ers. Expect, when boarding these vessels, to pay either a board-ing, admission, or cruising fee. The rates are not standard. The minimum is about $2.50 and prices go up sharply from there, especially on weekends, when the cost may be $20 per person.

These riverboats, since they cruise, are not open for a straight twenty-four hours a day. Special cruise times must be observed; it pays to check before making any arrangements to board the boats. Practically all of these boats have toll-free 800 numbers for this and other information.

Lake Charles

Three boats operate on Lake Charles at the present time. Two are owned by Players International, Ltd., and the other is the *Isle of Capri*.

Shreveport/Bossier City

Three boats cruise on the Red River. They are the *Isle of Capri*, owned by the same organization that runs the same-named boat on Lake Charles; the *Shreveport Rose*, owned by Harrah's, and finally, the *Horseshoe Riverboat*, owned by Horseshoe Entertainment, a subsidiary of the company that runs the successful Horseshoe Club in downtown Las Vegas.

Baton Rouge

Baton Rouge is the home of Louisiana State University, as well as the capital of Louisiana. This historic city, set on the Mississippi River, has two riverboats plying their trade. One, owned by Argosy Gaming, is named the *Belle of Baton Rouge*. The other is the *Casino Rouge*, which is owned by Louisiana Casino Cruises, a subsidiary of Carnival Cruises.

Lake Ponchartrain

This lake, located in Jefferson Parish, has Bally's *Belle of Orleans*, and the *Lake Ponchartrain*.

River City

The *Grand Palais* and the *Crescent City Queen* are both currently in bankruptcy, and efforts are being made to sell them to a major gaming corporation. Things don't always work out well in the gaming industry, especially in Louisiana, where competition is intense, and where the regulations requiring cruising hurt business. Riverboats have limited hours, and definite sailing times, and thus are not open to the public twenty-four hours a day the way they are in Mississippi. People cannot just walk into a casino and try their luck; and the admission charges for most of the riverboats are also a deterrent.

New Orleans

Originally, there were three riverboat casinos operating in the downtown area of the city, but all three have closed down, the last being the *Flamingo*, owned by the Hilton Hotel Corporation. The onerous tax structure, amounting to 18.5% of a casino's gross revenue, compared to 7% in other states, plus a head tax on gamblers, has pretty much doomed gambling in the "Big Easy." Another factor is legal restrictions on free meals and drinks, so as not to compete with New Orleans restaurants. Unless the legal climate changes, allowing lower taxes and more amenities, gambling in New Orleans will not be a viable enterprise.

Kenner

This suburb of New Orleans has the *Treasure Chest,* owned by Boyd Gaming, so the Crescent City is well supplied with gaming enterprises.

In New Orleans itself, Harrah's Corporation had the exclusive rights to a land-based casino. It had been operating this casino on a temporary basis out of the Municipal Auditorium. A permanent casino was to be built in the Canal Street section of the city.

The land-based casino has been a disappointment, and recently Harrah's has withdrawn from the project. Business was sub-par and employees had been laid off as a cost-cutting measure. The feeling in Louisiana is that the casinos will end up being dependent upon the residents rather than upon the tourists, and that the intense competition from the riverboats surrounding New Orleans will hurt any permanent casino in the city.

A Final Note on Riverboat Gambling

Gambling fever has certainly hit America. Who would have thought that a rural and poor state like Mississippi would develop into one of the gaming capitals of the USA? This was unthinkable up to the 1990s. Not only was it a poor state, but it is conservative, with strong ties to religious organizations. And yet there it is, a $30 billion industry.

Eventually, other big cities along the great rivers and lakes of America will get into the gambling act. Laws are constantly being introduced in state legislatures, and referendums are being prepared for voters in several states. Alabama is considering riverboat gambling, and Missouri, which permits it, is in the process of easing its laws regarding loss limits because the riverboat operators complain they are both onerous and unenforceable.

Eventually, riverboat gaming will reach a saturation point, but that point is still far off. It will be interesting to see just how legalized gaming will spread from the heartland and southern delta regions of America to other areas, as states scramble for the easy revenue. Easy for them, but someone is losing money. That's why I suggest you read the appropriate sections of this book before going on any riverboat. Don't be one of the many losers; be knowledgeable, and use the information presented here to good purpose. Taking a cruise can be fun, but winning makes it even more so.

The New Las Vegas Atmosphere

On my last visit to Las Vegas, I was walking along the Strip one evening, with mobs of people all around me, and I thought back to a time some twenty years ago when I was walking on that same Las Vegas Boulevard, heading with a friend to the Desert Inn, or DI, as it was and is known by Vegas insiders. At one time, it was known as Wilbur Clark's Desert Inn and Country Club, but Wilbur Clark never owned the joint. It was allegedly owned by the Mayfield Road gang from Cleveland, and was the class place on the Strip in the 1950s all the way up to the time Howard Hughes moved in and bought the place.

We were headed for the Skyroom in the DI, which had a piano and a small dancing area, where we'd meet women and friends and have a couple of drinks and relax. The Skyroom, once the highest spot on the entire Strip, was on the third floor! Now, the DI is a huge multistoried building completely unlike the original structure. The places I would pass getting there have also been transformed, or are gone. Gone are the Castaways and the Silver Slipper, which my good friend Bill Friedman ran. The Stardust has been practically rebuilt from the bottom up; the motel site on the corner of Flamingo and the Strip is now the Barbary Coast Casino. The Thunderbird has been renamed and bought and sold several times and its present locale holds a hotel–casino that is not yet open for business. I could go on and on.

Las Vegas, which I remember as a small city with some gaming casinos, is now a city of over a million souls and Clark County, in which it is located, is perennially on the list of fastest growing areas in the country. This is desert country, with water and electricity fed by the Hoover Dam and Lake Mead, about thirty miles away. The climate is dry and it is an ideal place for retirees. There is no state income tax in Nevada, the food is cheap, the housing is very affordable, and there is always something to do. This is a true twenty-four-hour town.

At one time, men came here to gamble. They brought their wives or girlfriends, who would indulge in bingo or the slots while the men played craps or blackjack. Children were not permitted in casinos; Las Vegas, which thought of itself as a rather sinful city, simply didn't cater to families. Everything was geared for the serious gambler. All this has changed. Vegas is now welcoming families with open arms. Monstrous hotels have been built with the family trade in mind. Hotels that once used every available bit of space for gaming purposes now have video game rooms for the kids. Kids are welcome; the welcome mat is out for them all.

Perhaps the first hotel to recognize the need for a family trade was Circus Circus. Kids had the run of a couple of floors there, which resembled those traveling sideshows that are the staple of small-town America. They could play games, toss balls, win prizes, keep amused. While they were kept busy, their parents were in the main casino gambling. And they were kept amused also by a constant circus. It was a heady situation—while you were playing blackjack, trapeze artists were flying overhead. But then America has welcomed this kind of sideshow atmosphere with all its heart.

Circus Circus, which has hotels in other areas of Nevada such as Reno and Laughlin, as well as a dockside casino in Tunica County, Mississippi, has been in the forefront of the gambling business ever since it welcomed the kiddies. They have two huge, very successful hotels at the southern end of the Strip, the Excalibur and the Luxor. The Excalibur is the ultimate in kitsch, with its pseudo-jousts and outlandish dealer costumes. Parapets in bright colors stand above the Strip welcoming the families of America. And they come. This is a very successful hotel, as is the Luxor, which is built in the shape of a pyramid, with a sphinx sitting moodily or happily, depending on the way you look at it, in front. The rooms are wonderful here, and the place is booked up all the time. Inside, there's a casino with a huge, empty space above it, leading to the top of the pyramid. You don't take elevators to your floor, you take an inclinator.

The atmosphere is ancient Egypt as seen by modern-day Vegas. There is an area for families with a city atmosphere, which is sort of incongruous in an ancient Egyptian setting. It contains fake buildings about ten stories high, and there is a big games room for the kids. You can even take a ride on the Nile, the Nile here being a waterway tour of the hotel and casino. The marveling tourists fill the boats up anyway.

Near these hotels stands the biggest of them all, the MGM Grand, a Kirk Kerkorian production, featuring a giant lion guarding the entrance. The outside is dark green, and looks rather good with its clean lines, next to the fake parapets of the Excalibur. Inside is the largest casino space in Las Vegas. The thousands of square feet contain the usual table games, slots, and electronic games, along with things for kids to do, like the Yellow Brick Walk of Dorothy in the Land of Oz, and fake lightning storms. The quick food places are geared to kids' tastes. Just to walk the walk is an exhausting process, but 60,000 people do it every day.

With these three new places stands an older hotel, the Tropicana, which has passed through various owners, and today is in the hands of the Aztar Corporation. Besides the jungle of slots in the casino, it features a walk during which you can see live exotic birds and animals on the way to your room. This hotel is also very big, with wings having been added on in all directions.

On this southern end of the Strip, these four colossi contain more hotel rooms than all of Los Angeles. And unlike the Los Angeles hotels, they are booked at about 95 percent of their capacity the year round. One of the strange things about the

Las Vegas scene is this—the more hotel rooms available, the more difficult it is to find one.

Further down the Strip, at the corner of Flamingo Road and Las Vegas Boulevard, stands Caesars Palace, which is now owned by the Sheraton division of ITT. This hotel-casino has stood the test of time. It is constantly being updated and upgraded, and has a concourse with a *trompe l'oeil* ceiling which changes according to the time outside. The hotel has a subdued and elegant atmosphere; within the walkway are fine and expensive shops, and restaurants like Spago's. A show is put on near the entrance to the concourse which somehow attracts people. It has to do with laser ceilings and ugly statues babbling something about ancient Rome. Other than that, the place is very impressive.

Caesars attracts almost as many walkthroughs as the MGM Grand, but a great many high rollers come here as well. The casino is usually packed, while the MGM Grand, which is much bigger, has a relatively empty feeling. Opposite Caesars is the Flamingo Hilton. When I first came to Vegas it was the Flamingo, Bugsy Siegel's brainchild which mimicked the elegant atmosphere of a Monte Carlo casino, with panelled walls and bountiful chandeliers. Now it is owned by the Hilton Corporation, and has been completely renovated and expanded. The other giant in the area is Bally's Grand, formerly the old MGM Grand. It is big and filled with slot machines, whereas the old casino had row upon row of table games like craps and blackjack.

The fourth corner was empty; Steve Wynn having dynamited the old Dunes Hotel with its gigantic neon sign into dust and rubble. In its place, Wynn, who owns the Mirage and Treasure Island, plans to build another hotel. It will be called the Bellagio, and will be an island on an artificial lake. It is expected to be a high roller's heaven, with luxurious accommodations. However, it is expected to share the space with a hotel managed by Circus Circus, called the Monte Carlo but equally owned by Mirage and Circus Circus. How this will work out will be interesting to observe, for the two hotels will be linked with a walkway.

The Mirage is one of the most profitable hotel-casinos in Las Vegas. It is located directly north of Caesars Palace, and features the Siegfried and Roy Tiger show. Entering the hotel from the Strip, you can see the huge white tigers reclining or doing whatever they do in a glass cage. They are part of the magic show produced by Siegfried and Roy, which is always sold out. The Mirage has a nice look about it, with a steamy atrium, an aquarium above the reservations desk, dolphins, a volcano that goes off at intervals during the evening, good restaurants and a fine buffet, and an extremely busy casino.

South of the Mirage is Treasure Island, another Wynn property, which stages outdoor pirate battles. Inside you are constantly greeted by fake pirate shouts, which gets annoying and distracting. In the end you simply wish for a little peace and quiet. This place, unlike the Mirage, which caters to the high rollers, is a family kind of hotel. The pirates, and the big game and video room for kids, are geared toward families.

Several new projects are planned for the Strip, all in keeping with a single theme to attract customers. Bally's, now owned by Hilton Hotels, is going with a Paris theme, Eiffel Tower and all, to be situated between its present hotel and the Aladdin. Circus Circus is building a huge hotel on the old Hacienda property on the south end of the Strip, tentatively called Paradise, with 3,800 rooms. The new New York, New York Hotel is a big hit, featuring a mock Statue of Liberty, and is located near the Tropicana. So, middle America will be able to walk along the Strip and see a pyramid, a Sphinx, the Statue of Liberty, the Eiffel Tower, volcanos, and pirate battles. Quite a spectacle, and sure to overwhelm the customers.

More than 20,000 new hotel rooms are expected to be added by the end of 1999. These include huge additions to places like Harrah's on the Strip, opposite the Mirage. Away from the Strip, on the west side of the city on Flamingo, the Rio now offers 2,500 suites, a 66% increase in rooms, after a monumental expansion of its facilities.

Downtown Las Vegas is also changing, but not in the same radical fashion. Rather than new hotels, an enclosed pedestrian walkway along Fremont Street has been completed. People won't have to worry about the traffic or the elements, especially the bruising midday heat during spring and summer. The

Horseshoe Club now has expanded by buying the Mint. The Freemont is now owned by Boyd Gaming, which is famous for Sam's Town on Boulder Highway, a local hangout.

There is something else I should mention, even though it is not in Las Vegas proper. At one time, on their way to Vegas from Southern California, tired drivers encountered a couple of dumpy casinos at Stateline, the spot where California blends into the Silver State. They looked like the kind of places where a few drunken cowboys might hang out. Now all this is changed. As you drive into Nevada, there are three hotels, all owned by Primadonna, right at Stateline. One is Whiskey Pete's, the original big hotel there. The others are Primadonna and Buffalo Bill's. They do big business, and are always filled with cars and RVs.

Some ten miles or so down the road on the way to Las Vegas, in Jean, stand two other hotels, Nevada Landing and Gold Strike. These have been bought by Circus Circus. They stand in the middle of a barren desert, two oases for tired travellers. They are both big casinos, with cheap rooms and meals. Many people now never make it to Vegas, their ultimate destination being one of these hotel-casinos.

As I mentioned before, the anomaly about Las Vegas is that the more it gets built up, the more difficult it is to get a room. Twenty years ago, there were worries that Vegas was overbuilt; now, the casino and hotel space has at least quintupled, and the casinos are still full and making money. A phenomenon that may eventually work against all this building is the lure of the new and different. People are drawn to a new hotel-casino with an exciting or different theme, but this gets old in a hurry. Eventually, the building will stop and it will all sort itself out. The places that offer good rooms, good food, and attractive gambling facilities will survive; the others will have a hard time. But this may be many years down the road; in the meantime, there is still that urgent push in Vegas for the new and overwhelming. For millions of Americans Las Vegas, Nevada, has become the ultimate vacation destination.

2

The Casino— Its Operation and Personnel

Running a casino is a complicated operation, and it takes a large staff of executives and employees to operate it correctly. For one thing, it's a cash business with money and markers being continually exchanged for casino chips which have a specific monetary value, and just keeping track of the casino bankroll is an enormous task.

Then there is the job of overseeing all the dealers and players because, since gambling involves cards, dice, and large sums of money, it is a field in which cheats and scam artists thrive. The security problem in casinos is a constant one, and many casinos have been burned by their own employees as well as by outsiders.

Just to stand in a crowded casino on a weekend night in the summer—to see the movement of people and the action and hear the screams of players at the craps table—is an amazing experience. All this must be carefully watched and controlled by the staff.

Most major casinos are connected to the hotels they operate in, and the hotel business is a world of its own, which would require several chapters to explain its proper operation. In this book, however, we're only dealing with the operation of the casino itself, and we'll concentrate on the men and women who handle that part of the business.

Why write about casino personnel in a book on gambling? For a very simple reason—these people are there not only to protect the casino bankroll and make sure that all runs smoothly, they're also concerned about and involved in customer relations, and this chapter will explain how to take advantage of this situation.

After all, the more you know when entering a casino, the better your chances of emerging a winner. You are dealing with several people at all times in the casino, whether or not you realize this, and you should know their functions and how they can be helpful to you.

Casino Manager

The casino manager runs the casino. Every aspect of the operation is under his control in one way or another.

At one time, when casinos weren't owned by public corporations, but were rather free-wheeling affairs, the casino manager's power was awesome. In those days, which lasted into the 1960s, the people running the big hotel-casinos in Nevada didn't really care that much about hotel, restaurant, or entertainment operations except as they affected the casino. At that time, all these operations were heavy money losers, but it didn't really matter, because the casino raked in the cash and made so much money that the losses became insignificant.

Then the economy changed; inflation increased and executives who ran these hotel-casinos became aware of the mounting costs. Every aspect of the operation today is expected to pull its own weight, except for the entertainment section. It still is a big loss leader, because the few performers who can attract enough customers to fill the showrooms draw tremendous salaries and other fringe benefits.

Perhaps the biggest star of them all, in Vegas terms, was the late Elvis Presley, who was a bargain to the Las Vegas Hilton no matter how many hundreds of thousands of dollars a week they paid him. For two months of every year Elvis was king of Vegas, and his show filled the giant showroom of the Hilton for every performance.

Frank Sinatra is another great star, not because he fills showrooms, but because he brings in the premium players from all over the world to the casinos he works in.

Although the hotel-casinos never have been able to show a

profit on their entertainment, the other areas of hotel operation do show profits, because prices have been raised substantially in the restaurants, and the hotel rooms show an amazing average occupancy of over 90 percent the year round.

As these operations were streamlined, as more and more giant corporations bought into Nevada hotels and ran them, the casino's role in the whole system was put into perspective. The casino was an important money-maker, but it wasn't the only aspect of the business that made money, and as its influence lessened, so did the role of the casino manager.

At one time, the moguls who ran the hotel-casinos left everything in the casino operation to the casino manager. He was the single most important employee, and his word on the casino floor was law. No one crossed a casino manager and stayed in the operation. Today the general manager or president of the hotel is a more important figure, and in many cases, the casino manager is subservient to the credit operation and its accountants. It is still his responsibility to run the casino, but now he does it in conjunction with others.

The casino manager still sets the tone of the casino— whether the employees are friendly or hostile to customers, whether there is a noisy atmosphere or the general ambience is subdued. He can't influence everything in the casino, because some of the huge hotel-casinos in both Las Vegas and Reno are run by corporation executives whose idea of success is the bottom line of profits. These people take the attitude that every customer is a potential robber of the casino bankroll. The atmosphere in these places can be deadening, not only for the many losers, but for those who play intelligently.

Casino managers come in two basic molds. Still lingering around are the generation that started in the illegal casinos and clubs of the Midwest and New Jersey, tough men who drifted or were called West when Vegas came alive. These are old-fashioned, hard men who didn't care to change with the times. When I first became seriously involved with the Vegas scene, I was sitting in a casino with one of these men, who ran a tremendous Strip casino with an iron fist. The casino wasn't very profitable, and I think a great deal of the fault lay with the casino manager, who was now working for a corporation listed on the New York Stock Exchange, but still thought that the boys from Detroit and Cleveland were running things. I was playing blackjack when Sammy (not his real name) came over and started a conversation. I was doing research at the time on a novel about Las Vegas, and I asked him about card counters (players who keep track of the cards mentally), since my main character was going to be an expert twenty-one player.

"Card counters? What do you want to know about them?" Sammy asked.

"You know what I'm talking about, right?"

"Sure. Sure I know. They crawled in this town after that professor or whoever he was wrote that book, but we can handle them."

"What do you mean, handle them?" I asked.

"Kick them out on their asses. We don't allow no card counters in here. No way. This is no strawberry patch."

"How do you spot a card counter?"

"It's the simplest thing in the world, let me tell you. They don't take their eyes off any of the cards on the table. They raise their bets suddenly from five bucks to five hundred. We've never been bothered by them."

At that point, I was playing blackjack at a $25 table, and the deck was superfavorable. I asked Sammy if he ever believed in hunches.

"Sure. I have a hunch, just one hunch, and that's we're gonna beat every player who comes in here and beat him bad if he plays long enough. And that goes for you."

"Well, I have my own hunch now, Sammy. I'm going to bet two hundred on the next hand."

"It's your money."

I stacked the chips and got my cards. The dealer had a 10 showing and peeked at his hole card, then waited for the only other player at the table to act on his hand. This player stood, and I still hadn't looked at my cards.

"Sammy," I said, "look at my cards. I feel lucky with you around."

"Why not?" He turned over a blackjack for me.

"Sammy, I knew you were lucky."

"Luck, schmuck," he said. "Take your money and run if you're smart, because in the long run, we're gonna bury you, the way you play this game."

"Don't I play it right?"

He gave me a condescending smile and left the table. This particular casino was heaven to play in because it hadn't adjusted to new concepts in blackjack playing. Sammy was still thinking of the suckers he had summarily dealt with in the old days. He had been talking to a card counter and didn't even know it.

I knew the casino's blackjack winning percentage was low, lower than average, because I was privy to computer runs at that casino, since I had *carte blanche* right from the top at that hotel. But Sammy was either too stubborn or too ignorant to learn what card counting was all about.

I was tempted to ask him to employ me just to point out card counters, since I can stand in any pit or at any table and immediately know who's counting cards and who isn't. I've been doing it so long myself that it's second nature, whenever I'm at a table, to know who's doing it along with me. And I knew he could really use me, because I was sure that card counters were denting the casino's bankroll, and the casino manager himself couldn't spot one sitting and talking to him.

The newer generation of casino managers are more attuned to the team concepts that corporations foster. Some of them are so devoid of power that they really have no say about the casino operation and are just there to make sure the premium customers are well taken care of.

One Strip hotel-casino, which once was the class place of Vegas, started losing money because the owners had stripped the casino manager of any power and had a nonentity running things. I sat in his office on several occasions and wandered about the casino with him a few times. He couldn't even tell me the house edge in baccarat.

Others are more knowledgeable, of course, but they don't have to be that smart in a business like gambling. The casinos have lucked out because they're in a business that everyone loves—gambling. They don't have to charge admission or pull the customers in, because the people are breaking down the doors to gamble. If you don't believe me, and live in the East, drive down to Atlantic City some weekend and try to get a seat at a table in the casinos there.

All that most casino managers have to do is control their money operations and protect their bankroll and that's enough.

Hell, give me a craps table to rent out in any casino on the Strip and I'll gladly pay a half million in rent for the year—and make another half million besides. In fact, practically anyone could do the same thing if he or she watched the action and made sure no one was cheating or stealing from the bankroll.

It's that simple, because people will always be at that table, day and night, gambling and throwing their money away recklessly. It doesn't take brains to run a casino; it takes knowledge of money matters and a mind that is just the least bit suspicious and therefore, supercareful.

Shift Bosses

All casinos run on a twenty-four-hour basis in Nevada, and these hours are divided into three eight-hour shifts. They're commonly called day, swing, and graveyard, and the hours vary, though a day shift usually lasts from 8 A.M. to 4 P.M., the swing from 4 P.M. to midnight, and the graveyard from midnight to 8 A.M.

Since even a casino manager must sleep at times, there is a shift boss for each eight-hour shift. These men are directly responsible to and under the control of the casino manager, and they have full responsibility for the action going on during the eight hours of their supervision. In addition, if there's a substantial jackpot at the slots, or the keno game has a winner of several thousand dollars, it's their responsibility to make certain that the payoff is correct and that the win was legitimate.

Pit Bosses

I've spoken to a lot of gamblers who talk about encounters with pit bosses. These players imagine that everyone in the pit, the area behind the tables, watching the action, is a pit boss. But that's not so. They are floormen, who work under the pit boss.

A pit may consist of six craps tables or nine blackjack tables placed in an oval arrangement so that the men inside that area can supervise the action easily. Some casinos have one pit for each game, while the giant houses may have several blackjack pits spread all over the casino.

Other casinos may mix up a pit, placing craps tables and blackjack tables together, but the casinos that do this have foolish men in charge, for each game requires its own expertise and it's nearly impossible to properly supervise a craps game and a blackjack game at the same time. The action is very different, the players are different, and, therefore, the supervision must be different.

In each pit, there is one pit boss for every shift. He works under the supervision of the shift boss, and each pit boss is responsible for the action, cash flow, and bankroll in that pit alone. The legendary Vegas pit boss is a hardened man with underworld connections, for the name "pit boss" invariably conjures up that image, but the pit bosses I've met are often high school graduates who've moved up the long hard way.

Many, now that the corporations are in full control, are college educated. Their main qualifications, though I may be getting a little rough here, is to look suspicious and jaded.

Pit bosses perform an important function in the casino because they are the highest of the executives with a specific area to control, and if that area is losing money or something is wrong in the pit, the trouble can be pinpointed and the blame laid on a specific individual's shoulders.

Floormen

The executives discussed up to this point rarely are in contact with most of the people who frequent a casino and use their facilities or gamble at their tables. On rare occasions, a casino manager will discuss credit arrangements or some special service with a premium player, and a pit boss will go out of his way to talk to a high roller or someone who has been specially recommended to him. But by and large, these men, together with the shift bosses, are in the background, supervising their areas of operation.

However, floormen are the casino executives the player will often come in contact with and see around the casino. At one time, all floormen were males, but more and more casinos are introducing women into the pit, so perhaps the term may eventually be changed to floorperson.

The floorman's job is much more confined than the pit boss's, for, whereas a pit boss deals with an entire pit of gambling tables, the floorman is given a more specific area to supervise—perhaps one craps table or three or four blackjack tables.

The floorman's job is varied. Being the one executive in constant touch with the players, he is supposed to put on a friendly front and to chat and be courteous to the gamblers. At the same time, he watches the games and makes certain that no cheating is going on, that no card counters are hurting the casino's bankroll, and that the bankroll is being protected at all times.

The job can be both grueling and boring at the same time, and the suspicious and unsmiling faces a player often encounters while at the table are not those of pit bosses, but of floormen.

If a high roller, a stranger to the casino, is at the table, the floorman may hover around, getting acquainted with the player as best he can, offering him the services of the hotel so that he continues gambling at that club.

Many players don't know how to take advantage of the floorman and what he can offer. In those casinos where he's not outwardly hostile to all winners, a floorman is prepared to offer certain amenities to players. For example, whenever I play at certain casinos in Vegas and bet at least five dollars a hand in blackjack, I always speak to the floorman, disarming him with aimless chatter.

Then, as conversation gets around to the casino itself, I mention the restaurants and/or shows and invariably am offered a free meal in either the coffee shop or the steakhouse.

I would never ask for one directly, but more often than not, the floorman is only too happy to comp me (comp meaning complimentary—the casino term for free services). He feels that if I am offered this service, I'll return to the tables again after the meal.

This service really costs the casino nothing, since they deduct the expense of free meals from their immense profits. They satisfy their customers, who will, in all probability, remain in a casino that comps them and be happy to play again at its tables.

Few gamblers realize that they can get free meals, free shows, and other courtesies from a casino they give moderate action to. And a player betting with $25 chips could ask for and probably receive a free room as well. Why not! The casino wants this player to be around its tables at all times, and there's a great likelihood that a gambler will play at the same hotel-casino he's staying at.

I personally don't care to be obligated to any casino and avoid asking or taking a free room, though I've been offered one on several occasions. I like to stay where I please, though I'm not against having a free meal in a casino.

Card counters should be loath to accept a free room, because if they're found out and barred in that hotel-casino, the hotel has their name, and that name will be given to all other casinos in Las Vegas, and they risk being barred at all the casinos there.

Floormen are always hanging around the tables, and anyone who is a big winner at twenty-one can expect heat from the floorman. But there are effective ways of dealing with that situation, which are discussed in the section on how to disguise counting methods in the chapter on blackjack.

The point is that the floorman is the one individual who is going to put heat on card counters and he's the one they're going to have to deal with. And the floorman's antennae can be rather sharp, particularly when one player gives advice to another constantly. The only times I've been barred was when I played with backers at the same table and helped them out with some hands. These backers were individuals who used their bankroll to stake my game, and when they played with me and asked my advice, it was as if a red light was shining over my head, an angry red light that spun around spelling out "expert" on one side and "card counter" on the other.

By giving advice, a player is signaling the floorman that he's a smart player, and that's the one kind of player the casino doesn't want at their tables. They feel that gamblers should only be losers and that no one deserves to win. But since smart blackjack players can and do win steadily, floormen bar them. Simple. In other businesses this might be illegal, but in the gambling industry it's a fact of life—a crazy and unfair one, but one that astute players have to live with.

Therefore, handling the floorman is of vital concern, since he is the man who's going to make the first move to bar you. When he comes around to the blackjack table, you must act like all the losers around you. Don't alter your bets downward after you win; no loser does this. Raise and double your bets after a win, only if the deck is neutral or favorable. That's what losers do; they raise their bets after a win in twenty-one hoping to catch a rush.

If you have a big bet out and the cards are reshuffled suddenly and without warning, leave that bet out. Taking it down, lowering it, is a sign of a card counter, and this is one of the key signals the floorman picks up on. In fact, he may order a reshuffle just to see what you are going to do about it, if he suspects you of card counting.

At the craps table, whether you win or lose makes no real difference to the floormen, for the game is pure chance, except for the skill involved in correctly managing your money and making the best bets on the layout. The floorman will prefer that you lose, but if you win a fortune, you won't get barred. In fact, you're encouraged to play again at their casino, so that the casino can try and get its money back. To encourage you, they'll offer free room, food and drinks, and sometimes women, anything to keep you there to gamble again at their tables. At the craps pit floormen are much more friendly, though even here greed sometimes permeates the air like poison.

I recall an incident at one of the Strip casinos, where, playing for a friend and handling his money at a craps table, I was involved in a really hot shoot myself. The floorman watching the action objected to the manner in which I was raising my bets, claiming I was causing the dealer too much trouble by increasing them after each winning roll. This is, however, a very solid method of beating the house (see the section on strategies for winning at craps).

The dealer, however, wasn't complaining. I had been making good bets for the boys so that the crew was winning along with me. The floorman wanted to break the rhythm of the game, somehow hoping that, by annoying me, the dice would change, just another stupid superstition held by casino personnel. At other times boxmen (the casino executives who supervise a craps table from a seated position) have objected to the way I threw the dice during hot rolls. When the dice are cold, they never object to the throw or the manner in which bets are raised.

In fact, in this instance, it wasn't the business of the floorman. I was raising my bets in a legal manner and wasn't slowing down or hindering the game. He was, with his constant interruptions. Finally, he got to my friend, who simply raised all the bets to the maximum on all the place numbers but the 4 and 10.

"Does that satisfy you now, friend?" my pal asked the floorman.

"Well . . ."

"Just tell me, yes or no, does that satisfy you?" He was really getting angry, because this was his first big win after a few losses, and here was the floorman interrupting the kind of roll that every gambler looks forward to.

The floorman backed away from the table, but kept his eyes on the action.

"That son of a bitch," muttered my friend. "I'm going to find out his name before I leave here and . . ."

"And what?" I asked, getting the dice back.

"Screw him . . ." My friend calmed down as I rolled an 8 and continued rolling numbers for another twenty minutes. My friend took away thousands more than he would have, had the floorman simply let us slowly progress with our bets.

Floormen get downright nasty with some winners, and these

winners mistake the rude individuals they are facing for pit bosses. But they don't have that exalted title. They have middle-level positions, get moderate pay for their work, and stand on their feet all day long in the midst of the noise and the smoke and all the rest of the activity that goes on in a casino. After a while it gets to them. They have essentially boring jobs, and they get jaded and especially annoyed when they see a player win a fortune and walk out, while they have to hang around for another four or five hours on their feet.

These men take out their frustrations not only on the players but on the cocktail waitresses and dealers. But most of all on the players, whom they despise for the most part as idiots and suckers.

As a player, unfortunately, you're going to have to deal with them. Some are good human beings, particularly if they haven't been in the job for too long a time. After a while, the action and the gambling gets to them.

Handle them the right way, firm and in a disarming fashion. Never cater to their whims or anger, especially if they are arbitrary and have no relation to the rules of the house, and never, never get into ego battles with them.

Above all, make them feel that they know all there is to know about gambling, and you know the rest. In other words, make believe that you're just an innocent waiting to be plucked, although the opposite will be true after you read this book. Your look of innocence will make them content and put them at ease, for few of these men can recognize the truth. They've been in casinos too long.

Dealers

Although dealers play an important role in casino operations and all players come in contact with them, their roles and functions will be discussed under the individual games.

3

Casino Credit

The average gambler at an American casino comes to the club with cash or traveler's checks that can easily be converted to cash with the showing of proper identification.

It is only a small minority that establish credit at the casinos, but those who do probably account for a greater volume of play than all the cash customers combined. Nearly all the junket players are credit customers, and the big casinos on the Las Vegas Strip count on half their profits coming from junketeers' play.

The high rollers, known as premium players by the casinos, generally have credit lines at one or more casinos in Nevada and Atlantic City. These players can't be bothered with cash; they like to be able to show up at a club at any time, and, within thirty minutes, without anything in their pockets but a driver's license, bet thousands at the tables.

The casino world, after all, often reflects the real American world outside. And today credit is the name of the game, and everyone who is anyone has some kind of credit. Just as the credit card has replaced cash in American life to the point where you can't rent an automobile in many cities without a credit card, so credit has replaced many cash transactions in casino operations. Many players who bet heavily don't like the risk of carrying cash, and the casino is only too happy to give its premium players all the credit they can use.

Casino credit has another lure as far as the casinos are concerned. When a person signs a marker and receives casino chips on credit, he is not only playing with abstract plastic disks (the chips), but the whole thing has a make-believe aspect. All this man has to do is sign his name and get money, and often this is treated as play money. It's only when the moment of reckoning comes, when he has to pay back what he has signed for, that the harsh reality of the situation becomes evident.

Thus credit can become a snare for the unwary, especially in a casino situation where the action is fast and hard, when gambling fever is contagious and money can be won or lost rapidly.

This is not to suggest that a player shouldn't try to get credit at a casino. I think it's advisable in many situations, especially if the player is going to do some serious gambling, but this credit line must be used as carefully as possible. It must be used for the player's, not the casino's advantage.

I'm supercareful about explaining the use of casino credit because I've seen too many players misuse their credit and really hurt themselves. I've seen them sign markers when drunk or in the middle of a horrible losing streak. I've watched them literally ruin their lives right in front of my eyes.

If it were up to me, I'd ban alcoholic beverages in all gambling casinos. I'd fine any casino executive who permitted a player to sign a marker for credit when drunk, but I'm not on any gaming commission. Since I'm not a gaming commissioner, players can use alcohol when gambling, and this is a deadly combination.

When you have credit, don't misuse it. Don't gamble when drunk and don't sign anything in a casino when drunk. The wisdom of this advice is obvious, but easy to forget or ignore when a player is at a craps table with six drinks under his belt and losing big money.

So if you have credit, I repeat and can't repeat enough, don't drink. If you gamble, don't drink. The best thing to do if you feel that you're losing control is to get away from the table as fast as possible and sleep it off. Keeping in mind some of the dangers of credit, we'll discuss how a player can obtain credit and use it to best advantage.

How to Obtain Credit

Most casinos are happy to give credit because it makes their wheels of fortune spin more smoothly, and the more credit, the merrier the bottom line of their profits. This is not to say that the casino will give credit to anyone who asks for it, or that anyone eligible for credit can simply walk in off the street and get it at once. But there is a correct way to obtain credit and most people can get casino credit if they apply for it in much the same way they would apply to a bank for a personal loan.

No bank is going to allow you to walk in and get a loan without having a credit application filled out and your credit rating verified. The same is true with a casino.

In many ways a casino is like a bank. Much of its business is a credit business, and it has to be very sure of its customers. Like a bank, a casino charges for its loans, but unlike a bank, which charges a fixed interest fee that is added to the loan when paid off, the casino's interest is in a hidden form. It comes from the casino's edge or advantage in the games and is expressed in gambler's terms as "vigorish" or "vig."

At both bank and casino a credit application will have to be filled out and credit references checked fully before money or credit is issued. When borrowing at a bank, the applicant will have to state the purpose of the loan, and the purpose has to be a valid one as far as the bank is concerned—to buy a new car, improve a house, or pay for medical expenses. The money is thus used for a tangible purpose.

The casino never asks what the money is going to be used for because it already knows. Credit extended at a casino is only used for gambling purposes, and that to a casino is tangible and valid use of its money.

This brings up a major difference between the casino and the bank. The bank's money, once borrowed, gives the borrower something of value in the end. The casino's money gets the player action at the table, and if that money is lost it has to be paid off, but the player has nothing really to show for it.

Therefore, when you obtain credit at a casino you should be aware of the pitfalls of that credit. By studying the contents of this book, you'll be in a position to use the credit wisely and without paying a cent for its use.

For most players who want credit the procedure will be pretty standard. They'll be given a credit application to fill out, listing information about bank accounts, credit cards, and financial references. The casino will then verify all this information, some by phone, some by correspondence. It can't be done at once. In most cases, it may take at least a couple of weeks before the applicant's credit is approved.

Because of this time interval, you should plan to get your credit approved before you arrive at the casino to gamble. To do this, you should either write to the casino well in advance, care of the credit manager; or, when visiting a casino, you should fill out an application on the spot so that on your next visit you'll have credit.

Sometimes a casino will accommodate a player by phoning his bank to verify his balance and issuing credit based upon the bank's information. But this will never be done after 3 P.M. on a Friday afternoon, and it is rare that credit will be issued just on the basis of a phone call to a bank. The casino is wary about phone calls, and with good reason. Some years back, a con man defrauded a great many Las Vegas casinos by having an agent (a fellow cheat) answer the phone and verify the man's bank balance and credit, well into the hundreds of thousands, at a bank on the East Coast, when in fact, the man getting credit didn't even have an account at that bank.

Every con man, every thief, every transient and scam operator eventually passes through a place like Vegas, trying to beat the casinos out of money with fraudulent schemes. The casinos are afraid of giving instant credit, of long-distance verifications. What they prefer is proper correspondence, seeing the person's credit references down on paper with a bank's letterhead above the information.

If a player has been a previous visitor to other Nevada casinos and has established credit at one or more of these clubs, the casino can easily check his or her credit through a central

Nevada agency. If the person's credit is good, if previous gambling debts have been paid in a timely fashion, then instant credit may be given at the casino on presentation of proper identification.

If, however, the player has refused to pay gambling debts at another casino or the casino has had trouble collecting and there still remains a sizable balance due, the person's name may go into a file called "the bad rack" and he or she won't be able to obtain credit at any Nevada hotel-casino until all previous debts are paid in full.

A credit line can also be established by putting up front money in the casino cage. This is cash that can be played against by signing markers at the tables. If money is lost, the casino has no fear about collecting because it merely deducts the losses from the deposited money.

If the casino sees that you give it action and have cash to back up the action, it will establish a credit line for you to use on your next trip. However, this should be discussed carefully with the personnel in the cage or the credit department to insure that front money won't be necessary on future visits.

When credit is obtained in the above ways, you will have two ways to exercise this credit. First, you will be able to cash checks up to the amount of your credit line and play with the cash you receive. Second, you will be able to get rim credit, that is, credit at the tables by signing markers against your credit line. A marker is an IOU, stating that the player owes so much to the house. When signing markers, the player receives only casino chips, never cash.

There is still another method of obtaining credit at a casino, though it is becoming obsolete as more and more casinos come under corporation control. This is by word of mouth from other gamblers, bookies, and people on the fringe of illegal gambling. An action player will advise the casino credit office that the person he's sending is good for such and such a line of credit and that he will vouch for that person up to the amount of the specified line. This was once a very common method of obtaining credit and it still works in some places, especially in those casinos where the underworld still has some control. The person vouching for the credit risk will be held liable for debts up to that amount. But should the credit risk pay back his gambling debts at that line and show the casino he's an action player so that he obtains a new higher line of credit, the person vouching for his credit is let off the hook as to any future credit. I've heard that there are underworld figures who have huge credit lines at some legitimate casinos. They use phony names, not to defraud the casinos, but because they don't want the IRS to realize the amount of money they play for or have available.

Some casinos will advance cash on a major credit card, such as Visa or Master Charge, but this is not a standard policy, for casinos are very wary about credit cards in the first place, since a great number of them are floating around, and some of these are stolen or sold cards. The casino, in advancing cash, will attempt to protect itself by verifying that the card is legitimate. This is done by calling a central number handling that firm's cards, but even when this is done, the casino is taking a chance, since a stolen card may not have been reported. Therefore, when trying to obtain cash by the use of a credit card, you should be aware that only a rather small amount will be advanced—generally no more than $100 or $200.

Cashing personal checks is a tricky business for out-of-towners. Many people show up at a casino and expect their personal checks to be honored, but very few casinos will accommodate them. Some will allow a $50, $100, and, in rare instances, a $200 check to be cashed upon presentation of a driver's license and a credit card. However, the casinos are getting stricter about their check-cashing because they've been burned too many times. Many people, after losing money in a casino, feel that the debt is not legitimate and stop their checks or refuse to issue payment on them.

Therefore, don't expect to get any serious gambling money just by coming to a casino and signing a check. In many cases, you won't get any money at all.

The most common, and the easiest way to get cash at the casino cage is to present traveler's checks plus appropriate identification, such as a valid driver's license. Many casinos will first check identification and then through a central num-

ber call the company issuing the traveler's checks to verify
that the checks are valid and haven't been reported lost or
stolen. Only then will they cash them.

Some casinos are stricter than others in this regard. I've
cashed a slew of $100 traveler's checks at a casino by just
signing my name and shoving them across the counter. In
another casino I tried to cash two $20 traveler's checks and
had to show my driver's license.

When going to a resort gambling city, always carry proper
identification if you want to establish credit or cash personal
or traveler's checks. By proper identification, I mean, best of
all, a driver's license. That's the first thing they ask for. If you
don't drive, some states will issue an ID for check-cashing
purposes. Get one of those. If you also have major credit cards,
bring them along.

But if you haven't established credit and want to do some
serious gambling, bring traveler's checks or cash. Don't expect
instant credit for big money, and you won't be disappointed.

Facts About Gambling Credit

Money is a very expensive commodity these days; if you dis-
agree, just go out and try to borrow some. Money on loan or
credit commands high interest. If you don't pay the balance
on your credit card within the designated monthly period,
you'll find yourself paying one and one-half percent interest
per month, or eighteen percent a year. That's a big bite. If you
go for a new mortgage on your home, the interest you'll be
paying will be at least 10 percent and in some states, much
more; in addition, you'll find that there are added charges,
such as lawyer's fees, origination fees, appraisal fees, and so
forth that will in reality drive that figure even higher.

There's no doubt about it. Money is not only expensive but
difficult to obtain. Banks want collateral for their loans, private
lenders want exorbitant interest, and both are reluctant to give
money for abstract reasons. They want definite proof about
where that money is going.

In many ways, as we have pointed out, the casino is like a

bank, and the credit it extends is like a bank's credit. A person must show that he or she is qualified for that loan; however, unlike a bank, the only purpose for which that cash is given on credit by a casino is for gambling purposes.

If you go to your friendly neighborhood bank and ask for cash to gamble with, you'll be quickly shown the door. Neither the banks nor private lenders want any of that business. They know that a gambler can lose it all in one shot and that they're going to have a lot of trouble collecting on a loan that shows nothing in the form of potential collateral.

That's not the only reason no one but a casino will give credit for gambling purposes. (We exclude from this discussion shylocks who are part of the underworld.) A gambling debt is noncollectible in any court in any state in the United States. Even a debt whose basis was gambling, though the debt was not in fact actually given for gambling, may not be collectible. And this applies not only in states such as New York or Texas or California; *the highest court in Nevada has ruled that a gambling debt cannot be collected in that state.*

Very few people know this, but it's a fact of life, one that the casinos know about. The court has also ruled that this works both ways; in other words, a casino in Nevada is not obligated to pay back cash for chips won at their tables. That's also a gambling debt, you see. However, if they refuse to honor their debts in this manner, the Gaming Commission would immediately step in and revoke the casino's license to do business.

Thus, the casinos are very aware of the fact that gambling debts can't be collected, and they also know that checks issued by gamblers can be stopped or dishonored and that there's nothing they can do about it, for there's no way they can legally collect on these checks unless fraud was involved. And by fraud, we mean the use of a phony name in obtaining credit or something like that. But most of the time that's not the case. What happens is that John Gambler, having lost a few thousand in a Nevada casino, is upset, and the more he thinks about it the more upset he gets, and when he gets back to New York City or L.A. or wherever, he stops payment on the check he issued to the casino. And the casino is left holding the bag.

If this is the case, one might ask, why do casinos extend credit at all to players? First of all, their uncollectible bad debts, those that will never be repaid, run to a very small percentage of credit extended, about 2.5 percent, the same as the average bank's percentage on its loans. Second, even though gamblers know they can stop payment on checks and dishonor their gambling debts, they also love to gamble, and if they don't pay back what they owe, they'll be blackballed from getting credit, not only at that particular casino, but at all legitimate casinos throughout the United States.

And despite all the rumors that swirl around the country about Las Vegas casinos, these places don't hire men to break legs and arms of those who owe them money. If it does go on at all, and I doubt this, it's limited to ''street guys'' who have gotten credit at casinos where the underworld has a big interest. In those exceptional cases, pressure may be put on these individuals. But the average legitimate person who dishonors a gambling debt in a Nevada casino or is overdue in paying back is not going to see men at the door with baseball bats.

What will happen will be annoying letters and phone calls from the casino itself, then dunning letters from lawyers in his area, then perhaps a few phone calls from people who represent the casino asking him to pay his debts and pointing out that, after all, the casino is owed money the man was given to play with in the first place, and it's a legitimate, if not exactly a legal, debt.

But no one will say ''pay or else!'' That's not done in these days of corporately controlled casinos. What most gamblers who can't pay their debts at once find is that the casino will allow them to make time payments, and as long as these are kept up to date, the casino may even extend some credit to the player.

That's what happens in most cases. The gambler makes time payments to the casino in the same manner as if he were paying off his car, and while he's making these payments, he'll be allowed a certain amount of credit at the casino and thus will have action. Most gamblers want that action, and that single important fact is the reason that gamblers pay their debts.

And even if a gambler ignores the casino's letters and phone calls and never pays a cent for years then suddenly comes into some money and repays the debt, the casino will not make any unfavorable judgment. The player can have credit there the next day.

How the Casino Protects
Its Credit Bankroll

If you go into a Strip casino in Las Vegas and linger near the cashier's cage, waiting to cash in some traveler's checks or casino chips, there's a sign posted nearby that's sure to catch your eyes. It states, in words to this effect, that "because of recent forgeries, chips of other casinos will not be redeemed at this casino." And if you go across the street to another Strip casino, you'll see the same sign posted at its cashier's cage.

The reason that casino chips can't be redeemed at any casino but the one issuing them has nothing at all to do with forgeries. Casinos will not honor chips issued by other casinos because most of the Strip clubs have a secret pact to protect their bankrolls and to make certain that players don't misuse casino credit. That's the real reason.

In the old days players with credit or those on junkets could go into Casino A on the Strip (at a time when junket members weren't carefully watched as they are today), take a marker for $1,000, play for a few minutes, then walk out of the casino, go across the street to Casino B, and cash Casino A's chips there.

This could occur in those years when casinos on the Strip honored each other's chips and would happily redeem them, for they figured that they were taking away a player from a competing casino. Even today in downtown Vegas or in the casinos in Reno and Lake Tahoe a player can hop from casino to casino and play at their tables with other casinos' chips and even turn them in at the cashier's cage.

This can be done because these casinos don't issue credit the way the Strip hotels do, and if they do, it will generally be for smaller amounts, to allow a player to cash a check up to a few hundred dollars, for example. Junkets are rarely, if ever, arranged for these hotels, and for the most part the players who wander into these casinos are known as "grinds," or small players. The few high rollers who try their luck usually bring cash with them or have a credit line at some of the casinos, but it really doesn't matter if they take the casino's chips outside to another club. It won't hurt the casino at all. It is only the Strip hotels and those casinos that cater to junkets that worry about their credit being abused.

How does the customer abuse his credit by taking chips from Strip Casino A and turning them in at Strip Casino B? Here's how. If a player had a $10,000 line of credit at Casino A and simply took out markers till he depleted his credit without giving the casino much play, his money would be intact, and he'd have $10,000 in cash in his pocket by cashing these chips at Casino B.

When his stay ended, he'd tell the cashier that he couldn't pay up on the $10,000 he owed, but would be happy to give them $1,000 and repay the rest within six months. The casino would prefer to get paid at once, but there'd be nothing they could do but wait for their money. And since the player took out $10,000 worth of markers, they'd figure that he gave them $10,000 worth of action, which was not the case at all.

The player now takes $9,000 of the casino's bankroll home with him to use as he sees fit. He may use it in his business, buy Treasury notes, put it in a bank and get the interest, or whatever. And what interest is he paying the casino for the use of their money? Not one red cent. In fact, he could, if he were shrewd enough, be using the casino bankroll to draw interest or invest in stocks or buy supplies for his business, all free of charge to him. It was a sweet racket.

Today this kind of maneuver is difficult to carry out. For

one thing, if a player establishes credit at a casino, he can't cash in his chips at a competing Strip hotel. He must cash in at his own casino.

And if a player has credit at a casino, his play is watched closely. If he signs a marker at one table and then leaves abruptly, returning to the cashier's cage to cash in the chips, he'll fool no one. What will happen is this: either the pit will call the cashier, advising him that this player has taken out a great many chips without playing them, or the cashier will ask the player if he has taken a marker for his chips.

If he answers affirmatively, the cashier will call the pit to find out what happened and then ask the player to redeem his marker. If there aren't enough chips to redeem it, the cashier will give him cash, but the next time he does this, the player will be asked to stay around, and the credit manager or someone in authority will speak to him, asking why he's doing this. If they get no satisfactory answer, the player's future credit may be cut off. The casino will take this kind of strong measure because it knows it's being taken advantage of by the player, and it doesn't want to wait months for its money to be paid back.

The same thing can occur when a player table-hops under the pretense of playing or giving action at several tables. For example, a player goes to Craps 1 and takes out a marker for $1,000, then goes to Craps 2 after a few minutes and plays for a few minutes there, then goes to Craps 3 and takes out another marker for $1,000, and then walks back to the cashier's cage to cash in his chips.

He won't be fooling anyone, not if the casino has an alert staff on the floor. Some players may get away with this scam in a crowded and poorly supervised casino, but for the most part, casinos will not allow this to happen with junketeers or players with big credit lines, not if they think the sole purpose of this move is to use the casino bankroll for the player's own personal use and purposes, free of charge.

The casino can't stop a player from cashing in or leaving a table at any time; what they can do is have someone talk to the gambler and explain their rules and tell him his credit might be cut off if he's not giving them action, but simply using their money to build up his own cash reserve.

Now, there are players who table-hop legitimately, who find one table cold and run to another and then another, looking for that one hot table. The casino knows that this happens often and knows that players are superstitious creatures at heart but it doesn't really care about these players as long as the intent is action.

If a player wants to gamble, if he's at the tables primarily to gamble, he can do what he wants to do and run from table to table or around the table three times before each bet if that's his pleasure (I guess I'm exaggerating a bit here). But if he's at the table, signing markers just to get the casino's money into his pocket, without paying interest on it, then he's going to be told abruptly to stop that scam.

How to Take Advantage of Casino Credit

This section is for those who do legitimate playing in recognized American casinos, and when I write of taking advantage of casino credit, I'm not writing about scams or about gambling in excess or going crazy at the tables with casino money. What I'm going to discuss is a sane way to handle your credit and to make certain that you don't hurt yourself in the process.

How can you legitimately take advantage of casino credit? The best way is by establishing credit at a few casinos that you are comfortable playing at, then using that credit in the best possible way.

First of all, most casinos will ask you to set a check-cashing limit of your own, an amount you don't want to go over, for your own protection. If they don't ask you, tell them you want this limit. In other words, even though you may have established a $10,000 credit line, if you state that you don't ever want to sign a check for more than $2,000 while staying at the casino or have your outstanding unpaid markers exceed

$2,000, then the casino will have to automatically cut off your credit *for your own protection.*

If they don't do this, if they allow you to play for more than the $2,000, you may very well have a legitimate reason for not paying any gambling debts in excess of that, and the casino may back down and forget about these debts in excess of $2,000.

By doing this, you'll prevent yourself from losing your entire credit line during one disastrous spree at the tables, when you're losing heavily or have been drinking too much. Once that limit is reached your credit is cut off, and you're out of action. This procedure is always suggested because it's saved a lot of people from really hurting themselves at the tables.

When obtaining credit from a casino, you'll be using their money free of charge, without paying interest or any other charges for it. To use it in the wisest possible way, play only at the games recommended in this book, with the methods outlined for best play. If you win with the casino's money, it creates a beautiful situation for you, and one the casino hates but can't do anything about. In other words, you're using their money free of charge to beat them with, and you're not investing a single cent of your own cash. Even if you lose a moderate amount, as sometimes happens, you can make arrangements to pay it off in an equitable and fair manner, and you won't pay one cent in interest for its use.

If possible, when using casino credit, play at a game like blackjack, which will give you an advantage over the house. If that's not your game, then make the best bets in a game like craps, giving the house a tiny edge. Or play baccarat and limit the house edge on bank bets to 1.17 percent.

What you'll be doing is using other people's money (the casino's) at a rate of interest (the casino's edge) much lower than money you could borrow anywhere else. And by not taking it out of a savings bank, you're still getting interest on your money there. With correct plays and proper money management, you can beat the house with their own money—the sweetest situation in the gambling world.

But also remember that having casino credit creates a great temptation to use it all up when losing just because it's there for the signing. Don't ever do that. Follow the advice given in the chapter "A Winning Approach to Gambling" before you ever use the credit and carefully study the chapters on the games you're going to play before risking a cent of that credit, so that you know exactly what you're doing at all times. Always keep a loss limit in mind at any session of play and never go beyond it.

At the tables you can sign markers if you have established credit, but you should never sign a marker for more than you need for that single session of play. If you need $400, don't sign one for $500. If you lose that $400, don't sign another marker. Leave the table and take it easy for a while before hitting another table.

Using the casino money free of interest, playing at only those games which give you the best chance to score a good win, playing correctly, setting a loss limit for each session of play, and, if winning, leaving as a winner, is the sane way to take advantage of casino credit.

4

Preferred
Treatment
of Gamblers

The majority of people who gamble in casinos are casual players, and their action is limited to a few hundred dollars, or a
thousand dollars at most, during their entire stay at a hotel. In
the Nevada casinos most of the gamblers come from California
and the neighboring states. For the most part, they are weekend players or people who have taken a couple of days from
their ordinary routines to try their luck at the tables.

Should these gamblers lose several hundred dollars, they
feel that the entertainment value of gambling, the thrill and
glitter of the casinos, is well worth the loss. To most of these
people gambling is innocent fun and excitement. As for the
casinos, many of them, particularly the ones in downtown Las
Vegas, Lake Tahoe, Laughlin, and Reno, depend on these
small gamblers for their income and welcome them with open
arms. In this age of computers and microchips, these casinos
fill their space with electronic games that require quarter or
dollar plays, rather than the expensive table games such as
craps and baccarat.

Another reason for these casinos using electronic games
other than the fact that they are made for gamblers with limited
funds, is the skill factor. Many of these electronic games require little or no skill. A slot machine, no matter how gaudy
it looks with its multitudinous payoffs, is operated by pulling
a handle or pressing a button. The machine engages and either
shows a winner or, more probably, another loss. The loss is
one to five coins, depending on the machine, and there are
constant payouts to keep the bettor engaged. In the long run,

he or she will lose to the house, but the losses will be limited. To further entice people, the casinos constantly advertise that they have the "loosest slots" or the "best payouts." In addition to these enticements, some of the payouts can be monumental. "Quartermania" machines and "Megabuck" slots pay a million or several million dollars to the lucky jackpot winner.

The players these casinos welcome are the "grinds" in the gambling business—small-time players who never make big bets and who are slowly ground down by the casino advantage. Of all the people who gamble these are the best for any casino in the long run. They will never make a big win, except for the lightning bolt big money jackpot, and if they do win moderate amounts while playing, their constant play will eventually return the wins to the casino. No matter how big the casino, no matter how opulent, these players give the house the bread and butter money that accounts for a good percentage of its profits. These players are never discouraged from the casino.

However, with the rise of monumental, thematically designed gambling palaces in recent years, such as the MGM Grand, Mirage and Treasure Island in Las Vegas and the Taj Mahal in Atlantic City, to name just a few, the overhead or "nut" is tremendous. Entertainment alone costs these hotels millions of dollars per year, and the free drinks, cheap food, and other services offered the players to get their "warm bodies" into the casino runs into more millions.

To feed this constant nut, the big and opulent casinos need action from gamblers, and their definition of action isn't players who are going to try their luck at the tables with a series of $2 and $5 bets for a couple of hours. The casinos do make money from these players, but what they really want are the big bettors, the high rollers, who will think nothing of losing $50,000 or more at the tables in the course of a couple of days.

If they can't get the $50,000 players, the $30,000 gamblers will do as well, and if they can't get them, a $10,000 limit player is still preferable to a grind who loses $40 at blackjack after getting three free drinks, eating the special buffet lunch, and cashing in a free coupon for a lucky buck or a roll of nickels.

Of course, people who run casinos aren't stupid. In order to discourage grinds or, conversely, to get small bettors to gamble at higher stakes, they raise the minimum limits at the tables. In the bigger, grander casinos, the minimum bet at a table game such as craps or blackjack may be $5 or $10. There also will be $25 minimum tables, or $100 minimum tables. Now, a $100 minimum table isn't going to attract a $2 bettor, but a $5 table might.

Even for $25 minimum bettors at blackjack, many of the hotels will set aside a private space. For example, going through the Golden Nugget in downtown Las Vegas, you may notice the baccarat pit, with a private area within it for $25 minimum blackjack players at a few tables. This holds true in other casinos. Casinos want the big bettors to feel important, so they are given privacy and extra attention. But the game is still the same, and all the trappings of grandeur can't disguise that. You must know how to play blackjack correctly to win in the long run—that's the bottom line for players.

At one time, the various hotels in Nevada, especially those on the Strip in Las Vegas, established junket programs to get the high rollers into their casinos. Junkets were planned excursions from a faraway point to the casino, organized by operators called junketmasters, who gathered together a group of qualified gamblers and accompanied them by plane to the hotel-casino where they'd gamble. These junkets usually lasted about four days and were only open to "action players" who met the criteria by previous play or who were recommended by junketeers. It was great while it lasted, for those on a junket. Everything was free as long as they gave the casino action, and the bills the casino picked up, such as the air fare, rooms, meals, and beverages, could run into thousands of dollars.

Today, alas, junkets are a thing of the past. Now, in the casinos catering to premium players, each player is dealt with individually. His action is watched by the hawklike eyes of casino personnel in the various gambling pits, and he is graded accordingly. If he meets minimum standards for that particular casino he will be given free RFB, that is, free room, food, and beverages. If his action is really whalelike, the casino will pick up his air fare as well.

Betting Limits and Play Expected to Receive Preferential Treatment

Just what kind of action is expected for free RFB? In the big hotels, a player will have to make $100 bets, minimum, and do this for four hours a day, minimum. That's a lot of action, and for what? A good room, some fancy restaurant meals, and drinks. First of all, a player is better off not drinking while playing, or even after playing; if he drinks to excess he won't be sharp enough the next day. This book is written for the player, not the casino, and at all times I try to protect the player from excesses.

Let's assume that a player wants preferential treatment. He introduces himself to a floorman or a pit boss, or a casino host or hostess. Usually, he already has credit in the casino, or has a large credit line at another casino that can easily be verified. He will usually ask for credit at the casino he is playing in, or he may have cash that he has moved from the safe deposit box of another casino and brought along with him.

Now that he's introduced himself, his play will be watched. As mentioned before, he must play at the amount and with the frequency required by the particular casino. I gave one example, but the requirements differ from casino to casino. Nothing is etched in stone, however, and casino personnel will be flexible. If they require $100 play for four hours, but the gambler drops $3,000 in thirty minutes and quits for the day, they're not going to hold that against him. Casino personnel understand that a quick loss may mean the end of play for a while. Basically, what they want is someone who plays steadily at fairly high stakes. It may be $50 play in one casino, or even $25 play in another, to qualify for free RFB. There are all kinds and sizes of casinos.

If you go to a casino and want a free meal, for example, speak to a floorman or someone in the pit and ask him or her to watch your play. If you are unsure of how long and at what level you must play to qualify for the meal, ask that also. You

might be told that a $5 blackjack table, for example, is suffi-
cient, if you play for two hours. If you are going to play for
a couple of hours anyway, fine. Go ahead and play, and get
your free meal. But if you want to play out $100 and figure
at best you'll be there for thirty minutes, don't change your
pattern of play just to get a free meal. That meal may turn out
to be very expensive indeed.

Essentially, what I'm saying is this—it doesn't pay to risk
thousands of dollars to get a free room and a fancy meal, nor
does it pay to risk hundreds of dollars to get a $15 dinner. If
you're uncomfortable gambling at a certain level, don't do it.
You're better off paying for your own room and meals. So
maybe it will cost you $100 a day in a fancy hotel. If you
haven't lost $2,500 by playing over your head, you're way
ahead of the game.

This is not to say you'll lose. This book will show you how
to play at the best level in any game you choose. Play those
games and those stakes you're comfortable with, and forget
about free meals.

You shouldn't always forgo the comps or free items the
casino is willing to give you. If you find that personnel at a
certain casino goes out of their way to welcome you, by all
means stay there. Staying at a friendly casino is much better
than being at a cold place where the executives think more
about the bottom line than about its customers.

If you're playing steadily, introduce yourself immediately
to one of the floormen, so he or she will take note of your
action. As long as you're playing a certain amount of time,
you might as well get the freebies the casino is willing to offer.
This may include meals, shows, maybe even a room, if they
feel your action is sufficient. As I mentioned before the free
room and meals, as well as beverages in the more expensive
hotels, may require playing at a high and uncomfortable level.
Don't make $100 bets for four straight hours if you can't
afford to do this either emotionally or financially.

But—and it bears repeating—do play at a level that is comfortable for you. If you find that the casino is friendly and
willing to give you some comps, you've done well. An easy
way to find out just what a casino expects is to ask someone

when you initially call about the availability of rooms. Ask to speak to someone in charge who can give you that information. If you find that the play expected is too much, try another place. You may eventually hit upon a casino that is just right for you; giving you comps at a level of play you can handle easily.

If you are a big bettor, and can play $100 hands for several hours without difficulty, you are in a bargaining position. Call up several hotels and find out what they'll offer you for your action. After all, you're a premium player and a valuable one for any casino. See what you'll get in terms of free food and rooms. Can you eat in any of the fine gourmet restaurants free of charge? Just what kind of accommodations will they give you? You can negotiate with a hotel with that kind of play. You can even try and get your air fare reimbursed. Just be sure to have your credit in order before you play.

As I said before, casinos are flexible, and will try to accommodate the high rollers. These are the gamblers they want. Be sure, once you've established credit and received the room and the meals, that you do give the kind of play you promised. Otherwise all the comps will rapidly evaporate and you'll have a huge bill to pay.

How the Casino Checks on a Player's Action

Once you've asked for comps, or asked to be watched in the hope of getting comped, the casino will select someone to watch your action. That someone will probably be a floorman in a gambling pit. If you're playing blackjack, the floorman will be assigned to the pit you're playing in, and you should stay there if possible. If one table seems bad, go to another table in the same pit. If you want to move to another part of the casino, let the floorman know you're doing this, rather than just leaving.

When you get to another pit in the casino, tell the floorman there that you were playing at a different pit where you were being rated as a player. He or she will make a call to the previous pit and speak to the floorman there, and your rating will continue. But just what do these casino personnel rate?

They generally break your action down into three parts. First they'll note the time you start playing. Then they'll note the average bet you are making. And finally, they'll put down the time you stop gambling. Note that I said they study your average bet. No one expects you to make the same bet over and over again. Gamblers run in streaks, no matter what kind of luck they're experiencing. Gamblers like to play the rush; that is, when they're winning, they like to press up or increase their bets. Conversely, when losing, they tend to lower their bets.

This is understood by casino personnel. As I keep mentioning, they are flexible when assessing gamblers. A player may test the waters with $50 bets, then start plunking down $200 wagers. If he gets on a rush of winning bets, he may go to $500. All this is taken into consideration by the person watching his action.

On the other hand, a player may start off horribly and never recover. Within an hour he's been wiped out. Let's say he took a marker for $3,000 and lost it all in that short space of time. He stops betting and retreats like a wounded animal to his room or the pool or wherever he can get some peace of mind and recoup his energy. The casino observer is noting this and the fact that he only played for one hour instead of four won't be held against him.

Suppose, however, that another player has a terrific winning streak at the outset of play. Everything goes his way and he keeps pressing his bets. At the end of one hour he's ahead $10,000 and he calls it a day. Well, he didn't give the casino the action they really wanted, which was for four hours. And on top of it all, the casino bankroll has been depleted by $10,000. Will this player's comps end? No way. He'll be given more and more, any enticement to keep his warm body at that hotel. The casino wants its money back, and casino operators figure that if he plays long enough, all the winnings will be returned to the casino's money trays. They don't want him to leave and play somewhere else. That would be a minor disaster.

If the player goes to another casino and loses all the money he won there, the first casino is still out $10,000, with no way to recoup it. On top of everything else, by taking away his comps, they're alienating a big bettor who probably won't return to their casino. So, big winner or big loser, the casino wants you to stay at its hotel and gamble in its casino. Casino personnel will be as flexible as they can; they'll stretch that rubber band all the way to make sure you keep gambling at their place.

Player Membership Cards

In recent years, the casinos have come up with a new way to keep track of gamblers' action and to rate the players without the necessity of someone in a pit watching their action. By issuing membership cards which are inserted in electronic games before the player starts gambling, casinos can keep track of slot, video poker, or any other kind of electronic game play. In some casinos the cards are also used for identification purposes at the table games.

Casinos are happy to issue membership cards. All you have to do is fill out a simple application. No bank references are required, no credit forms are needed; they are available to one and all. Basically, the following information is asked for:

Name, Spouse's name, Mailing address, Phone number, Birthday and voïlà!, you're in business. You are issued a card. The casino doesn't really care what credit you have, because they're not giving you credit. All this card does is follow your action at the slots or whatever other electronic games you play. You just slip it into the slot and start feeding the machine with coins. The card automatically monitors your action.

What's the purpose of these cards? Why have your action electronically followed? Well, for one thing, you get credits every time you play, and with these credits come complimentary awards. The more credits you have, the more awards you're entitled to. And getting a card is simple, and doesn't cost you anything. If you're at a casino and want to play the slots or video poker for a while, by all means get a membership card. In this age of computers, all your action is automatically credited to your account. When you go back to get your comps, they'll ask you for identification before giving you the awards. They do this because players sometimes leave their cards in the machines when they quit play, or they lose their cards in other ways. Providing identification ensures that no one else can take advantage of your action.

Credits and awards vary from casino to casino, but practically every casino, especially in Las Vegas, now issues membership cards. As awards, a player may receive simple things like key chains, money clips, or gold charms at the smaller casinos. With enough credits, the bigger casinos may reduce the rate of your room or give you free meals in its better restaurants.

Some casinos issue certificates that you can redeem for ready cash, or for discounts on goods purchased at the hotel's shops. In addition, once you become a member of a particular club, you may be invited to special events such as private parties or slot tournaments. You become someone special to the casino; not just a tourist walking through. Therefore it pays to become a member when you're staying at a hotel-casino. You've nothing to lose and everything to gain. If you walk to adjacent hotels, join their clubs as well. If you play the electronic games, take advantage of the credits you earn.

If you only want to play the electronic games such as video poker or slot machines, it pays to inquire about the comps and credits before making reservations at a particular hotel. Check various hotels, and find the one that best will compensate you for your action.

Just because you play video poker, for example, doesn't foreclose you from playing table games such as blackjack, where your skill can beat the house. Not only check on the membership clubs, but the comps available to you when playing a table game such as blackjack. Can you get a better rate on your room? Will it be difficult for you to get your meals comped? Don't be afraid to ask questions. It's much better to know just what to expect, rather than pick a hotel at random and find yourself unhappy with what awaits you.

On the other hand, if all you want is a bed, it might pay to get a cheap room somewhere, and to use the hotel as a base or center, roaming around whatever gambling city you're in and looking for action where it suits you.

For example, I recommend that you play progressive video poker games in the section on video poker. And I further recommend that these progressive machines have a payoff of at least $2,200 before they're worth playing. Stretching that figure, play nothing with less than a $2,000 payout. Now suppose you make a reservation at Hotel X. You join its membership club and receive a card, and you find that there are four areas where progressive quarter video poker machines are located in the casino. The first has a jackpot of $1,048.50, the second $1,236.70, the third $1,098, and the fourth $1,400.60. None are worth playing. What should you do if you want to put in some serious hours playing video poker?

Obviously, you're not going to play video poker at that casino. Your stay may be three days, and even at the end of that time you might find the largest payout is only $1,600 or $1,700. The best thing to do is go to a casino where there are payouts in the $2,000 range. Once there, immediately join the membership club at that casino. Speak to a host about a future visit to that hotel. If the casino personnel see that you're spending some serious hours playing the video poker machines, they may suggest you stay at their hotel-casino the next trip around. They may also offer you a special rate as an inducement.

They'll know about your action from the credits you're piling up on the card. But it's also a good idea to introduce yourself to a floorperson in the video poker section. There's bound to be someone around the area. Get to be known. It can only help you. Don't remain anonymous if you want future comps and benefits.

Remember, when you go to a new casino to play, look for the area that gives out membership cards. Casinos have different names for these areas. Some may call it a "Fun Club" or "Player's Club" or whatever name they deem feasible. But it won't be hard to find the area. If you can't find one, ask security. They usually will direct you. Or ask a floorperson anywhere on the floor, behind any pit. They'll help you out. And get that card before playing. While you're at it, ask if the card can be used for table games. Some casinos will allow this as a quick way to keep track of a person's gambling.

Summing Up

Casinos have special deals for preferred customers. The deals and comps vary from casino to casino, but expect the more opulent establishments to require higher levels of play. In a Strip casino or a downtown Las Vegas casino such as the Golden Nugget, expect to make minimum $100 bets for at least four hours to get a free room, gourmet meals, and beverages. That's a lot of action, so, if you can't afford this either financially or emotionally, don't play at these levels just for the comps.

If you can afford it, however, and you like the idea of a fancy suite of rooms and personal attention, by all means go for it. I suggest that you study the sections on the table games, such as blackjack, so that you end up a winner because of your skill as a player. Then everything is doubly sweet. You're treated like royalty, and you come home with more money than you started with.

In smaller and less fancy casinos, the minimum requirements are lower. Always ask what they are before playing if you want to be comped. It doesn't pay to play at a quarter ($25) table for four hours only to find you're entitled to nothing, if your main reason for playing at this particular casino was to be comped to a room and meals. Once you find out the limits required, see if they fit into your financial and emotional setup. If uncomfortable with the limits, let it go. Take a pass and go to another casino.

Of course, doing it this way is not the best plan. What I suggest is making inquiries before heading to Las Vegas or Atlantic City or wherever. If you find limits to your liking, establish credit before landing at your destination. Then you're all set.

But suppose you get to a particular casino, and first you don't like the ambience, the attitude of the dealers, or the general setup. You get the feeling things won't go well—that you're going to end up a big loser. You're just not comfortable. Well, forgo the free room and meals and don't play there. If possible, move to another casino that is more to your liking. If you leave Hotel A and walk over to Hotel B and tell them what your credit line at the other hotel is and how much you expect to play for, they may welcome you with open arms and move you right in. If they don't, and if you can't find another room in town for the weekend, play wherever you wish at comfortable limits, rather than trying to please the first hotel just to get a free room and some meals. They could end up as a pittance compared to your losses. Don't let the comps be your master.

If you're like most people who gamble, you're probably not pushing for a free room and board and the whole nine yards. You'll probably be satisfied with an occasional free meal or a free show. You may be staying at Hotel D and wandering around to find a good single deck blackjack game. You find it at a nearby casino. Just your speed. You decide to sit down and cash in a few hundred bucks. Ask the dealer to send over the floorman. Introduce yourself and tell him or her that you want your action monitored. He'll be happy to oblige.

Let's assume you spend two hours in the pit, playing at a couple of tables. At the end of that time, call over the floorman and talk to him. He or she may give you comps for dinner for two that night, or a free show at the casino, or both. He or she may like your action and suggest that you stay at that hotel the next time around at a reduced rate. You may even be told that four hours of play a day will give you the fabled free RFB.

Some players like to stay anonymous. They may be card counters who don't want the attention of a floorperson. We can understand that. Card counters aren't welcome in a casino, especially if they're big winners. If you make a terrific score at a casino featuring a single deck blackjack game, you might want to return again and again. And return anonymously. Let's assume you win $550. Why jeopardize other wins in that range for a $10 meal? That's another factor to take into consideration.

Finally, if you want to concentrate on the electronic games, I suggest video poker and that you join the casino membership club. The credits will add up and, in addition to the possible jackpot, you might get free meals or cash certificates. Why not take them? Video poker is not a game that you will be barred from, unless you're part of a team that seeks out monster jackpots and monopolizes the seats until they're hit. If you're playing by yourself or with a partner, no one is going to bother you when you hit the jackpot. In fact, the casino wants you back in order to recoup some of that money. Being a big winner galvanizes casino personnel to invite you back, unless they take you for a card counter. They're just as interested in a big winner as a big loser. The loser they figure will continue to leave his or her money at the casino. The winner, they hope, will come back and drop the winnings at a future time.

Whatever your level of play, whatever your game, study this section in order to take advantage of the comps and other goodies casinos will give you for your play. It'll make you an even bigger winner!

5

Blackjack—
Advantage
to the Player

Blackjack has overtaken craps in the last fifteen years to become the most popular of the casino games. While an individual baccarat or craps table may take in more money than the average blackjack table, there are many more tables in a casino devoted to twenty-one, as the game is sometimes called, and more and more people are playing the game.

Much of the recent popularity has been due to the publication of the book *Beat the Dealer* by Edward Thorp. Prior to its publication, blackjack was considered a game in which the house held a big advantage over the player, and few players knew the correct strategy necessary to beat the game.

With the advent of the computer it became possible for mathematicians to play out millions of hands of blackjack, eliminating certain cards from each deal to see the effect they'd have on the overall odds of the game. As a result of these studies, distilled by Thorp in his book, a player could now know the correct procedure for playing out each individual hand, and more important, he could know when the deck was favorable or unfavorable to him, and thus could raise or lower his bets accordingly.

When readers of *Beat the Dealer* converged on Las Vegas, the casinos first treated them with amusement, considering them "system" players, and they knew system players always lost. But as casino losses mounted, the operators of the Vegas clubs became panicky and started tampering with the blackjack rules. Some rule changes were merely temporary ones, while others have lasted to this day. Many were restored, not because it was to the casino's advantage to do so, but because thousands of players who liked blackjack and couldn't care less about card counting and correct strategy stayed away from the tables. When this happened, most of the former rules were reinstated, because the bottom line to any casino is its profit margin.

The game is different, however, than it had been before Thorp's book came out. No longer do all the clubs have single-deck games, and no longer do the dealers deal down to the bottom card or show the burned card. And no longer can players jump a bet from $1 to $500 with impunity or raise and lower their bets at will.

Today's casino personnel, who watch and supervise the blackjack tables, get paranoid when they see players constantly alter their bets. They're continually searching for card counters and are ready to bar them from ever playing twenty-one in their casinos again.

The worst offenders in that regard aren't the old-line, privately owned casinos, but the new corporation hotel-casinos, such as the Hilton in Las Vegas and Harrah's in Reno. They'll bar you in those places even if you're just a big winner. To them a winner is a card counter, and what these types of casinos want are losers, not winners.

It's a strange paradox that blackjack, being a casino game with rules of play set out by the casino, can be beaten by the players. It's stranger still that the casinos feel that only the ignorant and the losers should be allowed to play and that the solid players who make a study of the game and play correctly should be barred. It's a good thing that the casinos don't play their poker games directly against the players, for if anyone showed skill in poker, if the casino noticed a player raising with a good hand or folding his cards with a bust hand, they'd throw him out of the game and out of the casino, barring him for playing correctly.

I vividly recall an incident where a friend of mine was barred at a club in Reno, one of the biggest casinos there. Not only was he told to leave, though he was winning just a few dollars at that time, but he was publicly humiliated. He was asked for his name and proper identification, which he really didn't have to furnish, and he was forced to leave a table where he was doing nothing but idly chatting with a female dealer in hopes of getting a date with her that night.

He knew something about blackjack and knew a simple count to enable him to win at the game, but all he was doing was playing as any intelligent player would. Blackjack, after all, is a game of skill, and the measures this casino took were extreme.

Casinos have been taken to court by barred players, and until recently the casinos had won their cases against the players, hiding behind the legal charade of claiming to be private clubs, since they don't charge admission to the general public.

However, on December 1, 1979, the Casino Control Commission of New Jersey, in a surprise move, ordered the Atlantic City casinos to permit card counters to play blackjack. At the same time, the rules were modified to make it more difficult for card counters to maintain their edge over the casinos.

In order to weaken the counters, the new rules allowed the casinos to reshuffle their four to six decks more often by lacing the plastic insert about halfway into the decks instead of the more normal two-thirds and three-quarters in. The rule lasted only thirteen days before it was rescinded by the commission chairman. Card counters are again barred in Atlantic City.

There are ways to disguise your skills in blackjack; these measures are strongly advised for card counters and skillful players. By disguise, I don't mean a false mustache, but a manner of playing, betting, and acting at a table to lull the casino personnel into thinking you're eccentric or just lucky, not skillful. This is necessary because after you read this chapter on blackjack, you'll be able to beat any casino in America, and you must blunt the casino's countermeasures so that you can continue playing and winning.

Don't think, however, that winning at blackjack is that simple or that this chapter will present you with a golden key to riches without any effort on your part. Mastering the correct strategy, using it consistently, and curbing your impatience will make you a winning twenty-one player. Don't rush to the nearest casino with what you think is your golden wand, expecting the money to roll in immediately. Patience is one of the keys to winning.

You must learn the correct strategies and know them so well that you can unhesitatingly play the hand correctly each time. To do this requires many hours of study, practice, and actual play, first at home and then under actual casino conditions. Start with small games and work your way up, and you'll be pleasantly surprised at how the money and wins will slowly but surely accumulate.

Blackjack can be beaten, and this chapter will give you all the keys to victory you'll ever need.

The Basic Game

The basic game of blackjack is a rather simple one, but as in all simple games of skill, the complexities of best play are enormous. I don't mention this to frighten you off, but to prepare you to learn, to study and restudy the information in this chapter.

In the casino game one or more decks may be used, but we'll start with a single deck at the outset, since all strategies flow from the original single-deck version of the game.

The Single-Deck Game

Blackjack is played with a standard deck of fifty-two cards in which all four suits are of equal value.

In blackjack each card has a specific value or numerical count, with the exception of the ace, which has two values, but we'll discuss the ace last. The value of any card is determined by its spots. A 2 is worth 2 points, a 3 is worth 3 and so on to 10. The face cards: jack, queen, and king—are also worth 10 points apiece. The 10, jack, queen, and king, in blackjack parlance, are known as "10-value cards."

The ace is unique in having two separate values. It can either be counted as 11 or as 1, at the player's discretion, when playing out the hand. Having this dual value makes the ace the most powerful of all cards at blackjack.

Object of the Game

The object of this game is simple. It's to beat the dealer, but in order to do so, a player must have either a higher valued hand than the dealer, or the dealer must go over a total of 21 while the player has a valid hand with 21 or fewer points. In this game, a tie between the dealer and player is a standoff, with neither winning.

If either the player or dealer is dealt an ace and a 10-value card in the first two cards, he has a blackjack. A blackjack is an immediate winner, and if the player has one and the dealer has an ordinary hand, the player wins at 3-2. If the dealer has a blackjack and the player has an ordinary hand, the dealer wins. If both the dealer and player have blackjacks, it is a tie and thus a standoff, with neither winning.

In this game, the highest total a player or dealer can have is 21. Unless he has a blackjack, he will have to draw cards to get to 21. If either a dealer or player draws cards to his original two cards and goes over 21, the hand is a losing one, called a bust. A bust hand loses automatically.

Suppose a player is dealt a queen and a 6. He has a total of 16, which is a bad hand. He can draw, or "hit," this hand and get another card. If that card is a 6 or higher, it will give the player a total of over 21, and thus his hand will be a bust, and he'll lose at once. As outlined later in this chapter, a player either hits his hand or stands pat according to the card the dealer shows as his upcard (card dealt face up).

How the Game Is Played

The dealer always handles the cards and is responsible for dealing them out to the players. The dealer stands behind a blackjack table and faces seated players; usually from one to seven players can be accommodated at the average casino blackjack table. We'll assume that the dealer faces six players.

Prior to the outset of play, the dealer thoroughly shuffles

the deck of cards and then gives the deck to one of the players to cut. If that player refuses to cut the cards, any other player may do so.

After the cards are cut, the dealer restacks them and then removes the top card and either places it face up at the bottom of the deck or puts it to one side face down in a plastic box. This card, so removed, is called the burned card. It is out of play and never used.

If the burned card goes to the bottom of the deck, all used cards will be placed underneath it, also face up. If the burned card goes into a plastic case, then all future discards wind up face down on top of that card in the case.

The dealer is now ready to deal out the cards to the players. The dealer represents the casino, and all his wins go to the casino treasury. If the dealer loses, the losses are from the casino bankroll. So essentially the players are playing directly against the casino when they endeavor to beat the dealer at twenty-one.

Before the dealer will start dealing out cards, all the players must have made their bets by putting casino chips or cash into the betting boxes in front of each player.

Usually chips are used for betting purposes, but a player may bet with cash. If the player wins his bet, he'll be paid off with casino chips, not with cash, for the house discourages the use of cash in its games. Cash has to be carefully counted and slows up the game. The casino would rather have that cash in its drop box at the bottom of the table, and that's where it goes immediately after the player loses a hand betting cash.

After all the players have made their bets, the dealer deals out the cards, starting with the player to his left, as he faces him, so that the deal is clockwise.

The Deal

Each of the players is dealt one card face down, and the dealer gets his own card face down also. Then he begins a second round of dealing, giving each player another card face down, while his own card is dealt face up. The dealer always gets the last card dealt on each round, and always acts upon his hand last.

If the dealer's upcard is a 10-value card, he must peek at his hole card (card dealt face down) to see if he has a black-jack. If he has one, then it's an immediate winner for the house, and the dealer turns over his cards and collects all los-ing bets. If the upcard is an ace, before peeking, he asks the players if they want insurance, in effect allowing them to bet that the dealer has a blackjack. This will be explained in a later section.

At this point, the players are holding two cards apiece all face down while they see one of the dealer's cards. Although the players' cards are not seen by the dealer, it makes no difference at all, since the dealer has no options and is bound to play his own cards by rigid house rules, no matter what cards are held by the players.

Dealing two cards face down slows up the game, but it is a ritual of blackjack, and it makes the players feel as though they're doing something special by playing out their cards in this secretive manner. In reality, it makes no difference at all as far as the game is concerned.

After each player has received two cards, starting with the first player to receive cards, also known as the first baseman, each player can make one of several plays. For the time being we'll forget about the various options and concentrate on whether the player will hit (draw a card) or stand (not draw a card).

If a player is satisfied with his total, he may stand pat. If he isn't satisfied with his hand, he may want to draw one or more cards to increase the total of his points.

If a player wants to hit his hand, he need not say anything. The practice is to scrape the cards on the green felt surface of the table towards himself. He'll automatically get another card by doing this.

Scraping is used instead of words because in the casino there's a great deal of noise, and chaotic sounds and words are often misunderstood. The scraping motion is universally accepted. Should a player not care to hit his hand, he pushes his cards under his chips. And should a player have hit his hand and be satisfied with the total, he pushes his original two cards under his chips. No more cards will be dealt to him after he does this.

So now it's up to the first baseman to make his decision about playing his cards, whether to hit or stand. After he plays his hand, then the second player plays his and so on to the last player at the table, the one facing the dealer's right hand. This last player is known as either the third baseman or anchor man.

After all the players at the table have acted upon their hands, the dealer plays his. He first turns over his hole card so that all the participants at the table see both of his cards, and then plays out his hand according to the strict rules of the casino, either standing on his total or hitting his hand.

Although, as we shall see, a player has many options, a dealer has none. In most casinos a dealer must hit all his hands valued at 16 or below and he must stand on all hands valued at 17 or above. The only exception is in those casinos that require a dealer to hit a hand called a soft 17, which consists of cards adding up to 17 with the ace counting as 11. For example, a hand consisting of an ace and 6 is a soft 17.

For purposes of this section, however, we'll be playing in a casino where a dealer must stand on all hands totaling 17 or more, whether or not they're soft 17s. And no matter what hands the player holds, whether they be 18s, 19s, or 20s, even if the dealer knows he'll be beaten if he stands, he must still stand pat. He cannot deviate from the casino rules.

Let's now follow our six players and the dealer in an illustrative hand. The first two cards dealt to the players consist of the following:

Player A; 10, 4
Player B: A, 5
Player C: 9, 3
Player D: A, K
Player E: 6, 3
Player F: 7, J
Dealer: ?, 8

We are seeing the dealer's hand the way the players see it, with one upcard and one hole card.

Player A decides that 14 isn't strong enough against the dealer's upcard of 8, and so he scrapes his cards for a hit. He gets a 9 and now holds 10, 4, 9 for a total over 21. He has busted and loses at once, so he turns over his cards, showing his busted hand, and the dealer immediately removes the cards and the player's chips from the table. Player A is now out of the game; even if the dealer should bust later on, the player cannot redeem his chips. Once a player busts, and then the dealer busts, the player loses.

Player B has an ace and 5 for either a 6 or 16. By hitting, he cannot bust and stands a good chance of improving his hand, so he scrapes for a hit and gets a 3. Counting the ace as an 11, he now has a total of 19, which is a high total in blackjack, so he stands.

Player C, with a total of 12, scrapes for a hit and gets a jack. Since a jack counts as 10, he has busted and turns over his hand. His cards and chips are taken away by the dealer.

Player D immediately turns her cards over, since she has a blackjack. She is paid off at 3-2 on her bet, and her cards are taken away.

Player E scrapes for a hit and gets an ace. Since an ace can count as 11, with the original total of 9, Player E has 20, a very strong total. He now pushes his cards under his chips to indicate that he doesn't want any more cards.

Player F stands pat by pushing his cards under his chips. He has a total of 17, and although it's not that strong a hand in blackjack, the chances of hitting and possibly busting are too great to draw another card.

All the players have now played out their hands, so the dealer turns over his hole card. He has a 2 in the hole for a total of 10, and must, by the rules of the casino, hit his hand, since the total is below 17. He hits and gets a queen for a total of 20 and must now stand.

Player B loses because his total is only 19, and his cards and chips are taken away. Player E has a 20, so it ties the dealer's total, and only his cards are taken away, since a tie

is a standoff. Player F loses his bet, however, since he only
has a total of 17, which is lower than the dealer's 20. His
cards and chips are taken away by the dealer.

Now the dealer prepares to deal out another round of cards,
and the players, prior to this deal, must again place chips in
their betting boxes.

Double and Multiple Decks

More and more casinos are turning to multiple-deck twenty-
one games, in which two, four, and sometimes six decks are
used, rather than sticking to the original one-deck games. Casinos are doing this to speed up the game, to prevent players
from cheating, and to thwart card counters, who find it more
difficult to keep track of multiple decks. All games in Atlantic
City are multiple-deck games.

Card counters keep a count of the cards as they are dealt
out, usually in some sort of ratio of large cards to small cards.
This will be explained in the section on card counting, later
in this chapter. When these card counters play in a single-deck
game, it's rather easy for them to check out all fifty-two cards,
so many casinos, to stop them from taking advantage of this
situation, originally ordered the dealers to shuffle up the cards
after only two or three rounds of play. This continuous reshuffling slowed up the single-deck games, and since no
money could be bet while cards were being shuffled, the casino found itself making little money in its single-deck games.
As a result, they turned to multiple decks.

A number of casinos use two decks. These are held by the
dealer, although they're a little more awkward to deal from.
However, the majority of casinos using multiple decks now
deal out four or more decks at one time, and instead of a dealer
holding them, they're placed in a box, called a shoe, from
which they can be slid out, one at a time.

Dealing from a shoe speeds up the game, and these cards
can easily be dealt to the players face up, preventing the players from marking or changing cards. When cards are dealt
from a shoe, a plastic marker is usually inserted about three-

quarters of the way into the multiple decks, and when that marker is reached, the cards are reshuffled.

A multiple-deck game is much easier for a dealer to handle, and the casinos find that they make more money from multiple decks, so it's definitely the wave of the future. When cards are dealt face up, they don't ever have to be touched by the player. If he wants a hit, he simply points at the cards, and if he wants to stand pat, he waves his hand over the cards. When players don't touch or handle their cards, they can't tamper with them, and the casino can't be cheated.

Cheating is a continual problem for casinos. With four decks dealt face down, it's possible for a player to change or switch the cards he has been dealt, for there are many duplicate cards in a four-deck game, and if a player holds two jack of spades, for example, there is nothing wrong with that situation.

The card cheats who switch cards, replacing small cards with aces and tens, are called muckers or hand muckers. When cards are dealt openly, it's practically impossible for these cheats to operate.

Rules of Play

Strange as it may seem, the rules of play aren't standard in American casinos, not even in all the casinos in Las Vegas or in Reno, for example. This fault lies with the Gaming Commission of Nevada, which doesn't require standard rules and doesn't even require a particular casino to post the standard and prevalent rules in that individual club. In fact, the situation is so chaotic that rules may change from table to table in each casino.

I can mention personal experiences which have been frustrating because of this situation. Playing alone at a table, head to head with the dealer, I was making opening and neutral bets of $15, raising them to $30 when the deck was favorable and lowering them to $5 when the cards were unfavorable. I was also playing two hands at a time, since I was alone, and this enabled me to slow down the game and also made it easier for me to thoroughly count the cards.

I had played for about half an hour against one dealer, then he took his break and another dealer took over. When the deck next became unfavorable, I reduced both bets to $5, but this dealer informed me that if I played two hands at a $5 minimum table, I'd have to bet at least $10 a hand as my minimum bet. I told him that the previous dealer had allowed me to bet only $5.

"I'm sorry; you'll have to bet $10."

"Where does it state that I have to bet $10?" I asked.

The dealer disregarded my question and called over a floorman, who informed me that $10 was the minimum bet at a $5 table when playing two hands, even though this same floorman had been watching my play before and had seen me bet $5 a hand.

It's this kind of arbitrary rule-making that's not only irritating but illegal, as far as I'm concerned. If these are rules for the game, then the Gaming Commission should enforce them, or at least have them posted.

In most of the Vegas casinos it's impossible to know what the rules of that house are. Nothing is posted, either on the walls or at the tables. A player must ask for every option allowed. In Northern Nevada and Atlantic City the situation is a little bit better, since the important rules concerning doubling down and splitting cards are posted at the tables.

To clear up the mysterious Las Vegas rules, let's first deal with the Vegas casinos, which are the center of gambling in America.

Las Vegas Rules

Las Vegas is really two cities in one as far as gambling is concerned. There is the Strip, the area of Las Vegas Boulevard South that runs from Sahara Avenue up to the Tropicana Hotel and includes hotels near that boulevard, such as Bally's and Caesars Palace. The Strip also includes the Las Vegas Hilton, which is on Paradise Road, about a quarter of a mile from the

Strip. In other words, all hotels south of Sahara Avenue are lumped together as Strip hotels.

Then there is the downtown section, the center of which is Fremont Street. At the intersection of Fremont and Casino Center is the Fremont, Horseshoe, Four Queens, and the Golden Nugget. Other hotels and/or clubs run north and south on Fremont Street, ending with the Union Plaza at the intersection of Main and Fremont streets. Still other hotel casinos are on side streets, such as the Lady Luck on Ogden Street. All of this area is lumped together as the downtown section. The rules differ from club to club downtown, just as they differ from casino to casino on the Strip. However, there are some basic rules that generally prevail and we'll start with these.

Las Vegas Strip Rules

When we refer to the Strip, we mean the luxurious and ornate edifices that are known the world over, such as Caesars Palace, the Tropicana, and Bally's. The biggest blackjack games in Nevada are played on the Strip. After we discuss the general rules prevailing, we'll discuss individual casinos and their particular rules.

• The dealer must stand on all 17s. This means that no matter what 17 he holds, whether hard (10, 7) or soft (ace, 6), he cannot draw another card. This rule is to the advantage of the player.

• Insurance pays 2-1, and a player may bet half his original bet as an insurance bet. Although this bet is bad most of the time, there are situations where insurance is to the advantage of the player.

• A player may double down on any two cards he's dealt; that is, double his original bet. He then receives only one additional card from the dealer. This is a standard rule throughout Vegas and is definitely to the player's advantage, giving him more opportunities to double his bet than the more restrictive rules—prevalent in Northern Nevada—of doubling down only on 10s and 11s.

• A player may split any two cards of the same value and bet an amount equal to his original wager on the split card. If he receives a card identical to the split cards, he may split that card also. After splitting his cards, he may play out each hand separately, hitting as many times as he wishes. All face cards are considered as 10s and may be split. For example, a queen, 10 may be split.

However, if a player splits aces, he can only receive one more card on each ace after splitting them.

These are standard rules in all Strip casinos, making it the most liberal place in America to play blackjack.

There are even more liberal rules available, applicable in certain casinos. At times we'll mention the names of individual casinos, but rules change rapidly, and you should always inquire about the rules of the particular club you're playing in.

• Surrender is allowed. This means that the player may, if he doesn't care to play out his hand, surrender his hand and give up half his bet as a lost bet. He may do this only on the original first two cards dealt. Once a hand is drawn to, it cannot be surrendered.

This rule is allowed in several casinos, such as the Dunes, Caesars Palace, and the Aladdin. Some casinos display a printed notice at each table that surrender is allowed; others don't. A player has to inquire about this rule, for many times, even if it's allowed, there is nothing on the table to suggest that it's permitted.

The surrender option is definitely to the advantage of a player, especially if he's counting cards. When a deck is superfavorable for him, which means that there are many 10s and aces remaining in the deck, and he's dealt 10, 6 while the dealer shows a 10 as his upcard, surrender could be quite profitable. With favorable situations, the card counter will have a large bet out. In this situation, he's doomed. If he hits, he'll probably bust. If he stands, the dealer will almost certainly have a hand above 17. So, instead of losing his entire bet, the player can surrender his 16 and lose only half his bet.

There are several other instances where surrender is a valuable option, but they'll be dealt with in the section on surrender.

• After splitting cards, a player, when he receives another card on either hand, can then double down. For example, suppose that a player splits a pair of 8s, which is a smart play. And suppose that he receives a 3 on the first 8 for a total of 11. He would then be able to double down that hand, a very valuable option.

This rule is featured at several of the Strip casinos that have multiple-deck games, such as Bally's and Caesars Palace.

• More and more of the Strip casinos do not permit their dealers to peek at the hole card until all the players have acted on their hands first. In some casinos the dealer does not get a second card until all the players have acted first. In other words, an upcard is dealt for all the players to see, then the dealer deals himself another card after play is through, and acts upon his own hand.

In either case the casino is eliminating a problem area for itself. When a dealer is forced to peek at his or her hole card if the upcard is an ace or ten, two things can happen that might hurt the casino. First, the dealer may inadvertently disclose a "tell," or give away the value of that card by taking a long look at a four, for example, which resembles an ace in markings. Or an inexperienced or sloppy dealer may show the hole card to a player sitting at either end of the table, usually in the first seat. And there are instances where the dealer, in collusion with a player, will disclose the value of the hole card to his agent by some sort of hidden signal.

For the above reasons, the casino prefers that the dealer not receive a second card or not peek at his or her second card, the hole card.

It should now be assumed that the vast majority of casinos on the Strip do not permit their dealers to peek at the hole card.

Downtown Las Vegas Rules

• The dealer hits all soft 17s (ace, 6, or any hand where the ace counts as an 11, such as ace, 4, 2). This rule is fairly standard downtown and is unfavorable to the player.

• Insurance pays 2-1. This is standard throughout Vegas.

• A player may double down on any of the two original cards he's dealt. He'll then receive only one additional card from the dealer. This is another standard rule throughout Vegas.

• A player may split any two cards of the same rank. Thus, a player may split queen, king or 10, jack or a similar combination as well as two of a kind.

Once a card is split, if an identical card is dealt on the split one, it may also be split as well. Thus, if a player holds 9,9 and receives another 9 on either 9, he can split that also. But should a player be playing out his second 9, and already has received an intervening card on that 9, such as a 4, he cannot split again if another 9 falls. For example, on the second hand, he holds 9,4, then receives another 9. He cannot resplit that 9, for an intervening card has been dealt.

When a bettor splits aces, he can only receive one card on each ace, whereas with any other split cards he can hit as many times as he wishes to improve that hand.

The splitting of matched cards is standard downtown, but there are exceptions to the ace rule.

The following rules are found in only a few casinos downtown:

• Surrender. A couple of casinos may offer this option, but rarely are signs posted announcing this, even if surrender is allowed.

• After splitting cards, a player may double down. This rule is allowed in a couple of casinos downtown.

• After splitting aces, if a player is dealt another ace, he may split that also and receive one additional card on each ace. For example, a player splits aces. On his first ace, he gets a 5. He cannot draw another card. On the second ace, he gets an ace, and can split that one. Now on his next two cards (one for each ace) he gets a 6 and a 4. He cannot draw any more cards and is stuck with his hands.

The resplitting of aces is favorable to the player, and is allowed in the Horseshoe Club.

• The Las Vegas Club, a downtown establishment, has the most liberal rules in Vegas. However, it uses six decks and is frequented by small-time bettors, so that the atmosphere is not congenial to a player of even moderate means. In the Las Vegas Club a player is allowed practically every option known to the game. He can double down after receiving four cards if he desires. He can double down after splitting and can do this after receiving several cards on each split hand. There are other liberal rules at this club, but it rarely attracts serious blackjack players.

Northern Nevada Rules

The following are fairly standard rules in both Lake Tahoe and Reno:

• A dealer must hit soft 17s.
• A player can only double down on 10s and 11s.
• Insurance pays 2-1.
• A player may split any two matched cards, including 10-value cards and play out each hand separately. If he splits aces, he can only draw one additional card on each ace.

There are very few variations on these rules. Some casinos in Reno follow Las Vegas rules to an extent, allowing any two cards dealt to be doubled down, but the rules stated above are fairly rigid in Northern Nevada.

In Reno it's possible to find casinos that don't offer insurance. When insurance is not allowed, it's a definite disadvantage to the player.

The Northern Nevada rules are disadvantageous to the player, for the restrictions on doubling down and the dealer's hitting of soft 17s both are in the casino's favor.

In the Northern Nevada casinos, which includes not only Reno and Lake Tahoe but Sparks and Carson City, the dealer will always peek at his hole card when he has dealt himself an upcard of a 10-value or ace to determine immediately if he has a blackjack.

Let's further investigate peeking or not peeking at the hole card by the dealer. The reason for peeking is obvious. If a dealer's upcard is a 10-value card or an ace, he may be holding a blackjack, which makes it fruitless for the players at the table to continue to act upon their hands by drawing cards, splitting hands, or doubling down.

However, the casinos recognize that security is more important than this factor, and if players have already split their hands or doubled down, thus putting out more money or chips on the table, and the dealer discovers that he indeed has a blackjack after all players have acted, then the additional bets made by the players will be returned to them. Only the original underlying bet is lost.

For example, a player bets $10, and receives an 11 and doubles down by putting out an additional $10. If the dealer discovers that he has a blackjack, then the additional $10 on the double-down bet will be returned to the player, and he will have lost only $10.

Since casinos permit insurance bets, in which the player wagers up to half his original bet that the dealer *has a blackjack*, this bet is kept on the table until the dealer finally peeks at his hole card. If he has a blackjack, he'll pay off the bet at 2-1. If he doesn't have a blackjack, he'll collect the wager as a losing bet.

Atlantic City Rules

The rules governing play in Atlantic City casinos have been set by the New Jersey Casino Control Commission and should be fairly standard for all future casinos operating in Atlantic City.

• All games are played with multiple decks, either with six or eight decks dealt from a shoe. Occasionally, for special games for high rollers, the casino might put in a four-deck game, but this is rare. The general rule is that the smaller the game's limit, the more decks used. Thus, with a $3, $5, or

$10 table, eight decks are used. For a $25 minimum bet table (or higher limits) a six-deck game will be in operation.

At the $3, $5, or $10 tables the maximum bet is usually $500. At the $25 or $100 tables the maximum bet is usually $5,000. Sometimes higher limits will be allowed by previous arrangement with the shift boss, with the limits pushed up to $10,000 per hand and sometimes even higher, but this depends on the particular casino and the player involved.

• A dealer must stand on all 17s. This rule benefits the player.

• If a player's first two cards have the same (equal) numerical value, such as 8s or 10-value cards, he may split them at his option and play out each hand separately. If a player gets another identical card, he may not resplit his hand. For example, if he were dealt two 8s and were to split them and receive another 8 as his next card, he would have to play out the first hand with two 8s, for a total of 16. Let's see how this works:

A player is dealt 8, 8. He splits the 8s by separating them and puts down a bet equal to his original bet on the second 8. He now gets another 8 after he hits the first hand. Now his two hands would look like this: 8-8 and 8. He can no longer split the new 8. He has a 16 on the first hand and will play it according to our basic strategies, covered in detail later in the appropriate section.

If aces are split, only one additional card may be drawn to each ace; with other pair splits the player may draw as many cards as he desires to form the best hand. Let's give an example. The player has bet $25 and gotten A,A. He splits them by separating the aces and puts down an additional $25. He now hits the first ace and receives a king. He holds 21, a perfect hand. He hits the second ace and gets a 2. His total is A,2, or 3 or 13. Either way he would be able to hit with impunity to improve the second hand without danger of busting his hand, but he's prevented from doing so by the rules. Only one card can be drawn on each ace when splitting them.

• Atlantic City casinos allow doubling down after cards are split, a rule that is rarely in force in Las Vegas and practically unheard of in Northern Nevada. And it's very much in favor of the player. Here's how this works. Suppose the dealer's upcard is a 6, the worst card he can hold as far as the house is concerned, for it's the best one for the player.

Now, the player is dealt 7,7. By our rules of strategy, he should split them against the dealer's 6. So the player does this, receives a 4 on the first 7, and now holds 7,4 for a total of 11, a perfect double-down. He can now double this bet and draw a single card for his double-down. Let's suppose he gets a 10. Now he has 21 and can't lose. On the second 7 he draws a 3 for a 7,3 total of 10. He can double that down also. In essence, a single bet has become quadrupled, all in favor of the player. It's a great rule for the player. A bettor who's behind can get a couple of these situations working for him and catch right up, and even get ahead.

A player can double down on any two cards dealt to him originally, no matter what their total value, and after he doubles down, he can only receive one additional card on each doubled-down hand. However, he cannot double down a blackjack. Since a blackjack adds up to 11 as well as 21, it could be theoretically doubled down, but this is not permitted in Atlantic City.

• Insurance is allowed when the dealer shows an ace. The insurance bet is limited to one half the original bet.

• The dealer is never permitted to peek at his hole card until all the players have acted upon their hands, even if the upcard is an ace or 10-value card and he may be holding a blackjack. Players can still double down and split their hands, with no additional risk because if the dealer holds a blackjack, only the underlying bet is lost, not the doubled bet.

If an insurance bet has been made, it is settled when the dealer finally peeks at his hole card. If he has a blackjack, it is paid off at 2-1. If he doesn't have the blackjack, it is a lost bet.

Despite the additional casinos being built in Atlantic City, conditions can get very hectic and crowded during weekends and weeknights. Playing in the casinos under these crowded conditions is not conducive to expert play or counting of cards.

A good blackjack player prefers a table where the favorability of the cards will not be diluted by too many players.

Thus, when playing in Atlantic City, we suggest going at odd hours when the casinos aren't that busy. When a good run of cards favorable to you occurs, you want to be able to take maximum advantage of the situation, not watch the cards being used up by six other players.

Another point about Atlantic City blackjack games. To blackjack experts, an important consideration is the "shuffle point" of a multiple-deck game, that is, the point at which the cards are reshuffled by the dealer. The dealer knows it is time to reshuffle when he or she reaches an odd-colored plastic card inserted in the cards when they are first stacked in the shoe.

Casinos have rules about this shuffling point. They want the dealers to put in that odd card about two-thirds to three-quarters of the way into the deck. Thus about this proportion of the cards will have been played out before the cards are reshuffled. Obviously, the best shuffle point is when all the cards are played out. This way an astute card counter can keep track of all cards in the decks. The lower the shuffle point, the worse it is for the expert player. If the shuffle point is only halfway, for example, then the player can't take advantage of "end-play," a situation in which the deck may be very favorable, and he knows exactly how many aces remain. Also, if there is a quick shuffle point, the player may have to play against unfavorable cards and then have the deck shuffled up and face more unfavorable cards. In multiple-deck games the expert player must be patient, waiting for the decks to turn favorable for him. The sooner cards are shuffled up, the fewer chances he'll have for these favorable moments.

In most of the casinos monitored by expert players, they find that the eight-deck games are about in the 70–75 percent shuffle-point range, while the six-deck games are in the 67–75 percent range. Keep this in mind, and when playing, see where the dealer inserts that odd card. If it is less than two-thirds into the cards, go to another table or another casino.

Betting Limits at Blackjack

Most casinos post their limits clearly at the blackjack tables with a sign that usually reads $1–$500 or $5–$500. Betting limits vary from casino to casino. Within a casino it may vary from table to table. When no betting limit is shown on the table, the minimum game allowed may be $1 or $2.

Most players are comfortable playing at certain limits. Casino executives recognize this and know that a beginner betting $2 a hand will disrupt and slow down a game in which experienced players are wagering $100 to $1,000 a card. Therefore, they set various betting limits and restrict play at tables according to the minimum limits imposed.

The following are the minimum limits at twenty-one tables: $1, $2, $5, $10 (rarely), $25, and $100. The highest maximum bets are usually either $500 or $1,000. Sometimes a table will be given over to a player at limits higher than those mentioned. I watched a high roller at the Horseshoe Club in Las Vegas have a table to himself and bet with their gray $500 chips up to $5,000 a hand. It was a terrible mismatch, since the player didn't know what he was doing.

When a player wagers on two hands at one time, he must usually bet double the minimum table limit on each hand. Thus, if he's at a $5 table, he must bet $10 on each of his hands. This rule is sometimes in effect, sometimes not. In any event, it's an arbitrary rule that makes no sense, but is generally enforced. Why one player must bet double what two players would bet separately is a mystery to me.

Maximum limits have climbed over the years. Whereas $200 maximum limits were fairly common in the smaller Las Vegas casinos and $500 was fairly standard even on the Strip, today the smaller casinos allow $500 as a maximum bet, while the Strip casinos allow $3,000, $5,000, or more, depending upon the casino.

The Horseshoe Club in Las Vegas, which has expanded greatly since taking over the Mint, has a very flexible policy as far as limits go. Your first bet can often determine your limit. If you want to bet $100,000, that's okay with them and will be your limit from then on. And occasionally they get some really big players at their tables with that policy.

In Atlantic City the usual policy is this: for the smaller limit games, the $5 and $10 minimum tables, there is generally a $500 maximum bet allowed. Sometimes this is increased to $1,000 maximum. At the $25 minimum tables the limit will be $1,000 to $3,000, depending on the casino and the particular table inside the casino. At the $100 minimum tables the maximum bet will be $2,500 or higher. If you are a really big player, you can make a private arrangement with the shift boss to determine outside limits at the table.

When playing more than one hand at a time in those casinos where the cards are dealt face down, another arbitrary rule is enforced: A player may only look at one hand at a time and cannot peek at his second hand until he has played out his first hand. This rule is waived when a dealer shows an ace as his upcard and asks for insurance bets. Only then can the player examine both hands.

Dealer's Duties

Blackjack requires only one dealer to run the game. This dealer wears the uniform of the casino and stands during the entire game, although the players remain seated as they play and face him. His duties are as follows:

1. When players come to the table with cash, he changes the cash into casino chips, placing the cash into an opening in the table and thrusting the money down into a drop box with a wooden paddle. Cash is changed only prior to a round of play, never during the playing of a hand.

If a player has credit at the casino, the dealer calls over a floorman to verify the player's credit and then issues chips to the bettor with the floorman's consent.

2. The dealer shuffles the cards and deals them out. During the course of play he deals out additional cards to the players as they request them. Should the players lose by busting, he collects their bets and cards immediately. Should a player have

a blackjack, that player is paid off and his cards are collected at once.

3. After all the players have acted on their hands, the dealer plays out his own cards, according to the rules of the casino. If he beats a player, he collects the losing bet, and should he lose to a bettor, he pays off that player.

4. All the money and chips at the table eventually pass through the dealer's hands, and he is responsible for that money and thus makes certain that his collections and payoffs are correct.

5. The dealer should make certain that the game proceeds in an orderly fashion and that the players' needs are taken care of. If a bettor asks for a drink, the dealer calls the floorman or the cocktail waitress. Some dealers are very careful to please the players and will ask them if they'd like a drink, cigarettes, or other free amenities.

Player's Options

Although the dealer has no options in playing out his hand, the player has several at his disposal. Blackjack is really a game of skill, not luck, and a player may be faced with many decisions during the course of play. On any particular round a bettor may have to determine if he should hit or stand pat. He may have to ask himself whether or not he should split a particular pair. At other times he'll have to determine whether to double down on an apparently strong hand or surrender a weak one.

To determine the correct play in various situations requires many hours of careful study, but first of all, a player should know what his options are.

1. A player holding any total under 21 may hit his hand. This is not to say that he should hit when his total points equal 17 or higher, but he may do so if he desires.

2. A player holding any total 21 or below may stand. A player is not bound by the same rigid rules that a dealer must follow. He can hit and stand on any total.

3. A player may count the ace as either a 1 or 11. If a

bettor is dealt an ace together with another card having a value below 10, he may use the ace as either a 1 or 11, depending upon the situation. In casinos where dealers must stand on all 17s, the dealer must stand by using the ace as an 11 when combined with another card or cards totaling 6 or more points. A player, on the other hand, can and should always hit a soft 17.

4. A player may double down. In Las Vegas and Atlantic City he can double down on any hand using the first two cards dealt to him. In Northern Nevada a player can only double down on a total of 10 or 11.

Doubling down is a definite benefit to the player. When it is his turn to play, a bettor may either announce that he is doubling down at the time he turns over his cards or he may do it silently by turning over his cards and putting out additional chips equal to his original wager.

When a player doubles down, he is permitted to receive only one additional card, dealt face down. It's dealt face down traditionally, but there's nothing to prevent the player from looking at his double-down card. In Atlantic City, or where all cards are dealt face up, the double-down card is also dealt face up.

5. A player may split any cards of equal rank dealt to him as the original two cards, including 10-value cards (10, jack, queen, king) without the 10-value cards being matched pairs.

To split a pair, a player turns over his cards and then separates them, making a bet equal to his original bet on the split card. For example, if he has a pair of 8s, he turns them over and separates them. If he had bet $10 on his original hand, he places another $10 next to the split 8.

After cards are split, they're acted on as separate hands played one at a time. The player may draw as many cards as he wishes on each split card to form his best hand. The only exception to this rule is when splitting aces; then the bettor can only receive one additional card, dealt face down, on each ace.

When playing out split cards, it's necessary to receive additional cards face up, so that the player can easily add up his point total. Each split card becomes a separate hand, so that if one of the split cards turns into a bust hand, the other is still valid if its total is 21 or less.

When splitting aces, if a 10-value card is dealt to the ace, it is merely a 21, not a blackjack. A blackjack cannot occur after a split.

6. A player may double down after splitting matched cards. This option is allowed in Atlantic City and is very much to the advantage of the player. For instance, if a player had been dealt a pair of 9s and split them and then has received a 2 on the first 9 for a total of 11, he could double down. After doubling down in this manner he's permitted to draw only one additional card.

7. A player may surrender his hand. This rule applies in certain Las Vegas clubs. If a player doesn't care to play out his hand he may surrender it and lose only half his original bet.

A player may surrender only his original two cards and cannot surrender subsequent to drawing a card or splitting cards.

This option is favorable for the player and can be used effectively by card counters. For instance, if the deck is 10-rich (filled with 10-value cards) and the player is dealt a 15 or 16, while the dealer's upcard is a 10, the player would be wise to surrender. If he hits, he'll probably bust, and if he stands, he'll probably lose to a 17 or higher in the dealer's hand. By surrendering, the player saves half his original bet.

8. A player may take insurance. It's an option available to the player when a dealer shows an ace as his upcard, and will be discussed at length in the appropriate section.

This bet pays 2-1, and a player can bet only half his original bet as an insurance bet. Generally, it's a poor wager for the bettor to make, but under certain circumstances it is a good move.

Those are the basic options open to the player. All of them have some value, but only when used correctly. Understanding this, the player can make good use of these options, and combining them with basic strategy, he will find himself with an advantage over the casino.

Insurance

Imprinted on the green felt surface of practically all casino blackjack tables in America is the legend: "Insurance pays two to one." This insurance bet is a difficult one for many players to comprehend, and few players really know how to calculate the odds on the insurance wager.

The name of the wager is misleading. This bet is concerned with the probability of a dealer having a blackjack when his upcard is an ace. If the dealer has a blackjack, the insurance bet wins; if he doesn't have one, the insurance bet loses. In effect, the player, by making this bet, is hoping the dealer has a blackjack. If the dealer doesn't have that 10-value card as his hole card, the player will lose this bet.

The insurance bet can be made only when the dealer shows an ace. When the ace is his upcard, the dealer must ask the players if they want insurance. He must wait a couple of moments for everyone to make a decision about the insurance bet. After all the insurance bets are made, the dealer peeks at his hole card, except in Atlantic City casinos, where the dealer pays off or collects on the insurance bet only after all the players' hands have been acted on. If it's a 10-value card, he turns over his cards immediately, showing his blackjack, and pays off the players who made the insurance bet at 2-1. If he doesn't have a 10 in the hole, the dealer collects the losing insurance bets, keeps his hole card concealed, and the game goes on.

An insurance bet is limited to half the original bet and is made by placing the chips in front of the player's cards. Additional chips must be used; you can't use half your originally waged chips for this bet, but must place additional chips equal to half your original blackjack bet. For example, if your original bet was $10 and the dealer shows an ace as his upcard, you make an additional $5 bet as your insurance bet. If the dealer doesn't have a 10 in the hole, the $5 bet is immediately lost, and you must act on your hand to try to win your original $10 bet.

When a player has a blackjack, insurance works as follows:

Suppose you wagered $10 and received a blackjack. The dealer's upcard is an ace. You decide to make a $5 insurance bet. If the dealer doesn't have a blackjack himself, he collects the $5 as a losing bet, but pays you off at 3-2 or $15 for your $10 original bet. Your net gain is $10.

If the dealer had a blackjack, you would be paid $10 for your $5 insurance bet, but since both you and the dealer have blackjacks, the original bet is a standoff. The net gain here is $10. So either way, once you insure your blackjack, you are assured of winning your original bet.

Because of this fact, dealers, floormen, and other casino personnel are always advising players to insure their blackjacks, telling them they're foolish not to, since they can't lose their bet. They point out that should the player not take insurance and the dealer shows a blackjack, the bet is a standoff, and the player would win nothing on his original wager. However, this kind of reasoning is fallacious.

You should *never* insure a blackjack unless you're counting cards and the deck is favorable—that is, 10-rich. We'll deal with 10-rich decks in the section on card counting, but for now the rule is: Don't insure a blackjack and don't make an insurance bet unless you know the count. Most of the time the odds will be against you on an insurance bet. Here's why:

Let's assume that you are playing alone at a table, head to head with the dealer in a single-deck game. On the very first round of play you're dealt a blackjack ace, 10. The dealer shows an ace and asks if you want insurance. Should you make an insurance bet? Absolutely not!

You know 3 cards out of the 52 in the pack. You know your ace, the dealer's ace, and your own 10. That leaves 49 unknown cards remaining in the deck. Since there are originally 16 10-value cards (10s, jacks, queens, and kings) and 37 nontens, the remaining deck has 34 nontens (subtracting the two aces) and 15 tens (subtracting the single 10 in the player's hand).

The odds against the dealer having blackjack are now 34-15, more than 2-1. The house is only paying 2-1 on the bet, and thus the casino has an advantage of 8.1 percent on this insurance wager. That's why it shouldn't be made.

What if you held a 9, 6 on the opening round, and the dealer's upcard was an ace? The ratio of nontens to tens will now be 33-16, still higher than 2-1, and still giving the house an edge of 2.1 percent. Again, the bet shouldn't be made.

It is only when the ratio has fallen below 2-1 that this bet is worthwhile, but this fact is difficult to ascertain unless you are counting cards or can make an instant calculation at the table.

Suppose, for example, that on the first round of play you are playing two hands. One hand contains 9, 6 and the other 5, 4. The dealer shows an ace. Now the ratio is 31-16, or less than 2-1, and the player has a slight advantage of 2.1 percent. In this case the insurance bet is valid.

Most players don't know the proper time to make this bet. Some take insurance when they have a strong hand, such as 20, while others make the insurance wager when they have weak 15s and 16s, praying that the dealer has a blackjack, so that they'll be paid off instantly at 2-1, breaking even on their bet.

As you can see, it doesn't really matter whether your hand is good or bad, or you have blackjack; what is important is the ratio of nontens to tens. That is the only consideration for an insurance bet, which an intelligent player treats as a completely separate wager. If it's in your favor to make it, make it. If it's not in your favor, if the house has an edge on the bet, don't make it.

Once a game is in progress, the only way to know when to make an insurance bet is to count cards and know the ratio by the count. This will be explained in the section dealing with the counting of cards.

As to insuring all blackjacks because "you can't lose," this is wrong advice. When you insure a blackjack, you can only get even money for your original bet, instead of the proper 3-2 payoff. Since the odds are against the insurance bet most of the time, even though you will forfeit an occasional blackjack payout by not making the bet, you'll more than make up for these occasional losses by the extra 3-2 payouts you'll be getting on the uninsured blackjacks.

The Odds of Blackjack

Before computers came into general use, it was practically impossible to compute the correct odds of blackjack, since the game is so complicated because of the constant changes in the composition of the deck during each round of play. Before computers the casino executives figured that the game was in the house's favor, since their tables constantly won money.

Now we know that this was false reasoning. With the early liberal rules the house was at a disadvantage, and the only thing that made its blackjack tables show a profit was the fact that players didn't really know how to play the game correctly. This all changed with the computer studies made by Julian Braun and with Edward Thorp's book, *Beat the Dealer*.

Making extensive use of computer results, Thorp showed how the game should be played by analyzing strategies and showing which were to the benefit of the player. Before his book came out, players didn't realize that splitting 8s against any dealer's upcard was a beneficial move.

Nor did players double down on a soft 18 against a 5 or hit a soft 18 against a dealer's 9 or 10. All the books that had preceded Thorp's on casino gambling by so-called experts and authorities were dead wrong in their recommendation of strategies. One of these experts, who has conducted a personal vendetta against Thorp in his latest book on casino gambling and berates Thorp as a phony, changed his strategy after *Beat the Dealer* came out, and now, without crediting Thorp, claims that he knew what to do all along. Yet his early strategy disproves the claim.

So there was the situation before computers. The casino executives didn't know the true ōdds of the game, but their blackjack tables were making piles of money, so they figured the game was in their favor. Meanwhile, the players, who really had an edge over the house, didn't know how to play their hands correctly and thus couldn't take advantage of the opportunities afforded them. Then Thorp's book came along and the whole game changed.

Who does have the edge today, the player or the casino? The answer isn't that simple. It depends on the rules for a particular casino and whether or not single or multiple decks are being used. However, players are constantly being barred from casinos for counting cards and beating the houses, so it can be stated as an established fact that the player has a definite edge over the casino in many clubs.

In a single-deck game with standard rules of play, a player using correct strategy will have an advantage of about 1 percent over the house. This advantage can increase to almost 15 percent when the cards are favorable and be reduced to a 6 percent disadvantage when the cards are unfavorable.

However, a player need not make flat bets at the table. If you alter your bets so that you are betting the maximum when the deck is in your favor and the minimum when it is against you, you are bound to win in the long run. That's why casinos fear and bar card counters.

The more decks used, the worse it is for the player. When two decks are used, the player disadvantage becomes 0.4 percent and in a four-deck game this disadvantage rises to 0.6 percent. However, these figures are easily overcome with card counting and alteration of bets, so that it's not difficult to beat the casino.

The following are some rules variations which will affect the overall odds in blackjack. Where a minus (−) sign is shown, the variation hurts the player; where a plus (+) sign is given, the variation helps the bettor.

No doubling down on 9 or soft totals	−0.3%
Dealer hits soft 17	−0.2%
Surrender is allowed	+0.2%
Two decks	−0.35%
Four decks	−0.5%
Hole card not peeked at	−0.1%

Basic Winning Strategies

This section and the one on card counting are the keys to winning at blackjack. But card counting will be useless without a full knowledge of correct play. Unless you can make the right plays in blackjack, you won't have any advantage over the casino. To master these strategies, you should study them over and over again, playing out sample hands at home, by dealing to yourself. When decisions have to be made, consult this section. Only when you know this section thoroughly and then know how to count cards should you attempt to play casino blackjack for real money.

But once you've mastered these two sections, you'll have a constant edge over the house. You'll be a player the casino will fear, and you should, with proper money management and self-control, end up a big winner.

Hard Totals—Strategy for Hitting or Standing

To facilitate the learning process, many of the principles will be shown in illustrative charts. The first chart deals with hitting vs. standing with hard totals.

A hard total is (a) any hand in which an ace counts only as 1 and not as an 11. For example, the following are hard totals with an ace: 10, 6, ace; 9, 4, ace; ace, 5, 8, ace. (b) Any hand adding up to 12 or more without an ace. Examples are 9, 8; 4, 9; 6, 7; 10, 5; 3, 2, 7.

Hitting vs. Standing with Hard Totals

(H = Hit; S = Stand)

Hard Total	Dealer's Upcard	Decision
12	2, 3	H
12	4, 5, 6	S
12	7, 8, 9, 10, ace (7-ace)	H
13	2, 3, 4, 5, 6	S
13	7-ace	H
14	2, 3, 4, 5, 6	S

Hard Total	Dealer's Upcard	Decision
14	7-ace	H
15	2, 3, 4, 5, 6	S
15	7-ace	H
16	2, 3, 4, 5, 6	S
16	7-ace	H
17 and above	Any Card	S

When you hold a hand totaling 11 and below, you will always either hit or double down, depending on the situation (see double-down charts) since you cannot bust your hand no matter what additional card you draw.

When consulting the above chart, use it for hands totaling 12 or higher even if more than two cards form the hand. For example, if you hold 5, 3, 6, you should treat it simply as a hard 14 and consult the chart above for the correct strategy.

It's much easier to remember the chart if you understand the principles behind the moves. Since the dealer can't do anything but play according to the rigid house rules, the player has every advantage over the dealer but one. The dealer's single great advantage is this: if the player busts first, and then the dealer busts, the dealer still wins.

This advantage is so great that it more than makes up for all the player's options. The dealer always acts last, and plays his hand only after all the players have made their decisions regarding their hands. Therefore, you must avoid, if possible, busting your hand when the dealer has a chance to bust his also, for if you can force the dealer to bust while your cards are still alive, you will win.

When will the dealer stand a good chance of busting his hand? He is most likely to bust when he has a bust card showing—an upcard of 2 to 6. These are known as bust cards or stiffs because the dealer will have to draw another card to form his hand and can't stand pat unless he has a 6 showing and an ace underneath. In all other instances, he will have to hit his hand, and when he hits, there is a chance of going over 21 and busting.

On the other hand, when a dealer shows a 7 through an ace (7, 8, 9, 10-value card, ace) in all probability he will have a hand that is already pat, being 17 or higher. If you don't hit a hand valued at 16 or below, facing a dealer's 7 or above, you may simply be forfeiting your hand without any opportunity to improve it.

Those two considerations determine the construction of the above chart. When a dealer has a bust card showing as his upcard, you (except when you have a 12 against a dealer's 2 or 3) will give the dealer the first chance to bust his hand and will not draw to a stiff hand (12-16).

Why is there an exception with the 12 against the 2 and 3 upcards? Because computer studies have shown that in these two instances, the advantage swings to the player if he hits his hand.

When the dealer has a 7 or higher as his upcard, your strategy is to hit your stiff hand (12-16) to prevent the dealer from beating you automatically, by having a 17 or higher total while you haven't improved your weak hand.

If you remember these two principles which determine the player's strategy, the chart will be easy to memorize.

Soft Totals—Strategy for Hitting or Standing

Whenever you are dealt an ace, you can, at your option, value the ace as either 1 or 11. When you use it as an 11, your hand is said to be soft, with a soft total. Typical soft hands are ace, $6 = 17$; ace, $7 = 18$; ace, $8 = 19$. In all these hands, the ace is counted as an 11. But a soft hand can change to a hard hand. For example, if you hit your ace, 6 and get a 10, you now have a hard total of 17. Or if you hit an ace, 3 and get a 9, you have a hard total of 13.

The following chart is primarily useful in Northern Nevada, where you cannot double down except when holding a 10 or 11. Where you can double down on any total of the first two cards dealt to you, the chart following the next one, showing doubling down with soft totals, will be applicable.

Hitting vs. Standing with Soft Totals

Soft Total	Dealer's Upcard	Decision
A 6	Any upcard	H
A 7	2, 3, 4, 5, 6, 7, 8, Ace	S
A 7	9, 10	H
A 8	Any upcard	S
A 9	Any upcard	S

If you have a soft total less than 17, of course that hand should be hit and then played either as a soft or hard hand.

For example, if you are dealt an ace, 4, hit and get a 10, you now hold a hard 15, and must follow the strategy suggested in the chart on hitting vs. standing with hard totals. If the same ace, 4 was hit and you drew a 3, you'd be holding a soft 18 and would have to use the strategies of the soft-hand chart.

The only problem card in the above chart is the ace, 7 hand. The ace, 6 is always hit while the ace, 8 and ace, 9 are never hit. The ace, 7 is only hit against the dealer's 9 or 10 upcard because computer studies have shown that in the long run you will have an advantage if you hit, since there is a likelihood that the dealer who shows a 9 or 10 will have a hand valued at 19 or 20, higher than your 18. Against the dealer's ace as an upcard, a soft 17 is a dead-even proposition.

There are several reasons why an ace, 6 should always be hit. First of all, a 17 is a useless hand, since the only way you can win is for the dealer to bust his hand. Second, there are several cards that can improve the soft 17 and make it into a very powerful hand. Third, if you hit and get a 10-value card, you haven't hurt your hand at all. A fourth reason is that even if you get a card that weakens the total, such as a 6, giving you a total of 13 as a hard hand, it will make no difference if the dealer has a bust card as his upcard. In this case you now stand with your stiff.

When a dealer has an upcard from 2 to 6, you, in effect, are freerolling with your soft 17, since you have nothing to lose and everything to gain. You can improve your hand dramatically, or even if you weaken it, the dealer must still draw cards with a likelihood of busting.

Should the dealer hold a nonbust card such as a 9 as his

upcard, it's still worth hitting that soft 17, because the 17 will lose in all probability to the dealer's total of 19. Even if you receive a 6, giving you a hard total of 13, you still can draw another card, hoping to improve your hand.

Finally, an ace, 6 should always be hit because it can't be busted no matter what card is drawn. The same goes for any soft 17, such as an ace, 4, 2. This is played in the same way as the soft 17 of ace, 6.

Whenever a player stands on soft 17, I immediately know that he's a weak player and a loser. No strong player stands on that total. He either hits it, or if playing in a casino where doubling down is permitted on any two-card total, he doubles down against certain upcards.

Soft Hands—Strategy for Doubling Down

The following chart is useful in casinos in Las Vegas and Atlantic City or in any casino where doubling down is permitted on any original two-card total. Any time you have a chance to double down, you should do so, for it is to your advantage.

Soft Hands—Doubling Down

(S = Stand; H = Hit; D = Double Down)

Soft Total	Dealer's Upcard	Decision
A 2, A 3, A 4, A 5	2, 3, 7-ace	H
A 2, A 3, A 4, A 5	4, 5, 6	D
A 6	2, 3, 4, 5, 6	D
A 6	7-ace	H
A 7	2, 7, 8, ace	S
A 7	3, 4, 5, 6,	D
A 7	9, 10	H
A 8	Any upcard	S
A 9	Any upcard	S

At first glance, this chart may seem complicated, but if you know the principles underlying the doubling down of soft totals, it becomes much easier to follow the strategy.

When a dealer shows a 4, 5, or 6 as his upcard, these are

his weakest and most vulnerable cards, and you should take whatever opportunity you can to double down against those upcards. When you hold ace, 6, you should never stand, but either hit or double down. When you hold an ace, 7, your strategy becomes a little more complicated.

With an ace, 7 you hit against a dealer's 9 or 10. You know that from the previous chart. With an ace, 7, the dealer's vulnerable upcards are the 3, 4, 5, and 6, and so the hand should be doubled down against those cards.

Generally speaking, if you have a soft hand below 19, always double down against a dealer's 4, 5, and 6. That is the best strategy to follow in terms of doubling down.

A soft 19 and a soft 20 should never be hit, since they're strong totals by themselves and should be winning hands. Some experts suggest that a soft 19 be doubled down against a dealer's 6, but this is too skillful a play and might draw heat from casino personnel, so I don't suggest it be made. In any event, doubling down in that situation gives you a very slight edge, so it's not worth getting barred from a casino to pick up a few more dollars.

Hard Hands and Totals— Strategy for Doubling Down

In Las Vegas and Atlantic City any hard total may be doubled down, but for purposes of casino blackjack strategy you shouldn't double down on hard totals of less than 9. While there may be times when a hand could be doubled down, we don't suggest this move, since it will attract attention and possibly cause you to be barred.

You take a big risk when you double down on a hard total of 8, for this can be done theoretically with a 4, 4, or 5, 3 against a dealer's upcard of 5 or 6. Even though this move will give you a slight edge, it may jeopardize your future play at that casino, and it just isn't worth it.

Hard Totals—Doubling Down

Hard Total	Dealer's Upcard	Decision
9	2, 3, 4, 5, 6, (2-6)	D
10	2, 3, 4, 5, 6, 7, 8, 9 (2-9)	D
11	Any upcard	D

The chart above shows when these hard totals should be doubled down. If the dealer's upcard is not shown above, the hand shouldn't be doubled down. For example, if the dealer shows an 8, the player with a 9 can't double down; and if a dealer shows a 10, a player holding a 10 can't double down, except under certain circumstances, which will be covered later. But as far as basic strategy goes, this chart prevails and should be memorized.

Splitting Pairs

All American casinos give you the option of splitting any pairs and include all 10-value cards as pairs. Thus a jack and king are pairs for splitting purposes. When a pair of aces is split, practically every casino will allow only one additional card to be dealt to each ace. The exceptions are few, such as the Horseshoe Club in Las Vegas, where aces may be resplit, but when any other card is dealt to an ace, you must use only that card to form your hand.

When cards other than aces are split, you may use the split card as an original hand and draw as many cards as you wish to the split card to form your best hand.

In practically all American casinos, with the exception of the Atlantic City clubs, if a pair is split and another, identical card is dealt to a single split card, that card may be split as well. For example, if 8s are split and you receive another 8 immediately, that 8 could be split as well.

The general rule to follow is this: If the split is originally favorable to you and an identical card is then dealt, that card should be split also.

Some casinos, such as Caesars Palace and the MGM Grand in Vegas and in Reno, and the Atlantic City clubs, allow players to double down after they've split an original pair. This is a big advantage for the player and should always be done when allowed. For instance, if you receive a pair of 9s, split them, and get a 2 on the first 9, you could double down if you wished to. Since an 11 should always be doubled down, no matter what upcard the dealer has, this is the proper play.

Splitting Pairs

Player's Pair	Dealer's Upcard	Decision
A A	Any upcard	Always split
2 2	3, 4, 5, 6, 7	Split
3 3	4, 5, 6, 7	Split
4 4	Any upcard	Never split
5 5	Any upcard	Never split
6 6	2, 3, 4, 5, 6	Split
7 7	2, 3, 4, 5, 6, 7	Split
8 8	Any upcard	Always Split
9 9	2, 3, 4, 5, 6, 8, 9	Split
10-Value Cards	Any upcard	Never split

Rather than memorizing this chart by rote, it pays to analyze it by the principles of blackjack. Aces are always split because each is worth 11 standing alone, and if a 10-value card is dealt to an ace, the player has a 21. A 10-value card dealt to a split ace is not considered a blackjack, however.

Always split 8s because their total is 16, the worst possible total. Each separate 8, however, may form a more solid hand. Never split 4s and 5s because they already form the base of a strong hand and separating them may cause two weak hands to develop.

Never split 10-value cards because two 10s equal 20, one of the most powerful hands in blackjack. Why should you break up a 20 for two unknown and possibly weaker hands?

The 9s are split against all cards from 2 to 9, with the exception of a 7. Why not a 7? Because two 9s equal 18, and if a dealer shows a 7 as his upcard, he probably has a total of 17, which will lose to the player's 18.

The toughest decisions are involved with splitting 2s and 3s against a dealer's 7. It's difficult to do this, especially when losing, but these are the correct moves. The computers say so and the computers coldly calculate the odds.

Some Splitting Pairs Memories

As I look back at my career as a blackjack player, what I remember most are not situations in which I had a huge bet on the table, but various instances where I was faced with a pairs-splitting choice of play.

Some years ago, Caesars Palace had a couple of single-deck tables, where you could bet from $25 to $3,000. Other than those two tables, all the rest of the games were multiple-deck shoe games. I naturally gravitated to the single-deck games, because the rules were so loose that a player had the edge over the house on the *first round of play*.

First of all, as with all casinos on the Strip, the dealers at Caesars had to stand on all 17s, including soft 17s, a plus for the player. Then they had the surrender option, another plus when played correctly. You could not only split any pair, but you could double down after splitting. Another big plus.

I was playing there one afternoon with a backer, who agreed to split the profits 50-50 with me. The reason for this generous split was simple. In the course of years of play, he had dropped between $50,000 and $100,000 at the game, and he figured that 50 percent of something was better than a 100 percent loss. Having seen me play and having heard of my reputation, he had sought me out. This backer was a respected surgeon in the East and he liked to gamble. But he didn't really know blackjack, except for some basic moves that weren't going to win him any money. He came up with some big money and there I was, sitting in Caesars and facing a dealer. There were two other players at the table, betting between $100 and $500 a hand.

It doesn't take me long to gauge a player's strength. Give me five or ten minutes and I'll know just what kind of player he is—fool or expert or somewhere in between. Most players know something about the game, like my backer, but they don't know enough to take advantage of those extraordinary moments when you can really hit the casino. I began with $2,000 to test the waters, and started off with $100 bets, playing one hand.

It was a comfortable table, but the dealer was hot, and I

was coming in second best. The floorman drifted over to watch the action, but the three of us at the table were all losing, so he moved away to hold a spirited conversation with a cocktail waitress. As he was talking to her, I was counting down my chips. I had $900 left. I pushed out $100 on the first round of play, and pushed with the dealer. A number of small cards came out, but no aces. On the second round, the deck was plus 5 (there were 5 more tens in the deck than small cards valued from 3 to 6) and I put $500 out. I ended up with another push, with the dealer making a five-card 18 to tie me. Now the deck was plus 8, and the dealer was still holding the cards and not getting ready to shuffle up. I guess he figured he was invincible, for the other two players had taken a bad beating on the first round of play, and now had reduced their bets to $50 each.

My $900 didn't even give the dealer pause. He shot out the cards, and showed a 9. The other two players stood on their totals, but that could mean anything. They'd been standing on 16s against any high dealer's card, and sometimes with 15s.

I looked at my cards. Two 9s. Now, most players would stand on this total against a dealer's 9. The average player will split them against a 2–6 probably, but after that he's uncertain of the right play. The correct play is to split the 9s against a 9. After all, the dealer has a theoretical 19, and my 18 is a loser. I might buy a 10 or ace and really improve to a push or win. And all four aces were still in the damn deck. Then I saw one of the players reexamine his hand. He was holding an ace and an 8. Three aces left.

I split the 9s, and held my hand out behind me for more cash. My backer was standing right behind me, and he gave me $1,000. I put down another $900 on the table and told the dealer, "Money plays." He repeated the phrase to the floorman, who now took an interest in what was going on at the table. The dealer shot out another card. It was a 2. Now I had 11 on the first hand, and once more my hand went back and another packet of money was placed in it. I put down another $900 on the first hand as I doubled down. "Money plays," I said, and the dealer repeated the term.

He dealt me the double-down card face down. I never looked at it. If it was a bad card, such as an ace, I would react, and I wanted to keep my wits about me and play the hands the way they should be played. Now he dealt a card to the second 9, and it was another 9! The case 9. I had to resplit this 9. If an initial split is correct, always resplit. That's the rule. Out went my hand again, and another bundle of cash was placed in it. I could hear my partner muttering behind me. He had tested the waters with $2,000, but now was getting in extremely deep waters and I knew just what he was thinking. "That fool split 9s, and it doesn't look right to me, and now he's resplitting them. I'm gonna lose a fortune with this jerk."

On the second 9 I got an ace. OK. A 20. I certainly had improved the middle hand. Now I asked for a card on the third 9 and got another 2. Insane! My hand went back, for I sure as hell was going to double down on an 11 against the dealer's 9. Another $900 on the table. I now had $1,800 on the first hand, $900 on the second, and $1,800 on the third, for a total of $4,500 instead of my original $900 bet.

Again, the double-down card was dealt face down and I didn't peek at it. Now it was the dealer's turn. I should mention that while I was doing all this, not only was my backer muttering, but the other two players were groaning and shaking their heads. A fool was loose at their table and there was nothing they could do about it.

The dealer turned over his hole card. It was a king. He had 19. He turned over my first double down. I had hit a 10 for 21, a winner. My middle 20 was a winner, and my last double-down had hit a jack for another 21. I collected $4,500. Our loss of $1,100 up to this point was erased and we had a $3,400 profit. Instead of a straight $900 loss if I had stood on the original 9-9 for an 18. What a swing!

I was ready to continue, but my partner had had enough. We cashed in after that hand and went to dinner, and I explained the move to him. "I would never have done that in a million years," he said to me. "No wonder I can't beat this game."

But, hell, he was a great surgeon. And the steaks we were served were terrific.

The other split involved aces, and it occurred at the Horseshoe in downtown Las Vegas. This time I was playing alone, without a backer. Again, I had been caught in a bad streak and was losing. At my table was an insane middle-aged Chinese woman with a fistful of $100 bills, and I mean a fistful. She was playing two hands at once and just dumping mounds of bills on the table, without counting them. And losing. She, another player betting $100 chips, and myself were the only ones playing, taking up four spots since the woman played two at a time. And two of her cronies were occupying the other seats sitting and smoking, so the table was in effect closed to anyone else.

The personnel at the Horseshoe weren't going to antagonize this woman, so I played in the third baseman's seat and no one even paid attention to me. All eyes were on the crazy woman, including two floormen and a bunch of spectators. When she won, the woman would scream out loud, but that wasn't happening too often.

The cards weren't going too well, and it was rare for the table to have a favorable situation. This didn't make any difference to the madwoman, who poured out that money on her two hands, and eventually had no more bills. She said something in Chinese to one of her cronies, who then reached into a huge handbag and produced another wad of bills about four inches thick. And the betting continued.

After a half hour, I was down $500, with another $500 on the table. And then the cards suddenly turned favorable on one deal. No aces were dealt out at all for the first round, and only one ten, along with seven small cards. A plus 6 deck, and all four aces intact. I slid $300 in chips into my betting box, up from my usual $50 wager. As the dealer paused with the cards in his hand, waiting for the Chinese woman to make her usual bets, she suddenly shook her head in an agitated fashion.

"No, no bets." She had picked this one moment to stop betting insanely and wanted the deal to pass her by. So now it was the first baseman and myself. He had a $100 chip out, his usual bet. Didn't these fools know anything?

Since it was only two-way instead of four-way action, I pushed out the rest of my chips on my bet. I now had $520 there, counting some random nickel chips I had as extras after winning a small blackjack or two. Out went the cards. The floormen were still wondering why the woman stopped betting, and one was talking to her about comping her party to their fancy restaurant in the back as the cards floated down on the table. The first baseman quickly turned over his cards. He had been dealt a blackjack.

Now it was my turn. I saw an ace and quickly flipped over the cards. Snapper! But it wasn't a blackjack. I had two aces. The dealer showed a king of diamonds. Well, I had to split those aces.

I reached into my wallet, but had just a few dollars in there, along with about $1,200 in traveler's checks. Putting one ace next to the other, I said to the dealer, "Mark the bet."

He glanced at one of the floormen, who nodded, having seen me play often in the casino. He counted down my chips and put out $520 in chips in front of him to mark the bet. And dealt me an ace. Well, the Horseshoe allows resplitting of aces, so I pushed that ace aside, and now had a pretty row of three of them.

"Mark it," I said, and once more the floorman nodded and once more $520 in chips were put down on the table as my marked bet. Now, I thought, let me get three tens and cash in. But I didn't get three tens. I got three 8s, one after another. I had $1,560 out in bets, and right now I knew it was all lost, unless some miracle happened, because the deck was loaded with ten-value cards. I certainly hadn't gotten any.

The Chinese woman was clucking at my good luck, for she thought three 19s were terrific, but I knew better. The dealer took his time turning over his hole card as I stood up, ready to go to the cashier's cage just behind me to cash out my traveler's checks and leave myself practically broke.

He turned over an 8! The case 8. A miracle. Four 8s like that—it was something I never had seen before, not in a one-deck game. I collected my $1,560 and was now ahead over a thousand bucks. I've played a lot of blackjack in my life, but it's moments like these that stay fresh in my memory.

Counting Methods—
The Key to Winning

This section and the section on basic strategy should be read and reread until they are mastered, for they contain the key elements necessary to beat the casino game of blackjack.

If you understand the basic strategy and make flat bets, you will win about 1 percent from the house. However, if in addition to playing correctly, you count cards and alter your bets when the deck is either favorable or unfavorable, raising the wagers when the cards are in your favor and lowering them when the cards are unfavorable, you have a huge advantage over the casino, for you can grind out the casino's bankroll in much the same manner that the casino grinds out the players at games where it has the edge.

But in order to know when the cards are favorable, you must learn to count cards. Counting cards doesn't imply knowing all the cards played out or remaining in the deck; it means knowing certain ratios of important cards, which by themselves tell the whole story.

Counting cards is very important because the dealer, as we know, has no options, and the rules governing his play place a premium on the small cards remaining in the deck. Since a dealer *must* hit all his stiff and potentially bust hands, the more small cards, such as 3s, 4s, 5s, and 6s remaining in the deck, the better chance he has of forming a strong hand of 17 or more. Thus the more small cards remaining in the pack, the worse it is for the player, who will be beaten when the dealer makes a solid hand out of his "stiff."

On the other hand, when there are many tens and aces remaining in the deck, the cards become favorable to the player. You have the option of standing or hitting any hand you hold, and if you're dealt a stiff hand, let's say, 10, 5, and the dealer shows a bust card such as a 4, you can stand pat and let the dealer draw first. The dealer must hit his hand, and if he has a total of 12 or more with his first two cards, he stands a good chance of busting.

When there are many 10s and aces in the deck, you as a player stand a good chance of getting a blackjack. Even though the dealer has an equally good chance to get a black-jack, you are paid 3-2 for yours, while the dealer only gets even money. And should the deck be very favorable, and the dealer shows an ace as his upcard, you have the further option of making an insurance bet and saving your hand.

The Basic Counting Method

The important cards, as far as the card counter is concerned, are the small cards and the 10s, and more important, the ratio of one to the other. The earliest counting methods concentrated solely on cards like the 5, for computer studies showed that when the 5s were removed from the deck, the deck became favorable to the player. These methods had some value, but were rather primitive.

Then a 10-count was introduced by Thorp, but this was complicated and required the knowledge of several figures and ratios at one time, which was quite difficult for most players to put into practice under actual casino conditions.

Thorp modified the count to a simple point-count method after it had been initiated by others, and it is widely used today in different forms. Our point count is a rather simple one, using a plus and minus system, but it is very effective and differs from advanced counts by only minor degrees.

For purposes of this counting method, we'll be concerned with two groups of cards; the 10s (including all 10-value cards) and the smaller cards, the 3, 4, 5, and 6s. The 10-value cards are the most valuable for the player when they remain in the deck. On the other hand, the 3–6 cards are the most damaging. Since there are 16 10-value cards and 16 cards from 3–6, there is an even balance between the two groups, making for a simple point count.

Even though the aces are valuable assets to a player, they're not included in this count, but should be kept track of separately, since there are only four in any single deck.

This counting method can be used for one or multiple decks, but the player is advised to begin with a single or double deck at the outset. Until you become very familiar with this count and master it, you shouldn't attempt to use it on four- and six-deck games.

The reason why a single-deck game is preferred is simple. It's a matter of fatigue. With a single deck the count rarely gets to +6 or −6, and by then the deck will probably be depleted and reshuffled by the dealer. Two decks last longer, but there is still constant shuffling, to break the count. With four and six decks the deals go on and on, and there is relentless pressure to remember the exact count.

Here's how the simple count works:

Each 3, 4, 5, or 6 played out has a value of +1.
Each 10-value card played has a value of −1.

All other cards are excluded from the count, but the player should keep a separate count of the aces.

When counting cards, don't start the count until the cards have been removed by the dealer or played out. For example, if a player hits his hand and gets a 6, don't count that as +1. Wait until his cards are turned over by the dealer. In this way, a player can balance cards and can easily keep count.

What do I mean by balancing cards? If a king and a 6 show, the deck is neither plus nor minus; it's neutral, since the plus and minus cards balance out each other. If you always look for this type of balance it'll make card counting much easier.

Assume that you're at a casino blackjack table with four other players. You're the fifth player, in the last, or third baseman's seat. You draw cards last and act last in this spot.

Since all cards at practically every single-deck game are dealt face down, you'll be unable to take a count until the dealer turns over the player's cards to remove them, or until all cards have been played out and turned over by the dealer.

Here are the hands: (? stands for an unseen card)

Player 1. ?, ? He stands pat.
Player 2. ?, ? He hits and gets a 5, then stands pat.

Player 3. Ace, king This player has a blackjack. She turns over her cards, gets paid 3-2 for her bet, and the cards are removed. Now the deck is −1 because of the king.

Player 4. ?, ? He hits, gets a 10, then turns over his cards. He had held a 9, 6 and busted. The deck is still −1, since the 10 and 6 in this player's hand balance each other.

Player 5. 7, 5 Since you can see your own cards, you can keep a count going using them. You hit and get another 7, then stand pat. Now the deck is neutral, since you have a 5 and no 10-value cards.

Dealer. 9, 8 The dealer turns over his cards and must stand, since he has a hard 17. The deck is still neutral, since the 9 and 8 are not included in our count.

At this time, the dealer turns over the players' cards. Player 1 held a 10, 8. The deck is minus 1. Player 2 holds a jack, 6. The deck is still minus 1.

At the end of this round of play, you know the deck is minus 1, and therefore unfavorable to the player, since your minus count tells you that one more 10-value card than a 3–6 card was played out, and therefore there is an extra 3–6 remaining in the deck. Also note that two aces have been played out on this round, making the deck even more unfavorable.

A word about aces. Although they're not included in the count, there are important reasons for keeping special track of them. First of all, they're the most important cards in the deck as far as the player is concerned. You can form a blackjack only with an ace in your hand. If you get a soft hand, it can easily be improved into a strong hand.

Second, late in the game, under certain circumstances, it's important to know the count on aces in double-down situations. With four aces remaining in a deck, a double-down with a 10 against a dealer's 10-value card may be a feasible play. This kind of play is rarely made, but with a very favorable deck and one rich in aces, it can be used to good effect.

In a big game I once played, I doubled down with a 6, 4 against a dealer's 10, with the deck at plus 6 and three aces remaining, although the deck was almost two-thirds depleted. I didn't worry too much about the double-down, because the dealer had already peeked at his hole card, and since he hadn't turned over his cards, he obviously didn't hold an ace in the hole. Therefore, I doubled down and, to the casino's surprise but not to mine, I received an ace, beating the dealer 21 to 20.

To summarize the point count we're using:

Each 3, 4, 5, or 6 played out has a value of +1.

Each 10-value card has a value of −1.

All other cards are excluded from the count.

The aces are counted separately. They're useful for individual moves, such as the double-down situation just discussed. They're also useful in determining the value of the remaining deck. If the aces are depleted at the beginning of an early round of play, the value of the deck drops and you should be aware of this, since your chances of getting a blackjack are weakened.

Altering Bets With the Count

No matter what denomination chips the player is comfortable with, the betting method remains the same, so it doesn't really matter whether the player is betting $1, $5, $25, or $100 casino chips. Our betting method will be described in units, rather than in cash amounts, to make the betting strategy simpler.

At the outset of play, before the first card is dealt out, the single deck is considered neutral. The deck is also considered neutral when there is no plus or minus count during the course of play. For example, if the plus and minus cards balance out completely, it's considered a neutral deck.

With a neutral deck, the bet consists of two units.

When the deck is unfavorable, that is, has a minus count, the player will bet a minimum wager of one unit.

When the deck is slightly favorable, that is, either +1 or +2, the player will bet three units.

When the deck is more favorable, or 10-rich, at +3 or more, then the player's bet will be four units. Sometimes the deck is superfavorable, a +5 or higher, and there is a temptation to bet five, six, or more units.

This temptation has to be controlled, unless you have been winning all your previous bets and simply keep doubling up. But for a sudden move from two units to six units, you are tempting casino heat. This is usually the signal the casino needs to verify the fact that you are a card counter; their countermeasures will be swift and might include barring you from the casino.

Plus counts can be deceptive. A plus count of 2 on the first round of play is favorable for the player, but if more than half the deck is depleted, that plus 2 is even stronger and the player can bet more aggressively.

Likewise, if there are several aces remaining in the deck at the halfway mark, the favorable deck is that much stronger. It is sometimes better to combine the separate count of aces with the regular point count. For example, if two aces came out on the first round of play and the deck is +1, it pays to downgrade the deck to neutral, since those two aces are now missing from the remainder of the deck, and you have a lessened chance of getting a blackjack.

The ideal situation for a player is to have a favorable deck not only 10-rich, that is, full of 10-value cards with few small cards remaining, but one that is filled with aces as well. There's no more satisfying situation than having a maximum bet out and getting a blackjack. That's why the separate count of aces is so important.

When aces are depleted at the outset of play, it weakens the remaining deck enough to downgrade the playing hand, and if the aces are not played out, this situation upgrades the playing hand. For example with aces depleted and the count at +1, a neutral bet would be a better wager than a three-unit bet. With all the aces intact in the deck and the deck at +2, it would be to the player's advantage to up-grade the count to +3 for betting purposes and wager four units on the next hand.

These moves come with experience. Keeping count of the cards not only allows you to raise or lower your bets intelligently, but also to play out the hands with more skill, because you have a great deal of knowledge about the remaining composition of the deck.

Other Counting Methods

A great many entrepreneurs have made a fortune selling counting methods for blackjack players. A few have been valid, but the vast majority won't improve on the simple and effective method outlined in this book.

For the very sophisticated player, one interested in keeping track of practically every card in the deck, and also in weighing the strengths and weaknesses of every card, some of these systems will be worthwhile, though rather expensive. But the more complicated the system, the more difficult it is to play under actual casino conditions, and the difference in results will be negligible.

What is more important is to take advantage of the count to make certain plays in borderline or end play situations, and the next section deals extensively with this factor.

Changing the Playing Strategy According to the Count

For purposes of this section, we're going to stick with our simple count. Perhaps the word simple is a misnomer, for though the count is easy to remember and use, it is very, very effective, as many of my pupils can attest, and it has been used to good effect to truly damage the bankrolls of several casinos.

Before you study the variations presented in this section, you should be familiar with the basic playing strategy, knowing the correct moves for every possible situation. If you don't yet know these moves, go back and study them again and again until you do know them.

Then, after the basic strategy is mastered, study the basic counting method. Play out hundreds and perhaps thousands of hands at home until you can easily follow the count, which means not to linger over cards, raising your head in the air, thinking of what the count was and is now. To be able to use this count effectively under casino conditions, where you'll be playing at a table with other bettors, where the cards will be snapped at you, where a floorman will be watching your every move, is the bottom line. And if you are having trouble at home keeping track of the cards, imagine the difficulty you'll be facing in a casino.

Be patient. What you're learning in this chapter is the key to making a lot of money for the rest of your life. It's the key that unlocks the treasuries and bankrolls of casinos to your wallet. So learn and practice and be patient. When you can handle a count at lightning speed, immediately knowing the plus or minus figure, and you also know what moves to make under any condition, you're ready to learn the variations. After this section, you'll be ready to tap into the casino bankrolls.

First of all, the basic strategy outlined earlier should always be applied with a neutral count, either prior to the first round of play or during a later round of play, when the count is neither plus nor minus.

The following rules can be put into play during a running count; that is, a count taken during an actual round of play based on the cards the player sees.

It always pays to be in the third baseman's seat or a seat close to the end of the table, where you'll be able to watch the previous plays of bettors' hands. This seat placement also offers you the opportunity of taking a running count. Here's how this is done:

Suppose the count is neutral after a round of play. You are sitting in the third baseman's seat and have been dealt an 8, 2 for a hard 10. The dealer's upcard is a 9. The correct play here is to double down, for it gives you a slight advantage over the dealer.

However, the first player hits and gets a 10-value card (from now on called simply a 10), hits again, gets another 10, and busts. The next player hits and gets a 10, hits again, gets an ace, and stands. The other players at the table stand. From a neutral deck the deck has gone down to −3, with an additional ace played out. Those three 10s plus the ace would have been very strong cards for you to be dealt on your double down. In this case, with a running count, you would simply hit your 10, rather than doubling down against a dealer's 9.

Sometimes an alert player, without seeing cards that affect the count, will make a move determined by the cards played out on that particular round. Suppose that you, in the third baseman's seat, hold a 9, 3 for a hard 12, against the dealer's 2. The deck is neutral and the correct play is to hit the 12.

However, the first player hits and gets a 7. The next player splits 8s and gets a 9 on one of his 8s, and a 6 on the other and stands on both hands. The other players stand on their hands. You have now seen one 6, one 7, two 8s, and one 9, all cards that would considerably improve your hard 12. At this point you should stand and let the dealer draw. In all probability one or more 10s are coming up, to bust the dealer's hand.

For purposes of the following rules, we'll deal with plays other than surrender. For correct moves using surrender, study the section on surrender. Also, you should study the borderline hands in the section on that subject so that you can work out for yourself many of the variations under playing conditions.

Neutral −1 and +1 decks are always played according to the basic strategy.

If the deck is +2 or more, the following rules changes apply:

• Insure any hand against a dealer's ace.
• Do not split 3s against a dealer's 7.
• Do not hit a hard 12 against a dealer's 2 or 3.
• Double down on two-card total of 10 against a dealer's ace.

When the deck is −1, it is played as if it were a neutral deck.

When the deck is −2 or more, the following plays should be made:

• Don't double down a hard 10 against a dealer's 9.
• Don't double down a hard 11 against a dealer's 10.
• Don't double down a hard 9 against a dealer's 2.
• Hit a hard 12 against a dealer's 4.
• Hit a hard 13 against a dealer's 2 or 3.

To more fully understand these variations in basic strategy, we'll now list the borderline or trouble hands, where the basic strategy suggested gives the player only a very, very slight advantage, and any change in the card count should alter that strategy.

Borderline Hands

With the following hands, if the deck is a −2 or worse, you should change your strategy as follows: If the strategy calls for doubling down, you should merely hit. If the strategy calls for standing, you should hit. If the strategy calls for splitting, you should hit. In other words, when there's a −2 or more deck, you don't want to put out more money on the table, for the expectation of a losing hand is greater. On the other hand, you can hit hands with impunity that you'd ordinarily stand on, since you have a small bet riding in the first place, and your chances of busting on stiff hands is lessened with a minus count.

The following are borderline hands:

- Hitting a hard 12 against a dealer's 3.
- Standing on a hard 12 against a dealer's 4.
- Standing on a hard 13 against a dealer's 2.
- Standing on a soft 18 against a dealer's ace.
- Doubling down on a soft 13 against a dealer's 4.
- Splitting 2s against a dealer's 3.
- Splitting 6s against a dealer's 2.

Use these borderline hands in conjunction with the variations suggested in the previous section on variations in the basic playing strategy according to the count.

Surrender

Several of the Las Vegas casinos allow surrender, and at one time surrender was allowed in all the Atlantic City clubs, but that rule was done away with as card-counting experts got greedier and greedier, and were taking the casinos for large amounts of cash.

Instead of barring the counters, countermeasures were taken. More decks were used and the shuffle point was pushed forward to its present 70 percent. And surrender, which was a great option to an expert card counter, was eliminated. In those casinos in Nevada where it's still available, it's a great option for the player, especially if used correctly.

Surrender means surrendering your first two cards without playing them. To do this, you turn them over and announce that you are surrendering them. In casinos where the cards are dealt face up, you simply announce "surrender." The dealer will remove the cards and *half* your original bet to complete the transaction.

A hand can be surrendered only if it's not acted upon. Once you hit or double down or make any other move with that hand, it cannot be surrendered. Surrender means not having to play the hand at all, forfeiting any opportunity to improve that hand. For this privilege you give away half your original bet.

When is surrender valid? When should this option be taken advantage of? We'll show you in the next few paragraphs the essential strategy of surrender, one for the Las Vegas casinos and the other for the Atlantic City casinos. There's a difference in the strategical considerations between both places, for in Atlantic City the dealer doesn't see his hole card till all the players have acted upon their hands, while in Vegas the dealer sees his hole card whenever a 10 or ace is his upcard. In the Las Vegas casinos, therefore, you know when a dealer has no blackjack, but you don't know this in Atlantic City when you face a dealer's ace or 10.

The first rule to remember is this: Never surrender your hand when the deck is minus. It's a bad play.

When the deck is neutral of +1, surrender the following hands:

Single-Deck Games
Hard 16s, 15s, and 7, 7 against a dealer's 10.

Multiple-Deck Games
All hard totals of 13–16 against a dealer's ace.
All hard totals of 14–16 against a dealer's 10.

When the deck is +2 or more surrender the following hands:

Hard 16s, 15s, and 14s against a dealer's ace or 10.
Hard 16s and 15s against a dealer's 9.

Instead of splitting 8s, surrender them against a dealer's 9, 10, or ace.

As for games in which the dealer doesn't peek at his hole card, the same rules as applied in the neutral deck apply to the plus deck, because the player cannot know if a dealer has a blackjack if he shows a 10 or ace as his upcard.

Surrender can be a commonsense factor when used by the astute blackjack player. The richer the deck, the more 10s are in that deck, the more difficult it will be for a player to improve his weakest hands, the 14s, 15s and 16s, when they are hard totals. Therefore, he should take every opportunity he can to surrender them.

That's why it's preferable to surrender a pair of 8s against a dealer's 10 when the deck is favorable. Splitting the 8s when there are a great many 10s remaining may turn these 8s into two losing hands, and a player can ill afford to do this with a big bet out, which he'll have wagered in a very favorable situation. The expectation is that he'll make two 18s out of these cards, while he may already be facing a dealer's 20. If the player had bet $50 on that hand, he'd lose only $25 by surrendering it. If he plays out both 8s as split cards, he might lose $100. Quite a difference!

The beautiful thing about surrender is that it enables a card counter to play and bet that much more aggressively. If the deck is very favorable, he can make bigger bets than he ordinarily would without the surrender feature. Should he get his monster hand of 20 or blackjack, wonderful. Should he have bad luck and get a 15 or 16, he surrenders it and only loses half his bet. In essence, he's turning the odds 2-1 in his favor in certain situations. He has only half a bet to lose if his hand is terrible, while he has the whole bet to win if he gets a strong hand.

If possible, all other rules being equal, play in a casino that allows surrender. It will act as an umbrella over your bets. Whenever surrender is allowed, I always suggest that a player raise his base, or neutral, bet to take advantage of the feature, since the surrender option protects his very big bets should he get a poor hand. Thus, if a player ordinarily bets $10 as his neutral bet, I suggest a $15 or $20 neutral bet, so that when the deck is favorable, he can really sock in a bet of $50 instead of $20, protected as he is by the surrender feature.

Sometimes one can get creative in the use of surrender. I remember playing at a single-deck game on the Strip that not only had the very best rules, but had single-deck games in which you could go from $25 to $3,000 as the limits. When I sat down at that table, I had the edge over the house even on the opening deal. A few times, when they were testing to see whether or not I was a counter, the floorman would give the dealer's arm a little shove and he'd reshuffle when I had a really big bet out. Instead of removing the chips and lowering the bet, I asked the floorman for a drink and paid no attention to my chips. What difference did it make? I had every option going for me, including surrender. I was just a wee bit in front, and I like the front position. Better than being trapped in the back, with the mud thrown in your face by the faster ones.

Anyway, I was soon joined at the table by one of the blackjack legends, who is now unfortunately gone from this world. He was a brilliant player, and in the small world of blackjack experts we knew each other from way back. I was doing well, and he came right in with $1,000 bets. The time came when I had a $1,500 bet out, and the deck was favorable for the players. I was very relaxed and was not only counting the tens and aces and the small cards, but I could keep track of the 7s, 8s, and 9s. At this point all the 7s and 8s had been played out. I knew this because the last two 7s and an 8 were showing on the table. And all the 9s were intact, and the three players at the table, myself, the expert, and someone else had hands that had to be hit. The first player hit and drew a 7 and busted.

The great expert had two 8s, and split them against the dealer's 10. He got an ace on one and a 9 on the other, the first 9 showing.

Three 9s were left. I looked at my cards. 10,3 for a hard 13. With no 7s and 8s to hit, the best I could do was get a 6 for a 19. The deck was fairly rich with 10s. I had to figure the dealer for a 20. I surrendered and got this look of pathetic indulgence by the expert. "Ed," he said, "I thought you knew how to play this game."

I shrugged, got back $750. The dealer turned over a ten in the hole for his 20. I saved $750. I wasn't going to play out the hand just because I should play it out to please the expert. Knowing there was practically no chance of winning, I took the money. He was so disgusted with my play that he muttered something to some homely woman he had come with, something about a fool or jerk, implying me. I winked at the woman, gathered up my chips, and cashed in. I had a nice win. So goes it.

Where a Card Counter Should Sit at the Table

I always prefer the last, or third baseman's, seat, also known as the anchor man's seat, when playing casino blackjack. This gives me the opportunity to see the other players' cards if the hands are dealt face up, or enables me to see some of the cards dealt to the players with me as they hit their hands. I always take advantage of all possible information at a blackjack table, and knowing as many cards as possible can only be helpful to me when I have to make a decision concerning my own hand.

By sitting in the last seat, you can keep the best running count, counting cards as they are dealt out without waiting for the dealer to turn over all the players' cards. I've used several examples previously where this has been effective. For example, with a running count you can tell if a neutral deck has become favorable or unfavorable for purposes of playing out your hand.

However, the third baseman's seat is the one most often taken by card counters, and casino personnel often scrutinize the play of an anchor man. Sometimes, so as not to draw casino heat, I sit in a different spot, usually the seat next to the third baseman.

This is a very good seat as well. Often players will hold their cards high when examining them, and I get a quick look at the players' on both sides of me, which gives me more information about the deck.

A player can make money at any spot at the table. At times I was forced to sit at the first baseman's seat, and that was all right. If you can count cards, you will win money at blackjack, but it's best to sit where you can keep a running count, for those times when you have to make a decision about a borderline hand.

Multiple-Deck Games

More and more casinos are turning to the multiple-deck games, dealt out of a shoe. When playing in these games, a player can still use the basic strategic principles suggested in this chapter, for their validity is not changed by the fact that more than one deck is involved.

The same principles of card counting are used. However, there are some minor changes which should be noted. First of all, when playing either against a four- or six-deck shoe, the house will have a slight advantage over the player at the outset of play, and this disadvantage to you must be compensated for.

The easiest way to do this is to start off against a four-deck game with a −2 count. Since the deck is now considered minus and unfavorable, you will be betting your minimum wager of one unit. This one-unit bet must be kept until the deck changes to a favorable one. Here's how the unit betting will work.

At the outset −2	one-unit bet
Deck becomes even	one-unit bet
Deck moves to +2	two-unit bet
Deck move to +4	three-unit bet
Deck is +6 or more	four-unit bet

When playing against four decks, you will always start with a one-unit bet. If you're at a $25 table, then your minimum bet will be $25, working up by degrees to $100 as your maximum bet. Or you may wish to start with a $50 bet as your minimum, working it up to $200.

With a six-deck game, the deck is even more unfavorable at the outset, and here you will start with a −3 situation.

At the outset −3	Bet one unit
Neutral deck	Bet one unit
Deck is +2	Bet two units
Deck is +4	Bet three units
Deck is +6 or more	Bet four units

What you will find is that the decks may run neutral or unfavorable for a long period of time, and during that time you must be patient and not raise the bet just to have action. At other times the decks will stay favorable for a very long run, and at those times your previous patience will have paid off as you reap the harvest of good play and card counting.

With an eight-deck game, the deck becomes more unfavorable at the beginning of the play, and thus you'll be starting with a −4 situation.

At the outset −4	Bet one unit
Neutral deck	Bet one unit
Deck is +2	Bet two units
Deck is +4	Bet three units
Deck is +6 or more	Bet four units

Beating the Multiple-Deck Games

The handwriting has been on the wall for some years now. The casinos prefer multiple-deck games, and the more decks the happier they are. They prefer the multiple decks for several reasons. The game is faster for them, so they can make more money in a shorter period of time, and not waste time constantly shuffling up the single deck. In the multiple-deck games the cards are generally dealt face up, so that the player doesn't have to touch them, and thus they prevent cheating of the type called "hand-mucking," when the player exchanges other cards he's been holding for the cards dealt to him. Finally, they can now play with the rule of "no-peeking," so that the dealer doesn't give away a tell, or indication of the value of his hole card when he has to peek after holding an ace or 10-value card as his upcard.

It's getting more and more difficult to find these single-deck games. There are a number of them in downtown Las Vegas in the smaller casinos, and on the Strip as well. Here's a list that might come in handy for you, although new casinos are being built, new management is constantly coming in, and casinos change their rules and regulations constantly.

Las Vegas single-deck games: Circus Circus, Landmark, Palace Station, Royal Las Vegas, Silver City, Slots A Fun, Vegas World, El Cortez, Golden Gate, Gold Spike, Horseshoe, Park, Pioneer, Fitzgeralds, Nevada Palace, Jerry's Nugget, Silver Nugget, Eldorado.

Remember, this list will change as time goes by. Some of the casinos mentioned are in North Las Vegas or Henderson, close to Las Vegas, and included in the Greater Las Vegas area.

In Northern Nevada, which includes Sparks, Lake Tahoe, Reno, Carson City and that area, the rule is that single-deck games are available. However, the rules, such as permitting doubling down on only 10s and 11s, don't favor the player. But you'll get all the single-deck action you want up there.

In Atlantic City, there's no chance of finding a single-deck game. Their games are played with four, six, and eight decks. The bigger the game, the fewer the decks is a general rule, although a lot of gamblers don't really care if they're playing against four or eight decks. And these include some of the biggest players. They just don't know the game that well and have no conception of counting. But for those of us who want the edge, we should always play against the least number of decks possible. Play against four if you can in Atlantic City. Six, if four isn't available, and eight as a last resort.

In the previous section I outlined a method of dealing with the multiple-deck games, in which bets are altered according to the count. In this section we're going to take the principle one step further. Before we do, however, let's examine the concept of *running count* vs. *true count*.

Running Count vs. True Count

As cards are constantly dealt by the dealer, the count changes. In single-deck games, in which the cards are dealt face down, it's often difficult to know the exact count, since we have to surmise what players hold by their actions. So, generally, in single-deck games (and most double-deck games where the cards are dealt face down) our count is based on the last round of play.

The running count is easier to use in multiple-deck games. Remember now, in our count we gave a +1 to all small cards 3–6 dealt out previously, and a −1 to all 10-value cards previously dealt. Suppose we're now at a crowded six-deck game in Atlantic City, and we see the following hands dealt face up. The dealer shows a 7. A6, 9J, 3-4, 8-7, 5-5, 2Q, KJ. Suppose this is the first round. We can take a quick count here and get a +1 reading. Let's assume further that after all the players and the dealer has acted on his hand, the count is 0, absolutely neutral, and we make a minimum bet of one unit.

For our next bet we must use this information of a neutral bet. As new cards are being dealt out, we can say that our running count is 0. Perhaps after the next round of play, our running count is −4. Again a minimum bet is made.

There's no problem as long as the deck is minus or neutral. We won't raise our bet at all, but keep it at a minimum. But when the deck gets to a plus area, the true count gives us a quick and accurate fix on the relative value of the cards remaining in the deck. Here's how the true count is made.

First of all, we divide the deck into half-decks. In a four-deck game there'll be eight half-decks; in a six-deck game there'll be 12 half-decks and in an eight-deck game there'll be 16 half-decks. We use half-decks instead of whole ones in order to make our true count more accurate.

Generally speaking, you can depend on 20-21 cards being dealt out for each round of play at a full table in the casinos at Atlantic City. The same holds true for the Strip in Vegas. Thus, after three rounds of play a little over one deck has been played out. Or as we see it, two half-decks. We find the count is now +8 in a six-deck game. There were originally 12 half-decks, and now there are 10 half-decks remaining. If we divide +8 by 10 we get the true count, which is +.80, not quite +1. If the count at that point had been +10, the count would be +1. This is the true count.

Why a true count rather than a running count? Here's why. Suppose after one round of play in a six-deck game, the deck is +10. It sounds impressive, but there are a lot of cards remaining in the dealer's shoe, approximately 290 of them. A +10 sounds good, but divided by 12 half-decks, it's less than +1 as a true count.

Now, suppose that the count is the same +10 after ten rounds of play. Assuming that 21 cards have been dealt out on each round, the cards dealt out total 210 or approximately four decks, or eight half-decks. That leaves only four half-decks remaining. We divide our running count of +10 by 4 and get a +2.5 true count reading, much stronger than our earlier +10 divided by 12 half-decks or +.8.

The true count does give us a guide to the real power of our advantage over the house. A +10 after one round of play isn't as good as a +10 running count after 10 rounds of play. In fact, the +10 running count after ten rounds of play is about *three times* as powerful as the one after one round of play. And if it's three times as strong, it deserves a much bigger bet.

There's the key. With our true count we know how much strength our running count really has by turning it into a true count, and we increase our bet according to its power.

That's what the pros do. That's why they win in multiple-deck games wherever they play. Let's give some examples to make this absolutely clear. We're in a four-deck game, and the running count is +12. It's a crowded table and five rounds of cards have been played, approximately 102 cards (21 per round). That's about two decks, or 4 half-decks. Since the 4-deck game started with 8 half-decks, there are now four remaining. We divide our +12 running count by 4 and get a +3 true count, a very powerful plus count. We make a big bet.

Now, let's switch to a six-deck game. Eight rounds of play have gone by or approximately 168 cards have been dealt out. That's a little more than three decks or 6 half-decks. Since we started with 12 half-decks for our six-deck game, 6 half-decks remain. Our running count is +12. If we divide +12 by 6 we get a +2 true count, which is very strong. As can be seen, the true count is always less than the running count, and any plus value on a true count is powerful, and the higher the true count, the more powerful it is.

From here we go to an eight-deck game. After four rounds of play, our running count is +8. We have used up about 82 cards or three half-decks. We started with 16 half-decks and now have 13 remaining. We divide our +8 by 13 and get +.6. Not very strong at all.

In the previous section we showed how to get a quick fix on the favorability of the multiple decks by starting with a negative running count. For those of you who don't want to study the true count, that's a fair guide to increasing or decreasing bets. But for a more exact method of betting, we suggest the following when there's a true count.

True Count	Bet
Any minus or 0	1 unit
+1	2 units
+2	3 units
+3	5 units
+4	7 units
+5	9 units
Above +5	9-10 units

Of course, the above table takes into consideration the fact that there may be casino heat placed on you for altering your bets. However, since there is a long session at multiple-deck games for one shoe's worth of play, you can alter your bets upward steadily. Even if the running count goes up in one round of play, the true count will be a more gradual move.

With a true count you'll have a terrific fix on the value of your forthcoming hands. But you must pay attention to the number of rounds of cards played and keep dividing by half-decks. And be patient.

What happens if you are playing at a table that's not full, say, against six decks? Simply count the players and multiply by 3 to get an approximate fix on how many cards are dealt out each round. If there are four players, about 12 cards will be dealt out (including the dealer's). Thus, it takes about two rounds to approximate a half-deck. Use this guide of players ×3 to determine the cards in a round of play and you won't be far off the mark.

Let us consider shuffle points once more. If you recall, a plastic or other card is placed in the shoe about 70 percent of the way into the decks to mark the spot where the cards will be reshuffled. The farther in, the better it is for the player. A shuffle point of 90 percent is wonderful, for if the true count is plus and thus favorable for the player, near the end of the decks that true count can become very high. Suppose it's +12 and only 2 half-decks remain. That's a +6 true count. Bet heavily. You have a tremendous edge over the house.

In a four-deck game there are 208 cards; at a 70 percent shuffle point, that will leave 145 cards to be played out. In a six-deck game there are 312 cards; with a 70 percent shuffle point that leaves 218 cards to be played. An eight-deck game has 416 cards; 70 percent of that total is 291 cards to be played before the cards are shuffled. Of course, all of the second figures are approximate, because the marked card isn't placed exactly 70 percent of the way in. It varies from probably 65–75 percent.

To play like a pro in multiple-deck games in Atlantic City and elsewhere, do the following:

1. Keep a running count.
2. Know the true count at all times.
3. Bet a minimum stake when the cards are minus or neutral or below +1 true count.

4. Increase your bets when the decks go +1 or higher true count.

5. Try and find a table where the shuffle point is above 70 percent. It's to your advantage.

6. Be patient and wait for the cards to get positive before increasing your bets. Don't play hunches or try your luck.

7. Increase your bets but not by too much if you're drawing casino heat.

8. If you find that all high cards and aces are being dealt in a couple of early rounds, don't sit through a long, dismal losing session. Get up and find another table.

9. After you're ahead, put aside money so that you leave the table a winner.

Those nine rules will stand you in good stead, and will win money for you.

Money Management

This subject is of extreme importance in all gambling games, and particularly so in blackjack, where you not only must manage your bankroll, but your time as well.

When playing twenty-one, you don't want to be barred or have the casino put in countermeasures, such as constant shuffling up or harassment to discourage your participation. Therefore, you must be as inconspicuous as possible, especially if you have studied the methods of strategy and betting outlined in this chapter.

The single best method of avoiding casino heat is to hit and run—to make some money, leave the table, and go on to another table or casino before the management is wise to your expert play. To do this, you should never spend more than one hour at any one table. Besides limited play at one table, I would suggest never spending more than two hours in any one casino during any one shift.

As for money management, the following rules should be adhered to:

• Play with 50 times the minimum bet in reserve at any single table. If you are at a $1 minimum table and that's your minimum bet, you should have $50 either in your pocket or on the table as your reserve.

If $5 is the minimum bet, you'll need a reserve of $250. This doesn't mean that the whole sum should be placed out on the table. I like to put only about half that amount on the table, keeping the rest in my wallet. If I lose the $125 of the $250 I brought with me, I either pull out more money or move on to another table. This gives the appearance of having been tapped out, which casino floormen and pit bosses love to see. If all $250 is on the table and you've still got $125 of it, then you'll be table hopping and might draw the attention of the casino personnel.

• If you decide to stay at one table until you lose your entire single-session bankroll, or lose 40 of those 50 units, then it might be time to get out of the game, especially if the deck is now neutral or unfavorable. If it's favorable, stay around, bet the maximum, and try to salvage your losses with some wins. But only if the deck is favorable. Don't just trust to luck.

• Never reach into your pocket after losing all 50 units you've started with. *Never.* If you've taken a beating at a table—and this will happen from time to time—don't fight the cards. Get up and walk away. Rest and refresh yourself before attempting to hit another table.

• If playing seriously over a more extended period of time, perhaps a few days, perhaps a week or more, you should have between 7 and 10 times your single-session bankroll as your total bankroll.

If you are betting $5 chips as your minimum bet, you'd need $250 for one session of play and about $1,800 to $2,500 in reserve for a number of sessions of play.

If you can't keep that much in reserve, you shouldn't be playing in a $5 game. It's very possible to sustain a long run of bad luck before the cards turn in your favor. This can happen to even the most skillful of twenty-one players and could happen to you as well. To weather the temporary losses you must have money in reserve. Remember, if you use our basic strategy and count cards and alter your bets according to the count, you're going to end up a winner.

I can remember several instances of making good use of

my reserves. Once, on a trip to Lake Tahoe, I brought $1,500 with me. The first night there I lost $600, the next morning another $250. If I had been playing with scared money and had only brought about $1,000, between meals, room, and carfare I might have had only a few dollars left, packed it all in, and gone back to San Francisco.

But I still had about $650 in reserve, and my luck finally turned. Within a day I was even; by the end of my stay I left Tahoe with $1,000 more than I had come with.

I had a similar experience in Vegas, visiting the city one time to meet some friends who were due the next day. I arrived on a Thursday night, and by midnight I had dropped close to $900 of my $1,500. But my reserves again pulled me through. By the time my pals came, I had a big smile on my face and a wallet loaded with casino banknotes.

To summarize the formula for successful money management:

• Your total bankroll should be 7 to 10 times the single-table bankroll.

• The single bankroll should be 50 times the minimum bet to be played at the table.

• If losing 40 times the minimum, or 40 units, pack away the remaining 10 units unless the deck is favorable and get away from the table.

• If you've lost all 50 units, leave the table and never, never reach into your pocket for more money.

Winning Limits

I've been supercareful in describing the losing limits, because those limits are the danger signals. A player who doesn't obey them can go bankrupt from one or two disastrous sessions of play unless he has self-control in handling his money. He must learn to leave a table when losing without reaching in for more money. *The first loss is the cheapest,* and I can't emphasize it enough. Take your first loss and get out. Save your money for a better table, one where the cards will go your way.

Just as important as knowing what to do with losses is

knowing how to handle your profits. More players end up losers because they blew their wins than for any other reason. I've seen countless experts end up as big losers not because they didn't know what they were doing as far as the cards were concerned, but because they lacked the self-control to leave when ahead.

When winning, the time factor rears its ugly head as well. No matter how well a table is going, it may be necessary to leave it when the casino personnel become overly interested in your game. You may have to leave during a fantastic winning streak, especially if you're counting cards and alternating your bets. It's better to win less and return again for other winning sessions than to be a hog and lose any possibility of ever playing at the casino again.

Casinos bar experts and above all they bar players who are big winners if they feel these players know how to count cards. As a result of many hours of playing and observing the top players, I've come up with this formula for winning.

• If winning at least 20 units, put away 10 units plus your original stake and play out the rest. It's not necessary to put the chips in your pocket; that move alerts casino personnel. Just make a mental note of the 10 chips and when you've depleted the other chips, get away from the table with a 10-unit win.

• Should you keep winning, and the remaining 10 chips turn into 20 winning chips, make another mental move and add 10 more chips to your original pile. Now you can't help but leave with 20 units as your win.

• Work this way for the hour or until you double your chips, whichever comes first, and then get away. Take your money and run with your profits. You won't be there long enough to draw heat, and doubling your money is a beautiful win at a blackjack table.

• There may be a situation where you're ahead 40 chips and the deck is superfavorable. It might pay to make a large bet, perhaps double your original bet on the next hand, especially if you've won the previous one. Then if you win that and the deck is still favorable, make another big bet, even bigger than the one before. If you win, you might now start betting at a higher rate than you started with, hoping for one big killing. But do this only with chips you've won, not to get even.

However, don't linger more than that hour and don't reach for more chips from the ones you've previously won and put away. Never do that.

Using this stop-loss method of betting, you can't help but wind up a winner. Leave with your winnings intact, for there's nothing more debilitating and tiring than winning a great deal at a table, then blowing it all through too long a session or through stupid betting, using up all the previous hard-earned wins on some outlandish and wild bets in the hope of making a lucky killing.

One final note. If you've been at a table for a long time and lost most of your chips, then the cards finally turn and you get even, you should immediately leave the table. The long, hard struggle to get even is wearying, and a heavy loser should be happy to come out with his money intact.

There's nothing worse than losing practically all your chips, getting even finally, then losing it all back again. That kind of play is stupid, to use a kind word.

Tipping or
Toking the Dealer—Strategy

The general public doesn't realize how poorly dealers are paid by casinos. The usual pay scale for casino dealers at blackjack runs from a minimum of $25 to a maximum of $35 a day, which is peasant wages these days. The bulk of the dealers' earnings comes from tips, or tokes, as they're known among casino personnel.

I'm always in favor of tipping dealers, except when they're hostile or incompetent and their demeanor or play actively hurts the player. I feel that a competent and friendly dealer should be toked whether a player is winning or losing. Of course, if a bettor is winning, the tokes should be greater and more numerous; if he's losing, perhaps an occasional tip is in order to show the dealer that he's being thought of.

In blackjack, tipping a dealer so that he's friendly and on your side works wonders. Although the dealer has no options in playing out his hand, there are many other decisions, such as when to shuffle up the cards, that are his alone unless he's dealing in a rigidly controlled atmosphere where all deviations from the house rules are subject to reprimand or punishment. This isn't usually the case when a player is alone at a table with a dealer, or there are just one or two players at that table.

In most single-deck casinos in Nevada, where five or six players are filling the seats, the dealer will only deal out two rounds of cards and then shuffle up automatically, for these are the standard rules in many Nevada clubs.

But if a player is alone at a table, the dealer may have the option of deciding when to break a deck and reshuffle the cards. If a player is hostile or ungenerous, the dealer may break the deck at the most inappropriate moments, just when a player has raised his bet, for example. This will hurt an expert card counter badly, taking away all his favorable situations.

My advice is to keep the dealer happy, make him cooperative, and if possible, put him on your side helping you to win. If you accomplish that, it is sure to benefit you financially. And the easiest way to do this is not only to toke a dealer, but to do so in a manner that in effect makes him root for you to win a particular hand.

Even though dealers don't keep their individual tips, but share them with a whole shift of blackjack dealers, that doesn't lessen an individual dealer's interest in those tokes. Dealers want players to tip them, and they want players to be generous with their tokes.

After all, dealers aren't card-handling robots but human beings, and many of them are gamblers themselves. They realize that a losing player isn't going to give them big tips. But if a winning player stiffs them, their attitude can be downright nasty and they can do things to really hurt the player, such as shuffling up when the deck gets favorable, speeding up the game by dealing extraordinarily fast, thus making it uncomfortable for the player, or worse still, slowing up the game by calling over a floorman to watch the player's moves.

Dealers can sometimes spot a card counter, for some of the dealers are counters themselves, and their attitude is: Why help this jerk along when he has no interest in doing anything in return for me? It's a very human attitude, one I have no quarrel with. So treat the dealer as a human being and treat him fairly, and he may go out of his way to help you out.

My policy is to tip when certain playing or betting situations present themselves, to tell the dealer in effect, "Look, this is an important hand for me, and I want you to be partners with me at this time so that together we can win some money. Therefore, if you can give me any help, I'd appreciate it, and it will benefit not only me but you as well."

Of course, that long sentence is unspoken at the table, but to enforce this policy, I toke the dealer indirectly by making a bet for him rather than handing him a tip. Before I go further, let me explain how a dealer can be tipped at a blackjack table. There are four basic methods:

1. Tip the dealer only after the complete session is over.

The dealer will appreciate the toke, but this is the worst way to tip a dealer. Since the player hadn't given the dealer a single tip during the course of play, the dealer, in all probability, thought he had a stiff on his hands. Even though he's now pleasantly surprised by the unexpected toke, the dealer probably didn't help the player at all during the playing of the hands.

2. Tip the dealer directly by handing him a casino chip or money after a winning hand.

This method is appreciated by the dealer, but it's done after the fact (after the win) and won't aid the player on any particular hand he's betting on.

3. Tip the dealer by making a bet for him outside the bettor's box in the insurance area on the layout.

This is the most common way that dealers receive tips, for they win double the original tip if the hand wins for the player.

However, in most casinos (with few exceptions, particularly in Reno) the dealer must collect the winning tip immediately after the hand is played. This is a stringent rule in Las Vegas. In other words, the winning bet cannot ride for another round of play, so the player will be forced to either make another bet of this sort for the dealer or not tip him for the next round of play.

By being forced to make another bet instead of letting the previous bet ride, the player must put out more money instead of letting the casino win ride for him another time.

4. Place the bet for the dealer directly in your betting box, either alongside or on your own bet.

This is the correct way to toke a dealer. By doing it this way, you control the dealer's bet. You can let it ride or take it down or drag it or do whatever you want to do, since it's in your betting box and it can't be controlled by casino rules.

The dealer, seeing this bet, knows that he and the player are now partners for that hand and any subsequent hand that the bet stands for in that betting box.

The following example will illustrate the effectiveness of this kind of bet as a toke for the dealer.

I was playing at a $25 table in Vegas, head-to-head with a dealer. My range of bets ran from $25 (unfavorable deck) to $200 (very favorable deck) with my neutral bet at $50.

Playing alone at this table, with the floorman only occasionally drifting over, the dealer had a great deal of power in determining when the deck was to be broken and reshuffled. Of course, I wanted that deck reshuffled when it was unfavorable, but dealt down as far as it would go when it was favorable.

The game was a single-deck one. On the first favorable situation that developed, I bet $100 and put another $5 chip to one side of my bet in the box. The dealer eyed that chip, and I told him that it was his bet. I won the hand, and since the deck remained slightly favorable, I let his bet ride, though I kept my own bet at $100. We won that hand together, and now the dealer reshuffled the cards even though the deck was still favorable.

Well, I couldn't stop him from doing that by telling him the deck was still favorable and that I was a card counter, for that would have gotten me an early exit out of the casino. Instead

I took down the dealer's bet and gave it to him, and didn't tip him again until, after a few shuffles, the deck again became favorable.

Once more I made a $5 bet for the dealer. Again we won our bet, and now he had $10 riding for him in my betting box. We lost this bet, however, but the deck suddenly became superfavorable. I made a $200 bet and again bet $5 for him. However, he shuffled up the cards instead of dealing them out. I was disappointed, of course, but still there was nothing I could say. I simply took away his $5 bet and put it among my chips, waiting for another favorable situation.

Finally, the third time he got the message. As long as I had a bet for him in my betting box, he continued dealing the cards. When I took his bet down and paid him off, he shuffled up. There were times when he was dealing to the bottom of the deck, watching his bets win and grow in size. It was now an unspoken agreement that was working smooth as silk, and we were both making a lot of money.

There was a side benefit as well. When the deck became unfavorable, I didn't make a bet for him, and if there were a couple of rounds with no bet out for the dealer, he simply reshuffled the cards.

The floorman drifted over a few times, luckily while the cards were being shuffled because there was no bet for the dealer and I was betting a minimum $25. Seeing the cards continually reshuffled pleased the floorman, who smiled at the dealer's loyalty in not dealing out too many cards to me, the player. The floorman didn't realize, of course, that the dealer was doing it for my benefit, not for the casino's.

I made a big score at that table through correct tipping, which created a tremendous unspoken rapport with the dealer. When the deck was favorable, I got the benefit of a constant deal right down to the bottom of the deck, and when the deck was unfavorable, all I had to do was lower my bet and stop betting for the dealer, and the cards were immediately reshuffled.

When tipping, follow these two additional points:

1. Try to tip only when you have a maximum bet out—when the cards are favorable. Make the dealer a partner in

your hand. Train the dealer by removing his bet if he shuffles up at the wrong time.

2. Sometimes, even if the deck isn't favorable, but you've won a big double-down or scored well with a blackjack, tip the dealer generously by placing the bet outside your box on the next round of play to show that you are tipping him for winning, but it's a different kind of toke.

He'll appreciate this gesture and will be on your side throughout your play.

Sometimes I've tipped a couple of times and never even gotten a gesture of thanks from a dealer. Some dealers are extremely hostile, for whatever personal reason. I don't want to play against a hostile dealer at all. It ends up hurting my game, and you should avoid hostile dealers.

Play only against a dealer who wants you to win, who's going to root for you if you treat him right.

Handling the Dealer and Other Casino Personnel

The casino personnel you will come in contact with are usually the dealer and the floorman supervising the table you're playing at. It's important to handle these two people correctly so that they don't harass or bar you from the casino.

To do this properly, I have a few suggestions that will certainly help the bettor. When I carry them out personally, I try to be natural in my approach, and you should be also. It doesn't pay to be cold-blooded, for any fool can see through those kind of tactics.

• Take an interest in the dealer. Ask him his name and where he's from. Try and get into a conversation with him and to find out something about him. Be interested in him as a person.

As a professional writer, I'm always interested in people, and so it's not difficult for me to carry on a conversation with a stranger. Many of my articles and stories have resulted from friendships I've developed with dealers over the years.

They're human beings in a rather difficult job. They're on their feet eight hours a day facing hostile players in a noisy and smoky atmosphere. Many of the losing players they face blame the dealers personally for their losses. Many of these losers claim that they're being cheated, an irresponsible claim, but losers tend to get suspicious and angry. A dealer will really appreciate a calm individual who shows an interest in him.

• Never blame the dealer for your losses. He has nothing to do with the fact that you've blown your money. The cards tell the final story in blackjack, and it's the composition of those cards that has led to your defeat.

If I'm involved in a losing streak I tell the dealer, "These cards are really miserable. Just cold and terrible. Maybe you can get a new deck put into the game."

If you talk to a dealer in this manner, he'll often go out of his way to get a new deck put into play, or he'll continually shuffle up the cards thoroughly to break their pattern. Dealers want a decent person to win and they'll go out of their way to help. One dealer even refused to accept my tip while I was losing.

• Make the dealer your partner. Show him that if you win, he'll win also. Too many players are greedy individuals who wouldn't think of doing this. They want all the money for themselves, and they look upon the dealer as a mere cipher working for the house or, worse still, as their enemy.

Most dealers, if treated decently, will be rooting for the player to win. And they'll try to help the player in any way they can, legitimately. This can be a tremendous benefit at times.

• If you face an angry or hostile dealer, as sometimes happens, you should get up and leave the table as soon as you can. Don't fight the dealer and don't stay around trying to win big to show him up. He couldn't care less and you'll end up making foolish and wild bets at the wrong times. Simply leave.

When I face an unsmiling dealer or one that deals at an uncomfortable pace, I'm off and running from the table. I don't need enemies, not when I'm playing for serious money.

Occasionally I've said something to the dealer or complained to a floorman if the treatment was particularly rotten, but generally I leave the bastard to stew in his own anger.

When I have complained, it was because the dealer's behavior actually cost me money. This has happened on occasion, and then I really get angry. One time I was about to double down by turning over my cards and putting out an additional bet and the dealer simply passed me by and dealt to the next player. And on another occasion, as I was about to make a bet before the cards were dealt, the dealer went right by me before I could make a bet.

• If a floorman comes over to watch your play, remember he's also a human being doing a lousy job. If you don't think his job is terrible, then stand in a noisy, smoky blackjack pit eight hours a day, trying to look busy while watching the same old thing day after day: a bunch of players grumbling about their losses and asking for more credit. The faces of losers bent over their cards are tiring and disheartening to anyone.

And most players are losers. That's why a winner stands out at the table, and that's why we write about all these strategies and methods of dealing with casino personnel. After you learn the basic strategies and card-counting methods shown in this chapter, you're going to be a winner, and eventually you're going to have to handle casino personnel who will be watching you closely.

When I first encounter a floorman, I treat him with courtesy. I may tell him that he has a good crew of dealers and that the dealer I'm facing is competent (loud enough for the dealer to hear). If the floorman asks how I'm making out at the table, I never lie. If I've been winning, I tell him I'm winning, but that these wins won't make up for the losses I've had previously at the casino.

If I'm losing, I tell him I'm taking a beating, but I'm not really complaining, because I play for the hell of it and don't expect to win. I never give the impression that I've been an overall winner.

• Since floormen also serve in another capacity, as public relations representatives for the casino in dealing with players, I take advantage of this knowledge and put it to good effect.

If I'm playing at a $5 minimum table or a higher minimum table, I always ask about the food in the casino restaurant. Most of the time the floorman will comp me to a meal. As cold-blooded as casinos are, they want to give out a message of warmth, and they'll gladly give action players free meals and free shows and sometimes other amenities.

I never ask directly for any comped item; I merely ask about the meals, the show, and so on.

How to Disguise Counting Methods

This is a favorite topic of mine, for I'm intrigued with disguises, and when I discuss disguises, I don't mean physical changes. There are some card counters who have been barred from practically all casinos, and they must resort to false beards and things like that. The disguises I refer to are emotional and intellectual ones, for they are more effective than physical changes and are necessary to a card counter who is winning.

The following are the best methods of disguising play:

• Don't stay at any one table more than an hour or in any casino more than two hours at one time.

If you play often enough at a particular casino you'll be recognized by the casino personnel. That's all right as long as they don't recognize you as a card counter or winner. By hitting and running, you stand the best chance of not being barred. Long play at any one table gives them the opportunity to really scrutinize your play, so don't linger.

• Change your betting patterns when you have to. Even though the methods outlined in this book give you the best chance of winning by altering your bets according to the count, there will be times you won't be able to do this and survive in a casino.

Sometimes if you've put out a big bet in anticipation of a favorable hand and the dealer shuffles up instead, it pays to leave the big bet out. If you constantly change your bets at the last minute when the dealer breaks the deck, it will raise a red flag in front of both the dealer's and floorman's eyes. I always wait until the last minute to make my bet, eyeing the dealer surreptitiously, waiting to see what he is doing with the cards. If he breaks them, I then make my normal or neutral bet without having to remove chips from a previous bet.

I can remember one incident vividly, at a Strip hotel-casino where I had done very well on many occasions. I was playing head-to-head with a dealer at a single-deck game. The minimum bet allowed was $25, and I was altering my bets from a minimum of $25 to a maximum of $200.

I had played many times there, almost daily for long periods of time when I lived in Vegas, and yet I never was barred even though I beat them for a lot of money. The floormen and pit bosses had their suspicions, but any time they came close to barring me, my actions disarmed them.

On this occasion I had a $200 bet out with a favorable hand coming up when the floorman came over to the table. The dealer immediately shuffled up the cards. The logical move was to reduce the bet to $50, since the opening round would be a neutral one, neither plus nor minus. However, to do this might have been the final straw, and the floorman might have taken the opportunity right then and there to bar me.

Instead I let the bet ride and started a conversation with the floorman.

"Can I get a drink?" I asked.

"Sure." He snapped his fingers for a cocktail waitress.

"I've been running some good luck tonight," I told him.

"I see that." I had a huge stack of chips in front of me.

"Were you here yesterday?" I asked.

"Yes."

"Did you see what happened to me?"

"No."

"It was at lunchtime. I sat down just before eating, and by the time I got to the coffee shop I blew three big ones. Three thousand. I couldn't even eat."

I made up this story with impunity, because floormen work on shifts just as dealers do, and there was no way a floorman would be on at noon and at ten o'clock in the evening, when this conversation was taking place.

"I can't get over losing that much. I'm going to have to

win ten more times just like this just to break even." By this time the cards were given to me to cut. I cut them, the dealer restacked them and dealt me my cards face down. His upcard was an ace.

"Insurance?" the dealer asked.

"Should I take insurance?" I asked the floorman.

"First take a look at your cards."

"Okay." I had gotten a blackjack, a lucky break for me with a maximum bet riding.

"Should I insure it?" I asked.

"You should always insure a blackjack," the floorman said to me. "You can't lose that bet."

Of course this was bad advice (see *Insurance*), giving the house an 8.1 percent edge.

"I have a hunch he doesn't have his blackjack," I said.

"It's up to you, sir."

The dealer waited patiently.

"No," I said, "I don't want insurance."

I waited. The dealer peeked and then prepared to deal, not having seen my cards. I turned over my blackjack and got paid $300 instead of the $200 I would have received if I'd taken the floorman's advice.

The floorman shook his head and walked away from the table. He didn't bother me again that evening. After all, how could I be a counter? I left my big bet riding and didn't alter it. I asked for a drink. I asked his advice and didn't take what he considered correct advice. And I told him I had a hunch. This isn't the way card counters operate. Many card counters are stubborn individuals who don't roll with the punches. Such a counter would have reduced his bet, considered the floorman as an enemy, and immediately not have taken insurance without consulting the floorman. And in that situation he might have been summarily barred from the casino as a card counter.

• Make the wrong plays at times if the floorman or pit boss is watching your play. I do this often, especially when I have a minimum bet out and the deck is unfavorable. Some of my plays are so dumb and crazy that they'd confound me if I was watching a stranger make the same moves.

A floorman had been watching me closely for about fifteen

minutes when the deck got very unfavorable. I split 6s against the dealer's 10 and managed to break even; then on the next hand I stood on a soft 16 against the dealer's 5, mumbling that I figured he'd break first. After these two plays the floorman left me alone.

Other times I've split 5s instead of doubling down, stood on soft 17s (a real amateur move), and doubled down on a hard 9 against dealer's 10. In short, I've done ridiculous things to impress a floorman with my stupidity, just to be left alone. After I make these moves, floormen think I'm just an idiot having a good run of luck.

• Ask a lot of questions. I'm always asking questions at a table. I ask the dealer if I should split certain cards, such as 2s against a dealer's 6, or 8s against a dealer's ace. If he gives me the right answer, I follow his advice. If he gives me the wrong answer, I tell him he's probably right but I have a hunch. If he's silent or noncommittal, I act flustered, then make the right decision anyway, muttering about my ignorance.

If a floorman is around, I direct questions at him till he runs away to the tranquillity of another table. I've asked floormen to suggest books for me to read so I can learn how to play blackjack. They invariably give me the name of the most worthless one written by a fellow casino executive, which I sometimes ask them to write down, so I won't forget the title.

If you ask enough questions, no dealer or floorman will consider you more than a nuisance.

• If the game is big enough and there's going to be casino scrutiny from the start, the following steps have to be taken to protect your interests. This is what I do when a game is big and there's going to be immediate heat from the casino.

a. I come to the table with a glass full of liquid. It can be a weak drink of water. I'm the only one who knows what's in there, and I don't disclose the contents, except to intimate that it's a strong drink.

b. Instead of taking the money out of my wallet in an orderly fashion, I sometimes shake out the cash as if I'm slightly drunk.

c. After I get my chips, I drain my drink and ask for a

strong drink, such as gin and tonic, which I'll nurse during the remainder of the session.

The casino loves a drinker, and they don't figure that a card counter will be drinking.

d. My betting pattern is not rigid. In a big game I'll be at a casino that has favorable rules, and I might make my biggest wager on the first round of play, when I have a slight edge over the house. Thereafter, my bets will appear haphazard. If I win a previous hand, I double up the bet if the deck is neutral or slightly favorable.

e. I ask the dealer and floorman for advice, and sometimes I show my cards to a fellow player and ask his advice as well.

f. I joke around and keep up a constant patter. Casino personnel have an image of a card counter: a serious type who's always looking around at the cards to keep the count going. They don't believe that card counters would engage in idle chatter.

However, I am so attuned to the game that I can joke with the dealer, talk to the other players, and still keep an accurate count, including aces and, perhaps if I'm really sharp, a count of the neutral cards as well.

g. With a minimum bet and the deck unfavorable, I make crazy, strange bets only a fool would make.

h. I tip the dealer generously, keeping him happy.

Writing about this brings up many fond memories of the times floormen would be shaking their heads and smiling at my stupidity, wondering how an idiot like myself managed to be a winner. And they welcomed me back the next time with open arms, knowing that sooner or later a fool and his money are parted, as the old saying goes.

Keeping the Edge

The following was told to me by a man who makes his living entirely by playing blackjack. He's someone you'd not look at twice in a casino, and he likes it that way. Unobtrusive, quiet, reserved, or loud, arrogant, annoying: It all depends on what persona is necessary for the evening's work. What he's out to do is beat the casino in any way he can without actually cheating. Here's his story.

"I first learned the game by reading Thorp's book years and years ago, but circumstances kept me in a straight job in the East. When people ask me where I'm from, I always say the East, because practically everything in America is east of Las Vegas. I don't ask questions and I don't like being asked questions about my personal life.

"It took a number of years before I could hit Vegas. I had come on a couple of vacations, playing according to *Beat the Dealer*. Although Thorp suggested that all you had to do was sit down, count the cards, and the chips would be rolling into your pockets, it didn't happen that way. For one thing, his ten-count was complicated, and if you didn't get the cards, you lost. And the few weekends I spent in Vegas, surreptitiously slipping away from my family, well, I lost.

"It was discouraging, but the computers were saying you could beat blackjack. So I persevered. I kept working and practicing, then, as other books came out, I could see that a count could be simplified. But I had nowhere to play. Atlantic City was years from opening. I kept working and then a whole bunch of circumstances developed. I lost my job to my boss's son-in-law, my wife was cheating on me, and suddenly I was without work and without a wife. I gave her a divorce, and everything we owned. After all, I had two kids. I took part-time work to support myself and to send off the support checks, but found myself going from a three-bedroom house in the suburbs to a room in a ratty rooming house. Not for me.

"There was always Vegas beckoning with its blackjack tables. One day I just packed up a suitcase, which by that time contained all my belongings, and headed for the Greyhound station, and a couple of days later I stepped out into the bright sunlight of Main Street. I had a few hundred dollars in my pocket. Not much to start a gambling career with. But I worked two jobs a day, took a small room in a local motel where I shared the bath, and saved up. And practiced.

"In my spare time I hit the smaller casinos and played $1 and $2 blackjack. I started winning. First meal money, then rent money. I was at the $5 tables before I knew it. I made some mistakes. Biggest mistake was not knowing when to quit. I had to learn to quit when ahead. Divide up my money on the table and when I reached a point where the chips told me, 'You're ahead, but soon going into the hole,' I got up and cashed in. A few times I was ahead over $100 in the early days, and ended up taking more cash out of my pocket and losing that. The two worst things a blackjack player can have is ignorance and no self-control. Well, if you're ignorant, you shouldn't be playing the game. You should know the basic strategy cold. And by basic strategy I mean every play that comes up. Sometimes when I'm at a party and people start talking about gambling, usually the subject of blackjack comes up. I hear all kinds of stories of big wins or, more usually, bad luck at the tables. A few people will commiserate with each other on how unlucky they are at twenty-one, how they really know the game, but still can't win.

"And then there are others who say you can't beat blackjack, and their opinion is determined by the fact that *they* can't beat the game. Well, that's understandable, because 95 percent of the players are losers. And they're losers because they don't really know the game. When I tell this to some complainer, he informs me that he knows the game, that it's a simple game. So I might ask a few questions. I never ask personal questions, as I've mentioned, but I ask blackjack questions, like, 'If you're holding an ace-6 and the dealer has a 7 showing, what do you do?'

"Now, to an expert that's one of the elementary plays in the game. In Vegas you're either hitting the soft 17 or doubling down. There's nothing else to do with those cards. And you never, ever stand on that hand. You can't bust it, and you can improve it in a few ways or end up where you started, this time with a hard 17. Or sometimes if you draw poorly, you'll get a bind and bust, but that's a rare occurrence. Anyway, if I ask what they do with the soft 17, these fools will give me a blank look and then go into a long thought process. They need time to figure it out. They can't even make the most elementary play and they tell me they know the game and are unlucky.

"I don't even bother asking them anything else. In fact, I've stopped asking questions. Maybe I'm getting cynical. No wonder the casinos welcome these players with red carpets and all the drinks they can handle when they rush in with money in their grubby fingers. But the point I want to make is, learn the game right. You must know the basic strategy. And then you should learn how to count cards. And with those two things under your belt, the tables are reversed; now it's the casino worrying about its bankroll, not you.

"If you know how to count and you know correct play, you have the edge. And you make that edge bigger if you change your bets according to who has the advantage. If the casino has the advantage on the next hand, you lower your bet. If the edge is in your corner, you raise the bet. Simple as that. I wish it was all that simple. I can beat the house, been doing it for a number of years. What wasn't simple is fooling the casino into thinking you're just another fool playing the game, and if you win, it's because of stupid luck, nothing else. Now, that takes work.

"One of the best ways not to draw heat from the casino is to play at a game with big bettors, really high rollers. That's who they'll be paying attention to. Meanwhile you gather in the chips bit by bit. I like a table with a couple of other players who are betting the black $100 chips while I'm betting the green $25 chips. The minute a black chip shows, the dealer has to yell back to the floorman, 'blacks in play.' That's a rule in most casinos. They're not paying any attention to my bets.

"Sometimes I pass up situations in a casino where I can play head-to-head with a dealer. If I play at that table, he's got all his attention focused on me. So does the floorman. I bide my time. It's not winning that's my first goal; it's being able to stay in action without being barred.

"And speaking of dealers, while they're playing with the cards, I watch them closely. That's called 'reading the dealers.' They give away a lot; at least some dealers do. What they give away are tells. A tell is an unconscious signal on their part, showing the value of their hole card. Believe me, they have tells. Some dealers like to straighten out the upcard perfectly over the hole card when the hole card is a ten. Now, tells can only be given when the dealer peeks at his hole card in those casinos that still permit this. He or she peeks when there's a 10 or ace as the upcard, and they must make sure they don't have a blackjack. With the ten showing, they peek immediately. With the ace, they first ask if you want insurance. I take insurance only when it's in my favor. That's based on mathematical calculations that I won't go into now. The important thing is, the dealer's peek and his subsequent actions. If it's a 10 upcard, they're looking for an ace. Now, a trey or four resembles an ace, especially if you're bending up just a corner of a card. All you'll see with those two cards, like an ace, is a lot of white space.

"If the dealer has to peek a couple of times, I figure that the hole card is a stiff, probably a three or four, and play accordingly. Then I see what the hole card actually is. If my figuring is correct, I now have a tell on the dealer. Sometimes dealers sandbag you. I had one look at his hole card three or four times, and end up with a king of spades. I knew he had double-crossed me, because I stood with a hard 15, but I didn't say anything. I wanted to ask him if he wanted to make sure that the king had one or two eyes when they were staring at each other's mugs.

"Can't do that, of course. I simply left the table. Who needs that kind of aggravation? I'm playing for serious money; it's my business. If a dealer squares the two cards perfectly after looking at the hole card, and it constantly turns out to be a 10 underneath, that's a tell. Some dealers do it by reflex. They're satisfied with their total. But often I find the opposite. A dealer will leave the hole card slightly removed from the upcard when it's a 10, so he can quickly turn it over and collect all the losing bets in front of him. Either way, I try and be alert to the situation.

"Or a miserable wretch of a dealer may have a secret smile he thinks I don't catch, when he's going to beat the table. I'm observing everything. Sometimes it's a movement forward with the body when giving out cards after he's peeked. When he does this, I figure he's got a stiff in the hole and he wants players to bust. But whatever the body movement, head movement, smile or sullen face, squaring of cards or sloppy cards on the table, I make no assumptions until they're confirmed. But when I get a tell, it's great. I now have an even bigger edge on the dealer and on the money he's holding in the tray.

"Then there's 'first-basing.' This is a term for being able to peek at the dealer's hole card while he's looking. It can only be done easily from the first baseman's seat. If you sit far enough over and the dealer is right-handed, then he's going to lift the card in the hole in your direction. He's holding the undealt pack of cards in his other, left hand while he does this, and he should protect the hole card with that left hand. But dealers get sloppy, or are inexperienced, or haven't been trained correctly, and they don't protect it. So the first baseman sees it. The first time this happened to me, I was playing with a drunken friend, who was sitting in the first baseman's seat. We were just killing time at a $5 table waiting for the crowds to thin out before we went in for dinner. My friend had had a few, and he was a little bent out of shape, enough to teeter in that first baseman's seat. But in that position he was seeing the dealer's hole card, and he would bend over and tell me the card.

"Suddenly I forgot about dinner. I started betting quarter chips, and we got away with a win close to two thousand dollars before we were finished. The floorman came over when we switched gears, betting up, but all he saw was a drunk and another guy ordering stiff drinks. That was me. I didn't mind getting a buzz. I could still count and anyway that dealer's hole card was always available to me.

"After that, I cased casinos looking for sloppy dealers and occasionally found a good situation. I would stay only for about a half hour and move on. And I would be careful not to make myself obvious. It rarely happens that you can first-base, but if the opportunity affords itself, I do it. Some casino bosses consider this cheating, but I have no pity for the casino. They'll allow drunks to play and lose everything they have. To me, that's cheating also. Make the game fair for all concerned. Since they don't, I don't.

"The way most casino bosses figure twenty-one is this: Anything that doesn't allow them to put a vacuum cleaner in your wallet and draw up all the loose bills is cheating on your part. Card counting, tells, playing correctly, altering bets when you have the edge on the hand—to these greedy guys, it's all cheating. Well, they have tables in their casinos to play the game, and I play the game. And you have to be a natural-born fool not to play the best you can when you're playing for real money. Now, who can argue with that?

"Before, I mentioned that the two important things to have are knowledge of the game and self-control. You can learn both, I had to. Knowledge is a matter of studying books and charts and practicing. Be patient. You can make a lot of money with this knowledge, so take your time and learn it all. Don't hurry. As for self-control, that can be learned only in a casino setting under actual play. I mentioned how I'd divide up my money at the table, so I knew when to quit when ahead. Fine. But when losing, and you're bound to have losing sessions—days and sometimes a whole week of losing—then you have to see what you're made of. You can't panic. You have the edge in the long run. And you can't go crazy. Don't increase your bets hoping for luck. Forget about luck. Your luck will come, good and bad, and you can't force it. When you are winning, leave a winner and increase your bets. What I mean is this: If I'm betting $50 as my basic bet, I go up to $75 as my basic bet, then $100, then $125, as long as the cards keep going my way. They turn and I'm gone. But if I'm losing and am betting $50, I stick with it and never go up as a basic bet. If the cards are running badly, roll with the punches. Raising your bets to get even is only going to mean you'll lose more money. And when you've lost everything on the table, don't reach in for more. Leave.

"You never want to get in a position of taking a beating so bad you can't recover. Take small beatings and try to win big. That's my philosophy.

"I've made a nice living out of the game for quite a while now. I have my own condo, good wheels, money in the bank, solid investments. All from twenty-one. I've done it by keeping that edge over the house. Always one step ahead of them, never falling into their traps, never getting greedy, never losing control. And always studying, always refining, especially with the 8-deck games now in operation.

"Remember, above all, that if you want to play like a pro, think and act like a pro. A pro has the edge. Sometimes that edge looks like the thin end of a razor blade, but it's still an edge. Never give it up."

Casino Countermeasures

The casino discourages winners, and especially winners who are card counters, and they'll take whatever measure is necessary, short of cheating, to harass and beat them. I leave out cheating because, despite what several writers have written of casino cheating, it's been my experience that casinos won't resort to this measure because they have too much to lose. For one thing, a license worth millions of dollars can be forfeited if cheating is discovered by Gaming Commission investigators.

When a player has an endless run of bad luck, it may appear that he's being cheated, but that's not really the case. I used to spend hours practicing the game, dealing out hands to myself, acting as both the player and the dealer. There have been times when I lost so many hands that if I didn't know I was dealing to myself, I could swear I was being cheated.

Sometimes, as dealer, I would hit four or five hands in a row, and make a stiff hand into a solid twenty-one. It was terrible for the player in that imaginary game, but the cards just ran badly and there was nothing that could be done.

If you play long enough, you'll run into incredible strings of bad luck. You'll have a very favorable count and watch helplessly as the dealer draws the last 5 in the deck to form a 21 out of a worthless 16 hand. It happens all the time, and a player must expect bad luck as well as good luck. The important thing to remember is this: *Luck evens itself out, but skill remains a constant.* That's a principle an astute player should live by.

The following are countermeasures and what steps the player should take if they occur:

1. *Shuffling up*

This is the first and easiest of the casino countermeasures. The house, to bother, harass, or invalidate the card counter's methods, will order the dealer to shuffle up every time the player raises his bet. When this happens, the player should make no comment, but simply leave the table.

Or the dealer may shuffle up after depleting only a small part of the deck, so the player never gets a chance for a favorable run of cards. Again, no comment is called for. The player should simply get up and go to another table or another casino.

Sometimes the harassment depends on the particular shift at a casino. One shift may be easy on card counters while another is murder. If you face trouble at the graveyard shift, from midnight to 8 A.M., it may be that the day shift will not care at all about your betting methods.

If one shift gives you heat, try another shift. If that's the casino policy, then play a different casino. But remember, at a crowded table with a single-deck game, the usual policy is for no more than two rounds of cards to be dealt out. That's pretty standard, not a casino countermeasure.

Sometimes you can turn the countermeasure around and make it work for you. I did this once at the Dunes on the Las Vegas Strip.

I rarely played there early in the morning, but one day at 6 A.M. I found myself in the casino after saying goodbye to a couple of friends who were staying at the hotel. I went over to an empty $25 table and sat down. The dealer shuffled up the cards, I cut them, and the game began.

From the moment I sat down, a floorman came over and watched my game. He had the usual floorman smirk, waiting for a loser to get tapped out. I made a $50 bet, won my first hand, and the deck became slightly favorable, so I raised my bet to $75. As I did this, the floorman walked by the dealer's side, tapped his arm, and the cards were reshuffled.

I brought my bet down to $50 and again the cards were cut and dealt out, with the floorman watching from about six feet away. I lost this hand; the deck became unfavorable, and I lowered my bet to $25. Again the floorman came by and tapped the dealer's arm, and the cards were once more shuffled up.

On my next $50 bet, it was a standoff with a neutral deck,

so I left the $50 bet stand. This time the floorman did nothing. On the next hand I lowered my bet to $25, and back came the floorman, with the cards shuffled up again.

I realized that every time I altered my bet, whether up or down, the cards were going to be shuffled up. I didn't know why this was being done. I had never seen this particular floorman before. Perhaps he was playing a little game with me to pass the time of day, or perhaps he was a sadist at heart. The dealer realized my predicament, looked me in the eyes, and shrugged. I put out a bet for the dealer to show him that it was nothing personal between us.

With the new round starting, I made another $50 bet. I won it, and the deck became favorable. I kept the $50 bet going. It stayed favorable for four hands, with the $50 bet remaining, then became unfavorable. I raised my bet to $100. The deck was now terrible for me, but the dealer obligingly shuffled up.

My new bet was now $100. I kept this bet constant so long as the deck was neutral or favorable. When it was unfavorable, I raised it and had the cards shuffled up. So now I had a perfect situation, playing only with a favorable or neutral deck. I started to win some heavy money as a result.

Meanwhile the floorman conferred with another floorman, both watching my play. What could they do? I was making constant bets, and never was allowed to raise my bet without the deck being shuffled. How could I be winning? So these wise men let me play on and on. After about an hour I left with my pockets bulging with Dunes casino chips. The last time I saw that floorman, he was no longer smirking.

2. *Changing dealers*

Instead of a friendly dealer, the casino brings in a hostile one. Sometimes, for whatever reason, a male dealer will be replaced by a female dealer, generally a woman in her forties or so. There are some women dealers who look as though they hate the world, and men in particular. They never smile and never even look at a player's face. They deal fast and pay out and collect even faster and never say a word or acknowledge a question. I've met up with bad male dealers, but only a few were as bad as the witches these casinos dig up.

When facing this kind of hostility, this repressed anger, all one can do is play out a couple of hands and leave. I simply get up, take my chips, and walk away. I wouldn't tip them to save my life.

Instead of a hostile dealer, a dealer of another kind almost as bad is sometimes brought over. This character takes a deck of cards, shuffles through with the speed of light, and when the cards are dealt, they're flung at the player with blinding speed. Sometimes the cards fly into the player's hands or chest. When they hit the knuckles, they can really hurt.

One dealer who was brought in to handle me dealt so fast the cards were hitting my hands or falling on the floor. I made no effort to pick them up, but just sat there until a floorman came over and put the cards back on the table.

"Listen," I told the floorman, "tell your dealer to take it easy. Those cards are missing my eyes by inches."

The floorman didn't even answer me and didn't tell the dealer to slow up the game or to deal the cards in an easier manner. Instead he stood to one side and watched my discomfort. On the next play, one hit my hand and really bruised it. I picked up the card, put it with my other card, and stared at the hand.

I didn't do anything for five minutes while the dealer and floorman stewed. The floorman then told me I had better play the hand and not slow the game down, or he'd throw me out of the casino.

I stared him in the eye to let him know that he'd better not try it personally. However, I realized he wouldn't bother. In casinos there are all sorts of security guards around, ready to deal with players. So instead I asked the floorman for his name.

"Why do you want it?" he asked.

"I'm a stockholder in the corporation that owns this casino, and your kind of rudeness must be driving away customers. For one thing, I'll never play here again if you're around. So let me have your full name."

"What's yours?"

I told him my name, but he still wouldn't answer my question.

"Well, if you don't want to give me your name, at least tell me where the casino manager's office is."

"He's not in."

"Okay, I'll find the president's or general manager's office and tell him the situation. This is table 14, right?" Then I asked the dealer for his name.

He refused to answer.

"Okay, I'll find it out, don't worry." Meanwhile I laid down my hand, which was a blackjack, got paid off, and walked away from the table.

I didn't go to the general manager's office. I knew I'd never play in that casino again, but I wanted to make my point and let them worry a little. My hand still hurt, and I was very angry. Later, when I cooled down, I thought I shouldn't have even bothered with the questions; I should just have left those bastards alone.

3. *Scrutiny by several casino personnel*

This is the prelude to the final measure—barring a player. A whole group of executives come around to watch your game, and don't do anything but stare at you. You know the end is near, and it's best at that moment to get up and simply walk away from the table.

Sometimes this is accompanied by a change of deck every few minutes, a thorough count of new and old cards, and other measures that slow the game to a crawl.

4. *Barring the player*

This is the final step. Since I've been barred, I can tell you what happens. After you finish playing and cash in, a couple of men come over to you and ask your name. You don't have to give them your name or show any ID, but they'll ask just to harass you. Then they'll tell you that you're not to play in the casino ever again. Sometimes they accompany this remark with a threat—that if you ever are found at a blackjack table there again, you'll be arrested for trespassing.

Or you can be barred while sitting at the table. The casino executive comes over with a security guard and asks you to please get up and accompany them. You ask "Where?" They say, "Just get up and come with us." Of course, you're in their casino among their men. When that happens, the best thing to do is head for the exit, not the back of the casino. They'll generally let you leave. If they want to detain you, explain that you'll sue them for every penny they're worth, and create a commotion. Don't swing or use your arms or do anything physical, but ask in an extremely loud voice what this is all about.

Barring usually follows the first route, unless the casino is really out to scare you. But remember, counting cards is not cheating and is not illegal. Unfortunately, the casinos have the right to bar a player, because the courts have held that they're private clubs. But that doesn't mean they have the right to take your name and address or to physically detain you.

A final word: If you play according to our methods, you're going to be a winner, and you're going to come under the scrutiny of the casino. But disguise your play as we have suggested and you won't run into any trouble at all. Your goal should be to win money without being conspicuous about it, to win as though you're just plain lucky. In that case, you won't draw any heat at all.

Blackjack Etiquette and Miscellany

• When you first get to a table, put out the cash you want converted to chips. Be patient, for the dealer will change your money only after a round of cards is played.

• After you make a bet, keep your hands off the chips in the betting box. The casino is worried about cheats who do past posting, that is, alter their bets depending on the cards they receive.

• After you've been dealt your cards, keep them on the table in full view of the dealer. Never, ever hold them so that they are below the surface of the table. If you lower your cards this way, you'll be suspected of cheating.

• If you want a hit, scrape the cards toward you if they've been dealt face down. If dealt face up, point your index finger at the cards for a hit.

• If you want to stand pat, slide the cards under the chips

in your betting box if the cards were dealt face down, but don't touch or lift your chips when doing this. If dealt face up, wave a hand, palm down, over the cards.

• If you want to double down, turn the cards over and place a bet equal to your original bet next to the previously bet stack of chips. You'll receive one card face down as your double-down card.

• If you want to split a pair, turn the cards over and place a bet equal to the amount of the original bet on the split card. You can now play out each card as a separate hand.

• If you want to make an insurance bet, place half your original bet above your cards, in the area marked "Insurance pays 2–1."

• If you hit and bust your hand, turn it over at once so that the dealer can remove your cards and chips.

• If you are dealt a blackjack, turn it over at once so you can be paid and the cards removed.

• At the showdown, after the dealer has played out his hand, let him turn over your cards for you. Don't touch them, let him do that.

• Don't complain about your bad cards. If you don't like what's happening at the table, leave but don't annoy the other players or the dealer.

• Tip the dealer by either placing the bet for him in the insurance box or in your own betting box.

• While playing twenty-one, you're entitled to free drinks or cigarettes or cigars. If you want any of these things, ask the dealer to send over a cocktail waitress. He'll be happy to oblige.

Glossary of Blackjack Terms

The following are terms commonly used in casino blackjack. Knowing them will help you better understand the game.

Anchor Man. See *Third Baseman*

Bar, Barring a Player. The casino's refusal to let a player, usually a card counter, participate in a blackjack game at that casino.

Blackjack. 1. The name of the game, also known as

twenty-one. 2. A winning hand, consisting of an ace and a 10-value card, dealt as the original two cards of a hand.

Break the Deck. See *Shuffle Up*

Burn a Card. The dealer's act of taking away the top card from the deck and placing it unseen face up at the bottom of the deck or in a separate plastic case.

Bust, to Bust. To hit a hand so that the total goes over twenty-one, making it a losing hand.

Bust Card. The designation of a 2, 3, 4, 5, or 6 as the dealer's upcard.

Bust Hand. A hand totaling from 12 to 16 points, which, if hit, is in danger of busting.

Card Counter. A player who keeps track of cards played out from the deck to determine if the deck is favorable or unfavorable.

Counting Cards. To keep track of several groups of cards in the deck, such as the 3–6s and 10-value cards, to determine the favorability of the remainder of the deck.

Dealer. A casino employee who runs the blackjack game by dealing out the cards, collecting, and paying off the players' bets.

Deck. The 52-card pack of cards the game is played with.

Double Down. A player's option to double his original bet by turning over his first two cards and placing an amount equal to the original bet on the layout.

Draw a Card. See *Hit*

Favorable Deck. The remainder of the deck which is so composed as to be in the player's favor.

First Baseman. The player in the first seat, the one who acts first upon his hand.

Hand. The cards originally dealt to the player or the dealer. Also, the final total of the cards held by the player or the dealer.

Hard Total. Any total not including an ace or where the ace is counted as 1 in a hand. Example: 10, 6, ace or 10, 7 are hard 17s.

Hit. To draw a card to the original hand.

Hit Me. A term used by players to indicate that they want to draw another card. In most casinos this is done by scraping the cards toward the player.

Hole Card. The dealer's unseen card forming half of his original hand.

Insurance, Insurance Bet. An optional wager by a

player that the dealer has a blackjack when his upcard is an ace.

Insure a Blackjack. An insurance bet by a player when he himself holds a blackjack.

Mucker, Hand Mucker. A cheat who adds favorable cards to a multiple-deck game.

Multiple Deck. A game in which more than one deck of cards is used.

Natural. The combination of an ace and a 10-value dealt on the first two cards, forming a blackjack.

Paint. A picture or face card: a jack, queen, or king.

Reshuffle. See *Shuffle Up*

Round, Round of Play. A complete series in which all the players and the dealer act upon their hands.

Shoe. A box containing multiple decks of cards, which can be used to easily deal out the cards one at a time.

Shuffle Up. To mix up the cards prior to dealing them out. Also known as reshuffling the cards.

Single-Deck Game. A blackjack game in which only a single deck of cards is used.

Snapper. A slang term for a blackjack.

Soft Hand, Soft Total. A hand in which the total value is determined by using the ace as an 11. Example: ace, 7 = soft 18.

Splitting Pairs. The player's option to separate cards of equal rank, such as pairs, and play each hand as a separate hand; 10-value cards are considered pairs for splitting purposes.

Stand Pat. Refusing to hit or act upon a hand.

Stiff, Stiff Hand. A hand containing 12 or more points as a hard total, in danger of busting if hit.

Ten-Value Card. The 10, jack, queen, and king, all valued at 10 points.

Third Baseman. The player sitting in the last seat at the blackjack table; the one acting upon his cards last.

Twenty-One. Another name for the game of blackjack.

Unfavorable, Unfavorable Deck. The composition of the remainder of the deck not favorable to the player.

Upcard. One of the dealer's original two cards, which is dealt face up.

6

Craps— The Fastest Game

Of all the games the casino offers, craps is by far the fastest and most exciting, and it's a game in which a great deal of money can be won or lost in the shortest possible time. It's traditionally the game of the high rollers, the premium players who want a great deal of money action. And they get it in craps. This is not to say that the game only attracts big bettors, for it's a game beloved by many small gamblers, who are also intrigued by its speed and excitement.

It is the most vocal of games. At the other table games— blackjack, baccarat, and roulette—the atmosphere is more sedate. The players sweat out their wins and losses quietly, with only an occasional murmur or comment after a big win or a discouraging loss. But at craps the table is alive with sounds, as players scream for the seven, as they cry for numbers, when a hot roll is in progress. And when that hot roll comes, where the whole table is making money, the entire casino knows about it. The enthusiasm is contagious.

Craps is a great game to let loose in, to let out one's inhibitions. Since the yelling and screaming have no effect on the outcome, it's permissible and encouraged by the house. In a game like blackjack, where a great deal of skill is required and where the players must constantly make decisions affecting the play of their cards, such a noise level would hamper and interfere with the concentration required, but at the craps table the dice roll merrily along, not bothered in the least by the clatter.

Only blackjack offers better odds to the player, but in order to take advantage of favorable situations in twenty-one, a blackjack player must know the basic strategy thoroughly and must be able to count cards. Having this information, he will play even with the house or have a small advantage with the most favorable rules. The craps player, without having to count anything and without having to make continually new decisions, will give the house no more than 0.8 percent or 0.6 percent with best play.

Craps also offers a much broader spectrum of bets than does blackjack. Players can bet with or against the dice, while in twenty-one, players can only play against the dealer. At craps gamblers can also make continuous bets with each roll of the dice, not having to wait for an ultimate decision by the dealer, as they must in blackjack. Only roulette offers such a wide variety of bets, but in American roulette, the house has an unyielding advantage of at least 5.26 percent on every bet, a much greater edge than it enjoys in craps.

What intrigues most players, however, is the speed of craps, and the chance to win a great deal of money in a short period of play. Since bets may be made on every roll, and these bets can be won or lost with each throw of the dice, the opportunity to win a small fortune in a short period of time is always there. All players dream of that hot roll, and when it comes, when points and numbers come forth in profusion, and the dice are held by one player anywhere from thirty minutes to an hour and sometimes longer, the chance to make a killing becomes a reality.

In no other game can money be won so fast with small bets, since a right bettor is nearly always paid off at better than even money. And unlike the other table games, where once a bet is made it is rigidly frozen, in craps bets can be raised and altered after every roll, even without a final decision being made by the dice. Players on a lucky winning streak can compound their wins as the roll or shoot is progressing, something they cannot do in the other games.

The game can be beaten, for although the house holds a small advantage over the player on most bets, there are odds bets in which the casino has no edge whatsoever, and like all gambling situations, craps runs in streaks, and a smart player making only correct bets, giving the house a small edge and increasing his bets as a favorable roll moves along, can come away from the table with a tremendous profit over the short run.

I've seen players come to the table with $100 and leave with $10,000. It was as though they were coining their own money. More fortunes have been made in craps than in any other game, and alas, more lost as well. But players who know what they are doing, who follow the procedures outlined in this chapter, can win at this game with correct play, proper money management, and self-control.

It's the most thrilling of all the casino games, and it's even a great spectator game, but the ultimate thrills are reserved for those who lay their money on the line and play to win.

With all the excitement and speed going for it, in addition to the vistas it holds for really huge wins, it's no wonder that craps has many adherents, who will play no other casino game. These people can't wait for the moment when they arrive at the table, when the dice are rolling and a hot roll is just around the corner.

Casino Personnel Staffing a Craps Table

The casino employs a basic staff of five people to service any craps table properly. There is a crew of four dealers, three of whom are always at the table, while a fourth, in rotation, is on a break. With this crew is a casino executive known as the boxman. The boxman is not part of the crew and may not work with a particular set of dealers all the time, while the crew is a functional unit, trained and kept together to work fluidly.

The Boxman

The boxman is a casino executive who is in charge of the craps table. He supervises play, and his word is final in any dispute arising between a player and a dealer.

Unlike the other personnel at the table, who wear house uniforms, the boxman generally wears either a suit or sports jacket. Also, unlike the dealers, he remains seated during the course of play.

Near him, under his constant supervision, are most of the casino chips for the game. His principal duty is to protect the casino's bankroll at the table, and he keeps both arms close to the stacks of chips under his supervision. The boxman's other duties are as follows:

• He collects all cash coming to the table, pushing the money through an opening in the table to a drop box below, which holds all the money and markers (IOUs) collected during a particular shift.

• He makes certain that players who have changed cash for casino chips get the correct amount of chips for their money.

• He runs the table, watching the moves of the dealers and also watching the payoffs made to the players on one side of the table. The stickman watches the side the boxman cannot cover.

• He settles any dispute between a player and a dealer as to an incorrect or alleged wrong payoff or bet. His decision is the final word on these matters in practically all cases.

• If a die or both dice have fallen or been thrown off the table, it's his duty to examine the die or dice for imperfections, tampering, or changes before putting them back into play.

Sometimes at a crowded and busy table two boxmen are seated by the casino, each in charge of one side of the table. The casino is paranoid about its bankroll and will put as many people at or near the table to protect its money.

The Stickman

Standing opposite the boxman is the stickman, who is part of the dealer's crew. He is called a stickman because of a flexible stick he holds in his hand, which is used to push the dice around the table. (The dealers never touch the dice with their hands.)

The stickman, being part of the crew, is on break one quarter of the time, and on the stick one quarter of his shift. Most crews move their dealers around the table, so that each in turn is on base, that is, a standing dealer at one of the two end sections of the table, or on the stick or on break.

The following are the duties of the stickman:

• He is in charge of the dice, pushing them to a new shooter at the commencement of his or her roll. After the shooter has picked two from a choice of four to eight dice, the stickman returns the unselected dice to a box, which he keeps in front of him at all times.

• The stickman calls the game, announcing each roll of the dice and whether it is a winner or loser. For example, on the come-out, if the shooter has rolled a 7, the call might be "7, a winner on the pass line."

If a 7 has been thrown after a point was established, the stickman might say "7, loser on the pass line, line away," or words to that effect. There are no standard calls, this being mostly an individual matter, and each stickman has his own method of calling a game.

• After each roll of the dice the stickman returns the dice to the shooter, just waiting for all payoffs to be completed. At times, while waiting for the payoffs to be made, the stickman will fiddle with the dice, turning them over to make certain that each die is correctly numbered. This often happens during a hot roll, when the casino wants to make certain that the dice in play are legitimate and have not been tampered with.

• The stickman is in charge of the center of the layout and places all bets made on these center proposition situations. He also informs the standing dealers when to make payoffs from winning center layout bets. If a center bet is lost, he removes the chips and hands them to the boxman.

• He keeps up a continuous patter during the game, even when the dice haven't been rolled. For instance, while the shooter is shaking the dice, the stickman may say, "Hot roll coming up, bet those hardways, bet the craps eleven, get those field bets down." His patter is generally used to entice the players to make disadvantageous bets and also to make legitimate bets, such as on the come, in order to keep the game exciting, and to make certain that there is plenty of betting action at the table.

Some common terms the stickmen use are "yo-leven," when an 11 is rolled, "9, center field," when a 9 is thrown, for the 9 is at the center of the field bet. If a 2, 3, or 12 is rolled, the usual call is simply "craps," rather than the more exotic terms used for those numbers in private games, such as snake eyes for the 2, and boxcars for the 12.

After a shooter sevens out, the stickman generally calls the point that had been established and then the losing roll as follows: "Seven, line away, five (the point) was."

A good stickman can really talk up a game and make it hum. Some stickmen root for the shooter; others, either through indifference or through house policy, root against the shooter or remain neutral.

The Standing Dealers

The two other dealers, like the stickman, are part of the crew that staffs the table. They remain standing during play and wear the house uniform. Each standing dealer is in charge of one end section of the layout and deals directly with the players in that section of the table. A dealer's duties are as follows.

• When a player first arrives at the table, the dealer will convert the player's cash to casino chips by turning over the cash to the boxman. After the boxman counts the money, the player will be given the correct number of casino chips. If a gambler has credit at the casino, the dealer will give him chips to bet with after his credit is approved.

• During the course of play, if a gambler wants to change his chips for those of lower or higher denominations, known as "changing color," the dealer will do this for him.

• After a point is established on the come-out roll, the dealer will move a plastic disk (also known as a buck) to the corner box number to indicate that this number is the point.

If a new shooter is coming out, or if there is a new come-out roll, he will move the disk to the don't come box, leaving it there. This disk is sometimes black on one side and white on the other. When it is on its black side in the don't come box, this indicates that no point has been established and the roll is a come-out roll. When it is on its white side in a box number, that number is the point.

• The dealer will pay off all winning bets and remove all losing bets made on the layout in his section of the craps table.

• If a come or don't come bet has been made, he will place that bet and all odds bets in the correct box. If these bets should win, he pays them off and takes them down. If these bets lose, he removes them and takes the chips for the casino.

• He will handle all place bets, keeping track of them in correct sequence so that the appropriate players will be properly paid off should their numbers repeat.

In addition to this basic staff, there may be other casino personnel hovering around a craps table. In the smaller clubs and in the Northern Nevada casinos which get little play at the craps table, the player may see none but the crew and the boxman.

However, on the Strip in Las Vegas and in clubs that get heavy action at the craps tables, there will be at least one floorman watching the play. This floorman may merely supervise the game, or he may be involved watching the play of junket members to make certain that they give the casino sufficient play to warrant all the free services that the house offers them (see the section on junkets for a fuller explanation of services and supervision).

If a player has credit at the casino, it is the floorman who will verify it by having the pit bookkeeper call the credit manager or the cashier's cage. In some of the more modern casinos he may quickly verify it by use of a computer placed in the craps pit. The floorman is a casino executive and is usually dressed in a suit or a sports jacket. He ranks above the boxman, but below the pit boss.

The pit boss is in charge of all the craps tables in the pit. The term pit is used to designate an area inside a cluster of gaming tables, and this area is the pit boss's exclusive domain. The pit boss supervises the dealers, boxmen, and floormen under his control.

Most casinos, even some of the larger ones on the Strip in Las Vegas, have only one craps pit. However, other casinos with huge floor space, such as Harrah's and Harold's Club in Reno, may have several craps pits in their casino, each under the supervision of an individual pit boss.

Mechanics of Play

Only one player at the table has control of the dice at any one time, and the numbers he throws with the dice determine the payoffs of all bettors at the table.

The shoot, as a series of rolls is designated in casino parlance, goes around the table in clockwise fashion, with each player in turn having an opportunity to roll the dice. Once a person is the shooter, he has control of the dice as long as he doesn't seven-out, that is, roll a 7 after a point has been established. A player may voluntarily relinquish the dice prior to any come-out roll and doesn't have to stay to the end of his shoot if for some reason he wants to get away from the table.

Players need not become shooters when it is their turn to roll the dice. Some players never care to throw the dice; others are wrong bettors and never want to bet against the roll when they are shooting. For whatever reason, a player simply may refuse to roll by merely shaking his head when the dice are offered to him.

When a new shooter is ready to roll the dice, or come out, the stickman pushes several dice toward him with his stick. The shooter selects two, and the others are returned to the stickman.

Before a player can roll the dice, he must make a line bet, either pass or don't pass, at the table minimum. After this bet is made, the holder of the dice may throw them onto the layout, and he will hold these dice until he sevens-out or relinquishes them voluntarily.

The dice are expected to be thrown the length of the table, hitting the back wall of the table so that they bounce in a random fashion. If the shooter doesn't throw them firmly enough to hit the far wall, he will be admonished by the boxman to throw them harder. The object of the throw is always to get a random bounce out of the dice so that the numbers that come up are not predetermined. If the dice aren't thrown against a wall, it may be that the holder of the dice has some way to control their spin, and this is why the casino is so strict about enforcing the rule that the dice always hit a far wall.

The Come-Out Roll

The come-out roll is the most important roll in the game of craps, since it determines the point that must be repeated in most cases, and as long as that point is alive, right bettors can collect on a multitude of bets, often on every throw of the dice.

A come-out roll occurs whenever the dice have previously been rolled to effect a final decision on the line bets. Thus a come-out roll will occur in the following situations:

• When a previous shooter has sevened out (rolled a 7 before repeating his point)

• When a new shooter is throwing the dice for the first time

• After a shooter has rolled a 7 or 11 on the previous come-out roll, an immediate win for pass-line bettors

• After a shooter has rolled a craps (2, 3, or 12), an immediate loser for pass-line bettors, on the previous come-out roll

• After a shooter has made his previous point by repeating it before rolling a 7

The Craps Layout

The average craps table is the size of a large billiards table, and imprinted on the surface of this table is the craps layout. A layout lists all the bets the casino will book and shows the betting areas where these bets may be made. On some of the bets the correct odds the house will pay are listed as well. All bets made by the players are eventually placed on the layout in full view of the other players and the dealers, who handle the bets.

The layout is divided into three parts—one center section and two identical end sections. Thus players at either end of the table may make the same kind of bets and have these bets placed, paid off, or collected by a dealer close by without slowing down the game.

A craps table can accommodate anywhere from twelve to twenty-four players, though when a table is full the players really have to squeeze together. In front of each player is a rail, divided into the same number of sections as there are players, for bettors to keep their chips when they aren't in play on the layout.

The standard color of the layout is green, on a flat surface, with the lines, words, and boxes imprinted in white. Sometimes yellow is used instead of white, and sometimes the layout surface is of a different color, depending on the casino. In Las Vegas, the Hilton and Aladdin use blue to match their decor.

The casino layout illustrated below is a fairly standard one used in Northern Nevada, the downtown casinos in Las Vegas, and those in Atlantic City. Layouts differ slightly from casino to casino, but in most American casinos the same bets can be made, though at slightly varying odds. The Las Vegas Strip casinos use a layout that offers slightly less favorable odds on the center and field bets than those shown on the illustrated layout.

In foreign casinos there may be major differences, notably the absence of come bets, forcing players to bet on the place numbers at a disadvantage to themselves. Some other bets may be missing altogether, for there is no standard foreign layout.

The English casinos, however, have a layout that is more favorable to the player than the American layout, and their layouts are printed so that the average player can understand the game more easily. Instead of pass line, the term win line is used. Don't win line is written instead of the American don't pass line.

The following is the standard American craps casino layout:

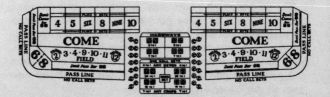

Looking at the craps layout shown above, we can readily see that two identical end sections surround a center area, which is the home of all proposition bets. Every center bet is one that gives the house too much of an advantage over the player to be worthwhile. This center area is under the control of the stickman, one of the dealers at the table.

The two end sections have both favorable and unfavorable bets for players, and each section is serviced by a standing dealer, who places, collects, and pays off bets for the players in his particular domain.

The heart of craps is the line bets—both pass line and don't pass. The pass line takes up a large part of the layout and swings around the table to accommodate all the players, since 90 percent of the gamblers at a table bet on pass line. By making this bet, they are wagering with the dice, hoping that they will pass, or win.

The don't pass area is much smaller, and has an additional statement in its box, barring the 12. This is done to prevent the don't pass, or wrong, bettor, from having an advantage over the casino. When a 12 is rolled on the come-out roll, it is a standoff between the casino and wrong bettor, with neither one winning, thus allowing the casino to retain a 1.4 percent edge over the don't pass bettor.

The come box is large, though it is infrequently used, since not many gamblers are certain of its use. The come bet is identical to a pass-line wager, except that it can only be made after the come-out roll. All of these bets will be discussed in full detail in the appropriate section of this chapter.

The don't come area also bars the 12, giving the house a 1.4 percent on this bet, and it is much smaller than the come betting area, since fewer players are wrong bettors, or bettors against the dice.

The field takes up a huge area, though this bet is not given that much action by astute gamblers who don't want to buck the high odds, since the house takes 5.5 percent as its edge on this wager. It is a convenient bet, since it is a one-roll bet, with the outcome dependent on the next throw of the dice, and gets some play from system and ignorant players who want an immediate decision.

The big 6 and big 8 is given a fairly sizable amount of space, though this is an extremely bad bet, giving the casino 9.09 percent over the player. This bet is made by gamblers who are completely ignorant about casino craps.

The other large dominating area is the box or place number section, at the top of the layout, with the numbers 4, 5, 6, 8, 9, and 10 showing in separate boxes. It is here that all come and don't come bets wind up, each in its particular space, depending on the previous roll of the dice. And it is here that players may bet on the place numbers, wagering that these numbers will repeat before a 7 shows on the dice.

The box and place numbers are handled by the dealer, whereas the line, come, and don't come bets are initially placed by the gamblers themselves. This is a minor distinction, however, and will be discussed in depth in the appropriate section of this chapter.

This leaves the center of the layout, with its wide choice of bets. For now, we'll simply state that all of these bets are unfavorable to the player and should never be made. They'll be fully discussed later on, showing why the house edge is so great that it would be practically impossible to overcome it in the long run.

That is basically the craps layout as seen in an American casino. As we examine and understand each of the bets available, it will become clear how intelligent betting can make a world of difference between winning and losing.

The Dice and Their Combinations

Casino craps is played with two dice, each die a nearly perfect cube having six sides, and each side of each die is imprinted with from 1 to 6 dots, representing the numbers 1 through 6. Thus, with two dice being used in the game, the possible combinations that can be thrown are 6 × 6, or 36. The highest possible number that can be rolled is a 12, while the lowest possible number is a 2.

Casino dice differ from ordinary dice used in games like

backgammon in several ways. First of all, casino dice are bigger, usually three-fourths to an inch square on all sides, and the edges, unlike backgammon and other game dice, are sharp and pointed.

Casino dice are usually red in color and made of a hard transparent plastic. The dice are transparent for a very good reason, since any tampering with the dice by weighting them (loaded dice) is nearly impossible if one can see through the cubes. To safeguard the dice further, each die is imprinted with the casino's logo and name and, in most cases, with a coded number.

All of these serve a direct purpose. Not only do they identify the dice as belonging to a particular casino, but should dice be switched by cheats during a game, the casino employees can verify their authenticity by examining and checking out the code number. It is the duty of the boxman, the seated casino executive who is in charge of a craps table, to look over any die that has fallen or been thrown off the table, checking not only for dents or imperfections, but also for the coded number to make certain that this was the same die that had just been rolled at that particular table.

The following table shows all the numbers that can be thrown with two dice (including the combinations) and the possible ways each number can be rolled.

Number	Combinations	Ways to Roll
2	1–1	1
3	1–2, 2–1	2
4	1–3, 3–1, 2–2	3
5	1–4, 4–1, 2–3, 3–2	4
6	1–5, 5–1, 2–4, 4–2, 3–3	5
7	1–6, 6–1, 2–5, 5–2, 3–4, 4–3	6
8	2–6, 6–2, 3–5, 5–3, 4–4	5
9	3–6, 6–3, 4–5, 5–4	4
10	4–6, 6–4, 5–5	3
11	5–6, 6–5	2
12	6–6	1

In the above chart it's apparent that there's a symmetrical curve with the 7 at the center and the 2 and 12 at either end. The 7 is the key number in dice and can be rolled no matter what number shows on either die; the only number that has this power.

Not only is the 7 the most frequently rolled of all numbers, but it has a unique status, since it is a winner on the come-out roll for right bettors, while it is a losing roll for those same players betting with the dice after a point is established.

The point numbers in the game of craps are 4, 5, 6, 8, 9, and 10. By the rules of craps these numbers must be repeated once they are established on a come-out roll, before a 7 is thrown, in order for the pass-line bettor to win. Since each of the point numbers can be made in fewer ways than the 7, the odds are against any of them repeating.

The following chart shows the correct odds against repeating a point number before a 7 is rolled.

Number	Ways to Roll	Odds Against Repeating Before a 7 Is Rolled
4	3	2–1
5	4	3–2
6	5	6–5
8	5	6–5
9	4	3–2
10	3	2–1

In casino craps, there are a variety of numbers that can be bet on a one-roll basis; that is, the player bets that they will appear on the very next throw of the dice.

The true odds against these numbers appearing are shown in the next table. Since there are 36 possible combinations, all odds are determined by that figure.

Number	Ways to Roll	True Odds Against Any Single Roll
2	1	35–1
3	2	17–1
7	6	5–1
11	2	17–1
12	1	35–1

These are the basic combinations and odds we'll be dealing with in this chapter, although, because of the wide range of bets available on the layout, we'll discuss other odds and combinations in the appropriate section of this chapter.

The Basic Game—Line Bets

There are two kinds of line bets available at the casino craps table—the pass line and don't pass bets. Sometimes the pass-line bet is called the front line and the don't pass called the back line, but we'll simply call them pass line and don't pass, to conform to the standard American craps layout.

These line bets can only be made prior to the come-out roll, and their final determination is involved with that throw in certain cases and with subsequent rolls when a point is established on the come-out roll.

The basic game of craps is involved with the line bets, and the vast majority of players make pass-line bets so that's the bet we'll discuss first.

Pass-Line Bet

This bet is made prior to a come-out roll, and to make this wager, the player must put chips in the area designated as pass line. In order to win this bet, one of the following must occur:

• On the come-out roll a 7 or 11 is rolled. This is an immediate winner on the pass line, and the bets are paid off at even money.

• If a 4, 5, 6, 8, 9, or 10 is thrown on the come-out roll, then that number is designated as the point, and it must be repeated before a 7 is thrown for the pass line bettor to win.

For instance, if the number rolled on the come-out is a 5, that is the point. If, after rolling the 5, the shooter rolled 2, 3, 6, 10, 12, 8, 11, and then 5, the pass-line bettors would win their bets. This is so because the 5 was repeated before a 7 was thrown. All numbers other than the point number 5 and 7 were immaterial and didn't affect the pass-line bettor's decision.

Pass-line bettors lose their wagers if the following occurs:

• On the come-out roll, a 2, 3, or 12 (all called "craps") is rolled. The shooter is said to crap out, and this roll is an immediate loser for the pass-line bettors.

• If a point number (4, 5, 6, 8, 9, or 10) has been established on the come-out roll, and a 7 is rolled before the point was repeated.

A losing sequence of numbers might look like this: 6 (the point), 8, 9, 4, 11, 3, 7. Since the 7 came up before the 6 was repeated, it's a losing roll for pass-line players. All the other numbers would have no bearing in determining a win or loss on this pass-line bet.

A pass-line bettor is called a right bettor. This term has nothing to do with morality, but is the expression used for a player wagering with the dice. Most players, approximately 90 percent of the gamblers at a craps table, are right bettors, for reasons we'll go into later.

To summarize the pass-line bet:

• On the come-out roll, a 7 or 11 is an immediate winner.

• A 2, 3, or 12 is an immediate loser on the come-out roll.

• If a point number is rolled on the come-out, that number (4, 5, 6, 8, 9, or 10) must be repeated before a 7 is rolled for the pass-line player to win. If a 7 comes up before the point is repeated, the pass-line bettor loses.

A pass-line bet, once made, cannot be removed or reduced.

Don't Pass Bet

This is also a line bet, but one against the dice, wagering that they will not pass, that the dice will lose. This bet can only be made prior to a come-out roll, and players betting don't pass will win their bets in the following ways:

• If a 2 or 3 is rolled on the come-out roll. This roll is called "craps" and the don't pass bettor is paid off at even money.

• If a point number, either 4, 5, 6, 8, 9, or 10 is thrown on the come-out roll, and a 7 is rolled before the point is repeated.

• If a 12 is rolled, the bet is a standoff, neither winning nor losing, since the 12 (in some casinos the 2) is barred as a winning bet for the don't pass player.

Don't pass bettors would win their wagers in the following sequence of rolls: 8 (point), 9, 4, 5, 5, 11, 9, 7, since the 7 came up on the dice before the point, 8, is repeated. All the other numbers and throws had no bearing on the result, even though some of the other numbers repeated, because it is only the point number that the line bettors are concerned with, and here the point number was 8.

Don't pass bettors lose if the following occurs:

• If a 7 or 11 is thrown on the come-out roll. This is an immediate loss, and the don't pass bettors' chips are removed by the dealer at once.

• If a point number is established, and then repeated by the shooter before a 7 is rolled.

A don't pass bettor is often called a wrong bettor. Again, no moral statement or inference is intended by the term wrong. There aren't many wrong bettors around, for the game of casino craps is dominated by right bettors, those anxious for the dice to win. There are several reasons for this, all of which have no actual bearing on the odds involved, since they're almost identical.

The odds against a pass-line bettor, who bets right, are approximately 1.41 percent, and the house advantage over a don't pass bettor, betting wrong, is approximately 1.4 percent. The difference in the casino edge on all line bets is negligible.

Most gamblers bet right because they are permitted odds bets, and when they take the odds on these bets, they are paid at better than even money. On the other hand, wrong bettors have to *lay odds*, and collect at *less* than even money. Thus wrong bettors are forced to put out more money on the layout than they will receive back if they win, which doesn't appeal to the majority of players.

Many players like to have continuous bets going on every roll of the dice, by betting either come or the place numbers, so that they will collect on every roll of the dice. Don't bettors, if they bet don't come or lay against the numbers, won't collect on every bet—they'll have to wait for the 7 to show before collecting. This is another important reason why most players like to bet with the dice.

A number of players wait for one hot roll, where the dice continually come up with come and point numbers, so that they win every bet they have out on the layout over and over again, compounding their wins at the same time by pressing or doubling their bets as the roll goes on. A right bettor can win a fortune with one continuous shoot while a wrong bettor makes money over the long run, with smaller wins.

Finally, most players think they are optimists when betting with the dice. They don't want to bet against dice and become pessimists, though there is no logic to that reasoning. And among right bettors a camaraderie develops, since all of them are rooting for the dice to pass, and all are pulling together in an enforced form of togetherness.

This is not to say that you shouldn't bet don't pass, for many astute gamblers have been successful as wrong bettors, the most famous example being the legendary Nick the Greek, who was a wrong bettor all his life.

To summarize the don't pass bet:

• On the come-out roll a 2 or 3 is an immediate winner for the don't pass bettor.

• A 7 or 11 thrown on the come-out roll is an immediate loser.

• A 12 (in some casinos a 2) is a standoff on the come-out roll. Whether a 2 or 12 is barred is immaterial to the players, since either number can only be made with one combination of the dice, and this doesn't affect the odds at all. When a 2 is barred, then, if a 3 or 12 is rolled on the come-out roll, don't pass bettors win their bets at even money.

• If a point number has been established on the come-out, and it is repeated before a 7 is thrown, don't pass bettors lose their wagers.

• If a point number has been established, and a 7 is rolled before the point is repeated, don't pass bettors win their line bets at even money.

Don't pass bets can always be taken down by a player after a point is established. The casino permits this because once a point is set, the odds favor don't pass bettors on their line bets. The odds in their favor range from 6–5 on the 6 or 8, 3–2 on the 5 and 9, all the way to 2–1 on the 4 or 10. The reason the bet now favors don't pass bettors is simple. The 7 can be made in 6 ways, and all these numbers can be made in fewer ways. Therefore, the odds favor a 7 coming up before any point number is repeated.

Needless to say, since the bet is now in favor of the player, once a don't pass bet is made and a point established, you should *never* remove your don't pass bet.

Free Odds Bets

Pass Line and Come

The free odds bet is the most important wager that a gambler can make, since it is the only bet the casino permits where the house has no advantage over the player. Yet if we examine the craps layout, there is nothing on the layout to indicate where or how this bet can be made. This is an intolerable situation in my opinion, but there's nothing that can be done about it, since the Gaming Commission in Nevada and the Casino Control Commission in New Jersey don't insist that casinos reveal all the possible bets and plays at their gaming tables.

A free odds bet can be made by all line bettors and by all bettors wagering on come and don't come. For now, we'll cover free odds bets made on the line bets, either on pass line or don't pass. The only qualification for these free odds bets is that the wager must be made in *addition* to a line bet. In private games this free odds bet can be made as a completely separate bet, but not at casino craps.

In most casinos the free odds bet can only be made in an amount equal to or less than the original bet, in which case the casino is said to permit single odds. There are exceptions to this rule, however, which will be covered in a later part of this section. For the time being, let's examine how a pass-line bettor makes a free odds bet, and what the bet is all about.

Let's assume that a right bettor has bet $10 on the pass line, hoping that the dice will win. After making the bet, the shooter, on the come-out roll, throws a point number, either a 4, 5, 6, 8, 9, or 10. After any of these numbers have been established as the point, the right bettor may now make an additional bet behind the original bet, or behind the pass line, at free odds.

The reason these are called free odds is that the casino will pay correct odds on these wagers. For instance, if the point were 4 or 10, the odds against either repeating before a 7 is thrown are 2–1. The casino will pay those exact odds, 2–1, on a free odds bet.

If the right bettor had bet $10 on the pass line, and the point were 4, he now bets an additional $10 behind the line* as an odds bet. If he wins by having the 4 repeat before the 7 is thrown, he'd collect $10, or even money on his line bet and an additional $20, at 2–1 on his $10 free odds bet. However, if the 7 came up before the 4 repeated, he'd lose both his line and odds bets.

If the point were 5 or 9, the payoff would be 3–2 on his $10 free odds bet, or $15–$10. If the point were 6 or 8, the correct payoff would be at 6–5, or $12–$10. Since the house has no advantage over the player on these free odds bets it is to the advantage of the player to make them, since they reduce the final casino edge on pass-line bets to 0.8 percent on single odds bets.

Where single odds are permitted, you may wager an amount equal to your pass-line bet behind the line as an odds bet. If you bet $5 on the pass line, you'll be paid 6–5 on the 6 or 8, and 2–1 on the 4 or 10, and this creates no problem. But almost no casino craps tables pay off in half-dollars, and if the point were 5 or 9, the correct payoff would be $7.50–$5.

---

* By behind the line we mean placing additional chips behind a line that separates the pass line area from the outside edge of the layout. The chips are just directly behind the original chips.

Therefore, where the point is 5 or 9, the house permits you to bet $6 behind the line, where your original line bet was $5. It is to your advantage to bet the extra dollar as an odds bet, since it reduces the casino's overall advantage on line bets.

In practically all casinos, if pass-line bettors had wagered three units on their pass-line bets, whether the unit be $3, $15, $75, or $300, they will be permitted to wager an additional five units behind the line if the point number is 6 or 8. Thus, with bets of $15 on the line and 6 as the point, players can bet $25 behind the line, to be paid off at 6–5, or $30–$25 should they win. This is also definitely to the players' advantage, and these enhanced odds bets should always be taken.

Some casinos permit double odds to be made, that is, players are allowed to bet double their original line bet as a free odds bet. Thus, players who had bet $10 on the pass line will now be permitted to bet $20 as their free odds bet, no matter what the point is. If the point had been 4 and won, players would collect $10 on the line bet at even money, but $40–$20 on the free odds bet at 2–1.

Free odds bettors, when backing up their bets on the pass line, will always receive more than the original wager if they win the bet. This is the great inducement for pass-line betting and explains why so many players prefer to bet right at the casino craps table.

Free odds bets can also be made on all come bets, at the same odds as on the pass line, since a come bet is the same as a pass-line bet, except for timing. A come bet can only be made after the come-out roll has established a point, not prior to that time. If single odds bets are permitted, the same single odds bets can be made on the come wagers, and if double odds are allowed, double odds can be made on come bets.

It is always to the players' advantage to bet the free odds and to take as much as they are allowed to take as their free odds bet. If single odds only are permitted, players should always wager three units on the pass line, to take advantage of the fact that they will be allowed to wager five units behind the line if the point is a 6 or 8, and four units behind the line if the point is a 5 or 9.

If double odds are allowed, players should take double odds on all points, since it is to their advantage to do this. When taking double odds, the house advantage on line bets plus odds is reduced to 0.6 percent. This is the smallest advantage the casino will ever have on the craps layout, and it is the lowest advantage on any casino game with the exception of blackjack.

Betting double odds gives a player an opportunity to win a great deal of money in a short period of time so, if possible, play at a casino where double odds are permitted. In Las Vegas some casinos, particularly the downtown ones and selected casinos on the Strip, offer double odds. In Reno practically all of the casinos offer double odds. The Lake Tahoe and Atlantic City casinos allow only single odds at their tables, though there may be exceptions in Lake Tahoe. But right now in Atlantic City none of the casinos permit double odds at their craps tables.

If you are at a casino and are unsure about the rules concerning odds, ask the dealer. If only single odds are allowed and a nearby casino offers double odds, go to the other casino. It is definitely to your advantage to do so if you're a right bettor.

I suggest this because it doesn't pay to give the casino one inch in terms of their advantage; the casino isn't going to give you one millimeter. Take full advantage of the double odds, and if you use the methods advocated by this book and get a good roll of the dice, you'll have the pit boss screaming for mercy.

I've seen a double odds table on the Strip in Vegas where the players in a couple of hours took the table for close to $300,000 because double odds were permitted. I've known instances of other monster wins at double odds casinos, where eventually the casinos gave up and wouldn't allow double free odds.

Double odds are the key to big wins for the players. Once you understand the game fully and study the basic strategies for winning at casino craps, you'll be in a position to make the casinos cringe if you get a hot roll going.

A final note—free odds bets may be removed or reduced at any time by a player, but since they work in favor of the gambler, they should never be taken down.

Don't Pass and Don't Come

The don't pass bettor can also make free odds bets. If single odds are allowed, the casino permits the wrong player to bet an amount *equal to the payoff*, rather than equal to the original bet. Let's explain this.

If don't pass bettors have wagered $10 on the line against the dice and the point is 4, they may now bet $20 as a free odds bet against the point, at odds of 2–1. That is, they are *laying* 2–1, or $20 to collect $10. If they win the free odds bet, they'll collect $10, or a sum equal to the original don't pass bet.

The following chart shows just how much wrong bettors will be permitted to wager as single odds on any point based on a don't pass bet of $10:

4 or 10	$20 laid at 2–1
5 or 9	$15 laid at 3–2
6 or 8	$12 laid at 6–5

In all cases the don't pass bettors are laying odds, not taking them, and their winner's payoff will be less than their free odds bet.

Sometimes, at a single odds table, players will be permitted to lay more than the original bet as free odds. For example, if they are wagering $5 on the don't pass line, they'll be allowed to bet $9 at 3–2 against the 5 and 9 as a point rather than just $6 at 6–4.

When double odds are allowed, players can bet up to double the payoff on their original bet. If the point is 4 and the wrong bettors have put down $10 on the don't pass line, they can now wager $40, laying 2–1 odds on the 4 since the payoff, should they win, will only be $20 on the odds bet. Where double odds are allowed, $10 bettors, betting wrong, can wager the following:

4 or 10	$40 laid at 2–1
5 or 9	$30 laid at 3–2
6 or 8	$24 laid at 6–5

When double odds are permitted, wrong bettors must put down an awful lot of money on the layout if they constantly lay full double odds. Even though the house has no advantage on these free odds bets, and even though they reduce the overall edge the casino has, many players are loath to lay double odds even when allowed.

In the later discussion of basic winning strategies for don't bettors we always suggest laying single odds, for an unlucky streak of repeating numbers can wipe out wrong bettors in a short time if they've been laying full double odds.

When a wrong bettor wagers only on the don't pass line, the house has an advantage of 1.4 percent on his bet. When single odds are permitted, the house edge drops to 0.8 percent, and with double odds, it drops down to 0.6 percent.

Don't come bets are the same as don't pass bets, except for timing, since these don't come bets can be made only after a point is established. However, where single odds are permitted on line bets, single odds are also permitted on don't come bets, and where double odds are allowed, a don't bettor can lay double odds on don't come bets.

All free odds bets made by right or wrong bettors, whether bet on the line or on the come or don't come, can be taken down at any time, or reduced. But again, it is not to the players' advantage to remove or reduce their free odds bets.

Come and Don't Come Bets

These bets are among the most difficult for a novice to comprehend, and many long-time players of craps don't quite understand them, yet the principle is simple and once grasped, the come and don't come bets will cease to be a mystery.

Come Bets

A come bet is ruled by the same principles as the pass-line bet, except for timing. A come bet can only be made after the come-out roll, that is, after a point number has been established. Otherwise, everything is the same. A 7 or 11 is an immediate winner, a 2, 3, or 12 an immediate loser, and any point number must be repeated before a 7 shows on the dice for the come bettor to win. And like pass-line wagers, come bets may be made at free odds.

After the come-out roll, players may make as many come bets as they like, while they are limited to one pass-line bet. This means that prior to every throw of the dice after a point has been established, players may put chips into the come box.

Making the bet is simplicity itself. On the layout, in a large area, is the come box. Prior to the roll of the dice the gamblers place their chips in that box. If a 7 or 11 is rolled next, they are paid off at even money. If a 2, 3, or 12 is rolled next, their chips are removed as a losing bet. If a point number, now called a come number, is rolled (4, 5, 6, 8, 9, or 10), their chips are removed from the come box and placed in the center of the place box number that had been rolled.

For example, if the next throw of the dice was a 6, the chips would go into the center of the 6 place box at the top of the layout. After the chips are placed there, players may give the dealer additional chips to bet as a free odds bet, at correct odds. These chips will be placed on the original chips, but at a slight tilt, to differentiate them from the come bet.

After bettors place their come bets into the come box they no longer touch their chips, except when paid off. Otherwise, the chips are handled by the dealer, who places them into the appropriately numbered place box.

Players need not have bet on the pass line to make come bets. Nor are they limited to making their come bets immediately after the come-out roll. As long as the disk is on white and in a place number box, the roll is in progress and a come bet may be made.

Let's follow a theoretical roll of the dice to see how come bets are handled.

Let's assume that the shooter is a new one, and this is his come-out roll. At this moment there can be no come bets made, only pass-line bets, if a player is interested in betting with the dice. The shooter throws the dice and an 8 comes up. This is the point. The disk is moved to the place number 8, and now come bets may be made.

Players wishing to make a come bet now must put their chips into the come box. Our player puts in $10 in chips. The next roll is a 6. The $10 is removed by the dealer and put into place box number 6. The player now hands the dealer another $10 in chips and says "odds." This $10 in chips is placed atop the original bet at a slight tilt, showing that it is an odds bet.

The next rolls are as follows: 4, 3, 12, 10, and 6. Since the 6 repeated, the come bet is a winner. The dealer will now remove the $10 original bet and the $10 odds bet and place them both in the come box. He will then put $22 alongside that amount as winnings. Ten dollars of that amount represents an even-money payoff on the come bet; the other $12 is a 6–5 payoff on the odds bet. The player now takes the chips and puts them into his rail, or he may make another come bet if he wishes, by leaving some chips in the come box.

Once a come bet is made, it is always working, or subject to being won or lost on every roll, including the come-out roll. However, the odds bet on the come wager is off on the come-out roll. We'll illustrate how this works with the next playing example.

Come-out roll—5. The 5 is now the point. The player now bets $10 in the come box prior to the next roll of the dice.

First come roll—9. The player's come bet is removed by the dealer and placed in the place box number 9. The player now gives the dealer an additional $10 bet as odds, which is placed on top of the come bet.

The next roll is a 5, and the point is made. After all pass-line bets are paid off, there is a new come-out roll. The 9 is still working as a come number, along with the odds bet, but the odds bet is off on the come-out roll.

New come-out roll—7. Although the 7 is a winner on the pass line, it is a loser for come bets, since the 7 came up on the dice before the come bet 9 repeated. However, since the odds bet is off and not working on the come-out roll, the player will get back $10 (his odds bet), but will lose his underlying $10 come bet.

After a come-out roll both the come bet and the odds bet are working so that if the 7 had come one roll later, the player would have lost both the come and odds bet, for a loss of $20.

Come bets, once made, cannot be removed, but the odds bet can be removed or reduced at any time by the player. However, it is a bad policy to remove odds bets since they work in favor of the player. Come bets without odds gives the house a 1.41 percent edge, with single odds 0.8 percent, and with double odds 0.6 percent, the same figures as pass-line bets.

Don't Come Bets

Like the come bets, don't come wagers can be made at any time after a come-out roll where a point was established.

To make this bet, the players place their chips in the don't come box. If a 2 or 3 is rolled next, they have an immediate win at even money. If a 12 is thrown next, the bet is a standoff, and should a point number or come number (the same thing) be thrown next (4, 5, 6, 8, 9, or 10), the players' chips are removed from the don't come box by the dealer. He places them above the place box number that was rolled, on the very top of the layout, to differentiate them from come and place bets.

At this time players may give the dealer additional chips to wager as a free odds bet, laying the odds against the number just rolled. These chips are placed to one side of the original bet to designate that they are for an odds bet.

If that number is repeated before a 7 is rolled, then the players lose the don't come bet along with the odds bet. Should the good old 7 be rolled before the number is repeated, the players will win both their don't come and odds bets.

Don't come bets are always working, even on the come-out roll. And for some reason the odds bets on don't come wagers are also always working, even on the come-out roll. Therefore, if a 7 is thrown on the next come-out roll, don't come bettors will win their bet and odds wager. If the number they had as a don't come wager is repeated on the come-out roll, they will lose both the don't come bet and free odds bet.

Unlike come bets, the house will allow don't come bets to be removed at any time, but players should never do this, since now the odds are in their favor, because there is more likelihood of a 7 being thrown than any point or come number being repeated.

The free odds bets can also be removed at any time, but they should never be removed, because it is to the players' advantage to have them on the layout. Don't come bets, like come bets, can be made on every throw of the dice after the come-out roll. The odds against this bet are identical to those on don't pass—1.4 percent without odds, 0.8 percent with single odds, and 0.6 percent with double odds.

Place Bets

Place bets are very popular with those players who bet with the dice at the table, and these wagers usually receive heavy action, especially from high rollers and others who want to make a lot of money in the quickest possible time.

These bets are working only after the come-out roll, and they can be made in denominations ranging from the house minimum to the house maximum on each or every one of the place numbers—4, 5, 6, 8, 9, and 10. However, most casinos pay off to $5 on these bets at better than even money and even money when these wagers are for less than $5, so it is best to bet at least $5 on all numbers but the 6 and 8 and to bet $6 on the 6 and 8, because they are paid off to $6.

The house payoffs are as follows on place numbers: 9–5 on the 4 and 10, 7–5 on the 5 and 9, and 7–6 on the 6 and 8. Some casinos, particularly the smaller ones that cater to 25¢ players, will allow payoffs of less than $5, but for purposes of this section we'll deal with minimum bets of $5 and $6 on the place numbers.

The following chart shows the house payoffs, the correct

payoffs, and the house advantage as the difference between the house payoff and the true odds, which we've called the correct payoff.

Number	Payoff	Correct Payoff	House Edge
4	9–5	2–1	6.67%
5	7–5	3–2	4.0%
6	7–6	6–5	1.52%
8	7–6	6–5	1.52%
9	7–5	3–2	4.0%
10	9–5	2–1	6.67%

The casino has its biggest edge on the 4 and 10 and its smallest advantage on the 6 and 8. In fact, every place bet but the 6 and 8 gives the house much too great an edge for any player to overcome in the long run. You'd be better off making come bets with free odds, thus giving the casino no more than 0.6 percent or 0.8 percent.

Place bets can be made on all the numbers or on any one of them, and these bets can be removed, reduced, or added to at any time prior to the next roll of the dice. Place bets are working all the time, except on the come-out roll.

To make a place bet, the player gives the dealer sufficient chips and tells him what numbers he wants covered and for what amounts. If any of these numbers repeats or comes up, the player wins and is paid off at house odds immediately.

Most players cover all the numbers at once. For example, gamblers, if they are betting the minimum $5 and $6 on place numbers, will give the dealer $27 if the point is any but the 6 and 8, or $26, if the point is either the 6 and 8, and they will say "across the board" or tell the dealer to "cover all the numbers."

The dealer will then put down $5 on all numbers but the 6 and 8, and $6 on the 6 and 8 if either of these numbers is not a point. The usual procedure is for all numbers to be covered except for the point number, which has the disk in its box. But players may bet the point number as a place number also, if they desire.

Betting a point number after having a pass-line bet on that same number is foolish, for if players have made both a pass line and odds bet, they will be giving the house no more than 0.8 percent, while the cheapest edge the house will have is 1.52 percent if the point is 6 or 8.

Why do players bet the place numbers when they can get better odds by betting come bets with free odds? They do it because most gamblers are impatient people. When betting the come box, the number must first be established, and there is a payout only if that number is repeated. With place numbers the first time that number is rolled, there is an immediate pay-off. However, for the privilege of being impatient, the gambler gives the house a greater edge.

Another reason is that come bets are always working, even on the come-out, and sometimes, in the course of a hot roll, a 7 is rolled on the come-out, and all come bets are lost and must be taken down. Place bets, being off on the come-out roll, are not affected by these 7s.

Remember that the 7 is the great enemy of the place numbers except on the come-out roll. When a 7 comes up on the dice, all place numbers are lost and are removed from the layout. When betting place numbers, the gambler is betting that enough of them will repeat before the 7 is rolled to make the bet worthwhile.

Gamblers are generally unaware of the odds structure in craps, and for that reason, many of them love the place numbers. Also they are lazy, and instead of making continuously solid bets, they'd rather make just one bet and get the whole thing over with.

Therefore, we suggest that place numbers be not bet except in an aggressive strategy as outlined in this book, and then only the 6 and 8 should be wagered on. Never give the house more than 1.52 percent, and in the long run, you stand a very good chance of winning at craps.

Place bets can be called off at any time by the player for a limited number of rolls or they can simply be taken down, also at the player's option. If the bets are called off, the dealer will put a small off button on the player's chips and this will remain until the player tells the dealer that his bets are working again.

Place bets are very flexible. When making them, you need not bet in regular or precise amounts, so long as you give enough money to insure correct payoffs at house odds. For example, if you give the dealer $9 to bet on the 5, you will be paid 7–5 for the first $5 and only even money thereafter for the remaining $4. Therefore, you should either give the dealer $5 or $10 or multiples of $5 to insure that you get the proper house odds. And if you're betting on the 6 or 8, you must give multiples of $6 to get proper house payoffs.

And when making these wagers, you may bet, for example, $50 on the 4, $80 on the 5, $30 on the 6, $60 on the 8, and so forth. You need not bet the same amount on every number. And you don't have to bet every number. Some bettors prefer the outside numbers, the 4, 5, 9, and 10, and never bet the 6 and 8.

This is foolish, of course, but many players do this. Others never bet anything but the 6 and 8, and still others bet only on inside numbers, the 5, 6, 8, and 9. But no matter how many numbers they bet or in what amounts, the house odds remain rigidly against them and never change.

Buying the 4 and 10

Instead of placing the 4 and 10 at a disadvantage of 6.67 percent, you may buy these numbers. To do so, you give the house an immediate commission of 5 percent, and then you are paid off at the correct odds of 2–1. In this way you reduce the house edge to 4.76 percent on the 4 and 10.

To buy the numbers, you merely say to the dealer, "Buy the 4 and/or 10" and give him the proper chips plus a 5 percent commission. If you buy either for $20, you must give the dealer an additional $1 as the vig, or 5 percent commission.

A buy button is then placed on these chips to differentiate them from ordinary place bets on the 4 and 10. Buy bets, like place bets, may be removed, added to, or reduced at any time and are not working on the come-out roll.

Laying Bets

Numbers not only can be placed, but also can be wagered against by wrong bettors. For example, if you feel that the next shoot will be cold and a 7 will come up before numbers repeat, you may lay bets against the numbers immediately instead of making don't come bets.

To accomplish this, you pay a 5 percent commission based on the payoff. For instance, if you bet against the 4 and lay $40, you give the house only $1 as its commission. This represents 5 percent of the $20 payoff, should your lay bet win. When making these wagers, you give the casino the following edge: on the 4 and 10, 2.44 percent; on the 5 and 9, 3.23 percent; and on the 6 and 8, 4 percent. After this bet is made, a buy button is placed on the chips and they're moved to the same area as don't come bets. Lay wagers, like place bets, can be removed, reduced, or added to at any time.

Field Bets

On the craps layout, the field bet is prominently featured, though it gets relatively little play except for some bets placed by small-time gamblers, systems players, and ignorant bettors who don't understand the other bets at the table. They see before them a large selection of numbers and feel the bet is a worthwhile one, possibly in their favor.

Like all other one-roll bets shown on the layout, however, the field is unfavorable to the player. On our craps layout, where both the 2 and 12 are paid off at 2–1, the house edge is 5.55 percent. Where either the 2 or 12 is paid off at 3–1, as it is in most of the downtown Las Vegas casinos and in some casinos in Northern Nevada, the house edge is reduced to 2.70 percent.

At first glance, it appears that the players, with all those numbers going for them, have the advantage, but the numbers shown on the field bet—2, 3, 4, 9, 10, 11, and 12—though in the majority in terms of numbers, can be made in fewer ways than the missing numbers, 5, 6, 7, and 8.

Let's examine this bet mathematically. First, we'll put down all the numbers on the field and the ways they can be made.

Numbers	Combinations	Ways Made
2	1–1 × 2 (2–1)	2
3	1–2, 2–1	2
4	1–3, 3–1, 2–2	3
9	3–6, 6–3, 4–5, 5–4	4
10	4–6, 6–4, 5–5	3
11	5–6, 6–5	2
12	6–6 × 2 (2–1)	2
		Total 18

The missing numbers, 5, 6, 7, and 8, can be made in twenty ways, and therefore the chances of winning this bet is 20–18 against the player, giving the casino its advantage of 5.5 percent. When either the 2 or 12 is paid off at 3–1, the odds against the player are 20–19, giving the casino an advantage of 2.70 percent.

The field bet is always working, even on the come-out roll, and it is made by placing chips in the field box prior to the next roll of the dice. The field bet can be made in amounts ranging from the house minimum to the maximum bet allowed.

This is referred to as a one-roll bet since the next roll of the dice determines immediately whether the bet is won or lost. If one of the numbers shown on the field comes up, it's a winning bet at even money except for the 2 and 12. If a 5, 6, 7, or 8 comes up on the dice, then the player loses the bet and the chips are removed by the dealer.

There are much better wagers on the craps layout for the astute player, giving the house less of an edge, and therefore this bet shouldn't be made.

Big 6 and Big 8

This is another bet that appeals to unwary and uninformed players. Now and then it gets some play, usually from people unfamiliar with the odds of dice. Players are curious about these boxes and the dealer tells them that the bet pays off at even money if the number 6 or 8 comes up before a 7 is rolled, so they place a bet.

This bet can be made at any time and is always working. When betting on the big 6 or big 8, the player is wagering that the number 6 or 8, whichever he's betting on, will come up before a 7 is rolled, and the bet is made by putting chips into either or both boxes prior to the next roll of the dice, at any time. This is not a one-roll bet, and the player will receive even money if he wins this wager. If the 7 shows first on the dice, he'll lose.

What makes this bet a terrible one is the mathematics of dice. Since there are only five ways to make either a 6 or 8 and six ways to roll a 7, the odds against the bet are 6–5, giving the house a 9.09 percent edge over the player.

This edge is quite large, and if the player wishes to wager on the 6 or 8 or on both numbers, he'd be much better off making place bets on these numbers, betting a minimum of $6 and receiving 7–6 if he wins the bet. In that way the house advantage is reduced to 1.52 percent.

Always avoid the big 6 and big 8 bets except in Atlantic City, where, if $6 or multiples of that amount are bet, the house will pay off at 7–6. If less money is bet, they'll be paid off at even money.

Center or Proposition Bets

In the center of the layout stand a myriad of possible bets for the player. All these are under the control of the stickman rather than the standing dealer. At the outset of this section we'll simply state that *none* of these wagers, which we'll discuss fully, are worthwhile for the gambler, and all should be avoided.

The first bets we'll discuss are the one-roll bets, which last for only one roll of the dice, and are won or lost at once. Therefore, a one-roll bet is always working, since the next roll of the dice will determine its outcome.

Any 7

This wager gets hardly any play, since even the densest of craps players realizes intuitively that it's a terrible bet. Here's why. There are six ways to make a 7 out of 36 combinations of dice, and the correct odds paid on this bet should be 36–6 or 5–1. Since the house pays either 5 for 1 or 4–1 (the same thing) it has a staggering edge of 16.67 percent over the player.

Avoid this bet at all costs.

Any Craps

At the bottom of the center layout is the any craps bet. The craps numbers are 2, 3, and 12, and the chances of rolling any of these numbers are 4 in 36. Therefore, the correct odds against this wager are 8–1. The casino pays only 7–1, giving it an advantage over the player of 11.1 percent. Never make this bet.

2 or 12

These numbers can be made individually in only one way, and the correct odds against either one is 35–1. Since the house only pays 30–1, it has an advantage on this bet of 13.89 percent. In some casinos, this bet is paid off at 30 for 1, or 29–1 (the same thing) and in these clubs their edge is a whopping 16.67 percent. No matter which casino you play in, avoid making this bet.

3 or 11

These numbers can be rolled individually in only two ways, and thus the true odds against either number is 17–1. The casino pays off at 15–1, giving it an edge of 11.1 percent. In some greedier casinos, the payoff is at 15 for 1, or 14–1, raising the house edge to 16.67 percent. This bet should never be made.

Horn Bet

This single wager combines the worst features of a group of individual bets. When making a horn bet, gamblers are betting that the next roll of the dice will come up either 2, 3, 11, or 12. They cover all these numbers with one four-unit bet.

If the 2, 3, 11, or 12 is rolled on the next throw of the dice, they'll be paid off according to the usual casino payout on that number, at a terrible disadvantage to the players, and the casino will retain the other three units as losing chips. This bet allows players to make four bad bets at one time and should always be avoided.

Hardways

The hardway bets, unlike the other center proposition wagers, is not a one-roll bet. These bets allow the player to wager that the number selected will come up hard before it comes up easy or before a 7 is rolled. Let's explain this, to make it absolutely clear.

In craps parlance there are four hardway numbers, one for each of the even point numbers, 4, 6, 8, and 10. For a number to be hard it must come up as a pair. A hard four is 2 and 2, a hard six 3 and 3, a hard eight 4 and 4, and a hard ten 5 and 5. Each hardway can only be made with one combination of the dice.

To figure the correct odds on these bets, we must know how many ways a number can be rolled easy, that is, not as a pair, and add to that figure the number of ways a 7 can be rolled, which is six ways.

Hard 4 and Hard 10

Each of these numbers can be rolled easy in two ways. The 4 can be tossed 1–3, 3–1, and the 10, 4–6, 6–4. Since there are six ways a 7 can be rolled, the odds against either the hard 4 or hard 10 are 8–1. These bets are paid off at 7–1, and therefore the house has an advantage of 11.1 percent over the player.

Hard 6 and Hard 8

These numbers can each be rolled easy in four different ways. A six can be rolled 1–5, 5–1, 2–4, and 4–2, while an 8 can be rolled 2–6, 6–2, 3–5, and 5–3. There are six ways a 7 can be thrown; therefore the odds against the hard 6 or hard 8 are 10–1. The casino pays off at 9–1, giving it an advantage of 9.09 percent.

Avoid making any hardway bets.

Hop Bets

Sometimes, the masochists at the craps table, not satisfied with the horrendous odds against them on center proposition bets, seek out other, more exotic bets. One of these is the hop bet. The gambler is wagering that the dice will come up in a particular combination such as 2 and 2 on the very next roll. The casino will accommodate this wager by giving him 30 for 1 that this will not occur. Since any single combination of paired numbers can only come up one way, the correct odds against this bet are 35–1, and the house has a sweet 16.67 percent edge for itself.

One final word. We've written about paying off at 30 for 1 instead of 30–1. Don't be misled when you see the term "for" at a craps table. Be wary. What "for" means is that the actual odds paid are reduced by one unit. Thus, a bet paying off at 5 for 1 is in reality being paid off at 4–1. Here's why:

When a bet is paid off at 5–1, you get back your $1 in addition to the $5 you've won. When a bet is paid off at 5 for 1, you get back only $5, including your dollar bet, reducing the payoff to 4–1. Remember that the next time you see "for" on the layout. Generally speaking, any for bet is a bad one and shouldn't be made.

Despite the fact that all the center proposition bets are bad ones for players, some get a lot of action. Prior to a come-out roll, many right bettors wager on any craps to protect their pass-line bets from a craps being thrown. This is stupid, since the house edge of 11.1 percent will eat them up in the long run.

There's no need to protect a pass-line bet that will ultimately give the house only a 1.41 percent edge by making a bet that gives the house an advantage of 11.1 percent. It just doesn't make sense, yet it's constantly done.

Many gamblers automatically heed the clarion call of the stickman and bet "craps, eleven," which is any craps and the 11 bet on the come-out roll. These bets, which are made out of ignorance or habit, are very bad.

During the course of a roll, players are constantly betting the hardways, especially if the point is one of the even numbers. They bet the hardway of that point to bring it out, to make it occur. Unfortunately, the dice don't have eyes and can't see the bets being made on the layout, so betting hardways has no real effect on that outcome.

The best policy at craps is to avoid not only the center proposition bets, but the continual calls of the stickman to make this or that foolish bet. And just because everyone else is doing it doesn't mean you should. The casinos get richer each year because of fools who crowd the tables throwing away their money against overpowering odds. Be independent, not one of the sheep. Avoid these wagers. Don't be tempted by potentially big payoffs. Save your chips for those bets which will give you the best odds and the best chance to win.

Strategies for Winning at Craps

Most craps players are losers, and some of them are very heavy losers. I've seen thousands of games played in casinos around the world, and I've watched and spoken to many craps players, some of whom consider themselves very knowledgeable. In addition, I've interviewed dealers, boxmen, floormen, pit bosses, shift bosses, and casino managers about the game.

My impression is that most players, even those who are battle-scarred veterans of the tables, don't have any idea how the game should best be played. They are forever talking in terms of hunches and feelings, and few of them even know the correct odds of the game.

As to casino personnel, some of them are so ridden with superstitions that their remarks were worthless except to show the blatant ignorance of so-called professionals in the field.

They talk constantly of how to stop hot rolls by changing the dice, by delaying the game, by changing dealers at the table. They act as though the dice themselves were observing all this casino action, as though the dice were waiting for the pit boss's next move before deciding what number they'd come up on the table. Of course, it's all nonsense, but so many casino people believe in superstitions that they've become an accepted fact in the casino industry.

In this section we're going to discuss strategies in broad terms, and in the next section, "An Analysis of the Best Craps Systems," we'll show how to put these strategies to best use.

The following are the basic strategies of winning craps:

• Go to the table with a sufficient bankroll to overcome short periods of temporary losses. If you're undercapitalized, this fact alone reduces your chances of ending up a winner. You'll find yourself around only long enough for the losing streaks, and by the time the hot hand comes, you'll be tapped out. Bring enough money for a full session at the table and have enough of an overall bankroll to withstand several losing sessions at the tables.

For a fuller discussion of the bankroll necessary, read the section on "Betting Limits and Money Management."

• Make only those bets that give the casino the smallest possible advantage. If betting right, limit the bets to the pass line and come areas of the layout, taking the maximum odds that can be obtained at the table. If possible, play only in casinos that offer double, rather than single odds. It'll give you a better chance to win.

Betting this way will give the house no more than a 0.8 percent edge over you. With double odds the edge will be reduced to 0.6 percent, which means that you'll risk losing a theoretical 60¢ for every $100 you bet, and in the short term you'll be able to overcome this disadvantage by raising your bets with the casino's money and leaving when ahead.

If you're a wrong bettor, you should only bet don't pass and don't come, laying single odds instead of double odds to prevent a sudden loss of your bankroll during a bad run of dice.

At no time will the house have more than a 0.8 percent edge over you, and if you play the don't side correctly, you can overcome this edge by proper use of your money.

• Use self-control at the table. Stick to the bets already discussed, no matter whether you're winning or losing. The one exception will be place bets on the 6 and 8 in an aggressive betting system, but putting this system aside for the time being, avoid any bets where the house has more than a 0.8 percent advantage.

This is fairly easy to do when winning, but often, when on a bad losing streak, you might look around the layout for big payoffs and be tempted by the proposition bets with their 30–1 payoffs. Don't make these bets under any circumstances. If you feel like betting this way, you're at a point where you just want to throw your money away so that you can leave the table in a hurry. I have a better suggestion; leave the table right then and there without losing all your cash; leave with the remaining money still intact.

The second phase of self-control comes when winning a great deal. There's a tendency to become greedy, and greed is the downfall of gamblers. As one astute president of a casino said to me, "We win because when players are ahead, they want to win more, and so they lose everything they've won. When they're behind, they try to get even in a hurry, and make bigger bets and go deeper into the hole."

Another casino executive put it more bluntly, "We win because most gamblers are willing to lose more than they're willing to win."

Don't be greedy. Don't spend an hour winning a great deal of money only to lose it all in five minutes of outrageous betting. There's a tendency, especially at a craps table, where action is so fast and money changes hands so rapidly, to play for the thrills of the game instead of for the money. When you're ahead, it's time to start thinking of getting out with some of the winnings intact. See the section on betting limits and money management for the rules of leaving the table whether winning or losing.

Never forget these three rules for winning:

1. Bring a sufficient bankroll to the table.
2. Make only those bets that give the house a minimum advantage.
3. Keep your self-control, whether winning or losing.

With these three rules as your guideline you can't help but be a winner.

An Analysis of the Best Craps System

We're going to cover four systems in this section; two for the right bettor and two for the player who bets against the dice. Of the two methods of betting shown for each kind of player, one is a basic system and the other a more aggressive one, but each gives the bettor the best chance of winning.

The Basic System for Right Bettors

Since we want to give the house a minimum advantage on all bets, the basic strategy is limited to two kinds of wagers—pass-line and come bets, both with maximum odds. The system works well with either double or single odds, but double odds are always preferable. When betting with double odds, we'll use a basic betting method of two units. With single odds, three units.

We'll use three units with single odds because the casino allows a bet of five units as a free odds bet if the point or come number is a 6 or 8, and four units if the point or come number is a 5 or 9. This extra odds bet reduces the house advantage and gives the player the best opportunity to make maximum profits.

Single Odds Game

• Your first bet is three units on the pass line. These units can equal $3, $15, $75, or $300. It doesn't matter how big or little you bet, because the principles are the same.

• After a point has been established, the maximum free odds bet that is allowed is bet behind the line. If the point is a 4 or 10, three units will be bet on the odds. If the point is a 5 or 9, four units, and if a 6 or 8 is the point, then five units will be the odds bet.

• You then make two come bets of three units each, taking the maximum odds on each come number. After two come bets are established, you stop betting. To establish two come bets, intermediate rolls of craps or 11 won't count. Come bets are continually made until those two come bets are placed.

• The basic idea is to have three numbers working for you —the point and two come numbers, all with odds.

• If a come number repeats, then you increase your next come bet to five units and again take maximum odds on the new come number.

• If that come number again repeats, the bet is raised to six units, and thereafter, as come numbers repeat, the bets are raised by three units at a time.

Thus, the increase is as follows: three units, five units, six units, nine units, twelve units, and thereafter the bet is increased by three units after each win.

• If the point is made (won), then the pass-line bet is increased in the same manner, from three to five to six to nine units and so on.

Let's follow a simple roll of the dice to see how this works. For purposes of this game, we'll have a bettor wagering with $5 chips, so that the opening bet of three units will be $15.

Come-out roll: 6 (point) $15 pass-line bet and $25 odds

The five-unit bet on odds is allowed in practically all casinos if the line wager has three units and the point is a 6 or 8.

| First come roll: 11 | $15 win |
| Second come roll: 5 | $15 come bet and $20 odds |

The player is permitted to bet four units if his line bet was three units and the come number was a 5 or 9.

Third come roll: 4 $15 come and $15 odds

It took three come rolls to establish two come bets, since the 11 was an immediate winner for the come bettor. With three numbers working for him, the point and two come numbers, the player stops betting.

Next come roll: 2   No decision on his bets
Next come roll: 5 $45 win on the come bet of 5

The 5 is now taken down by the dealer and returned to the player along with his profits, so that now only one come bet is working. Therefore the player makes another come bet, this time betting five units, or $25.

Next come bet: 6 $45 win on point bet of 6
                       $25 come bet and $25 odds

At this point, let's review the situation. The player has already won $90—$45 on the come bet of 5 and $45 on the point bet of 6. There are two come bets working, with $15 and $15 odds on the 4 and $25 and $25 odds on the 6.

Since the point was made, there's a new come-out roll. The player will now wager five units or $25 on the pass line, having won his previous pass-line bet.

New come-out roll: 4 $15 win on come bet of 4
                          $25 and $25 odds on pass line

Because come bets work all the time, the player has won the $15 on the 4 as a come wager. But since the odds bet is off on the come-out roll, it was returned to the player when the 4 was taken down, without any payoff on the odds bet. Now the player has only one come bet working, the 6, so he makes another $25 bet in the come box.

Next come roll: 10 $25 and $25 odds
Next come roll: 10 $75 win on come bet of 10 with odds

The 10 is taken down and paid off to the player. Now he must make another come bet. Since the previous bet was five units on the 10, he bets six units or $30, putting it into the come box.

Next come roll: 8 $30 and $50 odds

The player is permitted to bet five units as an odds bet when his come bet was three units and the come number was a 6 or 8. Since the gambler has two come bets working, he stops betting again.

Next come roll: 5   No decision
Next come roll: 12   No decision
Next come roll: 6 $55 win on come bet of 6 and odds

The 6 is taken down, and the player makes a $30 or six-unit bet in the come box, since the 6 had been bet with five units.

Next come roll: 7 $30 win on come bet
                      $80 loss on come bet on 8
                      $50 loss on pass-line bet on 4

The shooter has sevened out, and the roll is finished. Let's summarize the wins and losses.

Total wins	$280
Total losses	$130
Net win	$150

If the shooter hadn't rolled a 7 and the point had been made again, the pass-line bet would have been raised to six units. For purposes of raising bets, each come and pass-line wager is treated separately and is raised only when repeated.

It may be that, during a hot shoot, some of the bets will be at nine units, while others will be at five or six units. Each come bet is a separate entity in this system, for only when the come bet is repeated can the next come bet be increased. The same holds true for the pass-line wager.

Double Odds Game

When betting double odds, it's best to start with two, rather than three, units, since no matter what point or come number shows on the dice, the player can put at least double his basic unit bet behind the line as an odds bet. In the case of a 6 or 8 most casinos allow five units to be bet as an odds wager if the underlying bet is for two units. If the original or underlying bet is four units, then up to ten units can be bet as an odds wager on the 6 and 8. The basic structure of the 6 and 8 odds is five units for every line or come bet of two units.

When increasing bets after wins with double odds, raise the bets from two to four units and then by two units thereafter as points and come numbers repeat.

The same system is used for double odds as was shown for single odds. Make one pass-line bet, and then establish two come bets. Make enough come bets so that two are always working and then stop betting until a come bet repeats or the point is made. Thereafter, increase the bets.

Ten Times Odds

At the present time, ten times odds is allowed at only one casino, Benny Binion's Horseshoe Club in downtown Las Vegas. Let's hope it spreads to other casinos throughout the country, but I doubt it. But while it's at the Horseshoe, serious craps players would do well to test out their tables.

With ten times odds, what we want to do is bet those odds with each situation. We start with two units and bet ten times odds, then make two come bets and take ten times odds. Suppose we simply bet $2 on the pass line and $2 on each come point. We back all these bets with $20 in odds. This puts $66 on the table if all three bets are established. This is comparable to $10 as basic bets with double odds of $20 on each point, for a total of $60, but pays off much better.

If we win, then increase the bet by one unit only, and back up the $3, for example, with $30 in odds. We will now have $99 in chips out there to cover all our bets. If we keep winning, increase it by another unit and so forth, as long as the dice keep grinding out the points.

Aggressive System for the Right Bettor

This method of betting gives the house a slightly higher edge in certain situations, but it allows the right bettor to always cover the 6 and 8 and have these two numbers continually working for him.

Since the 6 and the 8 can each be made in five ways, they will come up more than any other point number and will be the heart of any hot, continuous roll.

When betting this aggressive method, either single or double odds games can be played, but the preference is always for double odds.

The same unit bets are made as in the basic strategy—three units where single odds are allowed and two units where double odds are permitted.

Single Odds

• Bet three units on the pass line and take maximum free odds on every point.

• Make enough come bets to establish two come numbers, then make no more come bets.

• If either the 6 or 8, or both, have not been covered by the pass line and come bets, then bet six units on the 6 and/or 8 *as a place bet.*

• If a come bet or pass-line bet repeats and is paid off, increase the betting as in the basic strategy, from three units to five or six and then increase the wager by three units after each win.

• If the 6 or 8 repeats as a place bet, increase the bet by two units. If the initial place wager was $30, increase it by $12 to $42. If the initial bet was only $6, then increase it by $6 after every repeat. Of course, if the basic unit used was a $25 chip, it will be increased by two units, or $50, after every payout. This is assuming that the initial bet was $150.

Using this method, it may be possible that a come bet other than a 6 or 8 will repeat and then the new come bet number will be a 6 or 8 while it's a place number. In that case, take down the 6 or 8 as a place number and continue it only as a come number. Let's explain this more carefully in the following example.

Suppose that the following roll ensued, with the bettor wagering $15 as his basic bet.

Come-out roll: 9 (point)	$15 and $20 odds
First come roll: 8	$15 and $25 odds
Second come roll: 5	$15 and $20 odds

The player now bets $30 (six units) on the 6, since it wasn't covered by any of the previous rolls, and stops betting.

Third come roll: 5	$45 win

The player now bets $25 in the come box, since the 5, being repeated as a come number, was taken down.

Fourth come roll: 6	$36 win as place bet
	$25 and $25 odds on the 6

The place bet is taken down by the player, and the come bet on the 6 is put up. It's always preferable to have a come bet on a 6 or 8, but the dice tosses can't be predicted, and both numbers may not come out on the first three rolls. In fact, the odds are against both the 6 and 8 showing on three rolls of the dice, and that's the reason for the aggressive strategy.

Should the 6 be rolled next, and it is taken down as a come bet, it need not be covered as a place bet until two come bets are established. The system doesn't call for the 6 and 8 to be covered immediately after the come-out roll or where only one come bet is working. Only after both come bets are established and either the 6 and 8 or both are missing as come or point numbers, should they then be bet.

With this betting method the player puts out extra money on the layout and gives the house a slightly higher edge on the place bets (1.52 percent), but it will enable him to make the most money should a hot roll develop.

Double Odds

Where double odds are permitted, the basic bet will be two units. The same system applies as in the aggressive system for single odds, with the 6 and 8 covered by six units. The increase in bets with double odds is by two units after each win, and two units ($12) after every place number 6 or 8 repeats, if the original place bet was $30. If the place bet had been $6, increase it only by $6 after each repeat. If the place bet had been more than $30, such as $150, still increase it by two units ($50 more).

Ten Times Odds

At the Horseshoe Club, or any other casino where ten times odds are permitted, we change the aggressive system as follows: We don't want to make any place bets, not with ten times odds available, so if the 6 or 8 isn't covered, simply make one more come bet.

Our basic bet is either two or three units, depending on the player's bankroll, with ten times odds made on all pass-line and come bets.

If two units are bet, and the bet is $2 on the pass line and $20 behind the line, and two come bets, also in the same configuration, then the player will have $66 out on the table. If $3 is bet with $30 behind the line and as odds bets on the come points, he'll have $99 on the table. With $500 as his stake, he can make the $2 bets, but will need about $700–$750 to make the $3 bets.

With wrong bettors, we don't suggest any modification of our basic or aggressive bettors, so the following sections remain intact, even when playing at the Horseshoe.

Basic System for Wrong Bettors

Whether a player bets right or wrong is a personal choice—one has no inherent advantage over the other. With right betting, players often find themselves taking many small losses waiting for that hot roll which will more than compensate for the losses and give them a monster win.

Betting wrong, on the other hand, means winning small amounts of money many times, only to sustain a big loss if a hot winning or passing roll develops. There are safeguards built into our system to prevent a really large loss, as you will readily see.

Most people prefer to bet right; they don't like the idea of putting out more money than they'll receive back if they win their bet. All right bettors *take* odds at better than even money, while wrong bettors *lay* odds at better than even money.

It's a matter of choice. We suggest that you be able to go either way. You'll know when a table you're at is cold, because no points repeat and sevens quickly wipe out the right players' bets. Sometimes, on the other hand, a table is running hot and numbers come up continually. Why fight the tide? To be a smart player is to be alert to the dice and the game. Dice can't be forecast, of course, but at times you can see which way the game is going. Be prepared to go either way with the dice, whether they're running hot or cold.

Some very solid players, such as Nick the Greek, were wrong bettors. Betting against the dice has no stigma attached to it. The house is betting wrong most of the time when it books the right bettors, who make up the vast majority of players at any craps table. If you feel comfortable betting against the dice, don't mind the dirty stares from the players at the table who hate wrong bettors, especially when the dice are cold. Bet to win. Bet with your feelings and use your senses to see what is happening at the table, and you'll come out ahead in the long run.

Here's how the basic winning strategy works for wrong bettors:

• Whether the table permits single or double odds, always lay single odds, since the 0.2 percent differential isn't sufficient to make up for a short losing streak which might quickly deplete your bankroll.

• Bet two units on don't pass and lay single odds on any point.

• Make two don't come bets or enough don't come bets to establish two don't come numbers. Then stop betting.

• If a don't come number repeats and you lose that bet, make one other don't come bet. If you lose a second don't come bet, *stop betting*. Do the same thing with don't pass. If one don't pass bet loses by repeating, make only one more bet on the don't pass line. If that loses by repeating, stop making don't pass bets until the shooter sevens out, no matter how long that might take.

This is your safeguard against a hot roll wiping you out by destroying your bankroll. Should you lose all your don't come bets and don't pass bets, stand back and patiently wait for the hot roll to end. Don't fight the hot roll; that is the death of all wrong bettors.

• Should you win your don't pass bet, increase the bet by one unit and then make all your don't come bets matching the three-unit don't pass wager, still laying single odds.

For example, if your don't pass bet was won by the shooter sevening out, and you now bet three units on the don't pass line, your don't come bets will also be in three units.

Should you keep winning during a cold roll of the dice, increase your basic unit bets by only one unit at a time, matching the don't pass bets with the don't come bets. One unit will be sufficient because your odds bets will be double that unit increase in some cases, and this can add up to big wins in no time at all.

• If a don't pass bet at a higher unit base is lost by a repeating point number, revert back to the two-unit don't pass bet and work your way up again.

This method has been tried many times in casino play and has proven to be a winning one. It doesn't fight the dice and attempt to throttle hot rolls. You work along with the game, taking your profits slowly but surely. Since you're always laying odds and putting out more than you'll ever get back, you want to increase your bets carefully.

When betting wrong, you can have only one number knocked out by any single roll of the dice when a don't pass or don't come number repeats. The right bettor, on the other hand, is always fearful of the 7 wiping out all his bets at one time.

The reason most wrong bettors don't come out winning, even when they have a good thing going for them, is that they get greedy and attempt to overcome a hot roll by betting larger and larger amounts after every loss. They fight that hot roll until they're completely tapped out.

One principle you must always follow in gambling, no matter what game you play is this: *Never increase bets when losing, only when winning.* In other words, if you've lost a previous roll of the dice, don't increase your wager. Only when you've had a previous win should you take your bet. If you follow this principle, you'll be breaking the back of a casino with their own money. That's tough playing and smart betting.

Aggressive System for the Wrong Bettor

Since you never give the house more than 0.8 percent by laying single odds on the don't pass and don't come bets, you don't want to increase the house's advantage beyond that percentage. There are three possible ways to play more aggressively and still hold the line on the casino's edge.

1. Instead of increasing each bet by one unit after every win, you can raise the bet by two units. This is a sane method to use when taking advantage of a cold table, always subject, however, to the safeguards outlined in the basic strategy.

2. You can increase your bets by one unit after each win, but instead of making two don't come bets, you can make three of them. This gives you another bet out on the layout, but at the same time it gives the dice another target for repeats. At a very cold table, where few numbers or none are repeating, a player will be able to make a lot of money in a short time betting this way.

3. The final and most aggressive alternative is to raise each winning bet by two units and then make three don't come bets. Be supercareful when doing this and be aware of the possibility of a hot roll repeating numbers till all the don't come numbers come down. If numbers start repeating, stop betting, take the temporary loss, and wait for the shooter to seven out before making another don't bet, either on the line or on don't come.

With this method, however, if you get a cold table, the money will pile up quickly, and you should net a beautiful win.

Betting Limits and Money Management

Betting Limits

At one time there were two minimum limits that could be found at craps tables. There were the 25¢ limits in the so-called "sawdust" joints, which catered to the really small bettors, and then there were the $1 minimum limits at the "carpet" joints. The 25¢ limit games could be found in downtown Las Vegas and in the smaller Reno casinos, while the Strip, Lake Tahoe, and Atlantic City houses imposed the $1 limit.

But gambling has expanded as more and more money is wagered at the tables, especially the craps tables. In Atlantic City it's difficult to find a table that doesn't require a $3 minimum bet, and other tables require a $5, $25, or even $100 minimum bet.

The same with the Strip hotels in Vegas. On crowded nights and weekends, many of them have $5 or even $25 minimum tables. These places cater to the premium players, the real high rollers, who come to the table with credit lines of at least $10,000 and aren't afraid to wager their entire lines in the course of an evening's play.

When you go to a casino craps table, before you change your money for chips or make any kind of bet, always inquire about the limits at the table. If the minimum is $5 and you have only enough of a bankroll to sustain a $1 game, you shouldn't force yourself to play over your head. This is especially true at the Atlantic City casinos, which are packed on weekends and have their smaller minimum tables quickly filled up with gamblers. Just because the only spot open is at a $25 table doesn't mean you should throw caution to the winds, and bet your entire bankroll with a few bets on the table. Or worse still, it doesn't mean that you should cash a check or get credit or use an ATM machine for more money just because it's the only game you can get into. That kind of behavior invites disaster.

Be patient. Wait for a table that is comfortable for your money. Don't press your luck, or hope for luck. You'll get luck, all right, bad luck. Patience is the sign of the winner, at gambling and in life. Wait your turn. Let the others play above their heads and regret it later. You play where you are comfortable, where you won't have to change your style of play, or strategy, because you just don't have enough money to cover all your bets at one time.

Maximum bets have also changed. At one time not so many years ago, it was generally $500 on line, come, and place bets, with a $600 limit on the 6 and 8 as place wagers. Where double odds were permitted, players were able to make a $500 line bet and put $1,000 behind the line. Now, maximum bets have gone through the roof as well. In most casinos the maximum bet is $1,000 or even higher. In the Atlantic City casinos you can usually bet up to $5,000 on the line, and place double odds of $10,000 behind that bet. That gives you $15,000 riding on the point. That's big money, in anybody's book, on one number. Then you're allowed big bets on come wagers, equal to your line wager. A few of those numbers out and you can have $75,000 wiped out by the roll of a 7.

If there's a $1,000 maximum line bet allowed, that usually holds for all come and place wagers. The exception is a place wager on the 6 and 8, which is now extended to $1,200 because of the 7–6 payoff. If the maximum bet allowed is $2,000, the same principle applies, with the 6 and 8 bet up to $2,400. But always ask if in doubt, because casinos are quirky and can change their rules at the drop of a hat, especially if they're in Nevada.

I used to come to see some exciting games in which $50,000 was on the layout at one time. Now in Atlantic City, you can see $50,000 being bet by one player on the table, with additional backup by ten other players, all pouring out the $100 and $500 checks, covering the layout in a mosaic of patterned chips. And when that seven is rolled and the stickman yells, "Seven, line away," ouch! There's a collective moan as those losing chips are scooped up. But soon the same bettors—fresh meat, as they are called—are at the table wagering heavily, and when the dice get hot and the casino is paying out hundreds of thousands of dollars in winning wagers, it's the pit boss and casino executives who are yelling "uncle."

Many of the players who can bet that kind of money can afford it. Others, who knows? I've watched a lot of big games in my life (long life!) and could sense those who were at the table with borrowed or worse money, needing a big win for one reason or another. To see them cringe every time the dice are thrown is a pathetic sight. Bet only what you can afford to lose, either emotionally or financially. Don't go beyond your limits, or the game will become a maze of anxiety and high blood pressure instead of fun and exciting.

The Horseshoe Club in downtown Las Vegas, which recently bought out the Mint next door, is unique in several respects. Although they have a nominal limit at the craps tables, which I believe is $5,000, that goes out the window if a gambler really wants action. They'll raise the limit up to the first bet of the player, or make separate arrangements if a big roller wants them.

Thus, a player can come to the table and make a $100,000 bet on the line, back it up with a million dollars—yes, a million dollars!—and he's faded, as the old craps shooters say. The Horseshoe will cover the bet. The reason he can put a million behind the line is that the casino will allow *ten times odds*. We're not talking about single or double odds, but ten times the initial bet on the line, come, or don't come bets.

Now, with ten times odds, what Binion's casino is giving you is the best game in town, because he's reducing the house edge to the bare minimum. With single odds, if you bet $1 and took $1 odds on the 4 or 10, for example, you'd be paid $3 for your $2 bet. If you bet $1 and took $2 odds (double odds), you'd be paid $5 for your $3 bet. But at the Horseshoe with your $1 bet, you're taking $10 free odds and being paid $21 for an $11 bet. The correct odds on a 4 or 10 is 2–1, so you're getting a trifle below that.

With this small edge, the free drinks, and the fact that you have them run a game for you, staffed with dealers, well, it's worthwhile taking your shot at craps here.

We were previously discussing the maximum bet allowed at the Horseshoe, and showed how a million dollars could be bet behind the line on a $100,000 bet. Just how much will the Horseshoe allow? I was speaking a few years ago to Teddy Binion, who was the casino manager at the time. He's Benny Binion's son, and Benny founded the Horseshoe. He said they'd definitely take a $2,000,000 bet. And above that? He shrugged and said it depended on the circumstances.

Then he told me a story about a man from Texas who had arrived at the Horseshoe with two big suitcases. One was empty, but the other was bulging with cash. He wanted the cash counted down, and it came to $777,000. Quite a sum in cold cash. Then he wanted to bet this at the craps table. Which table? He'd wait and see, but wanted the money turned into casino chips, which it was—1,554 $500 chips. These were wheeled over to the craps pit. Binion's has a number of tables near the front of the casino, and although the limits are monstrous, most of the action that day was with $1 and $2 players, for they're welcomed as courteously in this casino as any high rollers.

At one of the tables near the front entrance, a new shooter was coming out, a middle-aged woman who had $1 on the pass line.

"That's the table," the gambler said, and as the chips approached, the boxman held up the game. The pit boss and Teddy Binion were there watching, and all the chips were theoretically *bet against the dice*. A button was put down signifying his bet. The dice were moved over to the woman, who shook them and rolled them across the table. A 7 or 11 and $777,000 was down the drain. But she rolled a 9. Nine was the point. I guess the gambler breathed easier. Then she rolled a 6. Then she sevened out, and he won $777,000.

The cash was stuffed into his empty suitcase. After all, you had to give the man credit for being optimistic. He was escorted to the airport by a security guard and went back to Texas. A true story.

But that's not the end of the story. Some years later, the same man was back with his two suitcases. Again he wanted to bet against the dice, and again he picked a table at random and had someone else shoot the dice. I'm sure the Binions would gladly have reserved a table for him, but he preferred it this way. Well, this time, the shooter made the point, and all his lovely cash was down the drain, as far as he was concerned. He seemed pretty stoic about it, so I heard, and then asked for a room in the hotel. The Horseshoe has a small hotel upstairs from the casino, and it resembles a nineteenth-century hotel in a Western state, with matching bedspreads and curtains, but with modern conveniences.

The man went up there and blew his brains out. A weird ending to a strange story.

I always wondered why he didn't hedge his bets. That is, bet half the money against the dice, and if a point was established, then decide what to do. For example, if the point was 9 or 5, or 4 or 10, he might let the money ride against the dice. Or use the rest and back up the initial bet at the correct odds. If the point was 6 or 8, he might then place the rest of the cash on the 6 or 8, whichever was the point, at 7–6, and if the point was made, he'd have a small profit. But he couldn't lose once he did this. With all that money you have a lot of options. But then again, as I think about all this, with all that money, why bother risking it on one roll of the dice?

When allowed ten times odds, it seems foolish to make any place numbers, but at the Horseshoe you can still see fools covering all the numbers at one time instead of making come bets. They're giving up a rather sweet deal to play craps the useless and losing way.

A great many people love the game of craps, and many of the locals, as residents of Nevada are called, play at the 25¢ tables. They can get in a lot of action for $20 or so, though it's painful to watch a hot roll taking place among these gamblers, where they win a couple of hundred dollars instead of a couple of hundred thousand. I've watched a shooter hold the dice at a downtown club for about an hour, and during that time the biggest bet at the table was $50.

Strange things can develop at the quarter tables, where the house pays off with 25¢ chips on place bets. A player can cover all the numbers except the point number by betting $6.50 if the point is 6 or 8, and $6.75 if the point is any other number.

A dealer told me of a scam they constantly face. A player rushes over to the table during a roll, or is watching the roll go on, when suddenly he shouts, "Six fifty on the numbers!" He does this just before the shooter is throwing the dice, and as he fumbles in his pocket for his wallet.

If the unsuspecting dealer says, "You're covered," while the gambler still hasn't produced any cash, then he has the casino by the throat. If the next roll is any of the place numbers other than the point, the shouter takes out $650 and gives it to the dealer, collecting on a $100 or $120 bet. If the next roll is a 7, a loser on the place number, he hands the dealer $6.50 as his losing wager.

Needless to say, this is a terrific scam if the dealer falls for it. However, the experienced dealers at the downtown clubs know about this and they simply say no bet. That's why, on the craps layout shown, the words "no call bets" are printed. They're in bold letters to safeguard the casino's bankroll against con artists.

Money Management

Money management is one of the key factors in winning at the craps table, and is tied up to self-control, since leaving a table at the correct time often makes the difference between being a winner or loser.

Money management can be divided into several parts, as follows:
- The total gambling bankroll of the player
- The bankroll necessary for one session of play
- Betting limits to be followed
- How much a player should lose at any gambling session
- How much a player should win at any gambling session

Total Bankroll

Most players don't reside in the same city where they do their gambling. They may be visiting the gambling resort for the day, for a few days, and in some instances for a week or more. If a gambler wants to play seriously, he must take along a sufficient bankroll to finance his game; otherwise he'll either have to play wildly, hoping for an immediate big win, or he'll play too cautiously, since he won't have enough to ride out temporary losses and take advantage of winning streaks.

Playing without sufficient capital is playing with scared money—the gambler is scared to increase his bets and scared to lose and thus get tapped out.

Before going any further in this discussion, let's make one point clear. We're not encouraging anyone to gamble. We recognize, however, that most people love to gamble, and we want them to gamble intelligently if they play for money, but our first thought is always this: *Never play with money you can't afford to lose.*

No one likes to lose money, of course, but playing with cash that should be used for necessities such as rent, food, and medical expenses, among other things, is inviting disaster. Unless you have money you can put aside for the tables and lose without heartbreak, you shouldn't gamble at all.

If you do have some money set aside, that money, that total bankroll, should determine your betting limits. If a person goes to Reno with $100 for a weekend's play of craps, it would be foolish to get into a $5 game and lose it all within fifteen minutes.

That leads to desperation, and you don't want to become desperate. Never. You want to be cool and levelheaded at all times, and the best way to do this, besides gambling intelligently, is to bet at a level that is comfortable for your bankroll so that a temporary loss doesn't tap you out before you even get started.

Remember, craps is a game of chance, and there's no guarantee that you'll win every time you are at the table, no matter how shrewdly you play. So you must have enough in reserves to take those temporary losses in stride.

What I suggest is that you count your total bankroll, divide that bankroll by ten, and then play at a table using no more than that amount (one-tenth) at any session. That gives you ten lives instead of one at the craps tables.

And believe me, I've seen a single session of gambling wipe players out; clean them out and send them home like beaten dogs, because they didn't follow the basic principles of money management. I personally knew a man who flew out to Las Vegas with $10,000, took a cab to the Dunes where he had reserved a room, and since there was a large crowd waiting to check in, this man went to a craps table to try his luck.

He laid that ten grand on the table, took handfuls of black $100 chips, and started betting heavily, covering all the place numbers and making other foolish bets. Within forty-five minutes he had lost every cent of that $10,000. He lost by bad bets, by increasing his bets after every loss, and, after a while, he lost it all by making desperation bets on the center layout. He tried to fight the dice, but the dice and the house edge proved stronger. He picked up his bags, walked outside alone to avoid tipping a bellman, and got into a cab. Within an hour he was on a flight to New York City with his chest burning and a miserable headache gripping his skull.

Don't let that happen to you. Don't be out of the casino after an hour, searching for your loose change, tapped out by heavy and foolish betting, trying to overcome bad luck. Learn money management and keep your self-control and composure at all times.

Single Session Bankroll

The bankroll necessary for a single session at the tables should be the total bankroll divided by ten. If you come to Las Vegas with $1,000, you should play with no more than $100 at any table.

Players who want to be a little more daring, can divide their bankroll by seven, but not less than that figure. With $1,000 as a total bankroll, that will leave approximately $150 for each gambling session.

Many players don't pay attention to money management and don't think of dividing their bankroll for best use. They come to the casino with $1,000, take out $500 in cash, and start playing. After they encounter a minor losing streak, they raise their bets to make up the small losses and instead find themselves behind the $500. So they pull out the rest of the cash and now make really big bets to get even in a hurry and leave the table a short time later, flat broke.

To be certain that never happens to you, divide your bankroll in the manner suggested. If you lose one-tenth or one-seventh of the bankroll, you still have plenty left for the next table, and luck doesn't go only one way in any game of chance. Playing intelligently and raising your bets with the casino's money when ahead will make any player a winner, but no one can play without money, and if a player has blown his wad, that's the end of the ball game for him.

Table Bankroll—Right Bettors

The tough, smart player who uses the strategy outlined earlier in this chapter is in a winning position. He's giving the house only a minimal advantage on any bet, and a short winning streak can bring him a lot of their cash. To make his bets correctly, he must go through a complete cycle of betting— one pass-line wager with double odds and then two come bets established, both with double odds.

Your bankroll for any one session should permit you to complete seven to ten cycles of betting. If you're betting $2 on the pass line and taking double odds, you will invest about $20 on a full cycle of betting. Therefore, you should have at least $140 with you at the table to withstand a run of bad luck.

To reverse the situation, if you bring $150 to the craps table, you'd be foolish to bet more than $2 on your pass-line bet and risk the chance of losing your bankroll quickly after a few runs of cold dice. If you're betting $5 and taking double odds, you're in danger of being tapped out before you can get a winning streak going or before that inevitable hot roll comes along.

This isn't to say that the player should expect to lose, but losses do occur and dice run cold, and the right bettor should be prepared for this situation.

A player betting with $5 chips at a double odds table will need approximately $100 for a complete cycle of pass line and two come bets. Therefore, he should have at least $700 with him at the table, insuring that he won't be wiped out by a run of bad luck. If a player needs $700 for a single session of play, his total bankroll should be at least $5,000, or seven times the single table bankroll.

And a player betting at a single odds table, if he's a $5 player betting $15 (three units) on the pass line and come bets, backing up all bets with maximum odds, will also need about $100 for one complete cycle, so the single and double odds table require the player to have approximately the same amount of cash available.

These figures may seem high to someone who hasn't had experience at the craps tables, but if you want a lot of action for a few days, you'll need reserves like those mentioned to overcome the times when you're going to encounter bad streaks at the tables.

Again, this is not to suggest that all you're going to do is lose your money. But having these reserves will enable you to be around when the hot rolls develop and will give you plenty of breathing space so that you can retain your self-control and not be forced to make wild and foolish bets in an attempt to recoup temporary losses.

Table Bankroll—Wrong Bettors

If you're betting wrong, you should bet at least $5 on don't pass in order to lay the $6 against the 6 and 8 at 6–5 odds. If you follow a complete cycle of don't pass $5 bets, laying single odds along with two don't come bets, also with single odds, you'll have bet approximately $40.

To have an adequate bankroll for utmost protection against temporary losses, you'd need at least $300 in reserves for each session of play.

A $10 bettor, following the same cycle, would need about $80 to complete each cycle of bets and therefore would have to have $550 in reserve for that single session of gambling. The total bankroll would be about seven to ten times the single-session bankroll, or between $3,800 and $5,500.

Many players are going to look at these figures and shake

their heads in dismay. They expect to come to the casino for a few days' play with a couple of hundred dollars in their pockets, perhaps five hundred at the most, and get involved in heavy action. But they can't have heavy action with that kind of bankroll.

What should they do then? They'll just have to play the minimum games. With $500 they can't really afford to bet more than $2 at a time on line bets, not if they expect to be around for a few days. With $200 a $1 game will be more their speed. Otherwise, they're tempting quick disaster, and they can be wiped out before they even get the free drink from the cocktail waitress.

This is not to put down people with limited bankrolls. I'm simply stating a fact of gambling from life; craps is a game where, in order to make money, a player has to get a lot of cash down on the layout, even before he makes one winning collection. If he doesn't do this, he won't be playing the game correctly, and he'll be severely restricting his chances of maximizing his profits.

The best way to play is the way suggested in this book, but those bets cost money, and sometimes a great deal of money will have to be bet before payoffs start. That's the player's investment in the game, and it's an investment, if made correctly, that will pay him dividends.

How Much Should a Player Lose at One Table?

The answer to this question is rather simple. You should never lose more than the single-session bankroll you have brought to the table, and this amount should never be more than one-seventh to one-tenth of your total bankroll for gambling purposes.

If you've lost your single-session bankroll, you should leave the table and not dig into your pockets for more cash. If you follow this rule consistently you'll be smarter than 95 percent of the gamblers at the craps tables. Bad cycles and streaks do occur, and when you're caught in the whiplash, don't fight it. Get away from the table. Get a cool drink or go back to your room, take a walk and refresh yourself. Do anything but reach for more cash to gamble that money away at the table. Remember, *the first loss is the cheapest.*

What if you're not completely busted? What if there are still a few chips left in your rail? Leave when those chips aren't sufficient to cover another cycle of betting. If you've been betting $10 on pass line and come bets with double odds, it will cost you about $100 to complete another cycle of bets. If you have less than that in the rails, it's time to go, because more money will have to come out of your pocket to finish the next cycle.

How Much Should a Player Win at One Table?

At last we come to the good news. Betting with our systems, there will be times when the money will be flowing into your rails, when you'll have doubled your original stake in no time at all.

Above all, the right bettor should remember this single rule: *Leave when the hot roll is over.*

Expect only one hot roll per session and leave the table when it has ended. Take your money and run just as soon as that shooter has sevened out, after holding the dice for a half hour or longer. That's really the best advice I can give a right bettor.

If there's been no single hot roll, but you've been winning steadily, try to double your original stake. If you can't seem to get this far ahead, put away your original stake plus fifty or sixty units, taking them from the rails and placing them into your pockets. Play with the rest of your chips. If you keep winning, keep playing and then remove another fifty or sixty chips again. Keep doing this until there are no more chips in the rails or there aren't enough for a complete betting cycle. Don't reach into your pockets for more chips once you've salted them away. These are to be considered untouchable until you're at the cashier's cage, exchanging them for cold cash, green and crisp.

If you're betting wrong and you're ahead, leave in the middle of a hot roll when all your bets have been removed from the layout by repeating numbers. Leave with some winnings intact, but make sure to leave.

If you're betting wrong and winning, try to double your money, then either leave or put away your original stake plus all the rest of your chips except for one cycle's worth. Play them out. If you lose, leave. If you win, stick around and keep putting chips into your pockets until there are no more chips on the rails or until you don't have enough chips remaining for a full cycle of betting.

But never, never reach into your pockets for chips, once they've been placed there from the rails. Simply leave the table and cash in, and you'll find yourself a constant winner.

To be a winner, you must leave a winner. Always leave while ahead, and you can never go wrong.

Tipping the Dealers

If a crew of dealers is friendly and helpful, I believe the players should tip, or toke, them, whether or not they're winning. Sometimes a word or two from a dealer can make the players a bit of money or save them from losing money. If a player has forgotten to take odds on his come bet or hasn't backed up his line bet to the limit, competent and aware dealers will make it their business to correct this oversight.

Sometimes in a hectic game, after a player has received a payoff on a come bet or some other wager, he may forget to pick up the chips and will leave them in the wrong betting area. A dealer who is alert will point out this mistake and can save the player a bit of grief.

In the heat of battle, in the middle of a hot game of craps when a player has a lot of bets working for him, it pays to have a dealer who's on his toes and who has the interests of the players in mind. Tipping keeps that interest at a high pitch, but I don't suggest toking a dealer unless he's competent and helpful. Hostile dealers don't deserve anything, no matter how much a player wins. Neither do greedy dealers who push for tokes. But when a dealer is doing his best, by all means make a few bets for him and for the crew.

The most common way players toke dealers is by making center proposition bets for them. A player might throw out some chips to the stickman and say, "All the hardways, one and one." This means that all the hardway bets are covered, with one chip bet for the player and one for the boys, which is the most common term used for a crew of dealers.

Some players also bet on the 11 or 12 for the boys; others bet on any craps for them. However, it would be wiser to make a bet that gives the crew a better chance of winning, such as a line or come bet. If I've been doing well at the table, I always make sure to make a line bet for them along with my own, and if a point number is thrown on the come-out roll, I back their bet with proper odds. The dealers appreciate this kind of bet, because they know they stand a very good chance of winning it.

Some dealers don't deserve to be tipped. Some are nasty, impolite, incompetent, and disinterested in the game, and it makes the gambling session an arduous one. Dealers such as these make the player feel as though they're doing him a favor by taking his bet. When I encounter this type of dealer, unless I'm in the middle of a favorable roll, I get away from the table and take my business elsewhere.

Some players tip dealers just to keep them on the safe side, especially if they're big bettors and big winners. They don't want to make enemies among the dealers, because all gambling wins should be reported to the IRS, and some dealers who have been stiffed by big winners can get downright mean. I had dinner one night in Vegas with a craps dealer from a Strip casino, and he mentioned, after a number of drinks, a story about a player who had been at his table some months before. The player had a fantastic winning streak, taking in over $50,000, and in the end he tipped the boys $25, one green chip.

"And I worked my ass off for the sonofabitch," the dealer told me, well into his cups. "I made him a lot of bread just reminding him to take his odds, and I told just how much he could take on those free odds. I made him a few thousand just by reminding him, and the Tom (his term for a stiff; i.e., Tom

Turkey) gave us $25, as though he was doing us the biggest favor in the world.''

The dealer laughed at the recollection and bent forward, whispering, ''He was on a junket and I made it my business to find out who he was. And I made sure Uncle Sam found out just how much he won.''

''And then what happened?''

I got a smirk as the answer to my question.

So my advice is this—when dealers treat you courteously, treat them right. Their pay is just a small part of their income, and they depend on their tokes for their livelihood.

Sometimes dealers are very pleasantly surprised by good tokes. There's a popular and well-known car dealer in Las Vegas who likes to take a fling at the tables now and then. One night he went on a fantastic shoot at a Strip casino and took in almost $100,000. When he left the table, he hadn't toked the boys a red cent, but he did give all the dealers his business card and asked them to call him the next day.

The dealers expected a free simonize job, an oil change, or at best, a new set of tires. When they called, he had them all come down to his showroom and waved his arm around the room. ''Boys, pick out any car you see. It's yours.'' So the four dealers ended up with the most expensive sports cars they could drive out of his place.

What should you tip dealers? Some dealers think they should get 10 percent of the player's wins, but of course, that's crazy. Only the most drunken Georges do that, George being a term among craps dealers in Vegas designating a really good toker.

I would think that an occasional bet of $5 would be sufficient, if you're betting up to $25 on your line bets. If you're a very big winner, a couple of line bets and some come bets with odds while a hot roll is going on is more than sufficient. But there's no direct formula. If the dealer is helping you and his helpfulness has enabled you to avoid mistakes, tip him generously. If he's just there like a mute statue, doing his job but not doing any more than he's supposed to, tip him less. But tip the boys; they want you to win, and they'll do a little extra to make sure you come out ahead. If you're fumbling with the chips, the stickman may wait for you to make all your bets before relinquishing the dice. That can often make the difference between winning and losing.

It's not customary to tip the boxman or floormen. A boxman who's helped you in a dispute with a dealer can be thanked, however, for it never hurts to be courteous.

I wouldn't offer money to a boxman or a floorman, for some of them would feel insulted if you proffer them a tip, but should you be staying for a few days on a junket, it might be nice to remember them with a small gift, perhaps a box of cigars, a shirt or something like that. It's not mandatory, but it will be appreciated.

Gifts are rarely given to casino executives, but if a player has been dealt with generously and courteously, there is no harm in giving them a small token of your appreciation. When you return on your next visit to that casino, you'll be treated with all due care and courtesy.

Handling Hostile Casino Personnel

Not all boxmen are men of character and sterling qualities. Many of them are hard-bitten and mean. They sit dourly at the table, sneer, and take secret delight in the losses the players suffer. Unlike the dealers, they don't get tokes, so if the players win, all they get out of it is a trip to the pit boss to explain away the loss at their craps table.

Most boxmen don't like their jobs. Many are older men who have nowhere to go in the casino. They sit all day at the tables, watching dice fly across the layout, watching money and chips change hands till their eyes get blurry and their brains get razzled. I pay little attention to boxmen, unless they're super-friendly, which is not often, or unless they're rude and annoying, which is the case more often than not.

If a player is having a hot shoot, the boxman often makes it his business to interfere by continually examining the dice and slowing up the game any way he can. Or he may annoy the player shooting the dice by suggesting that he throw them in a different manner.

Some years back I was playing craps with a client at a Strip hotel-casino, showing him the fine points of the game. I had been standing at the table but not betting, and my friend, when it was his turn to throw the dice, quickly sevened out. I was about to pass up the dice when he suggested that I throw them for luck.

. He made a substantial line bet for me, and I shook the dice, then threw them in my own fashion, which is to fling them high and watch them bounce off the far wall after coming down from a height of three or four feet above the table.

The first three numbers I rolled were craps, which lost money for my friend. Then I got a really hot hand. Once I got started the numbers poured out of the dice. The boxman interrupted my shoot by telling me to alter my throw. I protested, saying I was hitting the back wall, and the roll was therefore perfectly legitimate.

He continued to badger me even though I modified my toss. Then I asked him what he expected me to do. He told me to shake them and fling them out.

I responded by flinging them with force across the table, so that one flew over his head, missing him by inches.

"Like that?" I asked.

He gave me a dirty look.

The next throw missed him by much less space.

"I'll have you thrown out of here," the boxman said to me. He was a pudgy man in his fifties with a face that hadn't crinkled or broken out in a smile for the last thirty years.

"Stand up," I said. "I want to see you do this personally."

The pit boss was called by a dealer, and the pit boss asked me to throw the dice the right way.

I flung them the original way, both hitting the back wall.

"Is that okay?" I asked.

"Sure. Now take it easy."

So I went back to my old tosses and the numbers kept hitting, and the boxman kept scowling. After this hot shoot we left the table. My friend suggested I complain about the boxman's behavior.

"To whom?" I asked. "That's the kind of boxmen these places often have. They think the players are all suckers, all losers, just dirt. The name of the game here is greed, not craps."

Other boxmen slow the game up so much that players get disgusted and angry and alter their bets, trying to hurt the house. Instead, they get hurt. My advice is, if you're having a favorable roll, stay to its end, as long as you're winning. Don't let these inadequate people bother you, but if they do, then get away from the table. There's enough pressure in gambling without the added burden of dealing with angry and discourteous casino personnel.

Bad News and a Good Job

I've been around gambling casinos and craps tables for more years than I care to remember. I've seen some hot shoots that made men hundreds of thousands of dollars, and cold tables that would freeze anything in sight. In the end, it's not only a matter of luck, but a matter of preserving your capital so that when that hot roll comes and the dice go your way, you have sufficient cash to back up your play to the hilt.

Once, going through a Strip hotel, I saw a dealer I had been instrumental in getting a job for at a smaller Strip hotel. He was living with a woman friend of mine, and she had a small kid and asked me if I could help him. I knew a number of casino bosses and presidents of hotels, and went to one, introduced this man, who I'll call Jake, to the president of the casino. The president owed me a few favors and agreed to have Jake audition as a craps dealer. The audition went well. By audition, I mean just what the word implies. It's not the same as trying out for a part in a Broadway play, but there is the same result if you succeed. You get the job.

Jake was allowed to become a dealer on a crew for an evening, and his work was examined by the pit boss. Jake had been dealing at a small casino downtown, then lost the job, or so he claimed, to politics going on in the craps pit. And I liked the woman he was living with and knew what kind of struggle she had had just to bring up the little girl. So I was happy he got the job. The casino had some high rollers, and the tokes were good here, and sometimes extraordinary, if a rich local guy got a hold of hot dice and made his hundred thousand or more.

I hadn't seen Jake for several months when I was strolling through the casino that evening on the way to a dinner date. He was standing at a craps table, waiting for the dice to swing over to him after the previous shooter had sevened out. I went over and tapped him on the shoulder.

"Hey, Ed," he said, "whatcha doing here?"

"Going to dinner. How about you?"

"Shooting some dice."

It was a different casino than the one he worked in, and he told me things were going well at the job and he had been making some really good money. And tonight he had a plan. As he spoke, the stickman said, "New shooter coming out," and moved the tray of dice over to Jake. He selected two and rubbed them on the surface of the layout.

"You haven't made a line bet," the dealer said, watching Jake's action.

"No problem," Jake said. And then he took a roll of bills out of the inside pocket of his jacket and dropped them on the layout. The roll was thick, larded with hundreds, fifties, and twenties. The dealer moved the money over to the boxman, who counted and recounted them, and then looked up at Jake with narrowed eyes before giving him the count.

"There's thirty-two hundred here."

"Right," Jake said.

"How do you want them?" the dealer asked, picking up a stack of black $100 chips.

"Across the board. Five hundred on all the numbers and six hundred on the 6 and 8. That's thirty-two hundred, right?"

"That is correct," the dealer said.

Jake then took a five dollar bill out of his pocket and placed it on the pass line.

"And that's my pass-line bet." Then he said to the dealer, "All numbers working on the come-out."

"All numbers working," the dealer said, loudly enough for

the boxman to hear. Now Jake received the attention of a couple of floormen and the pit boss, who was watching the action.

"Here's how I work this," Jake said as the chips were being placed on the numbers. "One roll of any number and I collect $700. I go for two numbers, make my $1,400, and leave. Sweet deal, huh?"

"What if a seven comes up. It's all lost."

"I know. But I've been dealing nights, and this guy keeps doing it. He shoots for one number, sometimes two. Small stuff. Fifty on the numbers, sixty on the 6 and 8. Never missed yet."

"You done it?" I asked.

"First time. Stick around, Ed, you been lucky for me so far."

Against my better judgment I stuck near him. He picked up the dice and flung them to the end of the table. One landed on a random chip, showing a 5, and the other spun around and then stopped.

"Seven, winner," the stickman said, and quick as a wink the $3,200 in chips were erased from the layout. Jake was paid $5 for his winning pass-line wager.

He picked up the two $5 chips and stuffed them into his jacket pocket. His normally ruddy face had gone gray. "Easy come, easy go," he said, trying to smile it off, but I knew that had been a big dent, maybe his entire bankroll. A crazy system. The odds were too much against him—he was giving away too much on the place numbers, hoping against hope that the 7 wouldn't show.

Normally the come-out roll is an "off" roll for the place numbers. That's so the right bettors don't have their place numbers lose while their pass-line bet wins. However, it can be on if the player wants it that way. And that's what Jake wanted.

I ran into Jake a few months later, downtown. He was dealing at a cheap club, dealing craps to 25¢ bettors. I asked what had happened at the Strip club.

"Politics," he said, forgetting that he had already told me that song and dance. I asked about my woman friend.

"Couldn't stand the kid. It was bad news."

I should have told him to look at himself in the mirror if he wanted to see what bad news was.

Craps Etiquette and Miscellany

• When first coming to a table, if you bring cash, don't hand it to the dealer. Put it on the layout, and he'll pick it up and give it to the boxman.

• If you want to make a quick bet while getting your cash converted to casino chips, tell the dealer the bet you want placed. He'll tell you you're on—it's the only call bet most casinos will permit. The dealer will make the bet for you, then deduct that sum from your cashed chips.

• You must make all line and come bets by yourself, placing the chips down in the appropriate area of the layout. After a point is established, you must make your own odds bets on line bets.

• After a come bet is established, you can put down additional chips for odds wagers. Place them in the come box, but don't hand them to the dealer. Don't hand anything to the dealer, because the rules of most casinos forbid actual touching or exchanging of chips hand to hand with casino personnel.

• If you want to make place bets, put the chips down on the layout within easy reach of the dealer and tell him what numbers you want covered and in what amounts. He'll make them for you.

• When the dealer pays you off, he'll put chips down on the layout as your payoff. It's your responsibility to pick them up before the next roll of the dice, or they may be deemed a bet you didn't want to make.

• If you're betting systematically, making two come bets with odds after a line bet, after a while you don't have to tell a competent dealer what to do. He'll automatically be placing the chips in the correct betting areas for you, accepting the odds bets, and putting them in the right places.

• After you make a bet, pick your hands up. *Keep your hands off the table when the dice are rolling.*

• When you roll the dice, make sure you hit the far wall of the table; otherwise you'll infuriate the boxman.

• If you smoke, make sure that you don't drop ashes on the layout. The dealers and boxmen will get very annoyed by this.

• Keep your eyes on your rails, watching and protecting your chips at all times. They're your responsibility.

• Also keep an eye on all your bets and make sure the dealer has made the proper ones for you. If he didn't, you'll bear the loss, should you not catch the mistake in time.

• You can yell and scream all you want at a craps table. No one cares, not even the dice, which may or may not heed your calls.

• The casino will provide free drinks while at the table, but don't drink alcohol if it dulls your senses or loosens your inhibitions. You're expected to toke the cocktail waitress who brings the drink.

• If no cocktail waitress is around, ask the dealer to have one sent over. He'll immediately accommodate your request.

• Treat the dealers like human beings. They're generally doing their best. Toke them whether you win or lose, if they've been helpful and courteous.

The Casino's Advantage on Craps Bets

Bet	Casino Pays	Casino Advantage (%)
Pass line	Even money	1.41
Pass line and single odds	Even money and odds	0.84
Pass line and double odds	Even money and odds	0.60
Don't pass	Even money	1.40
Don't pass and single odds	Even money and odds	0.83
Don't pass and double odds	Even money and odds	0.59
Come	Even money	1.41
Come and single odds	Even money and odds	0.84
Come and double odds	Even money and odds	0.60

Bet	Casino Pays	Casino Advantage (%)
Don't come	Even money	1.40
Don't come and single odds	Even money and odds	0.83
Don't come and double odds	Even money and odds	0.60
Place bet on 4 or 10	9–5	6.67
Place bet on 5 or 9	7–5	4.0
Place bet on 6 or 8	7–6	1.52
Buy the 4 or 10	2–1 (5% commission)	4.76
Lay bet vs. 4 or 10	1–2 (–5% commission)	2.44
Lay bet vs. 5 or 9	2–3 (–5% commission)	3.23
Lay bet vs. 6 or 8	5–6 (–5% commission)	4.0
Field bet (2–1 paid on both 2 and 12)	Even money or 2–1	5.55
Field bet (3-1 paid on either 2 or 12)	Even money or 2–1, 3–1	2.70
Big 6 and big 8	Even money	9.09
Any seven	4–1	16.67
Any craps	7–1	11.10
2 or 12	30–1	13.89
	30 for 1	16.67
3 or 11	15–1	11.10
	15 for 1	16.67
Hardway 4 or 10	7–1	11.10
Hardway 6 or 8	9–1	9.09
Hop bet	30–1	13.89
	30 for 1	16.67

Glossary of Craps Terms

The following is a large selection of terms commonly used in the casino craps game; knowing them will help a player better understand the terminology of the game.

Advantage, Casino Advantage. See *Edge*

Any Craps. A one-roll bet that the next throw of the dice will come up 2, 3, or 12.

Any Seven. A one-roll wager that the next throw of the dice will be a 7.

Back-Line. A bet on don't pass.

Bar the 12. A term shown on the craps layout, both in the don't pass and don't come betting areas, which bars the 12 as a winning bet for wrong bettors. In some casinos the 2 is barred instead of the 12.

Betting Right. Betting that the dice will pass or win.

Betting Wrong. Wagering that the dice will not pass, or lose; betting against the dice.

Big 6 and big 8. A bet, paying even money, that the 6 and/or 8 will come up on the dice before a 7 is rolled.

Boxman. A casino executive who supervises the craps table from a seated position between two standing dealers.

Bring Out. A term used by the stickman exhorting players to make certain bets in order to have the point come up on the dice. "Bet the hard six; bring it out."

Buck. See *Disk*

Buy the 4 and 10. Paying a 5 percent commission to the house in order to have the place numbers 4 and 10 pay off at correct odds of 2–1.

Casino Checks. The casino's term for chips issued by the house.

Change Color. To change casino chips into larger or smaller denominations. This is done by a standing dealer.

Chips. The common term for the tokens issued by the casino in place of money and having the equivalent value of cash, according to the denominations of the chips.

Cold Dice. Dice that aren't passing.

Come Bet. Betting that the dice will pass after the come-out roll.

Come Box. The area on the layout where come bets are made.

Come-Out Roll. The initial or first roll of the dice before a point has been established.

Craps. The term for a 2, 3, or 12 being rolled.

Craps Out. Throwing a craps number on the come-out roll.

Crew. The four dealers who staff a craps table.

Dealer. A casino employee who helps operate a craps table by dealing either directly with the players or by handling the stick and calling the game.

Dice. A pair of cubes, each with six sides and each numbered with from 1 to 6 dots, whose combinations, when thrown, determine the wins and losses in the game of craps.

Die. A single cube; singular of dice.

Disk. A round plastic object which is black on one side and white on the other. When on the white side and in a place box number, it designates that a shoot is in progress and that that number is the point.

Don't Come Bet. A bet made after the come-out roll that the dice will lose or won't pass.

Don't Come Box. The area on the layout where a don't come bet is made.

Don't Pass Bet. A bet made on the come-out roll that the dice will lose or won't pass.

Don't Pass Line. The area on the craps layout where a don't pass bet is made.

Double Odds Bet. A free odds bet made at double the original bet on a line, come, or don't come wager.

Easy, Easy Way. The roll of a 4, 6, 8, or 10 where the dice

are not matched as a pair. For example, a 5 and 1 is an easy six.

Edge. The advantage, usually expressed as a percentage, that a casino has over the player on a particular bet.

Even-Money. A payoff at 1–1.

Field Bet. A bet that the next roll of the dice will come up 2, 3, 4, 9, 10, 11, or 12.

Floorman. Casino executive who stands behind the craps table, overseeing the game and watching the play of junket members. He also determines whether credit should be given to a player.

Free Odds. A bet made in addition to a line, come, or don't come bet at correct odds. The house has no advantage on this bet.

Front Line. Another name for the pass line.

George. A dealer's term for a generous tipper.

Hardway. The term for 2–2, 3–3, 4–4, and 5–5 pairs of dice.

Hardway Bet. A wager that the dice will come up as a pair on any of the following numbers—4, 6, 8, and 10, before they come up easy or before a 7 is rolled.

Hop Bet. A one-roll wager on any number the player selects, at disadvantageous odds to the gambler.

Horn Bet. A combined one-roll bet on the 2, 3, 11, and 12.

Hot Hand. A shooter who is continually making points and numbers while rolling the dice is said to have a hot hand.

Hot Roll. A roll in which the dice are continually passing and are held by the shooter for a long period of time.

Inside Numbers. The place numbers 5, 6, 8, and 9.

Layout. The imprint on the felt surface of a craps table, showing all the bets that can be made with spaces for those bets outlined.

Lay the Odds. An odds bet by a wrong bettor against a number, which, if won, will be paid off at less than even money.

Lay Wager. A place bet by a wrong bettor, who pays a 5 percent commission in order to make this bet.

Miss, Miss Out. Another term for sevening out.

Natural. A term for a 7 or 11 being thrown on the come-out roll.

Nickels. An insider's term for $5 chips at a casino.

Numbers. The term for the 4, 5, 6, 8, 9, and 10.

Odds Bets. See *Free Odds*

Off. An oral call by a player that certain of his bets will not be working on the next roll of the dice, such as place wagers. Also a term signifying that certain bets on the layout will not be working on a come-out roll, such as place bets and odds bets on come numbers.

On Base. The term for the standing dealer who is not a stickman.

One-Roll Bets. Wagers whose outcome is determined by the very next roll of the dice.

On the Stick. The term to indicate that a dealer is a stickman.

Outside Numbers. The 4, 5, 9, and 10 as place numbers.

Pass. A winning decision for the dice.

Pass Line. The area on the layout where a pass-line bet is made.

Pass-Line Bet. A wager that the dice will pass, or win.

Payoff. The paying out of a winning bet to a player.

Pit Boss. A casino employee who is in charge of all the craps tables in one area of the casino, known as the craps pit.

Place Numbers, Place Bets. A wager on the 4, 5, 6, 8, 9, or

10, either combined or separately, that these numbers will repeat before a 7 shows on the dice. This bet is made in the place-box area of the layout.

Player. Another term for gambler or bettor.

Press, Press a Bet. Raising a previous bet, usually by doubling it.

Proposition Bets. The bets that can be made in the center of the layout.

Quarters. An insider's term for $25 chips.

Rails. The grooved area at the craps table where players keep their chips when not betting them.

Right Bettor. A player betting with the dice, wagering that they'll pass.

Roll. A single throw of the dice. Also, a complete series of rolls until the shooter sevens out.

Scared Money. Insufficient cash to gamble with.

Seven out. The roll of a 7 after a point is established, ending the shooter's roll.

Shoot. A complete series of rolls until the shooter sevens out.

Shooter. The player who rolls the dice.

Stickman. The dealer who calls the game and handles the stick during a craps game.

Taken Down. A bet that is removed and returned to the player, either at his request or by the rules of the game.

Take the Odds. An odds bet made by a right bettor, which, if won, will be paid off at better than even money.

Tip. See *Toke*

Toke. The dealer's term for a gratuity or tip.

Tom. The dealer's term for a poor tipper.

Working. A designation that bets are on and alive and thus that payoffs will be made or losing bets collected as a result of the dice's roll.

Wrong Bettor. A player who bets against the dice; one who bets that the dice won't pass.

7

Roulette—
The Quiet Game

Roulette is primarily a European game with a huge following on the Continent and in Great Britain. For centuries it has been *the* gambling game at places like Monte Carlo and at other elegant casinos. In the United States, though played in practically every legitimate gambling house of major size, its popularity has been nil.

This lack of interest in American roulette can easily be explained. The major reason is the American roulette wheel, which has, in addition to the thirty-six standard numbers (1–36) not one zero, as on the European wheel, but two.

Two zeros raise the house advantage to 5.26 percent on practically all bets but one, and that other bet, a five-number wager, gives the house better than a 7 percent edge over the player.

There may be other reasons for the unpopularity of the game in America. Americans are fascinated by two things—speed and numbers—and they get these in two very American games, craps and blackjack. Certainly the game of craps as played in a casino is the fastest of all gambling games and the one in which the most money can be won in the shortest period of time.

And while there may be numbers all over the roulette layout, they are, in essence, dead numbers, whereas in blackjack every card number is crucial, ratios and point counts abound, and, above all, it is a game in which at times the player has an advantage over the casino.

Of the four major table games (which include craps, blackjack, and baccarat), roulette offers the poorest odds to the gambler. In blackjack, players are even with the house at the outset and sometimes have an advantage over the casino if they know what they're doing; in craps they buck less than a 1 percent advantage by the casino if they make correct bets; and in baccarat, which is a static and controlled game in which odds and play remain rigid, the house has no more than a 1.36 percent advantage.

It is no wonder then that of all these games, roulette gets the least play. Many times I've passed the one or two roulette wheels at major casinos in Nevada and watched the croupier or dealer (as he is called in America) idly spinning the wheel or standing at an empty table with his arms crossed over his chest, waiting for some players to appear.

Other times, he may be occupied with a few gamblers, who are making minimum 25¢ or $1 bets on the layout. It is rare to see the roulette table pulsing with action. Occasionally, a group of Europeans, familiar with no other game, find their way to the roulette table and give it real action.

And sometimes a stray systems player wanders over with a surefire system for beating the wheel and plays it heavily for a while. Generally, in this situation, the action is small till the system goes haywire, and then the bets increase with rapidity, and usually the systems player staggers away, poorer but not necessarily wiser.

This discussion of roulette will cover not only the game as played in Nevada and Atlantic City, but the European game as well, including the terms used in that game, so that readers can play it as intelligently as possible whenever they find themselves in a foreign casino.

Roulette is, above all, a leisurely game, a game that can be played while seated, a game in which the spin of the wheel seems to take forever, in which much time is spent between resolutions of play. It can be a very quiet game, for there is little to root for openly. Most players, unless they're betting on the even-money chances, have so many chips spread all over the layout that it's impossible for them to remember exactly what numbers they've bet on. Most wagers are random or hunch bets, because the game is a purely random one.

Winston Churchill was once asked how he fared at the roulette wheels at Monte Carlo, for he spent much time on the French Riviera. He replied that he had done poorly. When asked why, he responded, "If only I had bet red instead of black."

Of course, that's how most gamblers at roulette feel after a loss. If only . . . if only they had bet high instead of low, odd instead of even, the second column instead of the first, and so on, but probably, if they had bet the other way, the results would have been the same. The roulette wheel, though kind to a very few, has been a great leveler and has separated many from their fortunes.

Differences Between American and European Wheels and Games

The major difference between the American wheel and the European is that the American, standard in practically all casinos in Nevada and Atlantic City, has two zeros, while the European has one.

This difference changes the game radically in terms of casino advantage. When two zeros are used, the casino edge is 5.26 percent on nearly all bets. When one zero is used, the house advantage drops by almost half, to 2.70 percent.

In some Nevada casinos a single-zero roulette wheel may be found, but I've never heard of a European wheel that has two zeros.

The American wheel is rather a simple affair, just a wheel and a relatively small layout showing all the possible bets and numbers, printed in English. It is usually staffed by one dealer, who spins the wheel, collects all losing bets, pays off winning wagers, and handles the changing of cash into chips.

When the game gets crowded, sometimes another dealer is called to the table to assist the original one, but this occurs infrequently. Even at a crowded and busy table, one dealer can handle all the action.

The American game is played by hand. Change is given in

stacks of chips shoved by the dealer to the player. If a player wins, he is paid with stacks of chips delivered or pushed by hand. The dealer wipes off the table by hand, gathering in the losing chips with both hands and quickly stacking them up according to color.

When even moderately busy, the average American wheel can get about 90 plays per hour with one dealer present. If two dealers are used, one primarily as a cashier, then 120 spins an hour is the rule.

All calls are in English, and basically the only call will be the number the ball has landed on. If it landed on 18, the dealer will merely say "18" without designating that it is also a black number, even and low. After the number is called, a marker, usually a plastic tube with dice inside, is placed on the winning number.

The American dealer is rarely called upon to aid the players at the table in making bets, because the layout is so small and everyone has access to almost all betting areas. The game is thus played in silence, and it seems as if there is little communication between the dealer and the players, certainly much less than occurs at other standard American table games.

On the other hand, the European game is played with what is known as a French roulette wheel. In England this same wheel may be used, or an American wheel may be in play, adjusted so that there is one zero on the wheel.

Instead of one dealer, a whole group of croupiers staff a table. The layouts are longer and the bets tend to be more complicated, all in French, including those made in many English casinos, which employ French croupiers and use French to give the game an aura of Continental mystery.

I remember my first visit many years ago to a club in London, on the Queensway. I strolled in, looked around the casino, then went over to the roulette table, and changed some pounds into chips. I made a few bets, then tried to make a corner bet that I couldn't reach. I handed the chips to the nearby croupier and instructed him in English. He looked at me as though I were speaking Hindustani and he made no effort to place the bet.

Finally, someone nearby told me the French expression for

the kind of bet I wished to make was called a *carré*. Thereafter, I tried to remember my high school French when betting on numbers, and in no time at all, from the other players and from my own simple knowledge of the French language, I was able to make all the bets I wished to.

Today, players won't have that kind of trouble. Many of the English casinos have lost their snobbishness and cater to Americans, so no real knowledge of French is required.

While American casinos wisely give different colored chips to each player, so that no two players have the same kind of chip, the European game is played with standard casino chips, all of the same color except for different denominations, and this can create problems.

In Monte Carlo, playing roulette one summer evening at a crowded table, I found myself continually getting into an argument with a wizened old woman who claimed that my winning bets were in fact hers. After a half hour of this I left the table, since the croupiers, knowing her as an old customer and not knowing me at all, were indifferent to the situation. If different colored chips had been used, the difficulty would never have occurred. In American casinos the colored chips stand for the basic minimum denomination of the game unless players want to put a higher value on their chips, in which case that color will be put on the flat edge of the wheel with a button or casino chip designating its value.

The European game, much slower than the American game, features many flourishes by the dealers, particularly when paying off winning bets, which is done not with stacks of chips, but by "running them out" across the table. And the dealers use a rake rather than their hands to move the chips, hence the expression "raking in the chips."

Even the mere changing of cash into chips is an elaborate process, and at a crowded table no more than thirty spins an hour can be expected. When the table is fairly empty with little action, the European wheel will get perhaps fifty spins an hour.

The nomenclature of roulette, which is a French game after all, is in French throughout the Continent, and in another section of this chapter is a glossary defining those terms.

Roulette Rules—Basic Differences

In Nevada, where two zeros are used, the house advantage is 5.26 percent. If a gambler wagers on any other bet but the 0 and 00, if either of those numbers comes up, all the other bets on the layout lose automatically.

When one zero is used, the house advantage is reduced to 2.70 percent. But the Nevada casinos that use one-zero roulette wheels are few and far between, and these casinos usually require a $5 minimum bet on their layout.

In Atlantic City, where two zeros are used, if the ball should land in either the 0 or 00 pocket, then only *half the bet* is lost, or surrendered, if the player had bet on any of the even-money outside wagers (red-black, high-low, odd-even). Or the bet may be held for another spin. If the bet wins, it is returned to the player intact. This is the *en prison* rule.

In the European and English casinos there is one zero only, giving the house a 2.70 percent advantage. However, there is also the *en prison* rule, which allows gamblers, at their option, to give up either half their bet if the 0 has been landed on while they had a bet on the even-money outside wagers, or to leave their bet intact and let it ride one more time. If the bet wins on this subsequent spin, they can remove it intact.

When the *en prison* rule is in force, the house advantage in European roulette is reduced to 1.352 percent, a substantial reduction from the 5.26 percent in most American casinos. This low advantage is why roulette is so popular in Europe and why countless thousands have been searching for centuries for the perfect system to beat the game.

Roulette Layout and Bets

The following layout is the standard one found in American casinos. Next to the layout is the wheel with its 36 numbers plus 0 and 00.

Each number is in its individual pocket, separated by metal from its neighboring numbers. A small white plastic ball is

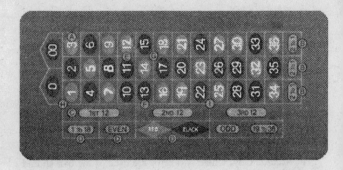

rolled around the outside rim of the wheel in the opposite direction from the wheel's spin. When the ball loses velocity, it eventually lands in one of the metal pockets, determining the winning number.

Each letter, from A to I, shows the various kinds of bets that may be made on the layout. The bets are divided into two groups—straight bets and combination bets.

Straight Bets

Letter	Odds	Position
A	35–1	Straight up

The letter A is in number 3, and this is known as a straight-up bet, a wager on a single number. The payoff for a straight-up bet is 35–1. The correct payoff should be 37–1, because there are 38 numbers all together, if we count the 0 and 00. Therefore the house has an advantage over the player of 5.26 percent on this and all subsequent bets to be described, with one exception, the five numbers bet.

A straight-up wager may be made on any of the numbers marked from 1 to 36, and also may be made on 0 and 00, which are considered numbers for straight-up bets. If a wager is made on either 0 or 00, it is also paid off at 35–1.

Letter	Odds	Position
B	2–1	Column

There are three B letters showing on the layout, all at the head of the table and each covering an individual column of numbers. A column wager is on all the numbers in that particular column. If wagering on the first column, players have the following numbers working for them: 1, 4, 7, 10, 13, 16, 19, 22, 25, 28, 31, 34. The house pays off this bet at 2–1.

The 0 and 00 are never included in any column bet and should the ball fall into the pocket containing either a 0 or 00, the column wager becomes a losing bet.

Letter	Odds	Position
C	2–1	1st dozen

This is an outside bet, payable at 2–1, since each dozen bet covers, as its name implies, twelve numbers. The 0 and 00 are never included in dozen bets, and should the ball land in 0 or 00, the dozen bet loses.

Letter	Odds	Position
D	1–1	Red or black
	(Even money)	High or low
		Odd or even

The heart of most roulette systems concern these outside wagers, which are paid off at even money. In the Atlantic City and European game, if the ball lands on 0 or 00, players lose only half their bet, or the bet is imprisoned for another spin. But in Nevada casinos all these even-money wagers are completely lost if the ball lands in 0 or 00.

Combination Bets

Letter	Odds	Position
E	17–1	Split

A player placing a chip on the line separating two adjacent numbers is wagering on both numbers at one time. For example, the letter E is between the 11 and 12, and therefore, if either number comes up on the next spin of the wheel, the bettor would be paid off at 17–1.

A chip can be placed between any two numbers as a split bet, including the line separating 0 and 00. For the convenience of bettors at the other side of the table, chips may be placed on the line separating the second and third dozens, and this is considered a split bet on 0 and 00.

Letter	Odds	Position
F	11–1	Trio

By placing bets on the boundary line between the numbers (inside position) and the dozens (outside position), players are able to make bets on three numbers at one time. Here the letter F covers 13, 14, and 15. In the same manner, 1, 2, and 3 could be covered, or 4, 5, and 6, and so on. When seated at a roulette table, players on the other side can bet on trios in the same manner. They could place chips on the outside line on 15 and have the same trio bet as shown in the illustration.

Letter	Odds	Position
G	8–1	Corner

When bettors decide to wager on four numbers at one time, they make a corner bet, placing chips at the point where all four numbers they are betting on converge. In the case illustrated, the chip G covers 14, 15, 17, and 18 at one time, and is paid off at 8–1. Corner bets can be made at any point on the layout where four numbers meet. For example, 1, 2, 4, and 5 could be a corner bet, as well as 32, 33, 35, and 36.

Letter	Odds	Position
H	6–1	Five numbers

This is the poorest of all bets the roulette layout offers in the American game, since the odds against the player are prohibitive at 7.89 percent. By making this wager, the player is covering the numbers 0, 00, 1, 2, and 3. This is the only five-numbers bet allowed on the layout and should never be made.

Letter	Odds	Position
I	5–1	Six numbers

When a chip is placed directly on the line separating six numbers, at the outside boundary of the numbers, it is considered a six-numbers bet and will be paid off at 5–1.

The bet can be made from the other side of the table as

well, and in this case, to cover the same numbers as in the illustration, the chip would be placed on the outside line separating 24 and 27. With this bet, 22, 23, 24, 25, 26, and 27 are all covered. Should any of these numbers come up on the next spin of the wheel, the player would be paid off at 5–1.

The European Game—French Terms

In the European game, as mentioned before, the dealers have more style and flourish than those handling the American game. When a croupier announces the number that just came up on the wheel, he also states whether red, black, odd, even, high, or low won. After the ball has landed in the 3 pocket, for example, the announcement would be "trois, rouge, impair, manque" meaning "3, red, odd, low."

The following are some basic terms in roulette:

English	*French*
Red	Rouge
Black	Noir
Odd	Impair
Even	Pair
Low	Manque
High	Passe
Straight up	En plein
Split bet	À cheval
Trio	Transversale
Corner	Carré
First four numbers	Quatre premiers
Six numbers	Sixain
Dozen	Douzaine
First	Première
Middle or second (as dozen)	Moyenne (deuxième)
Last (or third)	Dernière
Column	Colonne

In addition to the above expressions, players should familiarize themselves with the French equivalents of the numbers 1 to 36.

Betting Limits
and Money Management

There's not only a chip minimum value but a minimum betting limit as well at every roulette table. In other words, the cheapest chip may have a value of 25¢, but the minimum bet required using those chips may be $2. These limits are determined by the location of the casino and the type of players the club attracts. A Strip casino will generally have higher limits than one in downtown Reno or downtown Las Vegas.

At one time the standard chip was a 10¢ one, with a 50¢ minimum bet required. Today the minimum chip is usually valued at 25¢, and in some of the more ornate clubs it may be as high as 50¢ or $1.

When 25¢ chips are used, the minimum that can be bet is usually $1 or $2 on the inside numbers. This doesn't mean that players must bet that amount on one number. For instance, if the minimum is $1, they must have at least four 25¢ chips on the inside bets. More and more casinos that require 25¢ minimum chips also demand that the minimum bet on any number is $1 and that all even-money outside wagers be at least $2. As an example, players who wager on high and red must bet $2 on each choice.

Casinos are constantly raising the chip values and minimum limits to upgrade their roulette games, but they'd be better off upgrading it by offering roulette as the European game is played, with one zero only and the *en prison* rule. In this way, they'd attract more action and a whole multitude of players that have avoided American roulette because of the poor odds involved.

Since the outside bets, which include the even-money choices (red-black, high-low, even-odd) and the dozen and column bets at 2–1, have much lower ratio payoffs than the inside bets, the house maximum limit on these choices is much less than on the inside numbers. To avoid huge losses, most casinos set a house limit of $500 on even-money bets, but only $250 on the 2–1 dozens and columns bets.

As for the inside wagers, most casinos set a limit of $25 to $50 on these bets. Some casinos will offer lower maximum limits and others will offer a higher maximum, but not by much, because the casino doesn't want to get burned by paying off one monster bet at 35–1. They prefer to grind out the roulette players with their big edge.

Right now the biggest roulette game in America is held in Atlantic City, where $5 is the minimum inside or outside wager allowed at one time, though this bet can be spread out among various numbers. On the even-money bets, $1,000 is the maximum wager permitted; on the 2–1 bets, the maximum is $500. Any inside number can be played for a maximum of $100.

When in doubt about house limits, always ask the dealer. Many casinos put up signs at the roulette tables stating both the minimum bets required and the minimum value of the roulette chips, but rarely do they state the maximum wagers permitted. When 25¢ chips are used, more casinos will require a minimum buy-in of $10. In other words, to sit down at the table and play, gamblers must purchase at least $10 worth of 25¢ chips. They will be handed stacks of chips for their cash. Each stack contains twenty chips and is slid over to the player by the dealer.

Roulette chips are of various colors and have no denominational amounts printed on them. They have no intrinsic worth (other than their minimum value) and can't be cashed in anywhere but at the roulette table. If there is a minimum chip valuation at the table, for example, a 25¢ one, then all chips issued by the dealer will have that value.

Players are not bound by this valuation, however. If a bettor wishes chips to be valued at $1 each, for example, the dealer will issue that person roulette chips of a certain color and then put that colored chip on the flat edge of the wheel with a button on the chip, showing that either the chip is worth $1 or a stack is worth $20.

Cash as well as ordinary casino chips of any denomination can be played at the roulette table. Gamblers who are big winners may be paid off in regular casino chips during the course of play, since there is a limited number of chips of each color at the table.

When a bettor wishes to leave the roulette table, he's required to turn in all his roulette chips before departing. He will then receive casino chips or cash in return for the special colored chips. These casino chips can be cashed in at the cashier's cage, usually located in the rear of every casino.

Managing money correctly at roulette is a difficult problem because of the house edge. My best advice is to avoid the American game when gambling seriously, because with the two zeros, the casino advantage of 5.26 percent is just too much to overcome. Certainly better opportunities for profits present themselves at blackjack, craps, and baccarat.

If you decide to gamble at roulette, I'd suggest a limited bankroll. Buy four stacks of chips at the minimum price, play them out any way you wish, and relax and enjoy the game.

If you find yourself ahead at least two stacks of chips, either get out of the game, or make one big bet on the even-money choices with the winning two stacks and then, win or lose, leave. If you just hang around making small bets, the house will grind you out.

Systems for Roulette (and Other Games)

It's tremendously difficult for anyone to beat roulette with a system, because of the inherent house advantage. Even the European game, with its edge of 1.35 percent, has destroyed a whole slew of systems players. When the house has a built-in advantage, it's a negative game for the players, and raising bets and progressive methods of betting after losses aren't going to change the odds one iota.

Why do people still bet systems at roulette? Well, for one thing, the game is a leisurely one. Players sit while at the table; there's plenty of time to make bets between spins of the wheel. One can write down the past results and past losses and easily figure out the next bet before the ball drops into that slot.

Roulette is played even more leisurely in Europe. The European casinos, to encourage systems players, supply them with a score sheet on which to keep records of the numbers that have come up in the course of the game.

But the wheel and numbers and the ball have no memory whatsoever, and every spin is a random one. In other words, what has happened before has no effect on what will happen again. Then there is the law of large numbers, which shows that all the choices one can bet on, if played millions or billions of times, will come as close to their probable expectations as theoretically possible, but no one is at the table that long a period of time, and short runs have no effect on the ultimate expectations.

For example, if a player finds that red has come up more often than black the last fifty times the wheel has spun, at that moment, on that wheel, black may have come up 546,901 times and red 539,989 times, and red still has a long way to catch up. In short runs of fifty or even a hundred spins the law of averages doesn't prevail and gamblers might as well be outside of the casino, holding a net to catch the wind, for all the good it's going to do them.

When keeping track of numbers that have previously hit, the only hope is that somehow the wheel is biased (not perfectly aligned) so that some numbers will show more than others because of some imperfection in the roulette equipment or mechanism.

But this rarely happens, because these wheels are not only carefully manufactured but constantly tested to make certain that they're in perfectly balanced alignment. This leaves all to chance, and luck shines on very few individuals at the roulette table. Eventually, that old villain, the house edge, pops up and turns out the bulb to save energy and the casino's money.

Martingale System

This is the most popular and simplest system, and it's usually the first one that novice players come across or think about. They figure that, doubling up after every loss, they will eventually win one bet, and when that wager is won, they'll come out ahead.

The Martingale system is no more than a doubling up method of betting, doubling one's bet after a previous loss. If a player starts with a $1 wager and loses, then bets $2 and loses, he'll bet $4, and should that bet lose, he'll bet $8 and after that loss, $16, and so on, till he finally wins a bet. When he finally does win, he'll end up ahead the grand total of his first bet, or $1.

Betting this way, the numbers soon become astronomical, and after nine losses in a row, the tenth bet has to be $512. At this point, the player is exceeding the usual house limit of $500 and thus may only bet $500. Should he lose this wager, he would now be behind $1,011, with no way to break even or come out ahead using his system. Even if he won the tenth bet at $500, he'd still be down $11.

With all the escalating bets this system requires, running into the hundreds and sometimes into the thousands of dollars, we must remember that the ultimate win the Martingale system player is hoping for will net him a profit of $1!

This fact alone should explain the foolishness of the system. All those wagers, all that aggravation, all that heart-stopping anxiety to win his initial bet of $1. But if you tell the systems players that their scheme is insane, they'll come back with the ready rejoinder, "All right, what you say may be true, but how many times will I lose ten bets in a row?"

The answer, easily proven mathematically, is more times than they'll win 1,000 of these bets. Eventually that losing streak is going to occur, especially with a two-zero wheel. Even with one zero, more Martingale system players have been destroyed than I could name if I wrote a thousand pages of names.

The system doesn't work and never has. In the end all those small wins go right down the drain, due to that one bad streak of losing bets.

And no one knows when that losing streak will begin, for it can start at any time. Even more devastating is the fact that when playing at home with a toy wheel and making bets with toy money, a player is free from tension. After eight straight losses at a casino in a real-life situation and playing with real money, a player already down $255 may lose heart, as so many system players have, and either lower the next bet or skip it altogether. It's one thing to think up those systems in one's living room and quite another to play them out in a casino with actual cash. And the one that starts many a person on the road to ruin is the Martingale system.

Grand Martingale System

I won't linger on this one, except to explain it. Instead of merely doubling up, the system player now adds an additional betting unit to his losing unit, so that, with each bet he eventually wins, he wins a bit more than his original wager.

For example, after betting $1 and losing, the player now bets $3, which is broken down as follows: $1 for the previous loss, another dollar to make up that loss, and the third to give an extra dollar's profit.

If the $3 bet is lost, then the player must wager $7 on his next bet, adding another extra dollar. This method escalates the bets even more wildly, because after the $7 loss, the next wager would be $15. On the simple Martingale system the bet here would be $8.

With the Grand Martingale system the gambler will reach the casino's betting limit of $500 after eight losses instead of nine, and sooner or later he will lose those nine bets in a row, and he'll do this before he wins that $1,000.

To sum up, the Grand Martingale system is a faster way to destroy one's bankroll than the Martingale system.

D'Alembert or Alembert or Cancellation System

This system goes under various names, but in the end it works out the same. Instead of attempting to double up after every loss, the D'Alembert system player increases his bets on only the previous losing wager, and in this way, after nine straight losses at the outset, he would find himself well within the house limit. If the losses occurred in the middle of one of these runs, the situation changes radically.

Here's how the system works. The player writes down a

series of numbers, usually beginning with 1. The most common application of the system is to use three numbers in consecutive order, 1 2 3. These add up to 6. What the player wants to do after completing an individual run is win this total of $6 and then begin the system's run all over again.

To play the system, the gambler bets the total of the two end numbers. Since this particular one begins with the numerals 1 2 3, the total is $4 (3 + 1). If he wins the bet, he crosses out the 1 and 3, so that the numbers look like this now:

$\cancel{1}$ 2 $\cancel{3}$

Now he bets the remaining number, 2, or $2. Should he win this bet he crosses out the 2, and the run would look like this:

$\cancel{1}$ $\cancel{2}$ $\cancel{3}$

At this point the player has won $6. He won his first bet of $4 and the second of $2. Therefore he begins again by writing down 1 2 3.

What happens if he loses a bet? If he loses, he adds the previous loss to the end of the run, so that it would look like this after an initial $4 loss:

1 2 3 4

The total of the two end numbers is now 5, or $5. The gambler now bets this total. Should the $5 bet win, he would cross out the two end numbers, leaving the run looking this way:

$\cancel{1}$ 2 3 $\cancel{4}$

At this point, he must bet the remaining total of the numbers, or $5. Should he lose this bet, the run would look like this:

2 3 5

This next bet is 2 + 5 (the total of the end numbers) or $7. If he wins, they're crossed off.

$\cancel{2}$ 3 $\cancel{5}$

The next bet is the remaining number, 3. If that loses, the run goes on as follows:

3 3

The next bet is the total of the two end or remaining numbers, or $6. If that wins, these numbers are crossed off, and the run is complete. The gambler has won another $6.

In that last run the systems player has won three bets and lost three bets and yet wound up ahead by $6. What is attractive about this system is the fact that two numbers are crossed off after each win and yet only one number is added, so that if the player wins a little more than one-third of the time, he can close out the system and win his $6. And here with this system that doesn't require the doubling of bets after losses, a moderate losing streak cannot break the player.

However, like all systems, this one goes down the drain with too many loses. Once the system goes haywire, the bets grow larger and larger, and it's not necessary to have nine losses in a row to be destroyed. It's enough to have much less than one-third of the expected wins occurring in a run, in which case the player finds himself in deep trouble, with escalating bets and losses. Unlike the Martingale system, where a ruinous run will cost the player about $511, in the D'Alembert the losses can run into the thousands.

I'll show two actual runs, both of which weren't completed, for obvious reasons. The first will show how the system can escalate; the second will show how it can destroy.

~~1~~ ~~2~~ ~~3~~ ~~4~~ ~~5~~ ~~6~~ 8 9 ~~12~~ ~~13~~ ~~17~~ ~~19~~ ~~23~~ ~~31~~ 32 34 ~~43~~ 45 ~~58~~ 64 ~~83~~ ~~89~~ 98 132 168

With this run the system has become far removed from the early 1 2 3 bets. Now the bettor is wagering at least $200 a shot, and the worst is yet to come. It didn't take many losses for the system to begin its perilous descent into ruination. In this case, the player gave up, having run out of nerve and also having lost all confidence in his cancellation system.

The next run occurred a few years ago, and the person who bet it showed me his notebook with the figures still intact.

~~1~~ ~~2~~ ~~3~~ ~~4~~ ~~5~~ ~~6~~ 8 ~~10~~ ~~11~~ ~~14~~ ~~15~~ ~~17~~ ~~23~~ ~~25~~ ~~33~~ ~~36~~ ~~42~~ ~~58~~ ~~75~~ ~~83~~ ~~105~~ 125 ~~167~~ 183 241 ~~299~~ ~~324~~ 366 491

At this point it was impossible for the systems bettor to make the correct wager, since the two end numbers now totaled 616, and his losses were already $1,046.

The gambler told me that when he left the table at this point he was shaking like a leaf, had a blinding headache, and had sworn off gambling forever. I interviewed him in the coffee shop of the Golden Nugget in downtown Las Vegas, where he had just been playing roulette, trying out a different system. So much for a fool's resolve.

There are other systems, many other systems, all based on progressions after previous losing bets and thus all worthless. The correct gambling methods described in this book have nothing to do with these kinds of systems. Our methods are based on increased bets after wins, making additional money with the casino's money. These are the kinds of methods casino operators fear, because they know they can be very badly hurt if the player gets on a hot roll or hot streak.

A last word on systems. They're very seductive at the roulette table, but in the end they fail, as do all attempts to overcome a negative game by progressive bets after losses.

The Roulette Scam

I met Robert H. at the Four Queens, where we were both playing blackjack one night at opposite ends of the table. He was sitting in the first baseman's seat, and I could see that something was off with his game. He was making strange bets, raising and lowering them without any apparent purpose. Not only was he doing that, but he piled his chips in the betting box rather than stacking them one above the other.

Eventually, I caught on to what he was doing. He was past-posting, that is, adding chips to his original bet after he saw his cards. In other words, if he had a good hand, he readjusted the pile of chips, stacking them, but at the same time adding a couple of $25 chips to the stack.

The dealer was a beginner or else he was stupid, because he wasn't picking up this move. Eventually, we both left the table at the same time, and I got into a conversation with Robert H. Since this chapter is about roulette and not blackjack, I'll repeat his story as I remember it.

Robert described himself as a crossroader, and he defined the term as "anyone who would cheat at anything that's available, or seek out cheating situations whenever possible." Robert couldn't pass a Laundromat without trying to open the locks containing the quarters. He knew how to screw the telephone company when making long distance calls, and any coin-operated machine was subject to his thievery. He also loved to hang around the slot-machine arcades, where he'd be constantly testing slots that he could empty out through devious means.

One sunny morning Robert strolled into a Strip casino and went directly to the cashier's cage in the rear. He took out two bills (the term in Vegas for $100 bills) and got two $100 chips in return. Then he took these to the one roulette table in operation at this casino and stood at the end of the table, directly in front of the column bets, which is as far away from the dealer and the wheel as one can get at a roulette table.

The game was a small one, played with minimum 25¢ chips, and Robert stood and watched the action. Two old women were seated next to each other, betting $1 at a time on the even-money choices, and each had a few stacks of chips amounting to about $25. The dealer was completely bored with the players and spent most of his time watching for pretty women to pass by. When he could find none, he flirted with the cocktail waitress who scurried by behind him. Robert took this all in and watched the games with alert eyes.

There comes a moment in roulette, at the American game, when the dealer operating the table must look into the wheel to see where the ball landed. After he does this, he calls the number and turns to the layout, then places the house marker on the number showing on the layout.

Therefore, since there is a single dealer, there is a short moment when the dealer's eyes are off the layout and on the wheel, looking for the ball and the pocket it has fallen into.

After Robert had been there for several spins, the dealer looked down, yawned, called the number 4, and when he looked up, nothing had changed. The women still had their one dollar bets out, but, as he put down the marker on number 4, out of the corner of his eye the dealer saw two chips on the column wager, two $100 black chips parked in the first column.

"Hey, what's going on?" he asked Robert. "You didn't make that bet before . . ."

"Before what?" Robert asked innocently.

"I mean, you didn't have that column bet down. You put it down after I called the number."

"I don't know what you're talking about," said Robert quietly and gently, as is his wont. "I made those bets when the wheel was still spinning."

"Like hell you did."

By now the dealer was angry. He called over the pit boss and explained to the unsmiling man that Robert had made his bet after the number had been called.

The pit boss looked over Robert, who was neatly dressed in a jacket and open shirt, with creased trousers and shiny tasseled loafers. Robert was clean-shaven and his hair was neatly combed.

But all this didn't matter to the pit boss. "We can't pay you off," he told Robert. "You have to make your bets before the number is called."

"That's what I did. The dealer didn't notice my bet. He's too bored with his job to pay attention to this game. He was trying to date the cocktail waitress."

"No way we're going to pay you off. Take your goddamn money and get the hell out," said the pit boss.

But Robert didn't take away his chips. He stood there, waiting for his payoff. Then, breaking the tension, one of the women chirped in.

"Sir," she said to the pit boss, "if you don't mind me saying so, this gentleman is right. I saw him make the bet and it was way before the number was called. In fact, I nudged my friend here, when I saw him put those black chips down."

And the other woman said, "That's right, mister. This man made the bet. The dealer wasn't even looking at us at all, or at this man. He's kind of annoyed that we're sitting here, if you don't mind me saying."

With that kind of testimony the pit boss stewed in his juices. Then he cursed out the dealer and told him to pay Robert off.

Then the pit boss, who had to show his authority, called over a security guard and had Robert escorted out of the casino with a stern warning not to ever return.

Robert told the pit boss he had a lot of nerve calling over a security guard, that all he wanted to do was collect on a legitimate winning bet. However, he pocketed his chips and left with the guard.

"I was really desperate to pull that scam," Robert told me. "I got myself barred from a casino I could have made all kinds of money in. It's a perfect casino to knock off, because everyone's been there a long time and they're all bored and they think they know it all. They're just the ones I love to sucker."

"You were lucky," I said, "that the old ladies verified your story."

"I don't believe in luck," said Robert. "Anyone who believes in luck and trusts to luck, he's an idiot. Where the hell do you think those old ladies got their money to play roulette that morning?"

Roulette Etiquette and Miscellany

• There are chairs provided for the players at the roulette table, but at crowded tables there may not be enough chairs to go around, and you may have to stand during play.

• When seated, you can write down the previous numbers that have come up, and no one will bother or disturb you, but generally, the house will not furnish you with a pencil or paper.

• It is usually the custom to tip the dealer after hitting a number at 35–1 or when leaving the table if you've been given courteous service.

• You can place your bets while the ball is spinning around, but not once it starts its descent into the numbered pockets. The dealer will inform you if your bet has been made tardily. The first time you make your bet too late, he will probably warn you about it. The second time he'll disallow your late bet.

• You must cash in all your roulette chips after play. Don't carry them away with you, for the dealer will want them back and may send a security guard running after you. These are special chips belonging to that roulette table; they have no intrinsic value, and the dealer has just a limited number of each color.

• When playing at a European casino, keep track of your bets. All chips are casino chips and cheats or others may claim your winning bet as theirs.

• When at a European table, it's not absolutely necessary to know any French. You can play, if you can make all your bets yourself, or you can find someone to translate for you.

Glossary of Roulette Terms

Á Cheval. The French term for *Split Bet.*

Alembert System. See *D'Alembert System*

American Wheel. A roulette wheel containing 0 and 00 in addition to the numbers 1–36.

Ball. The plastic ball, usually white, which is spun counter to the wheel's spin, and which, when landing in a pocket containing a number, determines the payoffs for that spin of the wheel.

Cancellation System. See *D'Alembert System*

Carré. French for *Corner Bet.*

Colonne. French for *Column Bet.*

Column Bet. A wager paying 2–1, whereby players bet that the next spin will come up on any one of twelve numbers in the column they're betting on.

Combination Bet. A bet on more than one event or on more than one number, using a single chip.

Corner Bet. An inside, combination bet with one chip covering four numbers at one time.

Croupier. The house employee in the European game who operates the roulette table with other croupiers.

D'Alembert System. A progressive system of betting whereby two numbers are cancelled every time a previous bet is won, and one number, the total of two end numbers, is added whenever a previous bet is lost.

Dernière. French for last, as in a *Column Bet* or *Dozen Bet.*

Dozen Bet. A wager on either the first, second, or third dozens on the layout, such as 1–12, 13–24, and 25–36.

Double Zero. See *Zero*

Douzaine. French for *Dozen Bet.*

En Plein. French for *Straight Up Bet.*

En Prison Rule. A rule whereby the player has an option of either surrendering half his wager or allowing it to be imprisoned for another spin of the wheel, in which case, if he wins, the wager will be returned to him intact.

European Wheel. See *French Wheel*

Even-Odd Bet. An outside, straight bet on whether the next spin will be an even or odd number, paid off at even money.

Five Numbers Bet. A bet covering the numbers 0, 00, 1, 2, and 3, which gives the house an edge of 7.89 percent.

French Wheel. A wheel manufactured for European and English casinos containing a single zero.

Grand Martingale System. A doubling up system, in which a player attempts to gain an additional chip's profit after every previous loss.

High-Low Bet. An outside, straight wager on whether the next spin will be a high or low number, paid off at even money.

Impair. French for odd.

Inside Bet. A wager on any of the numbers 1–36, 0, 00 or any combination of these numbers.

Manque. French for low.

Martingale System. A progressive betting method in which the player doubles his bet after a previous loss.

Noir. French for black.

Outside Wager. A bet on any event at the table other than the numbers 0, 00, 1–36.

Pair. French for even.

Passe. French for high.

Première. French for first.

Red-Black Bet. An outside, straight wager on whether the next spin will be a red or black number, paid off at even money.

Rouge. French for red.

Sixain. French for *Six-Numbers Bet.*

Six-Numbers Bet. An inside combination bet on six numbers at one time.

Split Bet. An inside combination wager on two numbers at one time.

Straight Bet. A single bet on any one number, or any of the outside even-money or 2–1 bets.

Straight Up Bet. A wager on a single number, paid off at 35–1.

Transversale. French for *Trio Bet.*

Trio Bet. An inside combination bet on three numbers at one time.

Wheel. See *American* or *French Wheel*

Zero, Double Zero. These numbers can be bet on in the same manner as the numbers 1–36, but their addition to the layout determines the house advantage in roulette.

8

Baccarat—
The Glamorous Game

Baccarat was originally a European game invented and first played in Italy. The game became extremely popular in France, and it still is one of the biggest attractions in gambling casinos throughout Europe, with several casinos on the Continent specializing in the European version, known as chemin de fer. There is another version of the game, known as baccarat en banque. Both of these games will be discussed in later sections of this chapter.

The word ''baccarat'' is the French term for the Italian *baccara* which means zero, and this refers to the face cards (jack, queen, and king) as well as the 10, all of which have a zero value in the game.

What we'll be discussing primarily in this chapter is the American version of baccarat, played in the Nevada and Atlantic City casinos.

The original version of baccarat as played in American casinos was chemin de fer, in which the gambler holding the bank plays against all the other players at the table, who may also have a turn at the bank once a player hand wins. The game was introduced on the Strip in Las Vegas at the old Desert Inn Hotel and Country Club, and thereafter at other Strip casinos. In the 1960s the game was changed to baccarat, where the casino booked all the bets. Similar versions of this game are played in some of the European casinos. In the American version of baccarat the casino plays directly against all participants at the table, whether they bet bank or player. And since the bank hand, because of the intricate rules of the game, always has an advantage over the player hand, American casinos, to ensure their advantage, extract a 5 percent commission on all winning bank bets.

The American game is primarily a mindless one, for all the player has to do is make a bet on either bank or player and thereafter makes no further decisions. Although the rules are intricate, this need not concern a participant, since the rules are printed and followed by the dealers, who are responsible for all decisions involved in acting on the respective hands. In baccarat there are no optional plays permitted.

To attract bettors and primarily high rollers, the Strip hotels in Las Vegas have invested this game with a certain aura and glamour.

First of all, the large baccarat table on which the game is played is placed in a separate area of the casino, roped off from the other tables. Secondly, the dealers do not wear the standard casino uniform, but are sumptuously dressed in flashy tuxedos. And last but not least, to encourage players to enter the game, a bevy of beautiful and smartly dressed women are usually sitting around the tables, flashing their smiles and looking altogether seductive.

These young women are known as shills or starters. Once the game is in full swing, they slowly make their exits, for their seats are too valuable just to be wasted on beauty when hard cash calls to the casino.

At one time, there was another fascinating aspect to this game. It was played with cash, and it was quite a sight to see $2,000 in crisp $100 bills counted out rapidly by a dealer and placed on top of the player's original cash bet. This involvement with cash made the spectators' mouths water, and many participants were recruited from these same spectators, eager to get their hands on all that money.

The glamorous aspect of the game, though encouraging certain high rollers, has discouraged others who didn't understand the rules and were put off by the tuxedoed dealers and beautiful women, feeling that the game was too sophisticated for them. However, if one has the money, one can play. In the games on the Strip and in Atlantic City there is usually a $20 minimum running up to a $2,000 maximum bet. No one who can afford these stakes is excluded from the game, and in just a few minutes anyone can understand the fundamentals of baccarat.

Cash is no longer used, alas. State regulations in Nevada have discouraged cash use, and the casinos have gone along with this rule readily, because chips, after all, are abstract symbols, and while it doesn't feel quite as good to receive two thousand dollars in black chips as it does to get twenty crisp $100 bills, it probably doesn't feel as bad, either, to have the chips, rather than that cold cash, removed.

One quick story about a big cash game: Some years back, a Japanese industrialist sat down at one of the Strip casinos with his entourage. Not satisfied with the house limit of $2,000, which is the usual maximum on the Strip, the industrialist asked for a higher limit, with the right of his entourage to play along with him, using his money.

After much discussion with the casino bosses, it was agreed that $50,000 would be the maximum limit on any one bet by the entire team of players. Out came the suitcase full of cash, and the game began, played with American currency. The Japanese tycoon went on a rather lucky streak, and as the game progressed, the casino found itself running short of cash, and eventually the industrialist broke the casino's bank, literally. The casino had no more money to fund the game.

At that point the industrialist was ahead one million dollars, piled up in stacks of American cash. The casino, which was part of a number of clubs owned by one individual, had to send to their partners for more cash, and the game was held up till fresh funds came.

When the game resumed, the tide turned. When I heard the full story I could only shake my head in dismay.

The industrialist lost back not only the million, but another million and a half, the biggest cash win and loss I've ever heard about in Las Vegas.

If he had followed my basic principles of money management, when he was ahead a million dollars he should have put aside $750,000 in profits and played out the remaining $250,000. When that money was gone, he'd still be a tremendous winner, and there would have been a different ending to this story. But like most gamblers he was doomed to lose without proper money management and self-control.

Not all baccarat games involve big bettors. The downtown and Northern Nevada casinos are happy to play with a $5 minimum bet, and some casinos have introduced mini-baccarat, with the same rules as baccarat, except that it is played as an ordinary table game, with but one dealer servicing all the players.

The game of mini-baccarat hasn't really caught on, and it is unusual to see more than one mini-baccarat table in any casino. Usually, that one table isn't getting much play. The general public is still unfamiliar with the game and wary about playing, but since it involves no player decisions, it's one of the easiest to learn. Also, the house advantage is quite low; 1.17 percent on bank bets, and 1.36 percent on player wagers.

The Table and Layout

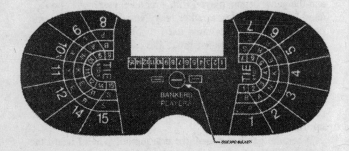

This is the table one will encounter at the American casinos. There are places for fifteen participants, and three dealers staff the game.

Players can sit in any seat they choose; the seating doesn't affect the play at all. The only difference is in handling the shoe containing the eight decks of cards used in the game. Each participant has the right to "hold the shoe," in which case he must bet bank while he does so, but any player may skip the shoe if he so desires.

A participant can be on either bank or player. If a bettor is in seat number 1, he makes a bank bet by putting his chips in the bank box marked "1." If he decides to bet on player, he puts his chips just over the line of his box into the player area.

Dealer's Duties

Three dealers are used to service the game. The dealer between positions 1 and 15 is known as the callman and he runs the game from a standing position. He receives all the cards, places them in the appropriate boxes, and then decides, according to the rigid rules of the game, whether any hand should stand or draw a card. After the final draw, he announces which hand has won.

After the winner is announced, the two other dealers, who remain seated throughout the game, pay off winning bets and collect the losing bets. If the winning wager was a bank bet, a record of the commission due on that wager is kept in the appropriate box area. If player 4, for example, had won a $100 bank bet, then he'd owe the casino a $5 commission, and a $5 marker would be placed in the box marked "4."

The commissions aren't collected immediately, but are due and payable after the eight decks in the shoe are depleted and before the cards are reshuffled for the next series of games. Commissions are also due when a player leaves the game.

Determining the Total Values of the Hands

All cards—ace through 9—are valued according to their spot or pip count, with the exception of the 10, jack, queen, and king, all of which are valued at zero.

In baccarat, however, no hand can total more than 9, and

since there are two cards in each hand, and sometimes three, all totals above 10 have 10 subtracted from the value of the hand. For example, an 8 and 5 total 13, but 10 is subtracted to make the hand into a 3.

The following are some other examples of card totals to make this concept clearer:

Cards	Hand total
6 and 5	1
4 and 9	3
2 and king	2
9 and ace	0
10 and king	0
8 and 8	6
6 and 4 and 9	9
8 and 3 and king	1
10 and 2 and queen	2

Rules of Play

These rules are printed clearly and available to all participants at the baccarat table. The rules are there for the players' convenience, because the dealer acts according to them without consulting the players at the table. They are as follows:

RULES:

Player When first two cards total:

1-2-3-4-5-10	Draws a card
6-7	Stands
8-9	Natural - Stands

Banker When first two cards total:

Having:	Draws when Player's third card is:	Does not draw when Player's third card is:
3	1-2-3-4-5-6-7-9-10	8
4	2-3-4-5-6-7	1-8-9-10
5	4-5-6-7	1-2-3-8-9-10
6	6-7	1-2-3-4-5-8-9-10
7	STANDS	
8-9	NATURAL — STANDS	

As previously mentioned, the highest total any baccarat hand can have is 9. A 9 dealt on the original two cards is called a natural and is an automatic winner, and no further cards are drawn. An 8 is the next best hand and that also is called a natural. If there is no hand equal to or higher than the 8, it is also an automatic winner, without additional cards being drawn.

Should one hand hold a 9 and the other an 8, the higher of the two naturals wins. Should both hands total 9 or both total 8, then it's a tie. All ties are standoffs, and neither bank nor player wins.

With any other total, the rules have to be consulted. You can see that the player never draws when holding a 6–7–8–9. The 9 and 8 are naturals, of course. The 6 and 7 are very strong hands, which might be weakened by drawing an additional card, and that's why they always stand pat.

When a player holds a 1–2–3–4–5–10 (0), he will always draw a card, except if the bank hand holds a natural, in which case the player hand would lose immediately.

The bank hands present a more complicated situation. Although the printed rules don't state this fact, the bank will always draw when holding a 0–1–2 (except if the player hand is a natural). When the bank hand is 3 or more, it is subject to the printed rules. However, if the player takes no card, the bank will stand on 6. Thus, when a player holds a 6 or 7 as his original cards and doesn't draw a card, the bank is foreclosed from drawing an additional card. If he holds a 6, the score will be 6–6, a tie, if the player's hand held a total of 6. If the player held a 7 and the bank holds a 6, the player hand wins, 7–6. And of course, if a player holds a natural, an 8 or 9, and the bank holds a 6, the player hand will automatically win.

Let's follow some illustrative hands to see how the rules govern the play of the cards.

Hand No. 1
Player hand: jack–4 = 4
Bank hand: 6–9 = 5

Player hand always acts first. Looking at the printed rules, we see that player must draw a card. He draws a 9 and now holds jack–4–9 for a total of 3.

Bank, with a 5, by the rules of play, doesn't draw a card

when giving the player a third card with a value of 9. Therefore bank stands with the 5.

Decision: Bank wins 5–3.

Hand No. 2

Player hand: 4–2 = 6.

Bank hand: 10–queen = 0

The player must stand with his 6. Remember, the bank always draws on its 0–1–2 unless the player has a natural. Bank draws a card and gets a 4.

Decision: Player wins 6–4.

Hand No. 3

Player hand: 2–2 = 4

Bank hand: king–5 = 5

Player must draw a card. He draws a 7 and now has 2–2–7 or a 1.

Even though the bank could win by standing pat, it must abide by the rules of the game and thus must draw another card. It's moments like this that provide the heart-stopping action of baccarat. Imagine betting $2,000 on bank and then worrying about drawing a 5 and losing, 1–0, when all you have to do is stand with your 5 and collect all that money. A bettor on bank would be praying for a face card to show now to keep his total of 5 intact. Or anything but a 5. The holder of the shoe slides out a card, turns it over, and gives it to the callman. It's another 7, for a total of 2. The bank hand has squeaked through.

Decision: Bank wins 2–1.

Hand No. 4

Player hand: jack–8 = 8

Bank hand: 4–3 = 7

The player has a natural and wins automatically, without any opportunity for the bank hand to improve. When a player or bank hand shows a natural, there is no further play and no drawing of cards. Remember, when referring to a natural, we mean the original two cards dealt, not drawing to get an 8 or 9.

Hand No. 5

Player hand: 4–ace = 5

Bank hand: 3–queen = 3

Here the player would be content to stand on his 5 and take his chances on winning, even if the bank drew another card. But by the rules of play, the player must draw another card. He draws and gets a 10. He still holds a 5. Now the player hand must sweat out the bank's draw. By the rules of play, when the third card drawn by the player is a 10 and the bank holds a 3, he must draw.

Bank draws and gets a 6 for a 9.

Decision: Bank wins 9–5.

Hand No. 6

Player hand: 3–4 = 7

Bank hand: 10–3 = 3

The player must stand on his 7, and is happy to, for there are a lot more cards to destroy or weaken that 7 total than there are to enhance it. Now he must once again sweat out the bank's draw. The bank gets a king and still holds a 3.

Decision: Player wins 7–3.

Hand No. 7

Player hand: 8–jack = 8

Bank hand: 9–queen = 9

Although both hands are naturals, the higher of the naturals wins, and therefore the bank hand wins. With naturals there can be no drawing of cards.

Decision: Bank wins 9–8.

Hand No. 8

Player hand: ace–2 = 3

Bank hand: 3–king = 3

Both hands start off equally, but the player must draw first. He gets a 9 and weakens his total. Now he holds ace–2–9 for a total of 2. The bank hand, happy with his 3, cannot stand pat on it by the rules of baccarat, so once more it is heart-stopping action in our theoretical game with a $2,000 bet at stake. The bank must draw a card and gets an 8, the one card it didn't want to see come up. 3–king–8 equals 1.

Decision: Player wins 2–1.

Hand No. 9

Player hand: 4–10 = 4

Bank hand: king–queen = 0

No rest for the weary! The player, happy with his 4 total, would probably prefer to stand, but cannot by the rules of baccarat. He draws a card and gets another 10 for a total of 4.

The bank hand must draw to his 0. He draws and gets a 6 and now has a total of 6. A terrific draw.

Decision: Bank wins 6–4.

Hand No. 10

Player hand: 10–7 = 7

Bank hand: 5–2 = 7

Under the rules of baccarat, neither the bank nor player hand can draw to a 7 as an original hand. Therefore, there's a tie.

Decision: Player 7, Bank 7. A tie.

Where ties can be bet on, the payoff is 8–1. This is a very bad bet, since the house has an advantage of 14.1 percent on this wager.

These ten illustrative hands should give you a clear picture of how the rules apply to the game in terms of drawing an additional card or standing pat.

The house pays even money to those bettors who wagered on player and won. Those wagering on bank collect their winning bets minus the 5 percent commission due the house.

The Play of the Game

Baccarat is now played with casino chips, using the standard denominations of $5, $25, and $100 chips. In the bigger games $500 chips may also be used.

If you wish to play baccarat, don't be put off by the roped-off area, the tuxedoed dealers, or the women sitting at the table. If you've never played the game before, it might be more comfortable to pick a table that has several players already there, with the game in full swing.

After you've selected a seat, change your cash for casino chips. If the limits are $20 to $2,000, you won't be permitted to make any wagers for less than $20, and you'll find that very few players bet $20 or use $5 chips. Most of the action will be with $25 and $100 chips.

Should you arrive at the table when the cards are being reshuffled, you'll see one of the ancient rituals of baccarat. The cards will be elaborately cut and mixed and then remixed by all three dealers, and then given to one of the players to be cut. To cut the cards, the player will be given a colored plastic insert to place somewhere in the cards just shuffled. The cards are then separated at this point, and the top card is turned face up. If the card is a 9, for example, the dealer will then remove nine cards from the deck without showing their faces to the players. These cards are dropped into the discard slot, and this is called burning the cards. The remainder of the decks are placed in the shoe and the plastic insert is then placed approximately three-quarters of the way into the decks.

When this card is reached during the course of play, the cards are taken out of the shoe and reshuffled. The elaborate ritual of shuffling can either be a fascinating spectacle or a tedious interval, depending on the player's mood or position at that time. Winners may sit back and enjoy the break; losers may be anxious for the game to get on, so that they can break even.

Or, in some instances, the reverse may be true. Winners who have been fortunate in betting on the correct side during the play of the cards in the previous shoe might now feel that they won't be so lucky with the next shoe. Losers who haven't had good luck might welcome a change of the cards.

After all, baccarat is a game of pure chance. There's nothing for players to do but decide on what side they'll place their bets, or the amount of the bets. They have no other options during the game.

If the game has just begun, the shoe will be given to the gambler in seat number 1, and thereafter, each time the bank hand loses, the shoe will move counterclockwise to the next seat till it reaches seat number 15, at which point it will then move along to seat number 1 again.

After all bets are made, the standing dealer, known as the callman, will nod to the holder of the shoe, who will then slide out a card. This first card is the player's. It will be dealt out face down and passed along to the dealer, who will either hold it until he gets the other player's card or immediately give it to the gambler with the largest bet on player.

This is merely a ritualistic move. The player hand could be given to anyone at the table betting on player, or it could be handled by the dealer himself. In fact, when there are no bets out on the layout on player, it is the dealer who handles the player cards. The holder of the shoe may bet on the player hand if he so wishes.

A second card is slid out of the shoe and placed to one side by the holder of the shoe. This is the bank's first card. Then a third card is slid out and pushed to the dealer who gives it to the same player bettor. A final fourth card is slid out, and this is the bank's second card. The card is placed with the first card put to one side by the holder of the shoe.

At this moment, no one knows the value of the cards just dealt. It is considered bad form for either the holder of the shoe or the bettor representing the player hand to look at the cards before all four have been dealt out of the shoe.

The dealer now calls for the player's cards. The player first looks at them and either hands them or flings them to the dealer, depending upon his position at the table or his mood.

The dealer takes the cards and then places them together face up in the player's hand area of the layout and calls out their total. If he has been given the jack and 3, for example, he'll say, "Player has 3" or words to that effect.

Now the holder of the shoe examines his cards, which is the bank hand, and passes these cards along to the standing dealer, who places them face up in the bank's hand area of the layout and announces their total. If he had been given the king and 4, he'd say, "Bank has 4."

At this moment, the rules printed on the cards go into effect. Since player has 3, he must draw another card. The dealer then says, "Card for player," and this request is answered by the holder of the shoe, who will slide another card out. This card is passed to the dealer face down. The dealer then passes it unseen to the player bettor, who then turns it over and returns it to the dealer. Let's assume this drawn card is a 9.

The player's hand has now been reduced to a total of 2. The player bettors will all have long faces and be disgusted by this turn of bad luck. But the bank bettors aren't home free yet. According to the printed rules, if the player has a total of 2 and the bank has 4, the bank must draw a card.

So, though the advantage is clearly with the bank at this moment, there is still a suspended uncertainty about the outcome of play. The dealer will now say, "Card for the bank," and the holder of the shoe will slide out another card, turn it over, and then give it to the dealer. Let's assume that this card is a queen, and therefore the bank's hand remains the same, at 4.

"Bank has 4, player 2. Bank wins," the dealer will say. Now all losing bets are collected quickly by the seated dealers. Then all winning bets are paid off, and the commissions due to the house on the bank's winning bets are noted in the small trays the dealers have in front of their seats. One dealer will handle seats 1–7 and the other seats 8–15.

The commissions on winning bank bets aren't collected immediately, but kept track of by the two seated dealers. After the cards in the shoe are used up and before they're reshuffled, the commissions are collected from those bettors owing them. A 5 percent commission works out to $1 for a $20 bet and $5 for a $100 winning bank bet. These commissions make little difference to a winning bettor, but if one has lost for the session and owes commissions, it can be quite debilitating.

After this sample round of play the same person would still be holding the shoe, for the bank hand had won. Only when the player hand wins does the shoe move on: otherwise it remains in the hands of the same gambler, who must bet bank and whose cards represent the bank at the table.

Most baccarat games are played with eight full decks, though some are played with six decks. The casino prefers the eight-deck game because there are fewer pauses for reshuffling, and therefore more hands can be dealt per shift. Whether a six- or eight-deck game is played is of little matter to the players, though the odds differ fractionally between the two games.

Mini-Baccarat

Unlike the elaborate game just discussed, with its rituals and traditions, the game of mini-baccarat is quite pedestrian. First of all, it's staffed by one dealer, and the table it's played on is similar in size and area to the ordinary blackjack table and seats about the same number of players, from five to seven. The mini-baccarat table, for there is rarely more than one in any casino, is placed among the other table games and, except for the layout on its surface, is indistinguishable from a black-jack table.

All the players remain seated and face a standing dealer. In front of each player's seat are areas marked for player and bank bets, and the bettor may wager on either one. Beyond these areas is a separate place for tie bets, which are paid off at either 9 for 1, or 8–1, which is in reality the same payoff.

The dealer has all the responsibilities of the three dealers at the baccarat table. He or she must shuffle up all the cards, deal them out, collect and pay off on all wagers, and keep track of the commissions due the house.

The limits are seldom as high as in the ordinary baccarat game. Generally, there's a $2 minimum bet required at mini-baccarat; sometimes a $5 minimum. When there's a $2 minimum, the game is played with dimes, for 10¢ is the commission due on winning $2 bank bets. In the $5 game, 25¢ coins are used for the commissions.

The game is played with a shoe containing either six or eight decks and moves along much more rapidly than the baccarat game. Like baccarat, the commissions on winning bank bets aren't collected immediately, but after the cards have been depleted, or when a player leaves the table.

The game isn't a popular one in casinos, and hasn't really attracted many followers. It's the same game as baccarat with-

out the frills. Baccarat, after all, could be handled adequately
by one dealer, but the casinos hang on to the rituals and aura
of the game, because this attracts the high rollers. Perhaps,
without its aura, baccarat would be a dying game, a fossil
among the table games the casino offers.

The Mathematics of Baccarat

Most players of the game are woefully ignorant of the mathematics and odds involved in baccarat. Many shy away from
betting on bank, because they feel that the 5 percent commission the house extracts on winning bets gives the casino a
5 percent edge on these wagers. This isn't the case, and for
the benefit of serious baccarat players here is the breakdown of wins and losses of both bank and player hands,
showing the house advantage for both bets and taking into
account the 5 percent collected by the house on all winning
bank bets.

Bank wins 50.68 percent of all bets.
Bank loses 49.32 percent of all bets.

Since the bank wins only 95¢ on its wins and loses the full
$1 on its losses, the exact winning percentage and house edge
is as follows:

Bank loses $1.00 × 49.32 = $49.32
Bank wins $0.95 × 50.68 = $48.15
Bank net loss – $ 1.17

The casino has a 1.17 percent edge on its bank bet.
The player bet gets paid off at even money without any
commissions due the house. However, this bet wins fewer
times than the bank wager.

Player wins 49.32 percent of all bets.
Player loses 50.68 percent of all bets.

The following are the winning percentage and house edge
on player bets.

Player loses $1.00 × 50.68 = $50.68
Player wins $1.00 × 49.32 = $49.32
Bank net loss – $ 1.36

The casino has a 1.36 percent edge on its player bet.

These advantages are quite small, much lower than the 5.26 percent the casino enjoys in roulette and less than the line bet advantage of 1.4 percent in craps. Therefore, with this low edge, and the fact that the bank wins more often than it loses, it is an ideal game for systems players. In the next section we'll discuss some methods of progressive betting useful in playing baccarat.

Winning Baccarat Systems

There are several basic reasons why we discuss betting systems for baccarat and dismiss such systems for a game such as roulette. First of all, in baccarat, each round of play, other than a tie, results in a win for either player or bank. There is nothing equivalent to the 0 and 00 in roulette to destroy a system. And ties, as we know, are standoffs, where neither bank nor player loses.

Second, we have a unique situation in baccarat. One side wins more often than the other. The bank bet wins 50.68 percent of the time, and this is an important factor in systems play. Even though the house takes 5 percent as its commission, it only takes a 5 percent cut on winning bank bets, not on all bank wagers, so if a player loses betting bank, he is not paying additional vigorish on losing bets.

We must mention a third factor, inherent in other gambling games as well. As any serious player knows, games run in streaks. Sometimes in baccarat the bank hand will win one round after another, and at other times the player hand will do the same thing. The odds of the game, however, favor the bank hand, and winning streaks tend to be longer and stronger on the bank side.

The following methods of betting put all these factors to good use. We'll use the bank bet as the basic wager and try to take advantage of winning streaks on that side of the layout.

When playing baccarat, it's very easy to keep track of

winning and losing bets on a scorecard furnished either by the house, or supplied by the player himself. The game is a leisurely one, and there's plenty of time to make the proper notations.

The card can be quite simply set up, showing bank, player, tie, and bet, and whether or not it was a winner or loser. The average card or sheet could look like this:

Bank	Player	Tie	Bet	Won or Lost
x			$20	W
x			$20	W
	x		$20	L
		x	$20	—
x			$20	W

In the above illustration there was no use of a progressive betting system, merely a notation of wins and losses, using $20 flat bets.

In setting up an effective betting method, we try to take into consideration the winning streaks rather than the losing streaks. To explain this a little more clearly, most betting systems are based on doubling up or increasing bets after a loss, hoping that one bet will either wipe out all previous losses and show a slight profit, or will substantially reduce previous losses.

In the roulette section we examined the Martingale and Grand Martingale systems, two methods of increasing bets after each loss, which run high risks with little reward.

Instead of raising bets after losses, the following systems are based on keeping them at the minimum, and only raising them after a previous win. Thus, if you run into a bad losing streak, you won't be wiped out by escalating bets. Here's how the first progressive method would work.

The first bet is $5. If you win that wager, raise your bet to $15 for the second round of play. If you win that one, next bet $20. Should that bet win, keep increasing each wager by $5, betting respectively $25, $30, and $35.

The betting method runs in cycles of six. Let's see the best possible results:

First bank bet	$ 5	Win	$ 5 profit
Second bank bet	$15	Win	$ 20
Third bank bet	$20	Win	$ 40
Fourth bank bet	$25	Win	$ 65
Fifth bank bet	$30	Win	$ 95
Sixth bank bet	$35	Win	$130

At this point, you've won $130, minus commissions of $6.50, for a net win of $123.50.

If you analyze the results more carefully, you see that after three wins you've won $40 and even if you lose the fourth bet, you'll be ahead $15 minus commissions of $1.75, for a net win of $13.25. Thereafter, even if you lose an escalated bet, you'll still be ahead, and after each winning bet your profits will increase dramatically.

This betting method may be played even more aggressively, with faster results, if you increase each wager by $10.

First bank bet	$ 5	Win	$ 5 profit
Second bet	$15	Win	$ 20
Third bet	$25	Win	$ 45
Fourth bet	$35	Win	$ 80
Fifth bet	$45	Win	$125
Sixth bet	$55	Win	$180

Betting in this manner, your final winnings will be $180 minus $9 commissions, for a net win of $171. Even if you only won three bets and lost the fourth, you'll still have a win of $10 minus commissions of $2.25 for a net win of $7.75. For this more aggressive method the shorter streaks don't work out as well as they did with the more conservative betting increases.

Although streaks come about quite often in baccarat, you might want to take advantage of shorter favorable runs and simply play for two wins in a row. In that case, betting bank, you might bet one unit on your initial bet, then increase it to three units, and stop there. In this way, with $5 units, your wins would look like this:

| First bank bet | $ 5 | Win | $ 5 profit |
| Second bank bet | $15 | Win | $20 |

At this point the streak is considered over, and you begin all over again with a $5 bet. I have found, however, that the best compromise is a three-tier method of betting, with one unit, three units, and then six units wagered. It would come out like this:

First bank bet	$ 5	Win	$ 5 profit
Second bank bet	$15	Win	$20
Third bank bet	$30	Win	$50

At this moment, there are two ways to approach the streak. One is to take the winnings of $50 minus $2.50 for commissions, for a net win of $47.50 and start over again with a $5 bet.

The second approach is to preserve the win by betting another $30 and continuing with $30 bets until the player hand wins.

Or you might bet $30 on the fourth bet, and if that wins, increase your fifth bet to $35 and add $5 onto each additional bet.

And finally, an effective approach might be to start all over again after three wins, with a $10 bet followed by $30, and then a $60 bet, hoping for another sustained streak. Since no one can foretell when a winning streak might end, these methods all have their merits and pitfalls. An interested player should examine all of these betting methods to find the one that best suits his goals and temperament.

Some players, after two wins, like to nail down their profits, but still want to take advantage of a longer streak, should it occur. They bet in the following units: 1–3–2–6.

The first bet is $5, then the next bet is $15 if the first bet wins. At that point they're ahead $20 minus commissions of $1, for a net win of $19. This kind of player wants to come out ahead even if the next bet is a losing one, so he only bets $10. If that bet wins, he increases his next bet to $30. Should he lose the $30 bet, he'd only be out $1.50, with the chance of winning $47.50 if he had won.

A real gambler, in that situation, already having three wins and $28.50 in profits, instead of betting $30, might bet $50, counting on a possible win of $76 against a loss of only $21.50.

That's really the whole point of betting on winning streaks. Once the streak is going, a player can take a chance somewhere along the way, hoping for an enormous win against the possibility of a smaller loss. Some players are happy with small but steady wins. Others are shooting for the sun, moon and stars, and try to parlay a $100 bet in baccarat up to the limit, doubling up after every win.

The best method is one that is not filled with greed, for rarely, if ever, does the greedy player come out ahead. With the betting methods we've outlined, it's possible to get a good win from a moderate streak, even when the final bet loses. If a bettor doubles up after every win, a final losing bet will wipe out all his previous wins, and besides that, he'll have a loss because of the commissions. It's best to compromise a bit to preserve the wins.

But most important of all, a gambler should never increase his bets after losses, hoping to double up and have one bet make up for all the other previous losses. These types of bets escalate very rapidly and invite financial disaster.

Betting Limits and Money Management

When playing baccarat, the betting limits a player usually encounters will be either $5–$500 or $20–$2,000. In Atlantic City, there are also minimum $50 tables with limits going as high as $10,000 a hand. If a premium player (high roller) comes along, they'll raise their limits in baccarat to accommodate the gambler. If you're really interested in betting big in baccarat, speak to the pit boss and see what limits you can arrange.

To properly play baccarat with any kind of progressive betting system, you should have at least 50 units of play available for betting. This means that in a $5 game, you should sit down with not less than $250. In a $20 minimum game, the bankroll should amount to $1,000.

If you run into very bad luck and lose your initial bankroll, end your play and leave the table. Avoid doing two things which spell financial destruction. Never reach into your pocket or wallet for more money or ask for more credit at the tables. And never make larger and larger bets while losing, in a desperate attempt to break even.

Everyone has to lose at some point or other, and baccarat, a game in which the house holds a small but nevertheless potent advantage of 1.17 percent on bank bets, is a game where you can find yourself losing an entire single session bankroll if the cards don't run your way.

When you're winning, you should first endeavor to double your money. If you can do this and leave the table, you'll have done well. There may be times when the cards are going so well that even after doubling your money, you want to stay around and test the waters again. In that case, you can attempt to get another winning streak going, but if you find that you've lost two or three bets in a row, get away from the table.

If you continue to win and build up another 50 units in profits, again you should try to make more money, still limiting yourself to those two or three losing bets in a row. In this way, you're putting no limits on your wins, but are protecting your previous wins and your bankroll.

Self-control is a very important factor in gambling, and often spells the difference between winning and losing. Self-control means never reaching into one's pocket after losing the original bankroll for that session of play, and it also means leaving the table when a winner without sacrificing the previous wins on a few wild bets. Don't ever leave a loser after being a winner. If you follow your precepts, you can't help but be a winner at baccarat.

Chemin de Fer

Chemin de fer, the French term for "railroad," is not played in the United States casinos, but is a widely played and popular game, especially in the French casinos. It is very similar to baccarat, except that in chemin de fer, or chemmy or shimmy, as some advocates call it, the players bet among themselves and not against the house.

The house provides the physical layout and table and also supplies a dealer, known as a croupier, who conducts the game. In Europe the dealer not only directs play, but makes certain that the rules are carefully followed.

Six or eight decks are usually used. They're thoroughly shuffled as in baccarat, and then placed in a shoe, known as a *sabot*. At this point, the game diverges from baccarat. Instead of the shoe going automatically to the player in seat number one, an auction is held, and the highest bidder gets the shoe and becomes the first banker. The winner of the auction then puts up the money for the bank, which is the amount he or she bid, and the game begins.

From this point on, whenever the bank hand loses and the player hand wins, the shoe is moved around the table, and along with the shoe goes the bank. The player to the right of the bank has the first option of taking the shoe and bank, by putting up money to buy the bank; or that player may pass up the bank completely.

If a player passes up the bank, it then moves to the next player in the rotation and that player has the same privilege of buying the bank or passing it up.

After a participant has gotten the bank, the money that bought the bank is placed in the center of the table. It is then counted by the croupier to make certain that the amount is correct.

This money will be covered in the course of play, that is, bet against, either partially or completely by the other players, who thus bet against the bank. The American term for this is "fading the bank."

Any player may decide to fade the entire bank by calling "banco." When a gambler calls banco no other player may be involved in that round of play. If two players call banco at the same time, then, by the rules and traditions of chemin de fer, the player closest to the bank's right hand fades the bet. This is known as banco prime.

Should no player fade the entire bank, then each player in turn, starting with the player to the bank's right, has the option of covering as much of the bank as he wishes.

Suppose the bank consisted of $200. If the player to the bank's right covered $50, the next player could cover all or part of the remaining $150. If he covered $50, then the third player could cover the remaining $100. When the entire bank is covered, or when there are no more players willing to cover the unfaded part of the bank, then play begins. If a player hadn't a chance to fade any part of the bank bet, he is out of play and cannot participate in that round.

The croupier will now instruct the holder of the shoe to deal out the cards. As in baccarat, two hands are dealt—one to the croupier and one to the bank. The croupier then gives the cards he was dealt, face down, to the player who has faded the largest bet against the bank. A round of play is begun, known as a coup.

Rules of Play

The rules are very similar to baccarat, but there are several exceptions. For one thing, unlike baccarat, the players holding the cards have optional plays. The following are the rules for the player's hand as to standing and drawing.

Cards	Play
8 or 9	Natural—the player's cards are immediately turned face up, and his bets are collected.
0–1–2–3–4	Draws a card
5	optional play—may draw or stand
6–7	Stands; no draw permitted

When holding the player's hand, unless it's a natural, the gambler doesn't display the cards to the bank. When the holder of the player hand is required to or desires to (on an optional play) draw a card, he says, "Card," and the holder of the shoe slides out a card face up. After this card is drawn, the player hand remains closed except for the drawn card. Now it's the bank's turn to play his hand.

The bank's rules of play are quite similar to baccarat, with two exceptions. The following are the standard rules of play:

One of the optional plays occurs when the bank holds a 3 and has given the player a 9 as his third card. Then he may stand or draw as he wishes. The second exception and optional play occurs when the bank holds a 5 and the player has drawn a 4. Then the bank has the option of drawing or standing. Otherwise, the bank has no choices.

Chemin de fer rules, while not as rigid as those of baccarat, are nevertheless compulsory for most plays, and are strictly enforced by the croupier. Should a mistake occur, the croupier must reconstruct the coup, and replay the cards from the beginning of that particular round of play.

French terms are used throughout chemin de fer. An eight dealt as a natural is called *la petite*, and a nine is called *la grande*.

What really makes chemin de fer an exciting game is its unique feature which forces the bank to double its size after every win. For example, suppose that the bank was originally $200. If the bank was fully faded and won, the bank size would now be $400. The banker cannot remove part or all of his winnings at any time without giving up the bank itself.

If the $400 is faded, the next win would bring the bank up to $800. If that amount is faded and the bank wins, the bank will stand at $1,600 and then $3,200 and $6,400 and will keep doubling if it wins while fully faded.

There are only two ways that the person holding the bank can get his profits out of the bank. First, if he wishes to give up the bank, he retains the entire proceeds of the bank, less 5 percent paid to the house on his *net win*. Or if the entire bank hadn't been faded on any coup, that amount is put to one side. If the bank hand loses, the unfaded money is his, less 5 percent to the house on his net win.

Some casinos give the bank the option of cutting the bank in half after winning three times in a row, so that the bank can clear a profit even if the fourth game is a losing one.

When the bank hand loses, the money in the bank is paid out to those players who faded the bank. Bettors wagering against the bank pay no commissions on their wins.

Should the banker decide to pass the bank and give it up

CHEMIN DE FER - BANK RULES					
		DRAW WHEN GIVING	STAND WHEN GIVING		
HAVING	3	1.2.3.4.5.6.7.10	8	9	**OPTIONAL**
	4	2.3.4.5.6.7	1.8.9.10		
	5	5.6.7	1.2.3.8.9.10	4	
	6	6.7	1.2.3.4.5.8.9.10		

before a bank hand has lost, the croupier will hold an informal auction and will give the bank to the player willing to put up an amount equal to the bank before it was passed.

Chemin de fer can be an exciting game, especially when the bank has won a few hands in a row and the original bank has escalated to monster proportions. Then, if the entire bank has been faded at the table, the holder of the bank is in for some heart-stopping action.

Should he lose the next hand, when he had the option to take his profits, the nagging thought would remain—"I should have stopped the hand before." However, if the bank had been passed and the next couple of hands proved to be winners for the bank hand, he would kick himself for not having the courage to go ahead and attempt to double his money and then quadruple it. Gambling, like life, can be full of regrets.

Baccarat en Banque

This version of baccarat, also known as *baccarat à deux tableaux* (double tables) is played mostly as a private game, and is usually backed by Greek syndicates or concessionaires of those syndicates. At one time it was perhaps the biggest gambling game in the world, with no limit set on play or bets.

In this game, unlike baccarat and chemin de fer, three hands are dealt—one bank hand and two player hands, one player hand going to each end of the table.

The bank is a permanent one, and participants and bettors can never bet on the bank or get the bank. They may wager on player hands at either end of the table, or may wager on both player hands at the same time by placing their bets on the line separating both ends of the table.

After all bets have been made, the croupier deals the cards from the shoe, first giving a card to the player hand on his right, then a card to the player hand on his left, then the third card to himself. When everyone has two cards, the hands are examined. An 8 or 9 are naturals and win immediately.

Should no hand hold a natural, then the game proceeds along the same rules used in chemin de fer for the player hands. The player hand to the right acts first, then the player hand to the left; the bank hand acts last.

In baccarat en banque, the bank has no printed rules governing its play. The banker must exercise his own judgment based on his cards and the play of both player hands.

Often this judgment will be determined by the size of the bets. The bank may make a safe play to be certain that he wins the larger bet, even though it may jeopardize the smaller wager. For example, if player A has bet $10,000 (not an unusual bet in this game) and has drawn a 10, and player B, without drawing a card, has a $5,000 bet, the bank, with a 5, would make a safe play.

The holder of the bank will know that player A, by the rules of chemin de fer, has started with a hand totaling either 0–1–2–3–4–5, and so the worst that can happen is a tie, which is a standoff, if the bank doesn't draw a card. The safest course here, one that will be in the bank's favor by odds of 5–1, is to stand pat with his 5.

This flexibility on the part of the bank against both player's hands bound by rigid rules gives the bank an extra edge in play.

Baccarat en banque is not played as a casino game in America, but is still found in some casinos in Europe, where large stake games are played. Because there are virtually no betting limits, the game is not for the poor or faint of heart.

Baccarat Etiquette and Miscellany

• Understand the limits at the table you're playing at. Don't come to a $20 minimum table and start making $5 bets.

• The player hand sees and acts upon his cards first. If holding the shoe, don't peek at the cards you've dealt till the player hand is opened. It's not prohibited but is considered bad form.

• The callman will run the game. Don't interfere with his decisions. An experienced dealer will know what he's doing.

• Dealers at baccarat can receive tips, and it's proper to toke them, especially after a big win, or at the end of your stay at the table.

• The dealers will be happy to get any player free beverages, cigars and cigarettes, and sometimes food if the game is a rather long one. Just ask them to call over a cocktail waitress.

• The game is slow and relaxed. There's no way to rush the game, so sit down and make yourself comfortable and play according to the rhythm of the game.

Glossary of Baccarat Terms

Auction. Bidding for the bank at chemin de fer at the outset of play and when a player voluntarily gives up the bank.

Baccarat (pronounced bah-cah-rah). The name of the game, derived from *baccara*, the Italian for zero.

Baccarat en Banque. A variation of chemin de fer, where three hands are dealt, and there are no set rules governing the bank's play. Also known as *baccarat à deux tableaux*.

Banco. The term used by a player who decides to fade the entire bank bet in chemin de fer.

Banco Prime. The privilege of the player to the bank's right to fade the entire bank bet in chemin de fer when there is more than one player calling banco.

Bank, Bank Hand. The hand in all forms of baccarat which is dealt to last and which acts last.

Burned Cards. Cards discarded after the decks have been cut and before actual play begins.

Callman. The dealer who runs or calls the game of baccarat.

Chemin de Fer. The European version of baccarat, where players bet among themselves.

Chemmy. The English slang term for chemin de fer.

Commission. The 5 percent the house takes on winning bank bets in baccarat. Also the 5 percent commission on net wins by bank in chemin de fer.

Cover, Cover the Bank Bet. See *Fade*

Croupier. French term for the dealer.

Dealer. An employee of the casino who staffs and services the game of baccarat.

Face Cards. The jack, queen, and king, which together with the 10, have a zero valuation.

Fade. In chemin de fer, to cover all or part of the bank bet.

La Grande. French for 9 dealt as a natural.

La Petite. French for 8 dealt as a natural.

Natural. The original hand consisting of the first two cards dealt, which total 8 or 9.

Player Hand. The hand opposing the bank hand, which receives cards and acts upon them first.

Rule Card. The card that shows the printed rules of play for baccarat and chemin de fer.

Sabot. French term for the shoe.

Shills. House employees, usually attractive young women, who sit around an empty baccarat table to attract players to the game.

Shimmy. The American slang expression for chemin de fer.

Shoe. The device which holds all the cards used in baccarat games, from which cards may easily be slid out one at a time.

Starter. See *Shills*

9

Keno—
The Imported Game

Keno is a game that could be classified as a modified form of
bingo. A player selects between one and twenty numbers out
of a possible eighty on a ticket called a blank, then the operator
of the game calls out twenty of the eighty numbers for each
game played. If the player's numbers match most or all of the
numbers called, he or she may be entitled to a prize running
up to $250,000 in some casinos.

The numbers run from 1 to 80, so that the game is simple
to play in its most elementary stage. In each game only 25%
of the possible 80 numbers will be selected by the operator,
which means that 75% of the numbers will not participate, and
this gives the casino operators a big edge over the players,
since the payoffs aren't commensurate with the odds against
catching the numbers selected.

In bingo, numbers are called until there is a winner. But
this is not the case with keno. If all twenty numbers have been
called and there are no winners, the game is over, and the
casino has kept all the money wagered. Another game is then
called. What usually happens when there are many players
during busy times is that there are some small winners, but no
big ones, and this condition can go on game after game after
game.

In fact, long periods of time may go on before there is a
big winner, one who has won the grand prize, whether it is
$25,000, $50,000 or a progressive prize beyond it. My feeling
is that in many casinos, no one has ever won the biggest prize
available, or, if won, it has happened once every few years

despite all the players involved. It's a very tough game to beat, and we suggest that no one play it as a serious gambling game. There are other games that give the players a much better chance to win, such as blackjack, craps, and baccarat, because the house edge is considerably less.

Yet despite the big house edge, keno remains one of the most popular of all games in Nevada. Thousands play it every day, enticed by the fact that they can win a great deal for a small bet, but of course, those small bets add up as loss after loss occurs. The game is pure luck, without any skill involved. There are serious players who keep track of the numbers coming up, and either play those numbers again or play the numbers that haven't shown for a while. Take your pick and put your money down, for it's all the same. There's no system to beat the game.

Despite the fact that all these people play keno, there are relatively few players who really know how to play it properly, and can take advantage of the opportunities it presents in the way of huge payoffs. By the way, if you want to play keno, you have to travel to Nevada. Atlantic City hasn't introduced the game. In many casinos in Las Vegas, the keno lounge has replaced the entertainment lounge permanently. I remember years ago going to several Strip casinos and watching talent like Vic Damone or Lionel Hampton performing for the price of a drink in the lounges. Now those same lounges are set up for keno, and the only way to see talent of this sort is to see a regular dinner or late show in the main showroom of these same casinos.

Most players betting on the game play it in its simplest form. They fill in what are known as straight tickets and select several numbers at random, then hope that they'll win some money if these numbers are called. The more sophisticated and knowledgeable players work in a different fashion, making wagers known as way and combination bets. We'll discuss these more complicated ways to play keno fully in this chapter, and will give examples of other kinds of plays, such as king tickets. By the time you finish the chapter, you'll know all the choices open to you in the game, and who knows, if lady luck decides to smile on you, you might come up with that big win.

For keno can be exciting as a side game, and the big excitement is in the big payoffs, extending up to $250,000. Since this kind of payoff can be gotten in some casinos for a $2 bet, it lures many players who hope to luck into that big win with an investment of a couple of dollars. After all, that same lady luck shines her winning smile in a random way, and nobody can foretell the future.

The trouble with the game, as we pointed out before, is that every time a huge payoff is promised for a small investment, the chances of winning are very slight indeed, and on top of this, the casino can take out a big chunk of the proceeds as its house advantage. In keno the edge is never less than 22 percent and can be as high as 40 percent, which is much too much for any serious gambler to buck. Why then, you might ask, should anyone even play the game?

As we stated, keno should never be played as a serious game, but it's a fine game to fool around with when eating in a casino restaurant or when killing time in one of the casino lounges. There are keno runners available, usually attractive young women, who walk around the restaurants and lounges, even near the regular gaming tables, collecting keno tickets and wagers and returning with the paid ticket after they've met the bet on your behalf. It's a free service, though the usual custom is to tip these runners.

And while you wait for the next game to go on, it's an easy way to pass the time, watching the called keno numbers light up on the keno board, possibly numbers that you've selected. These boards are posted all around a casino, and can easily be seen from practically every seat in any of the lounges or restaurants.

I've spent many a lunch and dinner hour in a casino restaurant, fooling around with $1 bets, talking with friends about what I was going to do with the $50,000 I was aiming at winning, if I indeed was lucky enough to win. Alas, I've never even come close. But it can be fun, and several friends or dinner mates can share in purchasing the tickets, and so the overall investment is quite small. On the other hand, under pressure from serious blackjack play, I wanted to eat a meal in peace without doing any further gambling, and so didn't participate with friends when they bought keno tickets. But it was available if I wanted to.

I have continually mentioned this as a fun game, because that's the way it should be played. The house has too great an advantage to overcome from this game to be taken seriously as a regular gambling venture.

Keno becomes more interesting when you know how to write tickets other than the regular straight ones, since you can then widen the scope of a single ticket to include all kinds of combinations. The various types of tickets will be fully covered in the appropriate sections of this chapter.

The game has many adherents, some of whom play nothing else. They're generally bored with the mostly even-money payoffs in games like baccarat or blackjack, or they don't understand or care to understand how to play these games. Various states in America have made millions of people gamblers when lotteries were introduced with their huge payoffs. It's the same principle. These people will go for a payoff that could dramatically change their lives, whereas they wouldn't even think of going to Las Vegas to play at a craps table. And unfortunately, many of the gamblers who play lotteries are people who can't really afford it, and the $5 or $10 a week that they invest in these lotteries sanctioned by the state is money that adds up to the hundreds at the end of the year, and could be put to better use for necessities.

However, some of the keno players can afford it, and feel that they can beat the game. Or, what happens is that they hit a big payoff early in their keno career and feel that all the money they're pouring back really belongs to the casino in the first place, so they have nothing to lose, a common gambler's fallacy. When you win at gambling, the money in your pocket is not the casino's, but yours, just as the money you hand over to the keno writer is the casino's and not yours. Just ask for it back. And you don't expect the casino operator to come over to you after a big win and ask for his money back. In fact, to me the ideal way to play keno is to take away a big win and never play the game again. You've done the incredible—scored despite the odds.

Don't press your luck. Such a fortunate player was a friend

of mine I'll call John, who won $15,000 and instead of giving it back to the casino in small doses, invested it in a route which enabled him to carry on a small business which he eventually sold for $300,000. Now, that was a nice keno win.

Then there's the gambler I know, one of the premier poker players of all time, who arrived in Vegas some years back after losing his entire stake in a high-rolling poker game. He was about to call his wife for a ticket back to Texas on the Greyhound, but before doing this, he sat down to a 29¢ breakfast in a downtown casino, all he could afford. At this time he was down to a couple of dollars. While he ate the greasy eggs and drank the bitter coffee, the board lit up with his numbers and he collected $12,500 for a 70¢ ticket. He took the money, left the food to die on the plate, ran across the street to a big poker game, and never looked back. He's a millionaire today.

So keno has done it for a few people, and there's the possibility of a big win if the game is played right and luck strikes. This chapter will show you how to prepare for the big win.

History of the Game

Keno is one of the oldest of gambling games still being played today, and its history can be traced back almost two thousand years to the time of the great Han Dynasty of China. It was invented by Cheung Leung, and, according to *The Gambling Games of the Chinese in America*, which has been published by Gambler's Book Club of Las Vegas, Nevada, this game of chance was introduced to raise revenues and provisions for the army.

From the very beginning it was a huge success. Not only did it raise countless thousands of pieces of silver for the state to support its army, but it kept its popularity long after its initial introduction and has maintained this popularity to the present time.

The earliest form of keno was played in Chinese and contained 120 Chinese ideograph characters, drawn from the

Thousand Character Book. This book, written by Confucius and his followers, is a classic work known to most literate Chinese.

As the game went on, the characters were reduced to ninety, and keno was played with this number for many centuries. When the game was brought over to America by the first Chinese immigrants, the number was reduced further to eighty characters, and it has remained at eighty to this day.

By the 1890s, the game had widespread popularity among the Chinese who were in America, and though it was never a legal game, it flourished nevertheless. During that period, prior to the turn of the century, the usual ticket purchased to play keno was a ten-number ticket, today known as a ten-spot ticket. The payoffs at that time were as follows:

Catch Spots	Payoffs
5	2 for 1
6	20 for 1
7	200 for 1
8	1000 for 1
9	1500 for 1
10	3000 for 1

Catch spots are those numbers selected at random by the operator of the game and matched on the player's ticket. Although the payoffs today would be much greater if a player caught nine or ten numbers or spots, the modern payoffs are surprisingly similar for the other numbers.

The game attracted other, non-Chinese gamblers, who were also anxious to invest a small sum of money to win a possible fortune. In those days a dollar was a great deal of money, and to win several thousand dollars for a small investment was quite an attractive prospect to laborers and others in the lower economic brackets, the same group that still invests in state lotteries and other games of chance where a huge payoff is possible for a small investment.

The difficulties presented to non-Chinese in this game were enormous. Since the game was played with Chinese characters, there were few Americans who could figure out or differentiate between these Chinese characters, and many wouldn't know whether or not they had won, since it was a laborious process to examine each and every character called by the operators of the game.

Gradually, therefore, the game evolved from Chinese to Arabic numbers 1–80, and thereafter Americans flocked to the keno houses. The same eighty numbers are used today in Nevada casinos.

To select the winning numbers, which were printed originally on small wooden balls, they were first stirred up by hand by operators of the game and then randomly introduced through what is known as a keno goose—a long tube that resembled a goose's neck.

Since the balls were continually touched by hand, there were many opportunities for collusion between players and those selecting the numbers. Today a goose is still used, but the numbers are imprinted on Ping-Pong balls, stirred by air and then randomly forced up two transparent tubes, one at a time, without being touched by the operator of the game.

When Nevada legalized gambling, keno was one of the games immediately introduced, except at that time it was known as racehorse keno. Not only did each Ping-Pong ball contain a number, but a name of a racehorse as well. All this changed, however, in 1951, when the United States government passed a law taxing off-track betting on horses. Since racehorse keno might be construed as off-track horse betting, the racehorse names were eliminated, and the game from that time on has simply been known as keno.

Today keno is played in practically every casino in Nevada. At first the game, which appealed primarily to those in the lower economic brackets, was shunned by the elegant casino-hotels on the Las Vegas Strip and was limited to the downtown Las Vegas and Northern Nevada casinos, which attracted smaller bettors to their clubs. In recent years the Strip casinos have gradually eliminated their lounge shows and converted these areas into keno lounges, and keno now can be played in nearly every casino on the Strip.

The keno lounge surrounds the area where the game is actually operated and called. The players' seats face a keno counter, where men and women, called keno writers, handle and mark the tickets, collect bets, and make payoffs. They do this not only for those players coming to the counter, but for the numerous keno runners who come from all corners of the casino and hotel, gathering players' tickets and bringing them to the keno counter.

Behind and above the writers is the operator and caller of the game. He or she sits on an elevated seat and when the game is to begin, presses a button which automatically mixes the Ping-Pong balls in a large transparent bowl, and then the air forces these balls into a goose, one at a time. There are generally two gooses, or tubes, extending from the bowl, each goose capable of holding ten balls. When twenty balls have been selected in this manner, the game is over.

As each ball is forced up, the number is read aloud by the operator, and at the same time is flashed onto every keno board throughout the casino, restaurants, and lounges of the hotel. In this way, no matter where the players might be, they can easily follow the game. It is not necessary for players to remain in the keno lounge in order to play the game.

How to Play Keno

To play the game, you first obtain a keno blank and mark the number or numbers you've selected. These keno blanks are available in the keno lounges and can also be found on tables in the casinos, restaurants, and lounges.

A keno blank contains eighty numbers in consecutive order from 1 to 80, with ten numbers on each line. You can mark from one to fifteen numbers on each blank when playing a straight ticket. A one-number mark is known as a one-spot, a two-number selection is called a two-spot, and so on up to fifteen. On other kinds of tickets more numbers may be selected, but payoffs are never made for more than fifteen spots.

These payoffs are based on three factors: first, the number of spots you select; second, the number of actual spots you catch; and finally, the price you pay for the ticket. In most casinos the minimum ticket is a 70¢ one, though on the Strip this price may increase to $1.40, while in smaller casinos and those catering to lower-limit keno players, the ticket price may be as low as 35¢.

After you have selected the number of spots you wish to play, you then write in the price of the ticket in the right-hand margin of the keno blank. When tickets are 70¢, you can bet the minimum or multiples of that price. For example, a ticket may be marked for 70¢, $1.40, $2.10, $2.80, and so on, at the discretion of the player.

Once the ticket is marked with both the number of spots you wish to play and the price of the ticket you wish to purchase, the blank is taken to a keno writer or given to a keno runner, who in turn takes it to a writer.

After the keno writer is paid for the ticket, he will keep the original player-marked ticket and return a duplicate ticket on which he has marked in india ink the numbers you have selected.

The blank that you fill in and present to the keno writer is called the *original* or *master ticket*. This is kept by the writer, and the one returned is the *duplicate* and is merely a receipt for the original ticket.

Each game is separately numbered and dated, and the number of the game appears on the ticket and also on the electric board which shows the numbers called during the game. All in all, twenty numbers will be selected by the operator of the game, and if you catch, or match, enough spots on your ticket with those called, you can win up to $250,000 depending on the spots marked and the price of the ticket.

If your selections have caught in sufficient number for a payoff, you must turn in the ticket prior to the calling of the next game or forfeit your win.

Let's now summarize what has been previously discussed with proper illustrations. First of all, you must obtain a keno blank, which appears on the next page.

After you obtain this blank, you take the crayon the casino supplies and mark up to fifteen numbers on this straight ticket. If you decide to play a six spot for 70¢, the completed ticket, together with the price showing, will look like the ticket on page 309.

You then bring the filled-in ticket to the keno lounge area, or to any counter in the casino that has keno writers available.

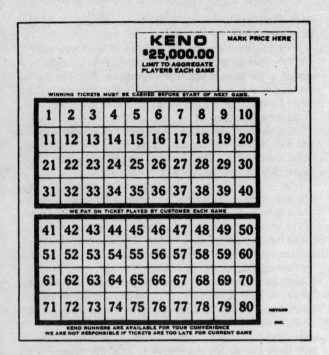

For instance, in Harrah's Club in Reno, there are keno writers outside the second-floor coffee shop to save both the patrons and keno runners the job of running to the main keno lounge located on the casino floor.

There will always be several keno writers available, and you should have plenty of time to get your ticket copied and paid for before the next game starts. The filled-in blank is handed to the keno writer along with 70¢, and you will receive back a duplicate ticket.

Both tickets are stamped by the keno writer: the one you originally handed him and the one you receive back, which is the duplicate. The stamping is done on the top of the ticket

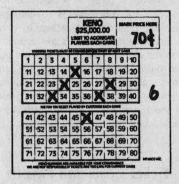

and shows the number of the ticket, the date, and the game played.

All of these procedures are taken so that the casino is protected from someone who either forges a ticket or works in collusion with an employee to present a ticket filled in after he has seen all the called numbers. Too much is at stake, namely the first prize of $250,000, for a casino to have sloppy controls in this game.

If you should win any prize money, the payoff will be based on the numbers marked on the original, and if there is any discrepancy between the original and your copy, you might forfeit a possible payoff. Therefore you must make certain that the writer copies your numbers correctly on the duplicate copy.

Should enough numbers catch for you to win, you must present your duplicate to the keno writer before the next game is played. If you examine the keno blank closely, it states in very small letters that "Winning Tickets Must Be Collected Immediately After Each Keno Game."

This statement is a very important one. It means that if you wait too long to cash in your ticket, you forfeit your payoff, even if that payoff was $250,000. Unless you submit your duplicate for payment prior to the next game being called, all you hold is a worthless piece of printed and marked paper.

To make certain that your ticket is a winning one, you can verify it by looking at the keno board and by checking it with a punch-out ticket. As the numbers are called, not only are they shown on the electric board, but they are punched out at the same time to doubly protect the casino. When you present your ticket for a payoff, the keno writer will automatically place the punch-out ticket over the duplicate presented, and in this way, by looking at the ink underneath, he can tell at a glance just how many numbers have caught.

Ticket Costs and Payoffs

All casinos that have keno lounges have a booklet with a rate card, showing the straight ticket payoffs. In most casinos there is usually one type of straight ticket available, but some casinos have special tickets, usually for $1, with slightly different payoffs. These rate cards should be consulted before a game is played, so that you know just how much you have to pay for your tickets and what the potential payouts are for your catches.

A typical rate card showing the 70¢ tickets with all payoffs from a one-spot to a fifteen-spot ticket is clearly shown on the opposite page.

Examining the booklet, you can see that, playing a six-spot 70¢ straight ticket, you can win as little as 60¢ if you catch three numbers, or as much as $1,100 if you catch all six numbers. If you had played the same six-spot for $1.40, the payout would be double, and if you played the game for $3.50, the payout would automatically be five times the original payout shown for the 70¢ ticket.

$50,000 and Progressive Payouts

Although some casinos still have 70¢ tickets with a grand prize of $25,000, most of the houses now feature a payoff of at least $50,000, with minimum $1 tickets. On the Strip the

70¢ Minimum Play

MARK 1 SPOT

Catch	Play .70	Play 1.40	Play 3.50
1 Pays	2.10	4.20	10.50

MARK 2 SPOTS

Catch	Play .70	Play 1.40	Play 3.50
2 Pays	8.50	17.00	42.50

MARK 3 SPOTS

Catch	Play .70	Play 1.40	Play 3.50
2 Pays	.70	1.40	3.50
3 Pays	30.00	60.00	150.00

MARK 4 SPOTS

Catch	Play .70	Play 1.40	Play 3.50
2 Pays	.70	1.40	3.50
3 Pays	2.70	1.40	3.50
4 Pays	80.00	160.00	400.00

MARK 5 SPOTS

Catch	Play .70	Play 1.40	Play 3.50
3 Pays	.20	.40	1.00
4 Pays	3.40	6.80	17.00
5 Pays	340.00	680.00	1,700.00

MARK 6 SPOTS

Catch	Play .70	Play 1.40	Play 3.50
3 Pays			
4 Pays	3.30	6.60	16.50
5 Pays	60.00	120.00	300.00
6 Pays	1,100.00	2,200.00	5,500.00

MARK 7 SPOTS

Catch	Play .70	Play 1.40	Play 3.50
3 Pays	.30	.60	1.50
4 Pays	1.20	2.40	6.00
5 Pays	15.00	30.00	75.00
6 Pays	220.00	440.00	1,100.00
7 Pays	3,500.00	7,000.00	17,500.00

MARK 8 SPOTS

Catch	Play .70	Play 1.40	Play 3.50
5 Pays	6.00	12.00	30.00
6 Pays	60.00	120.00	300.00
7 Pays	1,150.00	2,300.00	5,750.00
8 Pays	12,500.00	25,000.00	25,000.00

70¢ Minimum Play

MARK 9 SPOTS

Catch	Play .70	Play 1.40	Play 3.50
4 Pays	2.30	4.60	11.50
5 Pays	30.00	60.00	150.00
6 Pays	300.00	600.00	1,500.00
7 Pays	2,800.00	5,600.00	14,000.00
8 Pays	12,500.00	25,000.00	25,000.00

MARK 10 SPOTS

Catch	Play .70	Play 1.40	Play 3.50
5 Pays	1.40	2.80	7.00
6 Pays	14.00	28.00	70.00
7 Pays	98.00	196.00	490.00
8 Pays	700.00	1,400.00	3,500.00
9 Pays	2,660.00	5,320.00	13,300.00
10 Pays	12,500.00	25,000.00	25,000.00

MARK 11 SPOTS

Catch	Play .70	Play 1.40	Play 3.50
6 Pays	6.00	12.00	30.00
7 Pays	50.00	100.00	250.00
8 Pays	250.00	500.00	1,250.00
9 Pays	1,200.00	2,400.00	6,000.00
10 Pays	7,500.00	15,000.00	25,000.00
11 Pays	12,500.00	25,000.00	25,000.00

MARK 12 SPOTS

Catch	Play .70	Play 1.40	Play 3.50
6 Pays	.60	1.20	3.00
7 Pays	3.00	6.00	15.00
8 Pays	20.00	40.00	100.00
9 Pays	150.00	300.00	750.00
10 Pays	400.00	800.00	2,000.00
11 Pays	1,000.00	2,000.00	5,000.00
12 Pays	23,000.00	25,000.00	25,000.00

MARK 13 SPOTS

Catch	Play .70	Play 1.40	Play 3.50
6 Pays	1.20	2.40	6.00
7 Pays	12.00	24.00	60.00
8 Pays	50.00	100.00	250.00
9 Pays	471.00	950.00	2,375.00
10 Pays	2,500.00	5,000.00	12,500.00
11 Pays	2,500.00	9,000.00	22,500.00
12 Pays	23,000.00	20,000.00	25,000.00
13 Pays	25,000.00	25,000.00	25,000.00

70¢ Minimum Play

MARK 14 SPOTS

Catch	Play .70	Play 1.40	Play 3.50
6 Pays	2.20	4.40	11.00
7 Pays	5.50	11.00	27.50
8 Pays	22.00	44.00	110.00
9 Pays	17.00		
10 Pays	500.00	1,000.00	2,500.00
11 Pays	2,000.00	4,000.00	10,000.00
12 Pays	15,000.00	15,000.00	25,000.00
13 Pays	25,000.00	25,000.00	25,000.00
14 Pays	25,000.00	25,000.00	25,000.00

MARK 15 SPOTS

Catch	Play .70	Play 1.40	Play 3.50
6 Pays	2.00	5.00	5.00
7 Pays	5.00	10.00	25.00
8 Pays	15.00	30.00	75.00
9 Pays	75.00	150.00	375.00
10 Pays	600.00	1,200.00	3,000.00
11 Pays	1,500.00	3,000.00	7,500.00
12 Pays	5,000.00	10,000.00	25,000.00
13 Pays	15,000.00	25,000.00	25,000.00
14 Pays	20,000.00	25,000.00	25,000.00
15 Pays	25,000.00	25,000.00	25,000.00

REGULATIONS REQUIRE THAT ALL WINNING TICKETS MUST BE COLLECTED IMMEDIATELY AFTER EACH GAME.

KENO RUNNERS ARE FOR YOUR CONVENIENCE. Mark your tickets early to avoid missing a game. We are not responsible if tickets arrive too late for game played.

**$25,000 LIMIT EACH GAME
AGGREGATE PAY-OFF**

minimum can be as high as $2. Keno, if one keeps losing, can add up to an expensive undertaking.

Not only are $50,000 payouts the norm, but several casinos have instituted a progressive payout. It begins at $50,000 and moves up to as high as $200,000 or $250,000. Each time the huge payoff is not paid out, the progressive payoff increases in small increments. At one casino it was at $69,000, at another it was already up to the maximum of $200,000 when I visited Vegas last. Needless to say, if you want to play the game, wait for the maximum payoff before investing your couple of dollars.

The progressive payoff usually starts with a 9 ticket rather than with any of the smaller ones. The more numbers a player selects, the more the casino advantage and the less likely that player is of winning. So the casino entices the player with the big jackpot, but he or she must purchase a larger ticket picking at least 9 numbers. In the Horseshoe Club in downtown Las Vegas, you must purchase a $2 ticket with at least 9 numbers (you can choose more numbers) in order to be eligible for the progressive prize. Let's look at a typical rate card for the $1 game featuring the progressive prize, which in this instance can be as high as $200,000.

This is a dollar rate card, with no bet allowed below $1. If we examine this card closely, we see that at no time will a $1 ticket win us more than $40,000, and that is only when we select 14 or 15 numbers and hit them all, an extremely difficult task.

We'd be much better off playing the $2 tickets. If we bet as few as 8 numbers, we'd be eligible for the $50,000 payoff if we caught all 8 numbers. And believe me, it's much easier to catch 8 numbers than it is to catch 14 or 15. But we shouldn't be satisfied with $50,000. In a game such as keno, with the odds stacked against us, we want to win as much as possible if lightning strikes and luck is shining all over us. We go for the progressive win.

Before we do that, we should check on the amount it shows. It should be ideally the maximum $200,000 or $250,000, depending on the casino we're playing at. If it's at $50,000, pass the game. After all, $250,000 is five times $50,000, and why not get that enhanced payoff rather than the smaller one, all for the same price?

We should therefore concentrate on the 9 ticket, our easiest entry into the big payoff, when played as a $2 ticket. To do this, we select 9 numbers in a straight ticket, and hope all 9 catch. If they do, we win the big pot! Simple as that.

And remember, that should always be your strategy when playing keno. Go for the big win. Don't bother with the $3 payout by selecting 1 number and betting $1. You're much better off playing a column or a dozen at a game like roulette, where the odds against you are 5.26%, not the double figures of keno. After all, a $3 payout on a 1 number ticket bet for $1 is in reality 2–1, for you're getting back your original bet. The odds against are 3–1. Don't bother with this terrible bet. The casino has a 25% edge.

Let's now look at some other intriguing possibilities offered by casinos today.

The Special $1.25 rate card offers us our best shot if we select 8 numbers only. If we bet $1.25 and catch all of the numbers, we win $40,000. Betting $2.50 and catching 8 numbers gives us $50,000. But again, we might consider betting only $2 and selecting 9 numbers to get that progressive prize. No such prize is offered with the $1.25 Special. Remember your ultimate strategy—go for the biggest possible win in keno. That's the only way to play this game.

Even if you don't hit the big prize, there are some other good prizes to be gotten. But they decrease rapidly in size, so we always want to hit the big one. For example, marking 8 numbers on the $1.25 special and getting all 8 gives us $50,000. However, 7 gives us only $2,960.00 and 6 only $180. And getting 4 out of 8, no mean task, rewards us with only $2.

In the next group, we can see that $1.40 bet on a straight ticket will also make us eligible for the progressive prize.

With the $1.40 rate card, we have to select at least 12 numbers to be eligible for the progressive win. That's a lot of numbers to catch. Again, we suggest betting $2 and going after the 9 numbers. That is absolutely your best bet in this type of progressive keno payout.

DOLLAR RATES

MARK ANY 1 NUMBER

Catch	Bet	1.00	Bet	2.00	Bet	5.00
1	Win	3.00	Win	6.00	Win	15.00

MARK ANY 2 NUMBERS

Catch	Bet	1.00	Bet	2.00	Bet	5.00
2	Win	12.00	Win	24.00	Win	60.00

MARK ANY 3 NUMBERS

Catch	Bet	1.00	Bet	2.00	Bet	5.00
2	Win	1.00	Win	2.00	Win	5.00
3		42.00		84.00		210.00

MARK ANY 4 NUMBERS

Catch	Bet	1.00	Bet	2.00	Bet	5.00
2	Win	1.00	Win	2.00	Win	5.00
3		4.00		8.00		20.00
4		112.00		224.00		560.00

MARK ANY 5 NUMBERS

Catch	Bet	1.00	Bet	2.00	Bet	5.00
3	Win	1.00	Win	2.00	Win	5.00
4		14.00		28.00		70.00
5		720.00		1,440.00		3,600.00

MARK ANY 6 NUMBERS

Catch	Bet	1.00	Bet	2.00	Bet	5.00
3	Win	1.00	Win	2.00	Win	5.00
4		4.00		8.00		20.00
5		88.00		176.00		440.00
6		1,480.00		2,960.00		7,400.00

MARK ANY 7 NUMBERS

Catch	Bet	1.00	Bet	2.00	Bet	5.00
4	Win	1.00	Win	2.00	Win	5.00
5		20.00		40.00		100.00
6		380.00		760.00		1,900.00
7		8,000.00		16,000.00		40,000.00

MARK ANY 8 NUMBERS

Catch	Bet	1.00	Bet	2.00	Bet	5.00
5	Win	9.00	Win	18.00	Win	45.00
6		80.00		160.00		400.00
7		1,480.00		2,960.00		7,400.00
8		25,000.00		50,000.00		50,000.00

MARK ANY 9 NUMBERS

Catch	Bet	1.00	Bet	2.00	Bet	5.00
5	Win	4.00	Win	8.00	Win	20.00
6		44.00		88.00		220.00
7		300.00		600.00		1,500.00
8		4,000.00		8,000.00		20,000.00
9		25,000.00		PROGRESSIVE		PROGRESSIVE

MARK ANY 10 NUMBERS

Catch	Bet	1.00	Bet	2.00	Bet	5.00
5	Win	2.00	Win	4.00	Win	10.00
6		20.00		40.00		100.00
7		136.00		272.00		680.00
8		960.00		1,920.00		4,800.00
9		4,000.00		8,000.00		20,000.00
10		25,000.00	PROGRESSIVE		PROGRESSIVE	

MARK ANY 11 NUMBERS

Catch	Bet	1.00	Bet	2.00	Bet	5.00
5	Win	1.00	Win	2.00	Win	5.00
6		8.00		16.00		40.00
7		72.00		144.00		360.00
8		360.00		720.00		1,800.00
9		1,800.00		3,600.00		9,000.00
10		12,000.00		24,000.00	PROGRESSIVE	
11		28,000.00	PROGRESSIVE		PROGRESSIVE	

MARK ANY 12 NUMBERS

Catch	Bet	1.00	Bet	2.00	Bet	5.00
6	Win	5.00	Win	10.00	Win	25.00
7		32.00		64.00		160.00
8		240.00		480.00		1,200.00
9		600.00		1,200.00		3,000.00
10		1,480.00		2,960.00		7,400.00
11		12,000.00		24,000.00	PROGRESSIVE	
12		36,000.00	PROGRESSIVE		PROGRESSIVE	

MARK ANY 13 NUMBERS

Catch	Bet	1.00	Bet	2.00	Bet	5.00
6	Win	1.00	Win	2.00	Win	5.00
7		16.00		32.00		80.00
8		80.00		160.00		400.00
9		720.00		1,440.00		3,600.00
10		4,000.00		8,000.00		20,000.00
11		8,000.00		16,000.00		40,000.00
12		25,000.00	PROGRESSIVE		PROGRESSIVE	
13		36,000.00	PROGRESSIVE		PROGRESSIVE	

MARK ANY 14 NUMBERS

Catch	Bet	1.00	Bet	2.00	Bet	5.00
6	Win	1.00	Win	2.00	Win	5.00
7		10.00		20.00		50.00
8		40.00		80.00		200.00
9		320.00		640.00		1,600.00
10		1,000.00		2,000.00		5,000.00
11		3,200.00		6,400.00		16,000.00
12		16,000.00		32,000.00	PROGRESSIVE	
13		25,000.00	PROGRESSIVE		PROGRESSIVE	
14		40,000.00	PROGRESSIVE		PROGRESSIVE	

MARK ANY 15 NUMBERS

Catch	Bet	1.00	Bet	2.00	Bet	5.00
7	Win	8.00	Win	16.00	Win	40.00
8		28.00		56.00		140.00
9		132.00		264.00		660.00
10		300.00		600.00		1,500.00
11		2,600.00		5,200.00		13,000.00
12		8,000.00		16,000.00		40,000.00
13		25,000.00	PROGRESSIVE		PROGRESSIVE	
14		32,000.00	PROGRESSIVE		PROGRESSIVE	
15		40,000.00	PROGRESSIVE		PROGRESSIVE	

DOLLAR RATES

SPECIAL $1.25 SPECIAL

MARK ANY 4 NUMBERS

Catch	Bet 1.25		Bet 2.50		Bet 6.25	
3	Win	6.00	Win	12.00	Win	30.00
4		200.00		400.00		1,000.00

MARK ANY 5 NUMBERS

Catch	Bet 1.25		Bet 2.50		Bet 6.25	
3	Win	1.00	Win	2.00	Win	5.00
4		8.00		16.00		40.00
5	1	100.00		2,200.00		5,500.00

MARK ANY 6 NUMBERS

Catch	Bet 1.25		Bet 2.50		Bet 6.25	
3	Win	1.00	Win	2.00	Win	5.00
4		3.00		6.00		15.00
5		90.00		180.00		450.00
6		3,000.00		6,000.00		15,000.00

MARK ANY 8 NUMBERS

Catch	Bet 1.25		Bet 2.50		Bet 6.25	
4	Win	1.00	Win	2.00	Win	5.00
5		9.00		18.00		45.00
6		90.00		180.00		450.00
7		1,480.00		2,960.00		7,400.00
8		40,000.00		50,000.00		50,000.00

Next we come to an intriguing game, where we win by *not* catching numbers as well as catching them. And we can select 20 numbers at one time!

With this rate ticket, called the Twenty-Number Special, you can mark up to 20 numbers. You have to bet $5 to be eligible for the progressive payoff, which comes only with 16 catches, but there are all kinds of payoffs that sound intriguing. Are they? Let's see.

If you don't catch any numbers, you win $500. But the odds of not catching one number out of 20 doesn't make this payoff worthwhile. More likely, you might only catch 2 or 3, but then you only get your money back. Catching 4–6 numbers nets you nothing, and is a complete loser. What you're hoping for is at least 12 numbers to catch, so you get $1,000 or more back. Although there are so-called 18 out of 21 ways to win, with only 4–6 catches not paying anything, getting from 2–7

$1.40 PLAYS

70¢ Minimum

MARK ANY 1 NUMBER		
Catch	Bet	1.40
1	Win	4.20

MARK ANY 2 NUMBERS		
Catch	Bet	1.40
2	Win	17.00

MARK ANY 3 NUMBERS		
Catch	Bet	1.40
2	Win	1.40
3		60.00

MARK ANY 4 NUMBERS		
Catch	Bet	1.40
2	Win	1.40
3		5.40
4		160.00

MARK ANY 5 NUMBERS		
Catch	Bet	1.40
3	Win	2.40
4		30.00
5		680.00

MARK ANY 6 NUMBERS		
Catch	Bet	1.40
3	Win	1.20
4		6.60
5		120.00
6		2.200.00

MARK ANY 7 NUMBERS		
Catch	Bet	1.40
3	Win	0.60
4		2.40
5		30.00
6		460.00
7		7,000.00

MARK ANY 8 NUMBERS		
Catch	Bet	1.40
5	Win	12.00
6		120.00
7		2,300.00
8		25,000.00

MARK ANY 9 NUMBERS		
Catch	Bet	1.40
4	Win	0.60
5		4.60
6		60.00
7		400.00
8		5,600.00
9		25,000.00

MARK ANY 10 NUMBERS		
Catch	Bet	1.40
5	Win	2.80
6		28.00
7		196.00
8		1,400.00
9		5,320.00
10		25,000.00

MARK ANY 11 NUMBERS		
Catch	Bet	1.40
5	Win	1.20
6		12.00
7		100.00
8		500.00
9		2,400.00
10		15,000.00
11		40 000.00

MARK ANY 12 NUMBERS		
Catch	Bet	1.40
5	Win	1.20
6		6.00
7		40.00
8		300.00
9		800.00
10		2,000.00
11		10,000.00
12		PROGRESSIVE

MARK ANY 13 NUMBERS		
Catch	Bet	1.40
6	Win	2.40
7		24.00
8		100.00
9		950.00
10		5,000.00
11		9,000.00
12		20,000.00
13		PROGRESSIVE

MARK ANY 14 NUMBERS		
Catch	Bet	1.40
6	Win	4.40
7		11.00
8		44.00
9		350.00
10		1,000.00
11		4,000.00
12		15,000.00
13		30,000.00
14		PROGRESSIVE

MARK ANY 15 NUMBERS		
Catch	Bet	1.40
6	Win	2.00
7		10.00
8		30.00
9		150.00
10		400.00
11		3,000.00
12		10,000.00
13		30,000.00
14		40,000.00
15		PROGRESSIVE

TWENTY-NUMBER SPECIAL

Mark any 20 Numbers. Bet $5.00
You May Win up to $200,000.00.

CATCH	$ WIN
0	500.00
1	10.00
2	5.00
3	5.00
4	0.00
5	0.00
6	0.00
7	5.00
8	10.00
9	25.00
10	50.00
11	200.00
12	1,000.00
13	5,000.00
14	12,500.00
15	25,000.00
16	**Progressive**
17	**Progressive**
18	**Progressive**
19	**Progressive**
20	**Progressive**

18 out of 21
Ways to Win

P.S. Any vended ticket with more than 20 numbers or fewer is automatically null and void. **We will refund your money.**

catches, your most likely possibilities, will either lose for you or get you back your original bet of $5. However, for you players who constantly complain that you can't catch even a single number, this card might be worth a couple of shots. And as remote as it seems, there's still the very slim chance of catching the progressive payout.

There's a variation on this card, as follows:

K·E·N·O

WIN UP TO
$250,000

16 SPOT OR SWEET SIXTEEN
17 WAYS TO WIN
ALL-WAYS A WINNER
$5.00 TICKET

IF YOU CATCH	YOUR PAYOFF IS
0 of 16	50.00
1 of 16	5.00
2 of 16	3.00
3 of 16	2.00
4 of 16	1.00
5 of 16	2.00
6 of 16	3.00
7 of 16	5.00
8 of 16	20.00
9 of 16	200.00
10 of 16	600.00
11 of 16	2,500.00
12 of 16	12,500.00
13 of 16	25,000.00
14 of 16	50,000.00
15 of 16	50,000.00
16 of 16	50,000.00
Plus 100% of KENOPOT	UP TO TOTAL OF $250,000.00

Based on Kenopot Meter of $200,000

I came across this ''Sweet Sixteen'' card at the Palace Station casino, which is located on the western side of I-15 on Sahara. They have some interesting keno games going, one with a metered progressive payout that goes up to $250,000 for a $3 ticket with a minimum of 9 numbers.

On the Sweet Sixteen, there's money back all up and down the card, although you're either going to get $5 or less if you catch 1–7 numbers out of a possible 16, your most likely catch. There are two payouts of $50,000 for catching 14 or 15 numbers, and you get the progressive payout for 16 out of 16.

The ticket costs $5, and I would only play it when the progressive payout is close to $250,000. It might be worth a play or two to see if your bad luck will win you money, although, as can be seen by the payoffs, you start to get a serious pay-back only if you hit 11 or more numbers.

Replaying the Ticket

If you want to stay with predetermined numbers and contin-ually play these same numbers over and over again, it's not necessary to keep writing new tickets. The duplicate can be turned in to the keno writer, who then accepts it as the original for the next game, and this can be done time after time, saving energy and making everybody's task simpler.

Multi-Race Keno

The casinos have made it easier for those players who wish to play the same numbers over and over again. In some of the houses that feature keno, the concept of multi-race keno has come into use. Here's how it works: A player selects the num-bers he wishes to play, and then the number of games he wishes to enter with these numbers. In some casinos the max-imum is ten; in others one can play up to twenty games.

Let's suppose that a player wishes to play a three-way ticket as shown in the next illustration.

Let's see what the player has selected and played. First of all, there are two groups of four numbers, which is shown on the side as 2/4. Then there is one 8 number selection (com-bining the two groups, which is shown as 1/8). Underneath this is a statement 1.00R, which shows that each way is bet at a $1 rate. The combined total is shown on the side above the ways played as $3.00.

The player is playing this same ticket in a multi-race for ten consecutive races, so we see that he has paid $30.00 or ten times $3.00 for all the games to be played.

The first game he's entered in is number 116, and the last game will be 125. So for the next ten games, the player can watch the play or not, but when game 125 has been called,

KENO SPECIALS
MULTI-RACE KENO
FOR YOUR CONVENIENCE

MULTI-RACE TICKET SAMPLE

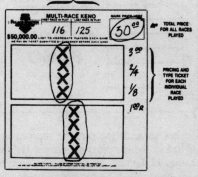

EXAMPLE OF A TICKET
PLAYED FOR 10 RACES

PLAY UP TO 10 CONSECUTIVE RACES
WITH JUST 1 TICKET
AND THEN RELAX AND ENJOY
YOUR MEAL, DRINK, OR
OTHER GAME.

YOU MAY PLAY 2 - 3 - 4 - 5 - UP TO 10
(MAXIMUM OF 10)
CONSECUTIVE RACES.

WINNING TICKETS CAN ONLY BE COLLECTED
IMMEDIATELY AFTER YOUR LAST RACE IN PLAY IS CALLED
AND PRIOR TO THE CALLING OF THE NEXT RACE.

which is the last game of the race, he must claim whatever wins he has had in the ten previous games. He can't do this before the calling of the tenth race, and if he waits till the next game, 126 has been called, he forfeits all prize money.

He can keep score on the back of a keno blank set for that purpose, as shown above.

Some casinos have more stringent rules. In the Horseshoe, where twenty games can be played in the multi-race, the rules state that the player is required to be present in a keno playing area (casino, bar, restaurant, card room, or other gaming area) during the entire calling of the game (i.e., all races wagered on). In fact, it's a good idea to do this because you should be aware of what you won, and if you've won big, you don't want to forfeit your profits by not being present when the last race of your sequence is being called.

Types of Keno Tickets

Straight Tickets

We've already discussed the most commonly used ticket in keno, the straight ticket—one on which you mark from one to fifteen numbers. In the smaller casinos they can be purchased for as little as 35¢. In most casinos the minimum price for a straight ticket is 70¢, while certain of the more ornate casinos permit only a $1.40 minimum ticket.

When purchasing a straight ticket, you are not limited to paying only the minimum rate. You may bet in multiples of that rate and receive a payout commensurate with that price. For example, if you chose a ten-spot ticket for 70¢ and caught eight numbers, you would receive a payoff of $700. If you play the same ten-spot ticket for $3.50, you would receive five times the basic payoff, or $3,500. If that same ticket had been purchased for $7.00, the payoff would be $7,000.

Straight tickets are the easiest to mark, the easiest to write, and the easiest to calculate. But there are other ways to play keno, using more complicated methods of choosing and marking the tickets.

Split Tickets

If you wish to write two or more straight tickets at one time, using one keno blank, the easiest way to do this is with a split ticket.

A split ticket utilizes two or more groups of numbers, separated from each other in some manner. The most commonly used methods are to draw a line between the groupings of numbers, or to circle one or both of the groups. The important thing when writing a split ticket is to make certain that the keno writer understands that he has been given this type of ticket.

The following is a usual way of writing a split ticket. Note that the fraction ⅖ means that the ticket contains two five-spots. The circled 70 means that each five-spot, or way, is

being played for 70¢. This ticket would be called a two-way five-spot.

The above example shows two groups of numbers, each bet and played separately on the one split ticket. But you are not limited to two groups of numbers. If you are willing to play smaller spots, such as two-spots and three-spots, you may play as many as forty individual two-spots on one ticket.

This is not recommended, but you should be aware that you can play more than one group, or way, on one ticket in this simple manner. When playing more than one way, many casinos will accommodate players by reducing the 70¢ house minimum to 35¢ per way. "Way" here is defined simply as a possible payoff. For example, if a split ticket has two circled groups, there are two potential payoffs, and thus, two ways.

When the minimum is reduced by half by the casino, you should be aware that the potential payoff is also reduced by half.

Way Tickets

A way ticket can be defined as a keno ticket marked with at least three equal groups of numbers, each group combining with the other groups to form several straight ticket combi-

nations. A way ticket might look like this, with the fraction ⅜ referring to a three-way eight-spot.

Note that each circled group contains four selected numbers, or four-spots. Therefore, when playing this ticket, each four-spot combines with the other four-spots to make three possible eight-spots. This means that there are three possible combinations of eight numbers from the three four-spots selected.

To show this more clearly, if we number each four-spot as A, B, and C, the following eight-spot combinations can result: AB, AC, and BC. Each of these groups now contain eight numbers and therefore this ticket will be written as a three-way eight-spot. We are using twelve numbers in all to catch an eight-spot winner, giving us a little more leverage in selection.

The ticket shown is written for $2.10, which means that you would pay 70¢ per way, but in many casinos it could be written for only 35¢ a way, even though the house has a 70¢ minimum.

Way tickets are simple to write and simple to figure out, and give you added possibilities for winning by having, in this case, twelve numbers working to win your eight-spot selections with.

Combination Tickets

These are some of the most complicated and versatile of all keno tickets, and few players use them or even know they exist. They are filled in, using the same keno blank that is used for other tickets, but they add to the gambling thrill of keno by making use of various combinations to try for a win.

First, let's look at a relatively simple combination ticket, using the previous way ticket as the base.

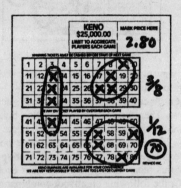

What we've done is combine the three eight-spots with one twelve-spot ticket. This can be done because the three groups of four-spots add up to one twelve-spot. Now we have a simple combination ticket of three eight-spots and one twelve-spot.

We can go even further with the same ticket on the facing page.

Now we have three four-spots, three eight-spots, and one twelve-spot.

Most combination tickets, however, are not based on rigid groups of numbers, such as the basic way ticket. A typical combination ticket wouldn't be made up of equal groupings of numbers, such as are found in a way ticket. The combination ticket on the following page shows this.

Here we have seven different combinations developed from

three simple groupings, one of two-spots and two of four-spots. This makes the combination ticket extremely versatile, though more complicated.

As with way tickets, casinos will allow a player to bet the tickets for less than the 70¢ minimum it requires for straight tickets, and most houses will permit a gambler to bet as little as 35¢ on each possible combination.

Some combination tickets are so complicated that they can really tax the mind and ingenuity of both player and writer. Therefore, when writing really complicated tickets it's a good idea to consult with the keno writer about minimum rates and the possible combinations resulting from the ticket, so that

there is no mistake concerning the payoffs that might result if any of the combinations hit.

Combination tickets can become very expensive because of all the ways inherent in even the simplest of tickets, and as game after game goes on, these costs really add up.

You should also be aware that the house edge, which is at least 20 percent in keno, doesn't get reduced or altered because combination, rather than straight tickets, are being played. All you are doing is combining many tickets in one ticket and playing them simultaneously when you play a combination ticket.

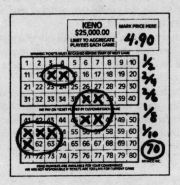

King Tickets

A king ticket can be defined in its most simple form as any ticket that contains a single circled number. But when you have one circled number in combination with other groups of numbers, also circled, you have the most versatile of all tickets. Let's look at a noncomplicated king ticket.

We have used the king (number 5) to combine with the two

three-spots to form two four-spots and one seven-spot. The purpose of a king number is to combine, not to be played as a single entity.

When two kings are used at once, the ticket can be extremely complicated, as you can see by looking at the next ticket.

This kind of ticket takes plenty of time to work out and write, and it is also quite expensive.

Some tickets can be written with all king numbers and are called all-king tickets. To write such a ticket, at least two kings must be used. King tickets, combined with way or combination tickets, make for extremely complex and versatile keno games. They are relatively expensive as well, but should the numbers catch, they can lead to lucrative payouts.

Since they are so complicated, it's important, after the numbers have been selected, to carefully examine them for possible payoffs, since winning catches can easily be overlooked in the more complex tickets. Any player in doubt about a possible win should immediately go to the keno writer and have him figure out the ticket. A keno writer will be happy to do this because that's not only his job, but if there's a good win on the ticket, he's glad to get toked for his efforts.

One final statement on the complicated tickets. You should always go to the keno writer on complex way, combination, and king tickets to make certain that they are correctly "conditioned."

The casino term for the player's choice is called conditioning, and on involved tickets, you want to be sure that you have all the possible ways you wanted covered on the ticket.

Special Tickets

Many casinos, as an inducement for unsophisticated or nonserious players, offer special tickets with varying prices and payoffs.

A few years back I was eating breakfast in a small casino in Lake Tahoe, away from the center of the town, and, having been given a keno booklet explaining a special three-spot ticket priced at 30¢ with a payoff of $35 if all three numbers caught, I picked my favorite numbers, 1, 11, and 30, paid the 30¢, and ate my breakfast.

After seventeen numbers were shown on the keno board, my ticket was worthless, with none of my numbers catching. Then 30, 11, and 1 flashed, and I was a winner of $35. I took that $35, went to the blackjack tables and parlayed it into $200. A pleasant morning indeed.

Casino Advantage in Keno

Since the house gives out cash prizes that can run as high as $250,000, and since a player can participate in the game for as little as 35¢ or 70¢ with a chance to win large payoffs, the casino makes certain that its edge in this game is very high. In fact, the edge is greater than on any other casino game.

To illustrate the house advantage, let's examine the odds on a one-spot ticket, the easiest and simplest of all tickets. When playing a one-spot, the player selects but one number, and if the number catches, he wins. If it doesn't catch, he loses.

The payoff on a one-spot is 3 for 1. This means that the actual payoff is 2–1. The player receives $2.10 for the 70¢

bet. There are eighty numbers that can possibly be selected in keno, and only twenty of them are called by the operator of the game. Therefore, the chances of winning with a one-spot ticket are twenty out of eighty, or 3–1 against. By paying only 2–1, the house has a 25 percent advantage on this wager.

This edge is even higher if the player bets a two-spot, for the chances of winning are slightly less, and the payoff is even smaller in proportion to the one-spot win. A two-spot wager gives the casino an advantage of 26.9 percent. A three-spot ticket gives the house 35 percent, a six-spot 37 percent, and the twelve-spot, the first ticket to pay $25,000 for a 70¢ bet, gives the house its greatest edge, 40 percent.

With these odds, betting keno as a serious gambling game is a treacherous course. It places gamblers at an enormous disadvantage, and those with limited funds can be tapped out quickly. This is a very tough game to beat.

Many gamblers are addicts of the game, however, and keep buying keno tickets game after game, afraid that if they should miss one, that particular game will be the very game that would have gotten them the big $25,000 payout. But these gamblers are operating under a delusion. On a few occasions, I've monitored the game for several hours after selecting twelve numbers, but not betting on them.

The first time I did this I went twenty-three games without any kind of payoff. Then, finally, I won $3 by catching six numbers. If I had been betting $7 a game, my net loss after those twenty-three games would have been $161. This kind of money really adds up. At 70¢ a game, losing twenty-three in a row totals $16.10.

Not only does this result in lost money, but wasted time as well, because there's nothing more boring and dreary than watching that board game after game with nothing of value showing up.

More than two hundred games are played in a single day, and at $5 a game, a whole day's loss would run about $800, counting on a few small payoffs. For most of the payouts are very small, rarely amounting to more than 5–1. It is rare to hear of any big winners. The casino is eager to broadcast and publicize wins by players amounting to thousands of dollars, but a player can sit in a casino for a month straight, hour after hour and day after day, and never hear of a payoff exceeding a few hundred dollars. Those $250,000 payoffs are events that have occurred once or twice in the casino's history.

Keno basically is a seductive game, appealing to those greedy enough to want to win a great deal of money for an investment in pennies. The house takes full advantage of the bettor's avarice and, in the course of catering to this greed, makes a small fortune for itself.

To get big payoffs, there must be a high percentage of catches, and the odds keep rising against getting those catches. The probability of hitting nine out of ten numbers selected on a ten-spot straight ticket is something like .00061.

Aggregate Prize Money

Each keno blank carries the legend, "$50,000 limit to aggregate players each game," or in some instances the figure given is $25,000, depending on the casino and the grand prize money it offers. What this means in plain English is that the casino is liable for a total payoff of $50,000 on any one game, not an individual payoff. If two players happen to catch enough numbers for each to collect $50,000, they'll have to split that $50,000 between them. No total payout on any one keno game will exceed this amount, except for the progressive payouts, which states ambiguously on the ticket, "Progressive limit $200,000 maximum." This means the same thing as the aggregate payout, and the casino will pay each winning player in one game his portion of that progressive payout. If it's the limit of $200,000 and two players have won, each will get $100,000.

By having this rule, the casinos lower their risk even further, though there really is no need for them to do this. I never heard of any case where two players were able to claim the top prize, and even if that's happened, it wouldn't make more than a dent in the casino's profits from keno.

I had written in a previous edition that the casinos in Nevada could give $50,000 or even $100,000 as their top prize and still not be hurt. Well, that day has arrived with the standard

$50,000 payouts and enhanced progressive payouts amounting to as much as a quarter of a million dollars. With the progressive payouts the casino takes no risk either, for to move from $50,000 up to $200,000 takes a lot of games in which no one has claimed the grand prize, and the casino has more than made back its money by the time someone is fortunate enough to win the $250,000.

When someone does win that kind of money, the casino gets a further benefit in the way of publicity. More and more players will flock to that game, hoping that lightning will strike twice. No matter which way they slice the keno pie, the casino operators get the biggest portion for themselves.

How to Select Numbers

There are four basic ways to select numbers in keno. Some players have a group of numbers they consider lucky or important, which they play in various combinations. These may include the player's date of birth, age, friend's or spouse's birthday or age, family's birthdays and ages, and so forth.

Other players do just the opposite. They select numbers completely at random, marking them on the blank without any predetermination whatsoever, until they have the required amount of numbers necessary to play their ticket. This method is as valid as the first one in selecting numbers, but a little more difficult to follow, since people tend to be aware of lucky and important numbers and immediately recognize them as they flash on the board.

The third method involves a scientific fallacy. Players decide to pick only those numbers that haven't hit for several games, and they keep track of all the selected numbers, game after game, on long sheets of paper marked from 1 to 80.

If after ten or so games, certain numbers haven't shown on the board, these numbers are played for the next game. In this way the gamblers hope that the law of averages will work in their favor, and reason that these numbers are due or overdue. However, the law of averages doesn't work for short series of plays. The law of averages is really the law of large numbers, and to really show a proper distribution, these numbers must be followed not for ten or twenty or a hundred games, but for many hundreds of thousands and possibly millions.

In the long run all eighty numbers should show up with equal frequency. Now, this might never happen, but the longer the game is played, the more equal the distribution of these random numbers will be.

A player might enter the casino, follow the keno board for two hundred plays and see that the numbers 1, 15, 26, 38, 42, 43, 56, 61, 67, and 76 haven't hit more than once or twice in all that time. So he plays these numbers, and they still refuse to show, or a couple of them hit at different times, but not enough times to cause a payoff on his ticket.

What this player doesn't know and cannot know is that these same numbers might in fact, in the course of a hundred thousand games at this particular keno board, be way ahead of the other numbers, and that other numbers have to come up hundreds of times more to catch up with the numbers he's playing in a vain attempt to take advantage of the law of averages.

Even if he had kept a record of all these hundred thousand games, that still might not be enough information for this player to predict the next winning ticket. If the game had gone on for ten million plays, all the numbers wouldn't be equally distributed but would be closing in on an equal distribution. The game is so random in nature that there's no way to predict anything based on the past.

The last method, which might be the best, is to continually select numbers that have shown board after board. I've personally observed the same numbers appearing on ten straight boards, and after a while I almost was sure that they would show again. When this occurs it is *possible* that the selection isn't completely random, and for one reason or another, certain numbers are coming up more frequently than others. A number of factors could cause this.

• The game is played with Ping-Pong balls, none of which weighs exactly the same as others. Some may be lighter and others heavier, even if this involves differences measured by

1/100 or 1/1000 of an ounce. The lighter balls may have a tendency to rise faster than the heavier balls when hot air circulates them in the bowl. Thus, these lighter balls might move upward, or "draw," which is the casino term for balls moving upward into the goose.

• A ball may have a pinpoint hole or crack, or in other ways be flawed, and these balls will be less likely to draw.

• There may be an imperfection in manufacture which deadens a particular ball or balls. Anyone who plays table tennis knows that occasionally you get a ball that looks perfectly normal, but in fact has a dead spot that keeps it from bouncing as well as other balls.

If any of these situations are present, there is a definite bias that can be taken advantage of by astute players. However, since they can't examine the balls individually, they can only surmise that one of these factors is present.

Since it is to the casino's advantage to have a random game, the balls are constantly checked and rechecked before use in play, and those with nicks, scars, dents, or other imperfections are replaced immediately.

Basically, keno is a game of pure chance—a random game that perhaps must be bet randomly for best results. This doesn't mean that players should be oblivious to certain events repeating themselves, but when these events do occur, players are in a poor position to know why—whether the reason is luck or some definite bias in the balls or equipment.

Taxes on Keno Winnings

Since there is the possibility of a huge payoff resulting from a relatively small initial wager, the IRS has demanded that all casinos record the social security numbers of certain winners.

The following is the schedule that is generally posted somewhere near the keno lounge of most casinos. If not posted, then let the following rules guide you.

Total Price of Ticket		Payoffs Reportable
From	*Through*	
$ 0	$ .59	$ 600 or more
.60	.89	1,200 or more
.90	1.19	1,800 or more
1.20	1.79	2,400 or more
1.80	2.39	3,000 or more
2.40	2.99	3,600 or more
3.00	3.59	4,200 or more
3.60	9.99	6,000 or more
10.00	and over	10,000 or more

Gambling losses may be deducted from gambling wins, so it's important to save losing tickets if you've won enough to have a reportable win. This places an uncomfortable and unfair burden upon the player, who may have lost a great deal of money in other games during the year. Suddenly he or she makes a big win at keno, which is completely taxable, while all previous losses at blackjack and craps are next to impossible to verify.

State Keno Games

Several states flirting with legal gambling of one sort or another have turned to keno as a way to boost their tax revenues. Usually keno is played as part of the lottery system already in force, as in California and New York, the two most populous states in the USA. Terminals are set up in various places such as quick-food outlets, delis, and other places that attract a brisk walk-in business or, conversely, in bars where customers tend to spend a great deal of time. Keno has become a very tempting game for those who want to risk a little to make a lot. A new game, or draw (as in drawing) gets off every five minutes, so the result is fast, and the betting limits don't appear to be that high. But this can be deceptive. If a person is betting $10 on each game, within an hour, without any wins, he can lose $120. And if he is in a bar, where his judgment may be clouded by alcohol, a player can soon find himself in serious financial trouble. As with all gambling, I suggest that when you're playing for money, don't drink. It's a bad combination, and the last thing you need is to have your good sense and judgment negatively affected.

Most establishments are set up with video screens that flash the selected numbers every five minutes, so that customers can see the results, and determine whether or not they have won anything.

To throw a bone in the direction of the problem gambler, New York puts an 800 number on its tickets for those who are or who know someone who is in trouble. I'll repeat it here: (800) 522-4700.

Differences between Casino and State Keno

There are a number of differences between the game played in casinos and the one played in the various states that have legalized keno.

1. Of the keno tickets I've examined, only ten, rather than twenty spots (casino keno), can be played.

2. There is a strict limit on how much money a player can bet per draw. In New York it's $10, in California, it's $20.

3. Only straight tickets are available for play, rather than the more complex combination and way tickets. A player selects up to ten numbers and that's it.

4. Since the game is computerized, Quick Picks are an option. In other words, instead of selecting your own numbers, you let the computer do it for you. This is a common feature of state lotteries.

5. A player is limited to a certain number of draws (games) he can bet consecutively. In California it's 100; in New York it's twenty.

6. The payoffs are different. The following tables list payoffs for New York and California, as representative states.

7. The odds against winning are listed after each game, so a player knows exactly what his chances are.

California Payoffs and Odds for 1–10 Spot Games

Spots	Match	Payoff	Odds
1-spot game	1	$2	1–4.0
2-spot game	2	$8	1–16.6

Spots	Match	Payoff	Odds
3-spot game	3	$20	
	2	$2	1–6.6
4-spot game	4	$50	
	3	$4	
	1	$1	1–3.0
5-spot game	5	$250	
	4	$10	
	3	$1	1–10.3
6-spot game	6	$1,000	
	5	$25	
	4	$4	
	3	$1	1–6.2
7-spot game	7	$2,500	
	6	$100	
	5	$10	
	4	$2	
	3	$1	1–4.2
8-spot game	8	$10,000	
	7	$400	
	6	$40	
	5	$10	
	4	$1	1–9.8
9-spot game	9	$25,000	
	8	$2,500	
	7	$100	
	6	$10	
	5	$4	
	4	$1	1–6.5
10-spot game	10	$250,000	
	9	$3,000	
	8	$250	
	7	$50	
	6	$5	
	5	$2	
	0	$4	1–9.1

Looking at the above payoffs, we can see differences between them and the casino payoffs. The 10-spot win, catching all ten numbers, is ten times the usual casino payoff of $25,000, but the other payoffs in descending order are less than those in casinos.

The 9-spot payoff at $25,000 is the same as in casinos, but the other payoffs are much lower than those in the casinos.

The other payoffs for the remaining spot tickets are much lower than what the casinos ordinarily pay. It should be noted that all the above payoffs are for $1 tickets. Multiply $1 prize payoffs by the dollars played to determine payoffs. For example, if you play a $10 ticket, then multiply the payoffs by $10.

Best Tickets to Play

By examining the overall odds against winning, it is apparent that the player should bet on the 4-spot, 1-spot, and 7-spot. Conversely, the worst tickets to play would be the 2-spot, 5-spot, and 8-spot.

New York Payoffs and Odds for 1–10 Spot Games

Spots	Match	Payoff	Odds
1-spot game	1	$2	1–4.00
2-spot game	2	$10	1–6.63
3-spot game	3	$23	
	2	$2	1–6.55
4-spot game	4	$55	
	3	$5	
	2	$1	1–3.86
5-spot game	5	$300	
	4	$20	
	3	$2	1–10.34
6-spot game	6	$1,000	
	5	$55	
	4	$6	
	3	$1	1–6.19
7-spot game	7	$5,000	
	6	$100	
	5	$20	
	4	$2	
	3	$1	1–5.46

Spots	Match	Payoff	Odds
8-spot game	8	$10,000	
	7	$550	
	6	$75	
	5	$6	1–9.17
	0	$2	
9-spot game	9	$30,000	
	8	$3,000	
	7	$125	
	6	$20	
	5	$5	
	0	$2	1–9.74
10-spot game	10	$100,000	
	9	$5,000	
	8	$300	
	7	$45	
	6	$10	
	5	$2	
	0	$5	1–9.05

Best Tickets to Play

The tickets giving the state the lowest advantage are the 4-spot, 1-spot, and 7-spot. The tickets giving the state the highest advantage are the 2-spot, 5-spot, and 9-spot. Obviously it is the latter group that you want to avoid.

If we compare the New York and California games, we see at once that the first prize for the 10-spot game in the Golden State is $250,000, while it is only $100,000 in New York. However, the 9-spot ticket pays $5,000 more for hitting all nine numbers in New York, while the 8-spot ticket pays out the same.

When you play state keno, you get a game ticket after making your selections on the blank ticket. The game ticket is your only valid receipt when you claim a winner. It is considered a "bearer instrument," which means whoever turns it in is considered the valid holder of the ticket. So keep your ticket safe and secure.

What's the best way to play state keno? I would play the

games with the lowest edge and forget about the 1-spot ticket. Even though the odds against it are pretty high, I might also take a fling at the 10-spot with its much bigger prize. But I'd play these games only occasionally and I wouldn't bet serious money, limiting my wagers to $1 per draw. The odds are too much against you, so state keno must be treated as a pastime and not a serious gaming venture.

Keno Etiquette and Miscellany

• When you place a bet with a keno runner, the house isn't responsible if for any reason the runner is unable to have your ticket written for the next game. If you would have won, there's nothing you can do about the situation. If you're playing for serious money (something we don't suggest you do), then you should go to the keno writer directly with your tickets, rather than rely on a keno runner.

• Keno runners and writers, though employees of the casino, want the players to win. If you receive exceptional or courteous service from them, or if you win quite a large sum on your ticket, it's customary to offer a gratuity to both the runner and the writer.

• When playing in the keno lounge, you can sit in comfort and also obtain free soft drinks or alcoholic beverages while playing. The usual custom, when given free drinks, is to tip the cocktail waitress.

• If there is an error on your copy of the ticket, if it differs from the original and is not corrected before the game is played, it may be declared void. Therefore, all keno tickets must be examined after they've been issued by the keno writer. Tickets are paid off according to the original ticket, not the duplicate held by the player.

• If you are entitled to a payoff, federal regulations require that you collect on that ticket before the start of the next game, or the ticket becomes void. Collect on your winners right after the board flashes the numbers. Don't take chances by lingering.

• Tickets can be replayed without writing a new ticket. Simply turn in the duplicate and that will become the original for the next game.

• Players should mark the ways as well as the individual spots on the blank, along with the price of the ticket they wish to play. The keno writer will do this as a courtesy if the player has forgotten to do so, but it's really the job of the player, not the keno writer.

• If you have any difficulty figuring out how to write a complex ticket, such as a combination or king ticket, the keno writer should be consulted. He'll be only too happy to help you out.

Glossary of Keno Terms

Blank, Blank Ticket, Keno Blank. A piece of paper issued by the casino, containing the numbers 1 through 80, which the player marks to play keno.

Blower. The device which blows air into the bowl or cage holding the numbered Ping-Pong balls, mixing them and forcing twenty of them into the goose.

Board, Keno Board. An electrical board showing the twenty numbers selected for each game of keno.

Bowl. See *Cage*

Cage. A bowl-like device holding the Ping-Pong balls used in the game of keno.

Caller. The person who operates the blower and goose and calls out the numbers selected during the game, as each is forced into the goose.

Catches. The numbers chosen by the player which correspond to those selected by the operator of the keno game.

Combination Ticket. A complicated and versatile keno ticket that may combine unequal groups of selected numbers to form various combinations or ways.

Conditions, Conditioning. The ways a bettor wishes to play his ticket; written in a manner resembling a fraction, such as ⅔, ⅛, which translates into two four-spots and one eight-spot.

Correct Conditioning. The writing of a ticket to correspond with the exact wishes of the player.

Draw. The movement of a numbered Ping-Pong ball into the goose, forced there by hot air from the blower.

Draw Ticket. See *Punch-Out*

Duplicate, Duplicate Copy, Duplicate Ticket. The ticket marked in ink by the keno writer and returned to the player, duplicating the original presented ticket.

Goose. A transparent tube which holds the numbered Ping-Pong balls after they've been forced there by the blower.

Groups. A combination of numbers separated from other numbers by either circles or lines.

Hits. See *Catches*

Keno Blank. See *Blank*

Keno Board. See *Board*

Keno Lounge. The area of the casino where the game of keno is called and operated and where players may sit while watching the calling of the game.

Keno Runner. A house employee who collects players' tickets throughout the casino and adjacent areas and presents them to the keno writers as a convenience to the bettors.

Keno Writer. The casino employee who collects the bet, writes the duplicate ticket, and pays off winners at keno.

King, King Number. Any one number circled on a ticket, whose purpose is to combine with other numbers to form ways.

King Ticket. A ticket played with one or more king numbers marked on it, making it a very versatile ticket.

Master Ticket. See *Original Ticket*

Original Ticket. The blank filled out by the player and presented to the keno writer, which is the basis for all keno payouts.

Player. A bettor at keno.

Punch-Outs. A ticket, also known as a draw ticket, which has the called numbers for the previous game punched out on a keno blank so that the keno writer can easily determine if a presented ticket has enough catches for a payoff.

Racehorse Keno. The term for the game of keno prior to 1951, when each number also had the name of a racehorse attached to it.

Rate Card. The booklet issued by the casino, containing the costs and payoffs on tickets containing from one to fifteen spots.

Receipt. See *Duplicate Ticket*

Runner. See *Keno Runner*

Special Tickets, Specials. Keno tickets other than the standard ones, with different payoffs and prices.

Split Ticket. A ticket by which a player can play two or more groups of numbers separately.

Spot. The term to denote the amount of numbers selected by the player for each individual payoff. A four-spot indicates that the player has selected four numbers for a particular ticket and possible payout.

Straight Ticket. The simplest and most common keno ticket, in which the player selects from one to fifteen spots or numbers and is paid off according to the amount bet and the number of spots chosen.

Way. Each individual group of numbers played separately by the player, or combinations of groups played the same way, for a possible payoff.

Way Ticket. A keno ticket consisting of at least three equal groups of numbers combining in various ways.

Writer. See *Keno Writer*

10

Slot Machines—
The One-Armed Bandits

Slot machines have been played in one form or another since a San Francisco machinist named Charles Fey invented the first one in the 1890s. Before the turn of the century they were placed in bars around the Bay Area, ostensibly winning the players free drinks if they lined up the correct symbols, but in reality the payoffs were in coins.

The symbols used on these early Liberty Bell slots were those of playing cards—hearts, diamonds, clubs, and spades. In addition to these card symbols, there were bells, horseshoes, and a star. The bell symbol is still used today. On these antique machines the payoffs ran from one nickel for lining up two horseshoes to the big payout of ten nickels for hitting all three bells.

The Liberty Bells were originally made of cast iron and manufactured by hand. They were small enough to be placed on bar tops and became extremely popular. Fey became hard pressed to meet the demand for his machines, for he operated the business and took care of the distribution and commissions himself. The profits were split down the middle with the saloon keepers, 50 percent to Fey and 50 percent to the owner of the bar.

The Liberty Bells proved extremely profitable, since they were designed to return only 86 percent of the coins placed in them. Because there was a federal tax on playing cards and since there were playing card symbols on each machine, Fey put a two-cent federal revenue stamp on each slot to keep within the law. It was essentially a one-man business, and it lasted all the way into the 1930s. The Liberty Bell Saloon and Restaurant on South Virginia in Reno, Nevada, run by the grandsons of Charles Fey, has a collection of many of the early slots, including the original Liberty Bells, which are no longer in operation in casinos.

A machine that took in and paid out coins without needing an employee to staff it was too appealing to remain exclusively in the hands of a local manufacturer like Fey. Since gambling devices couldn't be patented at that time, a successful manufacturer of carnival games named Herbert Stephen Mills got his hands on a Liberty Bell, hired away Fey's foreman, Mat Larkin, and soon was in the slot-machine business.

The first Mills machines were sold in 1906, and within a few years, Mills machines were turning up in every part of the United States. Two of the most popular were the High Top and Golden Falls. These machines were quite an advance over the original Liberty Bells. Like the Fey slots, they took in nickels, but whereas the early Liberty Bells hid the nickels in the bowels of the machine, the Mills slots had a window showing all the nickels accumulated, ready to be paid out, or so the player was led to believe.

The window showing the symbols was much wider than on the Liberty Bell, so that the gambler saw not only the symbols on the payout row, but the rows below and above it. Sometimes these other rows would be lined up with the symbols necessary for payouts, which enticed many players with the thought that the next spin would bring these symbols up or down to the center row.

Mills also introduced the symbols that most slots players the world over are familiar with—the lemon, cherries, plums, and other fruits, together with the bell and the bar. Lining them up in various ways meant instant payouts, and Mills also introduced the concept of a jackpot. The jackpot became the symbol of the grand prize of the slots, the ultimate payoff all slots players strove for.

The Mills handles were long and easily pulled, and in the 1930s, as one story goes, during a trial for operating slots as an illegal gambling device, the judge sentencing the defendant referred to the machines as one-armed bandits, and so they've been called that ever since, with good reason, for casino operators have made untold millions from these machines.

There were other manufacturers besides Mills and Fey. The Watling Rol-a-Top, with its escalator window on top, showing the last eight coins played, was a very popular model. It also protected the operator, since he could instantly see if slugs had been fed into the machine, because of the exposed coins. The Watling machines are real collectors' items today and among the most valuable of the antique slot machines.

Another interesting machine was the Caille Gum Vendor, which was used in jurisdictions where slots were illegal, since it dispensed gum for every nickel played, and this subterfuge was supposed to keep the police away. Still other slots dispensed inedible candy mints and had, in addition to the regular handle, "skill" buttons, which players believed had some bearing on the results, since they thought these buttons could stop the reels when pushed. But this was just another delusion in the long history of delusions produced by one-armed bandits.

Today the chief manufacturers of slot machines are the Bally Corporation and International Game Technology, both of which use modern electronic methods to upgrade the machines. Their newest entry into the field is the carousel of dollar machines, which one change person controls. These machines collect and pay off in dollar coins and their use has upgraded the machines in terms of more revenue for the casinos. The Bally $1 slots aren't owned by the casinos; they're rented from Bally under an involved lease arrangement.

Slots are found in all the legitimate casinos in Nevada and Atlantic City. They're also found in drugstores, airline terminals, supermarkets, grocery stores, and wherever a machine can be placed in Nevada. They're great moneymakers for all concerned, because they need no employees to staff them, except for an occasional change person. They collect and pay out money automatically, giving the owner or lessee of the machines an easy and lucrative income. Who could ask for anything more?

The machines provide a big side income for Strip casinos and the more elegant clubs in Reno, such as the MGM Grand, for these casinos depend upon the basic table games of craps and blackjack for their main income. In the smaller casinos in Nevada and in those houses which depend upon the lower income bettor, the grinds in casino parlance, a substantial portion of the club profits derives from the one-armed bandits. There are downtown Las Vegas clubs and others off the Strip that are filled only with slot machines. While these establishments may be small and limited, they're tremendous moneymakers.

The Lady Luck casino, whose main source of income is the slots, is a gold mine, though it's on a side street in downtown Las Vegas. Another downtown casino, the El Cortez, though it has a number of table games, caters mostly to slot-machine players and makes a fortune. There's big money in the slots; the players become addicted to them and never tire of pulling the handle and waiting for the payoffs and jackpots.

Who feeds these machines with endless coins? For the most part, they're placed by women in the lower economic brackets who would be hesitant to place a $5 bet on the blackjack or craps layout, but think nothing of changing a $5 bill for several rolls of nickels and fooling around with a couple of slot machines for a half hour or so.

The machines are also intriguing to those who want to land a big payoff for a small investment, and the casino operators know this and cater to these people. The people who frequent the downtown Vegas casinos and the clubs on and off Virginia Street in Reno are mostly working people thrusting their coins into the slots. They can't afford to play with a lot of money, but still want the excitement of gambling, and playing the slots is one of the cheapest ways to gamble.

After all, it only takes a nickel to play many of the machines, and a dollar bill still gets anyone twenty nickels and about ten minutes of action. Of course, losses do add up, however small they are, and gambling at slots steadily and seriously can become quite an expensive habit.

The great thrill of the machines is in the fact that no one knows what will happen next. After a player puts in a coin and pulls the handle, anything can happen. The slots may do its usual twirling act and come up empty, or there may be a jackpot on the very next spin of the reels.

This fascination with the unknown keeps everybody involved, and it's not only the lower income players who get a thrill out of playing the slots. Everyone likes to play them at some time or another, putting in a few coins and hoping to hit the jackpot. After all, some of the dollar machines have enormous jackpots, and occasionally one hears of a person hitting them for $1,000,000 or more. Recently, a friend of mine collected $1.68 million by lining up four jokers on the IGT Quarter Mania machine at a small casino off the Strip. The jackpots are always beckoning the gambler, and no one knows when they're coming up.

That unknown factor keeps the player at the machine. The next pull might be it! *Jackpot!* Or nothing. And more often, nothing happens. But what if one leaves the machine and the next person puts in a coin, and boom, *Jackpot*? What terrible luck. And so, many players hang around the slots as long as their money holds out, afraid to relinquish their position, for as long as they're there, they have control of the slots, and the jackpot might be theirs. Some gamblers have their favorite machines and anyone who inadvertently or otherwise tries to play that machine will be verbally abused, or worse.

The slots have been around for a long time now and will be for a long time to come. They're the perfect vehicles for the casinos with their steady profits and minimum maintenance. No one has to force players to put coins into these metal monsters, for the thrill of hitting a jackpot or getting a big payoff is enough incentive.

Slot machines may be placed in various denominations; at one time the most popular were the nickel machines, and these machines still make up a large part of slots actively in use. However, more and more of them are being phased out in favor of the 25¢ and $1 slots.

Some machines are *straight slots*, with only one series of payoffs and no deviations, because only one coin can be played at a time. Still other slots are variations on the straight theme, allowing more than one coin, but nevertheless having a fixed payoff system, which is shown on the front of the machine itself. For example, on a three-coin machine, one coin operates and lights up the center row, the second coin the top row, and the third coin the bottom row. If any of those rows have the proper symbols for payoffs, the coins will pour out.

Other machines take five coins, making operative not only the three rows showing in the window, but diagonal rows as well. And some machines, by accepting more than one coin, make each payoff greater. For instance, with one coin used, a cherry on the first reel would pay off two nickels; with two coins inserted, it would pay off four nickels, and so on. Should the maximum amount of coins be placed in the machine at one time, then there is an added bonus. The jackpot on the last line lights up, and it's now possible to hit it with a lucky pull of the handle.

Progressive machines, unlike the straight slots, aren't bound by permanent fixed payoffs on the jackpot. The jackpot increases with each coin played, till it can reach astronomical figures, sometimes into the hundreds of thousands of dollars. Other slots work on the principle of two progressions, each lit alternately, and if the correct symbols appear, then that lit jackpot is paid off.

Some of these payoffs are so enormous that the machine itself won't be able to pay them out; an attendant and slot mechanic have to be called over. The attendant makes the payout, while the slot mechanic sets the machine back to zero, beginning the progression all over again.

And there are still other kinds of machines—gimmick slots with many reels and strange symbols and exotic payouts, but no matter what kind of machine is played, no matter what gigantic numbers show on the machine, no matter whether a buckaroo, watermelon, or the house symbol has to line up on all three center reels, the house profit is basically the same.

The Mathematics of Slots

The casinos set slot machines to make money for themselves, and taking into consideration the initial cost of the machine, the various taxes for its use, its upkeep and maintenance, plus the servicing of its customers, the average nickel machine should return something like $2,000–$2,500 a year in net profits for the casino.

I had the opportunity during one of my studies of casinos to follow the full cycle of slots operations, from the mechanics shop where the payoffs were set to the final printouts on the computer, showing the profit margin for each and every machine in the casino. With 470 machines, most of them nickel ones, the club was taking in a net profit of over a million dollars a year. This study was made about eight years ago, and since that time this casino has upgraded its machines so that most of them are now 25¢ and $1 ones, and I'm sure its profits are much higher today.

These slots profits are always sure things, because they're mechanically set. At a craps table, a hot roll by one player can literally wipe out a month's income, and a bunch of card counters can wreck a blackjack pit's profits, but the one-armed bandits shrug off the human element and automatically churn out the profits.

The casino works out its profits on a purely mathematical basis. Since most machines are equipped with three reels and each reel holds twenty symbols, the total number of combinations possible are 20^3, or $20 \times 20 \times 20$. This adds up to 8,000.

With this 8,000 figure in mind, the casino operators decide how many coins they'll return for the 8,000 spins. If they allowed 8,000 coins to drop, then there would be no profit at all, since 8,000 coins would have to be used to complete the cycle.

If 7,500 coins dropped, the profit margin would be 1/16 or 6.25 percent. This is a very low percentage for any casino slot, and there is hardly a slot machine that retains so few coins. Such a machine would be known as an extremely loose one, and a player fortunate to find it would get a good run for his or her money.

If the machine retained 1,000 coins during its 8,000-pull cycle, then the profit margin would be 12.5 percent. Most slots retain even a higher percentage than that. The average machine in a casino (other than the Bally $1 slots in the carousel) will hold back between 16 percent and 20 percent of all coins placed in it.

When machines are geared to hold more than three reels or twenty symbols on each reel, the possible combinations increase dramatically. A three-reel machine with twenty-five symbols would hold 15,625 combinations, and a four-reel slots with twenty symbols on each reel runs to 160,000 combinations. But no matter how many combinations are involved, the house works out its edge over the player by setting the machine to retain a certain percentage of the coins played.

Straight Slots

For many years, the straight slots, with their fixed payouts, were the only type of machines in existence, and most of them could receive only one coin at a time. Each coin inserted required a separate pull of the handle, and the possible payouts were printed on the front of the machine.

These machines were in use for a long time, and many are still seen in casinos. Generally, they're the old Mills slots, with their cast-iron construction and large window showing all the coins already played. With these slots the profits were plentiful, but the machine took only one coin at a time, and no matter how fast a player could shove them in, there was still a limit to how many coins could be inserted per hour.

Inspired by prospects of more income, the casino operators, together with the slots manufacturers, devised methods to extract more money from slots players. They introduced machines that would receive more than one coin at a time.

To induce players to use these new slots, the payoffs were increased in proportion to the number of coins that were played. If one coin was inserted and the cherry (usually the lowest payoff symbol) showed alone on the first reel, two coins dropped. If two coins were inserted, then four coins would drop if the cherry appeared. It was really the same proportionate payout, but four coins looked better than two to the player.

Then machines were developed which, by taking more than one coin, allowed the player to win if any of the three lines showing in the window had the correct payout symbols. Now, if a cherry appeared on the top or bottom line, two coins dropped anyway. Various kinds of machines taking from one to six coins were put into operation, some paying out on all three lines and others paying more in proportion to the number of coins played.

The slots got more and more exotic. Today, machines pay off not only on straight lines but on diagonals as well, and still other slots will pay off a jackpot if the player has bet the maximum number of coins the machine will accept. In other words, if the machine can take six coins, there will be no jackpot unless six coins are played. The house advantage remains the same with these slots, but in effect, one machine does the work of six previous ones, and the house income rises proportionally.

The straight slots, with these advanced features, are still the most common machines to be found in a casino. At one time, most of them were nickel machines. With inflation and the devaluation of American currency, these slots have been overtaken in popularity by quarter machines. There have always been 10¢ machines, but somehow, the prospect of putting in the proverbial thin dime has never appealed to many slots players, and these machines get the least play of all.

Progressive Slots

To entice the slots players and to swell profits, casinos began introducing progressive slots. These were machines that, in addition to the straight payouts found in ordinary machines, had one added feature. As each coin was played, a number registered visibly on top of the machine and in full view of the player. This number increased step by step, and this figure, usually represented in dollars and cents, was the ultimate payout that would be made if the jackpot was hit. Unlike fixed jackpots, this one could increase with the use of the machine.

Depending on the slots and the kind of coins it accepted,

the jackpot figure could vary from $10 up to $285,000. Of course, these seven-figure payoffs didn't occur that often, and sometimes it would take a couple of years before anyone hit the jackpot, but sooner or later, someone was bound to hit it, and the higher the figure on the machines, the more likely it was that the payoff was imminent.

These machines became enormously popular the moment they were introduced, because the payouts were more exotic than those on ordinary straight slots. With a jackpot on a fixed payout machine, players could get $100 for their 25¢ play if they were lucky, but with some of these progressive machines, *they could become rich.* And to accomplish this, all they had to do was be in the right place at the right time and pull that handle that one lucky time.

Of course, the casino operators have never been known to be generous, and there was no way they were going to pay out hundreds, thousands, hundreds of thousands of dollars, and in some cases, millions of dollars without showing a profit, and to do this, these machines were rigged by mechanics not to hit a jackpot for as long as it took to get enough coins deposited to make certain that even with the jackpot paid out, the machine would be profitable.

With progressive machines there are other payouts besides the jackpot, but they don't come as often or in as large amounts as with straight slots. One might ask at this point— if a progressive machine that can pay out $100,000 won't do so for a couple of years, where do all those coins go? How many can the machine hold?

Each machine rests on a plastic table, and there is a hole in that table through which excess coins drop into a pail or other catching device. When a machine can't hold any more played coins, an automatic tripping device releases these coins through the bottom of the machine. They're dropped into a pail, and the pail is collected by casino personnel on a regular basis.

With the larger payouts it's not necessary for the machines themselves to have sufficient coins to pay off the lucky winners. A person winning a $55,000 jackpot, for example, isn't going to stand there and wait for 220,000 quarters to fall through the machine into the well. What will happen is that a bell will ring or a light will flash, or both will occur simultaneously. Then an executive of the casino, together with a slots mechanic, will come over and verify the win. Then the winner will get a check or cash from the casino, not twenty-five bagfuls of quarters.

When playing the progressive machines or any machines that have large payoffs, there are two things you must never do. I'll emphasize this statement: *Never do these two things:*

1. Don't pull the handle till you get paid in full. Pull the handle after a jackpot starts another cycle and you might lose your jackpot.

2. Don't walk away from the machine after a large number of coins drop into the well. By doing this, you may be forfeiting the balance of the payout, which won't be contained in the machine, but will have to be paid by an employee of the casino.

Many easterners, who have never played slots, have had this second problem at the Resorts International Hotel in Atlantic City. They hit a jackpot of $500 and walked away from the machine after collecting about $100 in coins. Then a cheat or sharp character would come along and demand the rest of the payout from the casino employees.

Both the casino and the gaming commission of New Jersey became wise to this scam, and several arrests have been made involving cheats who have wrongfully claimed jackpots. At this time, the casino has signs notifying slots players to remain at their machines until an attendant comes by and pays them off in full.

One final word about progressive machines. Expect smaller payouts and less frequent ones, for that must happen when a huge jackpot is in the works. And don't expect to have an edge over the house when playing progressive slots. The same house advantage is there, and it will be extracted from all players of slots, no matter what machines they put their coins into.

The $1 Carousels

To make the slots players bigger gamblers, the Bally Corporation, in conjunction with the casinos in Nevada and Atlantic City, have introduced $1 machines which take dollar coins and pay off only in dollars. These machines are owned by Bally, and except for unusual circumstances, are leased to the individual casinos. The $1 slots are grouped together in what is known as a carousel, an oval arrangement of slots which a single change person can service.

Unlike all other machines in the house, these Bally machines state the exact house advantage over the player. This edge is stated in a peculiar fashion, with signs showing that the slots are "96 percent in the player's advantage," or "92 percent in your favor." Translated into normal English, what these signs mean is that for every dollar you play the house will have an advantage of either 4 percent or 8 percent, and so, for every $100 played, the player will get back either $96 or $92. There is nothing in the player's favor at all.

However, these slots are worth playing if you want to do some serious gambling at the slot machines. For one thing, there are no other slots in the casino which have so small an edge over the player. And no other machines state the true house advantage.

Interestingly enough, some casinos balked about accepting the Bally carousels. One downtown casino in Vegas, when thwarted in its efforts to purchase the machines instead of lease them, put them into the worst and most inconspicuous areas of the casino, far from the normal pattern of casino traffic. Eventually finding that they were very profitable in spite of this, the casino moved them into a better area.

In a later section we'll show how to take advantage of these Bally $1 machines, and how to make the most of them. They're not progressive machines, and they accept from one to three coins at a time. There is a jackpot of $100, in some cases more, and in order to become eligible for that big payoff, three coins have to be played at one time.

These Bally machines, more than any other factor, have

conditioned the players into gambling for more money at slots. Now gamblers will place $1 into a gambling device that normally took a nickel, and it won't be long before the standard machine of the future will be a dollar one.

Specialty Machines

The casino operators realize that an exotic machine will be a conversation piece and will attract customers into the casino. Walking past the Four Queens on Fremont Street in downtown Las Vegas, one is immediately attracted to a giant machine, known as a Big Bertha, with eight reels running across its width and a handle that must be at least four or five feet long.

The usual fruit symbols are on this dollar machine, but the pulling of the handle and the slow but gradual roll of the symbols on each reel creates a spectacle that invariably attracts a group of interested spectators, and many of them eventually find their way into the casino itself, to try their luck on other slots or at the table games.

Most casinos, including some of the poshest ones on the Strip, have some kind of gimmick machine, whose huge size and giant payoffs make it an attraction in itself, and the spectators gasp and cheer as the wheels spin around and a payoff comes up.

With the advent of electronics, machines have been invented which require no handle at all; just a push of a button activates the mechanism that spins the reels, and these reels, instead of spinning in normal fashion, merely flash digitally. Eventually they stop at the center row, determining whether or not a payout is in order. These handleless machines have never really been much of an attraction, because players, when pulling the slots handle, feel that they are somehow participating in the eventual result.

However, whether one pushes a button or pulls a handle, if the machine is correctly engineered and in perfect working order, there comes a point when gears take over, moving the reels independently of the handle or button. So, it really doesn't matter if a player pulls the handle on a one-armed bandit with great grace or thumps down hard on the handle, the same result will ensue.

There are some interesting double or nothing slots in operation at various casinos. With these slots, after the center row shows a payout, instead of the machine spewing forth the correct number of coins, the player has the option of collecting at once or taking a chance by pushing a button that sets a smaller reel spinning. On this reel are just two symbols, running continuously in consecutive order—"double" and "nothing."

Should double come up, the player is entitled to twice the original payout, and again has the option of collecting, or once more pushing the double or nothing button. Generally, these machines allow players to make four consecutive attempts to double their money. After that they must collect the enhanced payout.

Once the machine has shown the correct symbols for an original payout, the double or nothing option is a 50-50 chance, since there are equal numbers of both symbols on the smaller reel.

These machines seem to pay out more consistently than ordinary slot machines, because the casino is counting on the greed of the players to blow their payout by spinning the wheel once too often and getting nothing.

Since one extra double or nothing spin gives the house no advantage, it's always worth trying that one spin. The smaller reel is so set up that each spin is independent of the previous one, so if the player should hit a double, the next spin will again be even money.

But the player should be aware of the law of averages. To get one double the chances are even money, with no advantage to the house. The odds against two doubles in a row are 2-1, for there is only one chance in three of accomplishing this. To endeavor to hit three doubles in a row, the chances now are only one in eight, or 7-1 against the player, and inexorably, these odds will hurt the gambler.

I've had a lot of fun playing a double or nothing machine at Circus Circus in Reno. It was a quarter machine that took multiple coins, and the payouts were rather large. My philosophy was this: if the original payout was substantial, I tried one double or nothing, and if it doubled, I collected. If the original payout was small, I tried to get two and sometimes three doubles.

After playing the machine for about fifteen minutes, my payout on the original bet was 80 coins. I pushed the double or nothing button, and it came up double. Now I had 160 coins to collect. This amounted to $40, and though I've bet substantially more at blackjack tables without thinking twice, to win $40 at the slots for a 75¢ investment changes one's perspective.

I now thought about my decision—collect or try one more time? I asked my companion for advice. He's a good friend and an excellent card player, but his luck had been running horribly that weekend, and most of his decisions had turned out wrong. He suggested that I collect, so I hit the double or nothing button one more time.

The double or nothing reel becomes hooded while the reel is spinning, so it's impossible to know what's happening. It generally spins for about fifteen or twenty seconds, and we both watched anxiously for the result. Finally it stopped on double. We let out a whoop—$80 to collect. But I still had the option of doubling once more. I asked my friend what I should do, as the sign blinked "double or nothing."

"You've been lucky so far. Try it one more time." I hesitated, moved my finger to the button and then moved it away. I thought to myself, "Maybe I should take another chance, after all, all I can lose is my original 75¢." But there was $80 ready to be collected. Prudence and good sense overcame my gambling spirit and I pushed the collect button. Out poured a mass of quarters which it took several paper cups to carry over to the change booth. I was rewarded not only with the cash, but an extra bonus, courtesy of Circus Circus, a pair of pantyhose. I decided to play safe once more. I ordered a neutral color, medium size.

The Best Way
to Win at the Slots

The difficulty with playing slot machines is that no one really knows the house percentage on any one machine. The rules of the various state gaming commissions don't require casinos to post their house advantage, and the casinos themselves are never gracious enough to do so. Therefore players are faced with a mystery every time they stand before a one-armed bandit. What is the house edge on this machine? There is even a more profound mystery—has this machine recently delivered a jackpot? If that's the case, the player is merely wasting time and money at that particular slots.

There are two theoretical ways to solve these two mysteries. One way is to study the computer runs of the casino and examine the payouts on every machine in the house, for each machine has an individual number to guide the casino in determining its profits.

I had an opportunity to do this at one time, when I spent several months at a Strip casino researching material for a novel I wrote about Vegas called *Snake Eyes*.

By studying the computer sheets, I found that the average percentage of profits the machines were throwing off to this particular club was 18 percent, with some slots paying as much as 25 percent to the house and a few paying as little as 12 percent.

Since few people, except for casino executives, ever see these computer runs, there is really no way for anyone to ever know the exact percentage or edge the casino has on any particular machine.

The other method is even more difficult and time consuming and in the end worthless. It would require monitoring one particular machine from the time the mechanic reset its mechanisms. Of course, it would take many days to follow the 8,000 pulls required to exhaust all the possible combinations, and maybe even longer, for no machine is constantly being used, minute after minute, hour after hour, day after day.

And even if one could do this, with a team of helpers, when the machine was once again reset, the mechanic might have orders to tighten it up a bit, so that the previous monitoring would have no bearing on the new results. Of course, I'm not seriously suggesting this method, but that's the only alternative, other than seeing the computer sheets.

When discussing slots with both the mechanic in charge and the president of the hotel-casino, they pointed out the reason for the discrepancies in the various machines' payouts. It would be much simpler for all machines to be set in one standard way; this way the casino would know exactly what the expected profit (or p.c., as they call it) should be.

However, in order to have a profitable slots operation, casino executives know that a proper slots mix is necessary. By slots mix, they mean a balancing of different kinds—some 5¢, some dime, some 25¢, and some dollar machines.

Slots mix also means placing certain loose, or well-paying, machines in proper locations in the casino and alternating loose and tight machines throughout the slots area.

The loosest machines are generally placed near the aisles, especially those aisles which are used by people waiting in line to see the shows the Strip casinos offer.

The easiest way for a Strip casino to attract potential customers or, as casino personnel refer to them, warm bodies, into a casino is to offer top-notch entertainment in the showrooms. When Elvis Presley was alive, when Wayne Newton was starring, when the Osmond Family brought in their clean-cut act, Middle Americans, the true slots players, poured into the showrooms by the thousands.

The casino operators aren't really interested in giving these people a fine show; what they want them to do is gamble, for all shows lose money for the house. Most of those waiting on line aren't big gamblers; if they were high rollers, they wouldn't be on line for an hour, waiting for a seat.

The casinos take care of their high rollers, their premium customers, and these people never have to stand on line for a wearying hour. All they do is go to the maitre d' and immediately they're given a reserved seat in the showroom.

Therefore, the casino executives know that the people waiting on line are either going to play for minor stakes at the table games, or more likely, try their luck at the slots. Knowing this, the lines are so arranged that they pass dozens of slot machines, and people on line, to pass the time, often try their luck on the nearby machines. If they have no luck with the aisle machines, after the show is over they'll simply run out of the casino and go to another club, where they may have a better chance at winning money.

To keep these warm bodies in the casino, the loosest slots are placed near the aisles where people wait on line for the show. Finding that these machines pay off quite well, these same people, once the show is over, linger in the casino, going to other slots areas to try their luck again. However, this time, they'll be encountering tight machines, and anything they've won before will quickly go back into the iron monsters.

Casino operators use their slot mix to separate players from their money by staggering their loose machines, alternating them throughout each row of slots. They know that most slots gamblers aren't satisfied playing one machine at a time; they like to play at least two and sometimes more. Sometimes a whole row of machines is reserved by one person.

And pity the poor man or woman who invades this reserved domain. They'd be better off going into a cage full of hungry lionesses. Some of the women who reserve machines for themselves guard them with their life, and not only have people been verbally abused for inadvertently playing a reserved machine, but some of these players go even further and start pummeling the poor unfortunate with pocketbooks and fists.

Not all players are so crazed, and I don't mean to disparage women who play the slots, but there are a small minority who are dangerous when provoked. What these players don't realize when they play two or more machines is that the casino operators know all about their habits and set the machines so that what one gives, the other takes away.

If a player, disgusted with a tight machine, then goes to the other side of her loose one, she'll find the same tight situation. This eternal battle rages between the casino operators and the slots players. The casino always wins in the end, because they have all the advantages, while the poor slots player loses but usually returns with more crumpled bills to once again fight the losing battle.

How then can you beat the one-armed bandits? First, you must realize that you stand little chance of coming out ahead when playing at a machine where the house edge is not posted. Therefore, if at all possible, limit your play to the Bally $1 carousels, where the house advantage is clearly posted.

At least now, knowing the small house edge, you have a chance to win in the short run. Bucking a 15 percent or 20 percent edge is a fruitless task, for it's practically impossible to win if you play for any length of time. At the slots, you have to take your profits and run, because the one-armed bandit, as tough as it is, can't catch you once you're out of the casino.

Here are a couple of hints concerning the carousels containing the $1 Bally slots. When I resided in Vegas, I got to know several of the change women who staffed the carousels. These young women stand on an elevated platform and spend their days giving change to the players of the $1 slots. Their pay is low, the hours long, and the work meaningless and boring. I became friendly with them and would spend time talking about this or that. It wasn't my flashing smile or wit that brought them over to my side; it was a common interest, making money.

Whenever I went to the carousels, I'd break $50 and get dollar coins, then immediately give the young woman staffing the machines a $1 tip. Yes, it's true, everyone likes money, and these young women, who rarely get tips to help out their anemic salaries, appreciate this kind of friendly gesture.

Then I'd ask about the machines in the carousel. Having nothing better to do, with time on her hands, and from her vantage point about six feet above the machines, the change person had a good idea of which machines had paid off the jackpots and which hadn't. She was also aware of those machines that hadn't paid out anything substantial in a while, and were long overdue.

After being directed to these machines, I played them to the hilt. Sometimes the machines she pointed out were several feet from one another. No matter. In the interests of impending fortune, I moved back and forth fearlessly, dropping in the coins. I'd always give the woman 10 percent of my profits, and I'm able to report that I'm way ahead on the Bally $1 carousel machines.

If you can't find these particular machines, or find the change person uncooperative, then the next best thing to do is search out casinos that have loose slots, the looser the better. If you get a good machine and find yourself ahead, you must flee with the profits. Don't put them back into the hungry iron monster, because no amount of coins will ever appease its insatiable appetite for American currency.

Where does one find loose slots? There is a pecking order in this regard, and we'll start with the worst places to play, places that should always be avoided. These are the groceries, drugstores, restaurants, supermarkets, and other establishments whose main business is other than gaming. In a city like Las Vegas, some of these machines, including the ones at McCarran Airport, will pay out no more than 50 percent of the coins it takes in.

If we use Las Vegas as an example, the next places to avoid are the Strip casinos. Their main interest is the gambling tables, not the slots, and they make an enormous profit from their slots, which rarely give them less than an 18 percent return.

The downtown casinos and some of the smaller places off the Strip give the player a decent chance to win, but even here, their idea of loose slots may be a 10 percent or 12 percent edge over the player.

Finally, there are those places on Fremont Street which have nothing but slots; they are veritable slots jungles with flashing lights and bells and all kinds of noise. If you can stand the atmosphere, they, along with places such as the El Cortez and Lady Luck, are your best bet as far as serious gambling on slots is concerned.

They cater to the slots players, giving them free food and drink, extra bonus prizes, and sometimes free drawings of really valuable items such as cars. They want the people who play slots seriously; that's the name of their game in gambling, and that's where a smart slots player should go for his or her best deal.

Cheating at Slots

One way to beat the slots is by cheating the casinos. It's not recommended on two counts: first, it's immoral and illegal to cheat; and second, if caught, the penalties in Nevada and Atlantic City are very harsh. In Atlantic City, which seems to have a much more benign atmosphere than Nevada, the slots cheats, even those claiming abandoned jackpots, have been prosecuted vigorously.

Cheating at gambling in Nevada is a felony, and the courts go along with the casinos in many cases, and neither the city jail in Vegas nor the state prison in Carson City is a nice place to spend time.

But people persist in looking for that extra, illegal edge, and many of them are attracted to the money available in gambling casinos. There are two basic kinds of slot machine cheats: the unsophisticated who try to take the casino's money away by force or guile and those who are more skillful, who have made a study of the engineering and mechanics involved in the manufacture of the slots. These cheats continually probe weaknesses in the machines, trying to score some quick money that way.

One of the gimmicks that common cheats use is the attachment of a string to a coin, so that, after thrusting the coin down the throat of the machine, they're able to retrieve it and thus play with the same coin over and over again.

Other crooks use finely fashioned slugs, but they have to be carefully manufactured, since most modern machines will quickly reject them. And it's more and more difficult to use the coin-on-a-string stunt, since the newer machines force the coin to twist in descent before the machine becomes operative, and once the coin is taken in, there's no way to get it back again.

We already mentioned those thieves who prey on unwary

and ignorant players and claim jackpots abandoned by the winners. This happens mostly in Atlantic City, but the casinos there have now posted signs, similar to those in Nevada casinos, warning the players that only a minor part of the jackpot is returned by the machine; the remainder is paid out by casino employees.

Finally, there are those crooks who don't bother to tamper with the machines at all. They walk around looking for coins left in the wells of the machines by players who are temporarily away from the machine, or they steal cupfuls of coins left by these same type of players, who may be down the line playing a whole row of machines at one time.

It's a common practice to leave coins in the well or in cups when players are working other machines, and most players are honest and would never dream of taking another person's money. However, thieves have no such moral compunctions, and will grab what they can.

The more sophisticated scam artists have other methods of cheating the casino. First of all, they make a study of a particular type of machine or a group of them made by the same manufacturer. Then they probe for weaknesses by looking for the simplest way to get the mechanism working without bothering to feed it coins.

For these thieves the most important part of the slots is the mechanism that trips the levers that set the reels in motion. Once these can be moved without coins, half the battle is won. The next thing they try to do is control the mechanism that stops the reels, so that the symbols can be lined up at will, giving constant jackpots. At this point, the machine is at the cheat's mercy, and will be quickly emptied of all its coins.

Crooks have also attempted to get to the inside of these machines by various methods, including the use of thin wires, electrical contacts, and even drilling devices. As the crooks develop new methods of probing, the casinos and slots manufacturers take countermeasures, continually fighting a battle with the thieves, trying to make their machines more and more secure from this kind of outside threat.

The battle still goes on to this day. Some cheats don't bother going into the machine itself, but probe for weaknesses in the one mechanism that they can play without attracting attention—the handle itself.

One thief developed a rhythm method of playing the handle and was able to make a fortune with it. He even had the nerve to teach his method to others, and soon he had a whole school of rhythm players, who bilked the casinos out of untold thousands of dollars.

The casinos eventually stopped this kind of cheating by adding new devices to the handle, making it work so that, once it reached a certain point, the movement of the reels became independent of the rhythm used to pull the handle. However, I was told by a crossroader (a person who will cheat at anything, anywhere) that the handles of some of the older machines can still be manipulated.

The machines are probed by moving the handle back and forth to see if the machine has proper safety features that have not worn thin or become inoperative. Once these safety features are missing or have been worn to a frazzle, the cheat steps in and manipulates the handle, lining up each reel separately to pay out a jackpot. Then these same cheats, called handle slammers, step back, slam the handle into place without disturbing the reels and get their payout.

Since many of these crossroaders are well known to casino personnel and their pictures are continually studied by security guards and slots mechanics, they can't afford to wait around for the payout. They hire assistants, called claimers, who are trained to handle slam the machine to assure the payout, and it is these individuals who claim the jackpot, later splitting the proceeds with the thieves.

These cheats don't bother with small jackpots. They go after the progressive machines and sometimes are able to score thousands of dollars, if they can get their hands on a machine that doesn't have the proper safety features.

As the machines get more and more sophisticated, as more and more safeguards are used by manufacturers and casinos, the thieves are also at work probing and trying to break down these same machines, always alert, as thieves will be, to the weaknesses of machines and men.

Slots Etiquette and Miscellany

• If you don't have the proper change to play the machines, there are change persons available. If one can't be found, there's usually a button on each machine for service. Ring that button and a change person will come to your aid. Change can also be obtained at the cashier's cage in the slots area.

• In addition to the change, ask for a paper cup to put the coins in. This is much easier than holding them in your hands, where they may drop to the floor.

• Before playing a machine, make certain that no one else has claimed it. Some players get very angry when their machine is taken away. To avoid a scene, play only at those machines that are not being used.

• You may play more than one machine at a time. It's possible to play a whole row if you wish to, but this gets cumbersome, and you may be leaving money in some of the wells, open to thieves.

• If you see a cup of coins near a machine, don't just take it. It probably belongs to an active player who is nearby, playing another machine.

• At some casinos free beverages will be served to slots players. At other casinos the slots players will have to pay for this service. Ask if you are uncertain and want a drink. In any case, whether free or not, it's customary to tip the cocktail waitress.

• Change persons aren't usually tipped, but they may be if you've hit a big jackpot and the person serving you has been helpful.

• When playing at the carousels, it pays to toke the change person, to find out which machines are due for a jackpot and to give the person a small percentage of the overall win if you do well with her advice.

• Set a limit on losses. Playing quarter or dollar machines can add up, and don't go overboard. Play slots for fun, and don't get into debt or lose control.

• Protect your money at all times; don't leave coins in the

well if you're away from the machine, and avoid leaving cups of coins out of your reach.

• Some jackpots are paid in full by the machine. Others, however, are paid mostly by the attendant. Don't walk away from a machine until you've been fully paid. Make sure you get your entire jackpot either from the machine or the house employee.

• Don't touch the handle on a machine that's just scored a jackpot. If you do, you might forfeit your entire jackpot, because, by the time the house employee shows up, there'll be nothing on the center row but losing symbols.

• For people who are handicapped or blind and want to play the slots machines, the Boardwalk Regency in Atlantic City has two dozen special machines for their use. Some machines are lower, so that people in wheelchairs can easily play them, while others have placards in Braille attached to their fronts to accommodate blind players.

Glossary of Slots Terms

Big Bertha. The slang name for a specialty machine that contains eight to ten reels and is oversize, with a gigantic handle.

Carousels. The area provided by the casino for a group of Bally $1 machines.

Change girl (boy) (person). The casino employee who makes change for the players and sometimes pays off small jackpots.

Handle Slammers. A term for a certain kind of thief who probes the weakness of the machine by manipulation of the handle and then slams it to complete his scam.

Jackpot. The highest payout on any machine.

Liberty Bell. The name of the original machine invented by Charles Fey of San Francisco.

Loose, Loose Machine. A slots that pays off liberally and gives the house only a small advantage over the player.

Mechanic, Slots Mechanic. The house employee who sets the machines for their payoffs. This person also repairs broken machines.

Mills Slots. The first machines used nationwide and the first to have a jackpot as well as the standard fruit symbols.

One-Armed Bandit. A popular slang term for the slot machines.

Progressive Machines. Slots that continually increase the possible jackpot each time a new coin is inserted for play.

Reel. A vertical and continuous holder of the symbols on the machine. There are generally three reels on each slot machine, though some machines may contain up to ten reels.

Slots. A common term for slot machines.

Straight Slots. Machines that pay out in fixed amounts according to the payoffs shown on the front of the machine.

Symbols. The various kinds of markings on a slot machine reel. The most popular are those originated by the Mills Company, consisting of fruits, bells, and bars.

Tight Machine. A machine that gives the casino a large win percentage by paying out relatively few coins to the players.

Well. The area at the bottom of the machine where coins that have been paid out fall to.

Window. The open area on the machine that shows the rows of symbols; or the area showing the coins already held by the machine.

11

Video Poker

With the computer age well under way throughout the world, it was no surprise that gambling should be affected by the new technology.

By being played electronically, without any casino personnel necessary to deal cards, make payoffs, or attend to customers, video poker greatly reduces the casino's overhead. And the casino loves situations where it can collect money without paying attention to the gamblers. Of course, for the video poker machines they need change persons and mechanics. But one change person can handle dozens of games, and one mechanic can handle a whole casino of video poker games.

Of all the games introduced in the last decade, nothing compares with the phenomenal growth of video poker. On my last visit to Las Vegas, I spoke with several long-time residents who had been able to resist the temptation to gamble, except for a fling of a couple of dollars every month on the slot machines. But they were hooked on the video poker games. With good reason.

When you play a slot machine, you simply put in coins and pull a handle. There will either be a payoff or a loss. Rarely will there be a jackpot. But there are no decisions to make, and you can bet mindlessly and endlessly as long as your coins hold out. You can play two or three or even more machines at once, going from one to another, feeding the coins, and pulling the handles. You'll know instantly whether you have won or lost. Coins will drop into the well, or a bell will ring indicating that you've hit the jackpot. If nothing happens, if you're greeted with silence on the part of the slots, you've lost. Simple and mind-resting.

Video poker presents choices, however. The game isn't one-tiered the way slots are. First, you see the hand you've been dealt by the computer chip; then you have to act on that hand. If you have a winner, you'll be rewarded with coins either dropping to the well, or a payout that will be given to you in the way of credits. When you have credits amounting to, let's say, 50 coins, you can simply press another button and get a cash payout. Or you can use the credits, which are reduced as you play another game using the coins accumulated in the memory bank of the computer.

Let's now see what you face when you sit down before one of these machines to play the ever-growing and popular video poker game.

A number of companies manufacture these video poker machines, and they fall into two basic categories as far as the money they'll accept is concerned. Some take only 25¢ coins, while others take $1 tokens. And some limit the player to only the use of five coins for each play, while others take up to 100 coins at a time. (Another kind of video poker machine, manufactured by Sigma, is a "Jokers Wild" machine. We'll discuss this type of game after examining the basic machines without the joker.)

The machines have fairly standard payoffs, though there is a slight variance in a number of the payoffs, as we shall see. And the payoff is multiplied by the number of coins used. Some machines encourage the use of five coins instead of less by making the royal flush payoff an enhanced one. For example, at the Golden Nugget the payoff for a royal flush is 250 for 1. If you put in one coin and win, you'll get back 250 coins. Two coins will give you 500, three will net you 750, four coins will win 1,000, but if you'd played five coins and hit a royal flush you'd get 4,000 coins back. Thus, the correct play when the royal flush is enhanced in this manner is always to play five coins and go for the big win. Let's now look at some of the standard payoffs. The payoff is for one coin.

5-Coin Play Machines

Royal Flush	250 coins
Straight Flush	50 coins
4 of a Kind	25 coins
Full House	9 coins
Flush	6 coins
Straight	4 coins
3 of a Kind	3 coins
Two Pair	2 coins
Pair of Jacks or Higher	1 coin
None of the Above	Loss

Included in "None of the Above" are no pairs and small pairs. All pairs below a jack are useless if caught alone; A pair of 10s has no more value than a pair of 2s. You're not playing against other players; you're playing against a machine.

There is a slightly different payoff with many progressive machines.

Progressive Machines

Royal Flush	300 coins
Straight Flush	50 coins
4 of a Kind	25 coins
Full House	8 coins
Flush	5 coins
Straight	4 coins
3 of a Kind	3 coins
Two Pair	2 coins
Pair of Jacks or Higher	1 coin
None of the Above	Loss

The payoffs are quite low. After all, in draw poker, anytime you have a hand of three of a kind or better, you probably have a winner when playing against other players. Four of a kind, straight and royal flushes are extremely rare, and yet the payoffs at the video poker machine are rather cheap compared to the power of the hand. It may very well take more than a hundred hours to get a straight flush; that's over a hundred hours of inserting coins into a video poker machine, and then all you get paid off is 50 for 1.

The more astute players always play at machines having a progressive payoff if a royal flush is hit. By progressive machine, we mean a machine that increases the payoff after each play in which a royal flush is not made. Even with an enhanced machine, which will pay 4,000 coins for your quarter if you hit a royal flush, that's only $1,000, and few serious poker players ever see that hand in their lifetime. But if there's a progressive machine that will give you a payoff of $2,500, now you're getting some value for that kind of monster hand.

If you do play a progressive machine, make certain that it has at least $2,200 before you start playing. Otherwise, look for one just below that figure ($2,000+), or pass up video poker. Normally, progressive payouts on royal flushes are tied to a whole group of machines. There may be as few as six or many more, and the more there are, the quicker the progressive payout increases. Look for those machines. You can tell the payout is progressive because there'll be a large screen flashing a number like $1,569.25 above a group of video machines and increasing in value as you watch. If you're uncertain if the machine you're going to play is tied to the progressive payout, ask a casino employee or change person. If you can't find any progressive machines, ask the same house employees if there are any in the casino. If there aren't, go to a casino where there are some. Go for the big payout in this game; otherwise the small losses will eat up your limited bankroll.

Poker Hands

Now, let's examine various kinds of poker hands, and what they look like.

For those readers who don't know anything about poker, we'll explain each type of winning hand. (A = Ace, K = King, Q = Queen, J = Jack.) All other cards have their numerical value, e.g., 10 = 10, 6 = 6.

The highest possible hand in poker is a Royal Flush. It consists of the A K Q J 10 of any suit.

The second highest hand is a Straight Flush. It consists of five cards of the *same suit* in order, such as K Q J 10 9 or 5 4 3 2 A. Note that the ace can be used as either the highest or lowest card in order.

Then 4 of a Kind follows. This hand consists of all four cards of the same rank, plus a fifth card that is an odd card. For example, 6 6 6 6 K is a 4 of a Kind hand. So is 9 Q 9 9 9 or 3 3 7 3 3.

A Full House is next. It consists of three cards of one rank combined with two cards of another rank. For example, J J J 2 2 is a full house, also called a full boat in poker parlance. Or 8 3 3 8 3 is a full house. I'm purposely placing the numerical values in odd configurations, for that's how they might show on the screen in video poker.

Below that hand is a Flush. A flush is all five cards of the same suit. Thus, 6 9 10 3 K all of hearts would be a flush. 2 A 8 Q 4 all consisting of spades would be a flush. Or any hand of the same suit, be it Diamonds (D), Hearts (H), Spades (S), or Clubs (C).

Then comes a Straight. A straight consists of five cards of consecutive rank or order, but not of the same suit. For example 10(C) 9(H) 8(S) 7(S) 6(C) is a straight. If all of these cards were of the same suit, it would increase in rank to a straight flush. But on the screen, be alert to cards out of sequence that would still be a straight. For example, you might see A(D) 4(H) 2(S) 5(C) 3(D). That's a straight, for we have the 5 4 3 2 and A all in one hand, and not of the same suit.

Three of a Kind is the next ranking hand. This consists of three cards of the same value or rank, along with two odd cards. The following is a three of a kind hand: 9 2 9 4 9. Since there are three 9s in the hand, it qualifies as a three-of-a-kind hand. Another would be K 7 K K Q. Or 3 2 2 5 2.

Below this hand is Two Pair. A pair is two cards of the same value or rank. When a hand consists of two pair along with an odd card, it qualifies. An example is Q 6 Q 6 2. We see two queens and two sixes in that hand. Another example is 5 A A 10 5. Here we have a pair of aces and a pair of 5s.

The final hand on which there is a payoff is one pair of jacks or better. Thus, if you get one pair of jacks, queens, kings, or aces, there is a payoff. Along with the high pair you'll have three odd cards, such as J J Q K A. The hand looks lovely, but it simply is a pair of jacks along with three odd cards.

Any hand consisting of a pair below the value of the face cards (jacks, queens, kings) or the aces doesn't qualify for a payoff. A hand of five odd cards is also a loser.

In essence, video poker is really draw poker played on a machine. In draw poker there are two rounds of playing and betting. In video poker there's only one round of betting, at the outset, before you draw your cards. Thereafter you can't raise or lower your initial bet (the coins you played). But you have another round of drawing cards, just as in draw poker, in order to improve your hand.

The Video Poker Machine

When you sit down at a video poker machine you'll be faced with the following buttons:

Draw	Hold	Hold	Hold	Hold	Hold
Deal	Cancel	Cancel	Cancel	Cancel	Cancel

Thus, there is a hold/cancel button under each card in addition to the draw/deal button off to one side. There may be other buttons for choosing credit or cash in payoffs, but for the time being we'll concentrate on the draw/deal and hold/cancel buttons, for they'll permit you to play the game correctly, and make decisions that will determine whether or not you're going to end up a winner on any particular hand.

There's also a slot to take in the coins. Let's assume you've put in five coins. What you'll see on the screen all this time is the previous hand that was played. Perhaps you've just sat down at the video poker machine. Disregard the previous hand played. It doesn't affect you at all. First, insert your coins. The previous hand will still show, but when you press the Deal/draw button, a new set of five cards will appear on the screen. Let's assume you see the following:

5(H) 10(S) K(C) 8(D) 2(H)

So far you see a pile of junk, with no payoff available immediately. Now, even if the hand was one in which you didn't have to draw a single card—if you had five cards of the same suit, which qualifies as a flush for example—you'd still have to go through the second step of video poker before you can get paid off. That step is the draw. With the flush, you'd press the hold/cancel button under each card, and a "hold" would show under each card. Make sure that you see that word "hold" under each card on the screen. After you do, press the deal/draw button, and all five cards of the flush will remain. Then you'll get your payoff.

Now, let's go back to the odd cards we drew for this example, the 5 10 K 8 2. The chance to draw a straight or flush here is remote. Our best hope for a payoff is to pair the king. If we do this, we get our bet back, and that's better than having a loser. So here's what we do. We press the hold/cancel button under the king, and "hold" will flash on the screen under the king.

At this point, you might ask, what is the cancel button? The button says hold/cancel, doesn't it? Right. Let's suppose in the previous example, instead of pressing the hold/cancel button under the king, we pressed it under the 8, and "hold" flashed on the screen under the 8. We don't want to retain the 8, so we again press the hold/cancel button under the 8 and the hold on the screen disappears. The cancel use of the button is to negate a previous action we don't want *before the draw*. Once we draw new cards, we can't do anything about a wrong decision.

After pressing hold under the king, and seeing it flash on the screen, we now press the draw/deal button. All the other cards will disappear from the screen except for the king, and be replaced by four other cards immediately. Let's assume we see this after the draw.

9(S) 5(C) K(C) 3(S) K(D)

We now have a pair of kings. Depending on the machine, either five coins will clink down into the well, or we'll get credit for five coins. The screen will proclaim, "Winner!" but all you've gotten are your coins back. It's stretching the definition of "win" when you're not paid more than you've bet, but in any event you haven't lost anything.

But remember, and this is important, there is a draw after you've been dealt out the first five cards, and even if you have a winner without having to improve your hand, you must hold all the winning cards and push the draw button in order to qualify for a payoff.

Now, let's examine other possible buttons on the machine. Many machines give you credit instead of payoff if you collect. The reason for this is simple: Not only do you avoid hearing the jangle of coins dropping, but you can more easily continue betting your credited coins, albeit, as often happens, using them up in a losing cause.

Thus, you'll see a button marked "credit/play" or something similar. A button may allow you to press down one coin's credit at a time until you have the desired bet, or a button may allow you to bet 10 coins at one time. And of course, there'll be a button marked "cash in" or something similar, allowing you to get all the coins you've stored in the credit part of the machine.

Don't forget to cash in before you leave the machine, or you'll give some newcomer all the coins you had won. There are video poker hustlers who do nothing but walk around looking for abandoned machines that have coin credits still valid. They sit down, press the "cash-in" button, and collect the coins someone else won.

Best Play

Before we analyze the best play for various kinds of hands, the reader should remember that he or she is playing against the machine and not against other players. To beat the machine, the hand must have the values that give a payoff. First and foremost, any pair of jacks or better (jacks, queens, kings, or aces) will get you your original bet back.

So we value these pairs as payoff pairs. All pairs from 2s through 10s as a final pair give us nothing but a losing hand. The higher pairs, jacks or better, give us our money back. Just as a pair of 10s is no better than a pair of 8s, as far as the machine payoff computer is concerned, so a pair of aces is no better than a pair of jacks. Either pair will get you your coins back and will be proclaimed a winner on the video screen. Of course, in a regular poker game played among individuals, if we have a choice of saving an ace or a jack, we'll save the ace. It has a higher value, but not for video poker. Each are equally valued as far as pair payoffs are concerned.

Now, let's look at the kinds of decisions we'll have to make:

1. Three to a Royal Flush vs. Four Flush

We are dealt 9(H) K(S) J(S) 4(S) Q(S).

We have 4 spades to a flush, the 9(H) being the odd card. However, we also have the K Q J of spades, a 3 to a royal flush. In this instance we go for the royal flush. Not only is there a monster payoff, but with some machines there is also an enhanced payoff tied up to a progressive jackpot that increases in value with each play of dozens of machines.

Even without the enhanced progressive jackpot, we want to go after the royal flush. Something else should be taken into consideration. On a number of machines, if you bet from 1 to 4 coins, the payoff on a royal flush is only 250 for 1, but if you bet 5 coins, it jumps to 800 for 1. This is on machines for the most part that accept only five coins. Our advice is always to play the five coins and go for the big payoff. Saving a coin here and there is foolish, for if you do get lucky, you're cheating yourself out of the monster payoff.

If you go for the flush and throw away the 9(H), all you can hope for is a flush, paying off at 6 for 1. Or a high pair, getting your money back. The other way, you have the chance for a high pair, two pairs, three of a kind, a straight, a flush, a straight flush, and a royal flush. It is therefore to our advantage to go for the royal flush, retaining the K Q J of spades.

2. Three to a Royal Flush vs. Four Straight

The hand is 10(C) Q(D) K(D) J(D) 2(H).

In this situation, again we hold on to the three to a royal flush, the K Q J of diamonds, and throw away the possibility of a straight by dumping the 10(C) as well as the 2(H).

3. Four Flush vs. High Pair

This is a very common situation, often misplayed.

The hand is Q(H) 6(H) Q(C) 10(H) 5(H).

In this situation, we dump the four flush and retain the queens. With the high pair we're assured of our money back, and have various possibilities open to us, such as four of a kind, full house, three of a kind, and two pair. Go for the high pair here, since all we can hope for the other way is a flush, and with small probability, pairing the queen of hearts again.

4. Four Straight vs. High Pair

The hand is Q(H) J(D) J(S) 10(H) 9(C).

With our high pair, we're assured of a payoff, plus all sorts of other possibilities, such as three of a kind. It's no contest. Retain the jacks.

5. Four Straight with Low Cards vs. One High Card

The hand is K(D) 4(S) 6(D) 7(S) 5(C)

We go for the straight here. Although there is a possibility of getting a high pair, we're not even assured of this. Our four straight rates an edge here, though mathematically it's not that much of an edge.

6. Low Pair vs. Two High Cards Not Paired

The hand is 9(C) A(D) K(S) 4(C) 9(S).

Although there are two chances to pair high cards, we already have a low pair that can be improved to three of a kind, full house, even four of a kind, as well as two pair. We go with our pair, even though it's low.

7. Low Pair vs. Four Straight with High Cards

The hand is 10(H) J(D) K(C) Q(H) 10(S).

This hand looks lovely, but in actuality all we have is a low pair, since a pair of 10s has no more value to us than a pair of deuces. It's a very close call whether to retain the small pair or go for the straight, but we should, by a very narrow margin mathematically, retain the small pair of 10s.

8. Two High Cards vs. One High Card

The hand is 3(D) 6(S) A(S) 10(C) Q(D)

This type of hand comes up quite often. We have two high cards, the ace and queen. If we were playing regular poker, there'd be no contest; we'd retain the ace and throw away the queen. But here we have two cards of equal value as far as payoffs on video poker is concerned. We should retain both high cards in the hope of pairing either one and getting other improvements, such as two pair and three of a kind.

9. Three to a Straight vs. Low Pair

The hand is J(C) K(D) 6(H) 6(S) Q(S).

This is another common situation, and once more calls into question the value of a small pair. But since there are only three cards to a straight, even if it is a high straight with possibilities of pairing, we don't want to give up the chances of getting a three of a kind, four of a kind, or full house, and so we retain the small pair.

10. Four Flush vs. Two High Cards

The hand is 6(C) A(H) 9(C) 2(C) Q(C).

You will recall that in hand no. 3 we showed that it paid to retain a high pair over a four flush. But then we had a pair, assuring us of our money back. Here we have two odd high cards, and it's no contest. It's much to our advantage to go after that flush. There's still an outside chance of getting a high pair as well in this situation, even if we retain only one high card.

11. Four Flush vs. Four Straight

The hand is 6(D) J(D) 10(C) Q(D) 9(D).

Another kind of hand that makes one pause. In ordinary poker we go for the flush, since it beats a straight. Here, of course, we just want to beat the machine and collect our payoff. Since the chances of getting a flush or straight are very close, and since the flush pays more, as in regular poker, we go for the flush. It's by far our best bet in this situation.

12. Middle Straight Draw vs. Two High Cards

The hand is 9(C) J(S) Q(D) 2(D) 8(H).

We need a 10 for the straight, known as a "gut-shot" draw. It's better to save the two high cards, the jack and queen, than go for the single draw possibility.

13. Middle Straight Draw vs. One High Card

The hand is 7(S) 8(C) 2(C) 9(H) J(H).

Once again we lack the 10 for the straight. And once again, it's to our advantage to retain the jack and take our chances with the draw than go for the gut-shot hit.

14. Four Straight High Hand vs. Three High Cards

The hand is K(C) 10(S), Q(D) J(C) 3(S).

Since we have two chances with an open-ended straight, it's to our advantage to go for the straight rather than retain just the three high cards. In effect, we're keeping the 10 as a kicker of a sort. The same situation would hold true if we had an open-ended high straight against two high cards. We go for the straight.

15. Low Pair vs. Low Pair and Kicker

The hand is 2(C) 2(D) 9(H) A(S) 3(C).

The concept of a kicker is the retention of a high card along with a low pair to improve the hand dramatically should the kicker pair. This concept is more valid in regular poker than it is in video poker, because in regular poker you're playing against other players. Drawing two cards in an ordinary draw poker game also has the psychological advantage of making the opponents believe you have three of a kind and are drawing to improve on that. But you can't psych out the machine, and it's to your advantage not to retain the ace kicker and to simply hold the pair of twos.

16. High Pair vs. High Pair and Kicker

The hand is Q(D) Q(C) 9(S) 4(H) A(D).

Just as with a low pair and kicker, it pays not to retain the kicker, but to go with the high pair. If you get two pair or a full house, it doesn't then matter if the extra pair or three of a kind consist of jacks or better. This concept is only important in a single pair.

17. Three to a Flush vs. High Pair

Hand is Q(D) 4(D) 5(D) 10(C) Q(S).

We've already seen that it's better to retain a high pair than have a four flush. Thus, by logic, it's even better to retain the high pair than have a three flush. Keep the high pair and assure yourself of a payoff, with the expectation of getting even better hands from the single pair. The same holds true with a three to a flush vs a low pair. Even though you're not guaranteed any payoff, it's still better to hold the single small pair, with the possibility of improving the hand. The odds are just too strong against getting a flush when you start with a three flush.

In the next instances we're going to examine hands that already will pay off vs. drawing to a royal flush.

18. Straight vs. Four to a Royal Flush

Hand is K(S) Q(S) A(S) 10(S) J(D).

In this hand we already have a straight and by holding all five cards are assured of a payoff of four units for each coin bet. However, a royal flush will give us a payoff of 800 units for each coin bet. We have to forgo the sure thing here and go after the monster payoff. Break up the straight by dumping the diamond jack and drawing one card.

19. Flush vs. Four to a Royal Flush

Hand is J(D) Q(D) K(D) A(D) 3(D).

Again, we can collect on our flush by holding all our cards, but it isn't worth going after the smaller payoff when we already have four to a royal flush. Go for the royal flush and throw away the three of diamonds.

20. High Pair vs. Four to a Royal Flush

Hand is A(C) A(S) K(C) J(C) Q(C).

We already know the answer to this from the previous examples. We dump the ace of spades to go for our royal flush. As a general rule, anytime you have four to a royal flush, go for it, and don't bother with a smaller payoff.

Jokers Wild Video Machines

Manufactured by Sigma, these machines are found in a few casinos. I first encountered them in the Palace Station Casino in Las Vegas, off I-15 and Sahara Avenue on the west side of town.

These machines are intriguing for two reasons. First, there's a joker in the pack—a pure wild card that can be used to enhance any poker hand. Second, there's a double or nothing feature that I've not found on other video poker machines. Let's now examine the payoffs on this machine.

Jokers Wild Video Poker

Royal Flush	500 coins
Five of a Kind	100 coins
Straight Flush	50 coins
4 of a kind	20 coins

Full House	8 coins
Flush	7 coins
Straight	5 coins
3 of a Kind	3 coins
Two Pair	1 coin
None of the Above	Loss

There are several differences in the payoff here, all based on one coin play. The royal flush is a much bigger payoff, giving the player 2,500 coins for a 5-coin win. There is no progressive feature, and players are limited to 5-coin bets. Five of a kind is a hand not seen on any other machines without a joker feature, since it's impossible to get this hand without a wild card such as a joker. There is no payoff for jacks or better hands; a single pair, no matter what, is a loser. This changes the strategy of play, since there's no reason to save high cards in the hope of pairing up. As a result there are many more losing hands here.

For example, if you're dealt 5(H) 9(C) A(S) 3(D) J(H), you have a complete bust, a hand that is known as "garbage" in poker circles. You'd throw away this hand in a regular draw poker game. In the ordinary video poker game you'd save the ace and jack, hoping to pair one or the other and at least get your bet back. But here if you pair them, it's still a losing hand, and there's as much likelihood of pairing the 5 or 3 as there is of pairing the ace and jack.

And you have to play the hand. What you have to do is hold two hearts or the ace and jack and hope for miracle draws, which rarely occur, giving you a winning hand.

On the other hand, if you have a pair of any value, you hold them, hoping for the joker to give you three of a kind. And if you have a four straight or four flush, then you definitely are hoping for a joker to make your hand. The minute a joker is drawn to a four straight or a four flush, you have a winner, for it's an automatic wild card. And a joker drawn to a four-straight flush or a four-royal flush is a very big winner.

If you have four of a kind without the joker, you're still going to draw, trying for five of a kind. And that goes for a hand of 3 3 3 JKR 9, for instance, where you'll hold the three

3s and joker and draw a card, hoping again for five of a kind.

With a joker in the deck, it's much easier to improve your straights and flushes. Normally, the odds against improving a four flush to a full flush is 4.2–1; with the joker it becomes 3.8–1. And open-ended four straights are improved 10% more often.

With the joker in play, here's a rundown of representative hands and the chances of improving them.

Odds Against Improving Hands

Hand	Odds
8–10–Q–JKR	5–1
6–7–8–9	4.3–1
Four-Flush	3.8–1
4–5–7–JKR	3–1
6–7–8–10 (same suit)	2.7–1
4–5–6–8 (inside straight)	8.6–1
9–10–J–JKR	2–1
5–6–7–8 (same suit)	2–1
6–8–9–JKR (same suit)	1.5–1
3–4–5–JKR (same suit)	1.2–1
Any Two Pair	8.6–1
Any Three of a Kind	6.1–1
Drawing Three to a Pair	2–1

To sum up play on these machines: You have a chance for some big hands because of the joker, but you're going to lose a lot more hands without any payoff whatsoever.

Double or Nothing Feature

The window of the video machine will display five cards at all times. First, there are the original five cards and then the cards after the draw. For example, we first see:

J(S) 9(H) 9(D) 3(C) 3(S)

Our play is to hold the 9s and 3s, and discard the jack. We do so and buy another 9, so our line of cards now look like this after the draw:

9(S) 9(H) 9(D) 3(C) 3(S)

Assuming that we put in 5 coins, we now have a winner

that will pay off 40 coins, at 8 for 1. We can now either collect the forty coins by pressing the cashout button or go for double-or-nothing. If we desire to try our luck with this double or nothing feature, we press the ''double'' button. The five cards will be erased, and instead we'll see the first card, and the back of the other four cards, all looking blank.

In order to collect on this double or nothing shot, we have to beat the first card by selecting any one of the other four blanks as the card we're hoping to beat the first card shown.

In other words, at this point the machine will display one card, which is the machine card. To collect double or nothing, we have to select a card higher than the machine card. We can select any of the four blank cards as our representative card. If it's higher than the machine card, our payoff is doubled. For example, let's assume we've pushed the double or nothing button, and see the following:

6 __ __ __ __. (The __s refer to blank cards.) We now have a choice of selecting any of the four blanks. Suppose we select the last blank, the fourth one. We press the hold button under it, and then all the cards are displayed. Let's say they look like this:

6 J 2 3 8

The 8 we selected is higher than the 6, so we get a double payoff. If we had selected the third or fourth button, the blanks would have shown us a 2 or 3 and we'd have lost, and gotten nothing instead of the 80 doubled coins we've now won.

What happens if there's a tie between the machine card and our selected card? We can try once more, since neither side wins or loses.

Now suppose, as in the previous example, we won and want to double down again. We can do that. We're now betting that we will win again. If we lose, we have no coins at all. Suppose we try again, and the following shows up as the machine card:

J __ __ __ __

Now we're in trouble. The only cards that can win for us is the queen, king, ace, or joker. Let's say we press the second hold button and make the second blank our card. The cards now show up as follows:

J 6 9 Q A

This time we picked the wrong button, and we lose everything.

If a joker comes up as the machine card, it's an automatic loss for us. If we get the joker as our card, we have an automatic win.

Should we select the double or nothing feature? It's really an even-money shot in a game where the odds are otherwise stacked up against us. I'd try it once. Winning twice in a row makes the odds 3–1 against us. However, the payoffs can get quite high with a 10,000 coin limit on doubling.

Video Poker Etiquette and Miscellany

• If you don't have the proper change to play the machines, there are change persons available who will be happy to accommodate you. You can easily change a $10 bill into a roll of forty quarters and have plenty of change to last a long time.

If a change person can't be found on the floor, you can go to a cashier's booth near the video machines, which are usually placed among the slot machines. Or you can ring the service button on a machine, and a change person will come to your machine with coins for you.

In addition to change, ask for a paper or plastic cup to hold the coins. Don't try to hold them in your hands, for you'll end up dropping and losing them.

Many machines now accept currency. For example, if you slide in a $20 bill, you'll get 80 credits on a 25¢ machine.

• Before playing a machine, make certain that no one else has claimed it by putting down something on the seat. If there's any doubt in your mind, avoid the machine you think has been set aside for someone else.

Unlike slots, it's hard to play more than one machine at a time, though it can be done. It will take a much longer time than a slots machine, because decisions have to be made constantly. To avoid mistakes, we suggest you play only one machine at a time.

• In most casinos the video poker players are catered to with free drinks. Either call a passing waitress or ring a bell for service. Even though the drink is free, it is customary to tip the waitress. Usually a quarter or two quarters is given.

Change persons aren't usually tipped.

• When playing the poker machines, don't expect to win. Manage your money so that you limit your losses. If you give the change person $10 for a roll of quarters, play out that roll and quit. That's plenty of action. If you find you're ahead, leave a winner. Don't give it all back to the machine. Suppose you've hit a four-of-a-kind hand, had bet ten coins, and now have 250 coins in the well. Play a few more times—if you lose the thirty coins you bet on three plays, leave a winner.

• Always go for the big win. That's the ticket. Try for that royal flush.

• Ask the change person if there is a progressive payout on video machines, and find out which machines are tied to that progression. Play those machines if you're after a win in the thousands of dollars. They're around in a number of casinos and are becoming the norm in casinos.

• Protect your coins at all times. Don't leave coins in the well, and don't forget to cash out all credits due to you when you leave the machine. Be alert and keep your eyes on your money.

• Some rather large payouts are paid out by the machine, others are paid out by an attendant. If you've hit a royal flush, don't walk away from your machine to find an attendant. Ring the service bell and be patient. And don't fool around with the buttons or do anything to disturb the machine. Don't inadvertently wipe out your big win.

• If you have problems with the machine—if it jams or hasn't paid you off properly—press the service bell and ask for a mechanic. You'll get one who will listen to your problem and solve it. The first time you have such a mechanical problem, you'll usually get a refund and the benefit of the doubt.

Other Video Machine Games

Blackjack Video Games

Blackjack video machines can be seen in most casinos, and can be played for either 25¢ or $1 tokens. Some machines limit the player to five coins bet at one time, and others go up to 100 coins at one time. The rules vary from machine to machine, but are roughly the same as the table game of blackjack.

However, although most options are available, such as doubling down and splitting of cards, and in some machines, even surrender, the usual payoff on a blackjack is even money instead of 3–2, and that fact alone makes these machines poor selections for an astute bettor. We're not going into the ramifications of video blackjack other than to suggest that you avoid the game. For one thing, each time you play a new hand, you're theoretically facing a newly shuffled deck of cards. Thus, you can't count cards, or know if the deck is turning favorable or unfavorable; with the rules of play it's always slightly unfavorable to the player. And there's no dealer to read for tells.

Your best bet is to play at a regular blackjack table against a single-deck game. Not only will you have all options available, including a 3–2 payoff for a blackjack, but you can also count cards and take advantage of solid situations when the deck is in your favor by raising your bets. If you're playing for $1 a pop at the video machine, find a $1 game (such as in the Horseshoe in Las Vegas) in which you face only a single deck. If you're playing against a double deck, that's OK also. You'll have a much better shot at winning if you read and study our chapter on Blackjack in this book.

Keno Video Games

Keno is also available as a video game. The payoffs are similar to those in the regular game without any of the monster payoffs now available, such as the $250,000 one at the Palace

Station Casino in Las Vegas. And the odds are just as bad, so we suggest that you avoid these machines entirely. The only advantage to video keno is that you can play more games in the same time it takes for a regular keno game to be consummated. To me, that means that you will be losing more quickly. Avoid this game.

The Expanding World of Electronic Gaming

The computer chip has done wonders for the gaming industry. Games can be played without supervision, and are programmed to give the casino a solid edge, while baiting players to put in more and more coins for bigger and bigger jackpots. Games like video poker have exploded in popularity, with large areas of casinos devoted to them. All casinos need in the way of personnel are change persons and mechanics, plus a supervisory floorman.

Even the use of floorpeople is optional, since no disputes will arise between a human dealer and a player. Change persons may also become redundant in the near future, as most machines now take cash directly. What happens is this: suppose you sit down at a video poker machine and you don't see a change person around and the nearest cashier is at the other end of the casino. Not to worry. You simply take a $20 bill from your wallet or purse and slide it into the machine. If you're playing a 25-cent machine, eighty credits will flash on the screen, and you can go ahead and play. This helps you and the casino.

It helps you because you can play at a much faster rate with credits, rather than constantly pushing in five coins at a time and waiting for a winner so you can get some credits to play off. With credits, all you have to do is touch the maximum credits button and the cards flash on the screen. This also aids the casinos because the faster the play, the more money they make. The customer waiting for a change person is an irritated gambler, as well as one who isn't playing a machine.

Electronic games are ideal for any casino. They can be set to pay back a certain percentage to the house, and casinos don't have to worry about any lucky players, as they do at their table games, going on a fantastic run and denting the casino bankroll. The electronic games are solid money makers for the casino, and, as mentioned, take up an enormous amount of floor space.

When I first got involved seriously with the world of gambling, most of the space in casinos was devoted to table games such as craps and blackjack. On the side there were banks of slot machines, primarily for the benefit of the wives and girlfriends of the high rollers, who stayed at the craps or blackjack tables. The slots made money, of course, but the big money was going to be made at the table games. Now the whole situation is reversed. There's still money to be made at table games, but the electronic games bring in a ton of cash.

The slots now make up a smaller percentage of these games. Video poker, video keno, and a host of new games are constantly being introduced to the gaming public. Both Bally and International Game Technology have installed machines that combine a number of games in one machine, and the world of interactive play and touch screen choices is also now upon us.

The Bally's machine is known as Game Master, and combines the following games in one machine: draw poker, deuces wild poker, keno, double bonus poker, blackjack, joker poker, triple trouble, lizard of odds, white lightning, and bonus poker. All players have to do is touch the screen to choose the game they want to play.

International Game Technology has come up with a machine called Winner's Choice, which includes the following games: bonus poker, blackjack, double bonus poker, deuces wild poker, double 4 of a kind bonus poker, jacks or better poker, keno, red white and blue, super eight line, and super sevens. As with Bally's Game Master, all a player has to do is touch the screen to select a game.

These games do not feature progressive jackpots, and I stand by my advice in the Video Poker section to look for and play the progressive machines. Basically, these multi-game machines are for the benefit of the casinos, since one machine offering so many games can save an enormous amount of space.

Most electronic machines are easy to master and easy to play. They attract a wide variety of gamblers, especially those who are willing to gamble a moderate amount of money. As a result, they fill casinos from coast to coast.

Recently, I went into a couple of casinos on the Las Vegas Strip to check out the action and the games offered. When I lived in Vegas in the 1970s, I used to frequent both of these casinos, and knew the people who ran them quite well. Both casinos were rather elegant, with a subdued atmosphere and large spaces devoted to the craps and blackjack pits. When I walked in this year, I couldn't get my bearings. Ahead of me was a forest of electronic games, taking up all the space. Both casinos had become different places, catering now to the family trade, to the small bettors, and the slots and electronic games players. That's where the easy money is now.

Glossary of Video Poker Terms

Cancel Button. The button that enables a player to cancel a previous decision to hold a particular card before the draw. When the cancel button is pressed, the term "hold" will disappear on the screen.

Cash Out Button. By pressing this button, the player will receive all coins previously credited to him by the machine.

Change person. The casino employee who makes change for a player prior to play, and who cashes in coins won in video poker after play is over.

Credit Button. This button allows the player to play out coins credited to him without using his own coins. Some machines allow one credit coin at a time to be pressed, up to the limit allowed; others allow ten coins to be played at once from the credit button.

Deal Button. At the outset of play, after coins are inserted in the machine, this button, when pressed, will show five new cards constituting the poker hand.

Draw. To receive new cards, up to five, after the initial poker hand has been dealt.

Draw Button. The button,

when pressed, that allows the player to draw up to five new cards to his original poker hand.

Four Flush. Four cards of the same suit, such as 8(H) J(H) Q(H) 3(H), together with an odd card.

Four of a Kind. A poker hand consisting of four cards of the same rank or value, such as K K K K.

Four Straight. Four cards in sequence, such as 5(C) 6(D) 7(S) 8(S), so that there are two ways to make the straight, either by buying the 4 or 9.

Full House. A poker hand consisting of a three of a kind plus a pair, such as 6 6 6 3 3.

Gutshot Straight. A four straight that can be made only one way, such as 5(C) 6(D) 8(H) 9(S).

High Card. A jack, queen, king, or ace, when paired, which pays the player back his original bet.

High Pair. A pair of jacks, queens, kings, or aces, which pays the player back his original bet.

Hold Button. The button that, when pressed, will hold a card in the original hand before the draw.

Jokers Wild. A type of video poker machine that has a

joker in addition to the normal 52-card pack. The joker is a pure wild card and can be used as any card to enhance or make any hand.

Kicker. An odd card, usually a high card, held by the player for the draw. Thus, a 3 3 A hand consists of a pair of threes plus the ace kicker.

Low Pair. A pair of 10s or cards of lower rank, such as 9s, which alone don't constitute a winning hand.

Mechanic. The house employee who repairs machines that are broken or jammed.

Progressive Machines. Machines tied to a single payoff that increases each time a new coin is inserted and a royal flush is not made. It pays off only on royal flushes.

Royal Flush. A hand consisting of A K Q J 10 of the same suit, the best in poker.

Straight. Five consecutive cards, but not of the same suit. For purposes of a straight, the ace can be the lowest or highest card in a straight sequence, such as 5 4 3 2 A or A K Q J 10.

Straight Flush. Five cards in sequence and of the same suit, such as K(S) Q(S) J(S) 10(S) 9(S).

Three of a Kind. A hand that consists of three cards of the same rank or value, such as 8 8 8.

Two Pair. A hand consisting of two separate pairs, such as 9 9 4 4.

Three Flush. A hand consist-ing of three cards, all of the same suit, such as 10(D) 8(D) 2(D), together with two odd cards.

Well. The area at the bottom of the machine into which coins that have been paid out fall.

12

Caribbean Stud Poker— The Tropical Game

In this book, I deal only with those games played against the house, or casino, and this game is no exception. Although it has the word "poker" in its title, Caribbean Poker is strictly a table game in which the player endeavors to win by holding cards that are stronger than those held by the dealer. In some ways this game resembles blackjack, but without the skill that is built into "twenty-one." There are only a couple of options open to the player in Caribbean Stud Poker (besides the size of his bet), and that is to either double his wager after looking at his cards and one of the dealer's five cards, or fold his hand and lose his initial bet.

There is one other option, which I should point out, and that is whether to bet an additional dollar to qualify for the progressive jackpot payoffs offered by the casino. As a general rule, this is an extremely bad bet, but all this will be covered in the appropriate sections of this chapter.

I first encountered Caribbean poker on a day cruise out of Fort Lauderdale. After watching it for a while, I realized how difficult it was to beat the house. Without knowing any of the correct odds, I could immediately see that it was structured heavily in favor of the casino. My feeling proved right, because after watching the game for about half an hour, I saw every participant go belly-up and lose his or her initial bankroll.

Caribbean stud poker is a popular game on the cruise ships and the Caribbean resorts that permit gaming. It has now spread to the legalized casinos in America, and it has attracted some interest among the players who want to try their luck at a fairly mindless game. Most people know the rudiments of poker, and are familiar with various poker hands, so they quickly understand the rules of this game. Another factor is that the betting is fairly simple. And if you make a mistake, it affects only your money. Many novices are nervous about playing a game like blackjack, because their decision to hit or stand may affect the outcome of the entire table, and if they make a mistake that costs the other players money, they get dirty looks or worse. But in Caribbean Stud poker you play only your hand. Actually, you don't really even play your hand, because there is no raising, no psychology, no real skill. Your basic decision is whether to fold your cards or double your bet. After that, the final outcome is out of your hands.

Rules of the Game

Caribbean stud poker is played on a table similar to a blackjack table with up to seven betting spots, accommodating that many players. A standard fifty-two-card deck is used, without the jokers. In a regular poker game, the players compete against each other. In Caribbean Stud Poker, all players have one goal in mind—to beat the dealer.

When a player sits down at this game, he will notice that the area in front of him or her contains three separate betting spots. First of all, there is one marked "ante," which is enclosed in a rectangle. Then there is a circle marked "bet." There is also a slot in front of each player, known as a "drop slot," which takes a $1 token or coin.

Usually, there is a minimum bet of at least $5 required in this game when playing on the Las Vegas Strip, though some casinos will allow smaller wagers to be made. The initial bet is made prior to the dealing of the cards in the box marked "ante." If a player wants to go after the progressive jackpot, he makes an additional $1 wager in the drop slot. When a $1 bet is made in the progressive jackpot slot, the dealer presses a button so that each $1 progressive bet drops. A red light goes on by the slot indicating that the player has made this wager.

After the initial bet of $5 (or more) is made, the player and all others at the table who have made this wager are dealt five cards. Many of these games use the Shuffle Master method of dealing, which automatically gives out five cards at a time to each player, and five to the dealer.

All of the players' cards are dealt face down and the rules of the game expressly forbid players to exchange information about their hands. While the players' cards are face down, the dealer reveals the last card he gets, which is known as the ''upcard.''

At this point, the player sees his own five cards and the dealers upcard, and now makes his decision either to ''fold,'' that is, give up his hand to the dealer and lose his bet, or to ''call,'' that is, to double his initial wager. Once the player folds he is out of contention, and doesn't participate further in that round of play.

After each player has made a decision, all players must put their cards face down on the table. First, the dealer collects all the ante bets from those who have folded. Then he turns over the four remaining unseen cards from his hand for the benefit of the remaining players who have ''called'' their bets, showing his entire hand.

If the dealer doesn't have at least an ''ace king hand'' or higher, that is, a hand headed by an ace and a king, such as ace king 8 5 3, he does not ''qualify,'' and now all the players that have called and remain in the game will be paid off. However, their payoffs will only be for the initial wager in the ante box. The double call wager will not be paid off, nor lost. The player removes it and includes it in his stack of chips.

Now, if the dealer has at least an ace king hand or higher, such as one pair or two pair or any cards of a higher value, and his hand does qualify, then the dealer's hand is compared with each player's hand. If the dealer's hand is higher, such as three of a kind against a player's one pair, or a pair of jacks against a player's pair of 10s, the player loses both his ante and call bets.

But, should the dealer have a ''qualifying hand,'' ace king or better, and it is weaker in value than a player's hand, the player will first be paid off at even-money for his ante bet, and will now qualify for the "bonus payouts," which are as follows:

1 pair	Even money
2 pairs	2–1
3 of a kind	3–1
Straight	4–1
Flush	5–1
Full House	7–1
4 of a Kind	20–1
Straight Flush	50–1
Royal Flush	100–1

What if there is a tie, where the dealer's hand and player's hand are equal? This situation is very rare indeed, coming up about 0.00160 percent of the time, but if it does happen, then it is a "push," a tie, and neither the dealer nor the player wins or loses.

Maximum Payout

One other factor should be mentioned at this time. In looking at the cards explaining the game in a number of casinos, I noticed the following disclaimer, "Bonus payouts may not exceed table's maximum payout." What does this mean to a player? In examining the situation further, I discovered that some smaller casinos had only a $5,000 maximum payout, while others went up to $60,000.

Here's what they mean by a maximum payout. The casino will only pay you the maximum amount that they set aside for bonus payouts. If the limit is $5,000, for example, and you wagered $50 on the ante and $100 additional on the optional call bet and held a royal flush, you'd be entitled to 100 × $100 (your call bet) + $50 for your ante bet. That would be $10,000 + $50 for a total of $10,050. However, if the casino only has a maximum payout of $5,000, you'd only receive $5,000 plus your $50 ante bet for a total of $5,050.

Therefore, if you intend to make some big wagers, find out what the maximum payout is before playing Caribbean stud poker. Then use the following formula: divide the maximum payout by 200 to set your maximum ante wager. You'll get the correct payoff if you hit a royal flush.

Let's assume that the maximum payout is $10,000 in the casino you're playing at. Using our formula, divide this by 200 to get 50. So that's all you should bet as a maximum ante wager. If you get the royal flush, then the $100 call bet will be paid off at 100-1, for the correct $10,000 payout.

Odds Against Being Dealt Pat Hands

At this point, it is interesting to see the actual chances of being dealt these "pat hands." By pat hands, I mean hands that are made up of only five cards, none of which can be discarded and replaced with fresh ones, as is the case in draw poker and most forms of video poker.

Holding	Odds Against
Any pair	1.37–1
Two pair	20–1
Three of a Kind	46–1
Straight	254–1
Flush	508–1
Full House	693–1
Four of a Kind	4,165–1
Straight Flush	72,192–1
Royal Flush	649,739–1

Well, with these odds, the player's situation doesn't look that good at all. A player will get 2–1 for two pair when the true payout should be 20–1. And the situation gets worse the bigger the hand. The odds against getting a pat flush are 508–1, whereas the payout is a paltry 5–1. Four of a kind comes but once every 4,165 hands, but all the casino will give you is 20–1. And a royal flush, the best of all poker hands, consisting of an ace, king, queen, jack and ten of one suit, comes but once every 649,740 hands. And the casino will pay you off at 100–1 for this beauty.

Just how often does a royal flush come up in Caribbean stud poker? I asked a floorman at a Strip hotel, where the meter on the progressive jackpot was at $243,000. I was told that it came up at that casino only twice in the last three years. A pit boss at a downtown casino said the hand had come up four times in the last three years. In other words, someone is going to get a royal flush less than once a year, playing at a particular casino.

Taking everything into consideration, Caribbean stud poker gives the house an advantage, as we will see, of about 5.27 percent.

The Progressive Jackpot

Let's discuss the progressive jackpot and the various payoffs that result from players being dealt big hands. Here is a list of the progressive jackpot payoffs:

Royal Flush	100% of meter (Jackpot)
Straight Flush	10% of meter
Four of a Kind	$500
Full House	$100
Flush	$75

In order to qualify for any of the progressive jackpot payoffs, a player has to place $1 in the drop slot or "progressive slot" prior to being dealt any cards. If he has been dealt one of the above hands, he must inform the dealer of this fact. A player, for example, may be dealt a pat flush and not show his cards. Once they're taken away, he's forfeited the right to the $75 payoff. This may occur when the dealer doesn't have a qualifying hand. Since the players' cards are face down, the dealer simply pays off the winning bets without looking at the gamblers' cards. It is the player's responsibility to turn over his cards if he has a hand that merits a progressive jackpot payoff.

The payoff on the progressive jackpot is made regardless of the outcome of the table bet. For example, suppose you were dealt a pat flush, and made a call bet in addition to your ante. You've also dropped a dollar into the progressive slot. The dealer has a bigger hand, however. Let's assume he holds a full house and beats your flush. Though you'd lose the table bets, you'd still collect on the $75 progressive jackpot payoff.

There is a rub to progressive jackpot payoffs. In some casinos, they are in the aggregate; that is, if two or more players hold the same hand and have placed $1 into the drop slot, they share the payoff. For example, suppose two players find themselves with straight flushes, a wild and improbable occurrence. The payoff is 10 percent of the meter. If the meter is at $100,800, instead of each player getting $10,800, they'd have to split that amount, collecting $5,400 apiece.

In essence, playing the progressive jackpot is like playing the lottery. Instead of selecting six numbers as in most state lotteries, the player must drop the dollar into the slot and hope for lightning to strike.

The previous chart shows that the chances of getting a royal flush are 649,739–1. With this number in mind, it seems at first glance that the jackpot should total at least $649,740 to make this a profitable bet. However, this is not the case, as we shall see later. As each progressive jackpot bet is made only a certain percentage of it is applied to the progressive jackpot, with the rest going directly to the casino as profit. As we shall also see, at certain payoffs, the progressive jackpot will be worth playing, while at lower numbers it should be avoided. Let's now look into the correct playing strategy for Caribbean stud poker.

Playing Strategy

Various computer studies have given us involved strategies for this game, but a simpler strategy yields almost the same values, and since this is a negative game, that is, a game in which the house has an edge, we will give you a simple strategy that nets the casino about 5.27 percent. Memorizing a more complicated strategy will bring the house edge down to about 5.20 percent. What does this mean in actual terms of money? With a house edge of 5.27 percent your loss expectation is $5.27 for each $100 bet over the long run. If we reduce the house edge to 5.20 percent, the casino win expectation is $5.20 for each $100 you bet.

Let's compare this with other games. The worst table game to play in terms of loss expectation is American wheel roulette, containing a 0 and 00. The casino edge in this game is 5.26 percent. This is comparable to the edge the house enjoys in Caribbean Stud. A game like craps, when played correctly, betting only the line and come and don't come bets, will be 1.4 percent in the house's favor, but taking double odds will reduce this to 0.6 percent, or a loss expectation of 60 cents for every $100 bet. Even a mindless game such as baccarat, where the only option is betting Player or Bank, will give the house 1.35 percent or 1.17 percent, whether betting Player or Bank. Finally, blackjack gives the player an edge over the casino when played correctly, and a wider edge when counting cards and betting more when the deck or decks are favorable to the player.

What then should we do with Caribbean Stud? I would avoid playing this game for any serious money because of the large house edge. To memorize a whole group of principles to bring this edge down another 0.07 percent is a waste of time.

So, now let's look at a strategy for the game.

1. Call with any pair or better

This rule must be observed if you have any chance to win in this game over the short run. Many players will fold small pairs, such as 2s, 3s, and 4s. A bad mistake. Remember this: Theoretically, you will be dealt a pair about 42.3 percent of the time. Most pairs you bet will give you an expected gain. Each pair you don't bet will cost you money. Plain and simple. Bet each pair, no matter how weak the hand you hold and no matter what the dealer's upcard. For example, if you hold 2–2–6–4–3 and the dealer has a queen, you should call this hand, not fold it.

These will be your bread and butter hands, making money for you, and coming up more than 42 percent of the time. Of course, a pair can be anything, such as aces or kings. Or they can be deuces or treys. But they will come up many times.

2. Ace–King–Queen–Jack–x

The "x" in this hand represents any card other than the 10, which would make it a straight. This hand is worth calling with because if the dealer just has an ace–king hand, he will probably be defeated. For example, if he holds ace–king–

queen–10–9, you win both your ante and call bets. The hand is even stronger if the dealer holds any one of your cards as his upcard, with the best possible card for you being an ace or king, since you've dramatically reduced his chance of pairing this card, and he has an opportunity to qualify, enabling you to win both your bets. Even with these cards, you don't have an overall win expectation. You are simply cutting your losses by calling with these cards rather than folding them.

3. Ace–King–Queen–x–x

With this hand you call if the dealer holds either an ace, king, queen, or any of your x cards. Let's assume your hand is ace–king–queen–8–3. If the dealer shows any of your cards as his upcard, call rather than fold. This is a marginal hand at best.

4. Ace–King–Jack–8–x

This is much weaker than the previous hands. As with the other non-pair hands discussed, it is taking an ace and a king out of the dealer's hand, giving him less chance of qualifying in this way. For example, the ideal hand you want the dealer to have when you play the ace–king–jack is an ace–king, with the third best card lower than the jack. Or if he gets the jack as well, then his fourth card will be lower than the 8. That's why you use the 8 here. Only two cards will defeat it, and six will fall to it, if the dealer shows an ace–king–jack and doesn't pair up.

But don't expect to win in the long run playing these non-pair hands. What you will do is slow your losses. The gain isn't that much, but it is a gain for you in that your losses will be less.

If you intend to play Caribbean Stud, study the examples of playable hands, and realize that you will be betting the one-pair hands most often. With hands of 10s or better, you will have a positive win expectation, as I shall show. Of course, stronger hands, such as two pair, "trips" (three of a kind), straights, flushes and full houses, as well as the more powerful four of a kind, straight and royal flushes will get you some serious money, but we already know that these hands seldom come up.

The other rub is that, when you do make these powerful

hands, we have to hope that the dealer holds a qualifying hand for us to collect on your call bets. This is quite a frustrating rule, and one of the main reasons the house has such an edge over the player in Caribbean Stud.

Losing Strategies

With the house holding such a big edge, players must be careful not to consider strategies which will increase its advantage even further.

1. Folding Small Pairs

Some players I have observed have consistently gotten rid of really low pairs, such as deuces, treys, and 4s. Their reasoning is that any higher pair in the dealer's hand will beat them, but they are wrong. First of all, just as the players will get a pair only about 42 percent of the time, so will the dealer. More than half the time he'll be holding five odd cards.

As I mentioned previously, the pairs are your bread and butter hands, even though they won't all yield a gain expectation against a higher upcard shown by the dealer. This is true especially of the 2s–4s as pairs, even when the dealer's upcard is of the same or lower rank, such as a dealer's 2 against a pair of 3s. But for all other pairs, there is a win expectation against a dealer holding an upcard of equal or lower rank.

For example, if you hold a pair of 7s, you have a positive win expectation if the dealer's upcard is a 7 or lower. When you hold a pair of 10s or higher, you have a positive win expectation against any card the dealer might have as his upcard.

Why then, as we have observed, not fold the 2s–4s as pairs, if there is a loss expectation? For the same reason I suggest holding certain non-pair hands. Your overall losses will be much less if you bet these low pairs than if you simply fold them. If a player folds his pairs of 2s–4s, he will be giving the house an edge of over 7 percent! Don't do this.

A comparable situation exists in blackjack. If you are dealt a pair of 8s against a dealer's 10, you should split the 8s, even though in the long run there is a loss expectation attached to this play. The same thing holds true when you are dealt a hard 16 against a dealer's 10. You should hit this hand, even though there's no winning expectation to the play. What you are doing in both situations is making a gain in the sense that your losses will be less by making these moves. For example, if you stand on the hard 16 against the dealer's 10, you give up almost 3 percent to the house.

2. Fold All Hands that Are Not Bettable According to Our Strategies

Some players feel that, because they immediately place their cards face down after viewing them, they're fooling the dealer into thinking they have strong hands when they make the additional double call bet. If the dealer doesn't have a qualifying hand, these players are paid off for their ante bet, and think to themselves, "Aha, I've bluffed the dealer." Thinking this way will only bluff your bankroll.

The surest way to lose money in this game is to play hands that should be folded. For example, you're dealt a king–queen–10–9–8, just missing a straight. Instead of folding, you make a call bet. At best, you're going to win an ante bet if the dealer doesn't have a qualifying hand of ace–king or better. If the dealer qualifies you lose three bets; your ante, and the double call wager. So what you're really doing is playing a garbage hand in the hope of winning one bet, while chancing three bets.

Don't even think of doing it. And don't play hunches in this game. It's a very tough game to beat, and in the long run the house edge is going to eat into your bankroll. If you are ahead in the short run, it will be because you were dealt some good hands, such as two pairs or trips or a run of pairs. Over 90 percent of your payoffs will come from these holdings. But if you don't get many of these hands, and are constantly dealt "rags" or junk hands, you may start losing patience and bet all kinds of hands you should fold. Once you start doing this, you are doomed to defeat. You will lose until you are tapped out at the table. Don't let this happen. If you find you're not getting any playable hands, get out of the game. Don't take out your frustration on your bankroll. I can't emphasize this enough.

If you avoid these losing strategies, you're giving yourself some kind of chance to keep the house edge at its level a bit above 5 percent, and with a bit of luck you might even take home a short-term win.

Betting the Progressive Jackpot

Remember, in order to win the progressive jackpot, a dollar token or coin must be inserted in the drop slot before the dealer deals the cards. He then presses a button that lights up the slot, signifying that you are now eligible for the jackpot and all attendant payoffs. Although there are payoffs for flushes and stronger holdings, what you are really after is that royal flush with the big bucks payoff. You'd also settle for a straight flush, another nice payoff. But these are really long shots. Remember that a royal flush comes up only once in 649,740 hands and the straight flush once in 72,193 plays.

How the Progressive Jackpot Is Increased

First of all, let's examine the level of the jackpot before it is increased, or just after a jackpot has been paid off. There is no set standard to determine at what level the progressive jackpot begins. In some small casinos, it is set at a measly $5,000, but most casinos begin it at $10,000. The Horseshoe in Las Vegas starts it at $50,000, but this is a rare exception.

Every time a player puts a dollar token or coin in the progressive slot, a portion of that coin is applied to the progressive jackpot. The more applied, the more quickly the jackpot increases. Just how much of that $1 is applied to incrementing the jackpot? The figure varies from casino to casino. The best estimate is somewhere between 45 and 75 cents, with the mean average about 50. Thus, in most casinos, half or more of the $1 bet on the jackpot is retained as profit. The most liberal paybacks on the progressive jackpot seem to be at the Mirage and Golden Nugget in Las Vegas.

When to Bet the Progressive Jackpot

The break-even point also varies from casino to casino, and involves several factors, including the incremental increase in the jackpot for each losing wager.

If you play for the jackpot when the meter is set at $50,000, the casino has over a 40 percent edge on your bet. It doesn't decrease that much even when the jackpot reaches $100,000. It's still a bad bet. Generally speaking, even if the jackpot is about $250,000, your bet isn't that good. However, if you want to gamble, try for the jackpot when it reaches $200,000. The casino still has an edge, but you may get lucky. Any bets below that figure in the hope of getting the royal flush is just fattening the casino's coffers.

A final note on Caribbean stud poker. As has been shown, it is a negative game, that is, the casino has an edge on the player no matter what strategy he uses. There are ways to keep the edge as low as possible, but again, as I previously advised, this is not a game to bet serious money on. If the meter shows a huge number, you might want to take a shot for a while, but set a strict loss limit. Don't chase the jackpot and keep losing. No matter how high the jackpot is, the odds against hitting the royal flush remain at a constant 649,739–1. And don't think in terms of the royal flush being "ripe." This is delusional thinking. Play this game sanely and for low stakes.

Glossary of Caribbean Stud Poker Terms

Ace–King Hand. A hand containing a holding headed by the ace and king of any suit, with no pairs. This is the minimum holding a dealer must have to hold a qualifying hand.

Ante Box. The rectangular box in which the initial bet is made before the cards are dealt by the dealer.

Ante Wager. The initial bet made by a player. In most casinos, the minimum ante bet is $5.

Any Pair. A hand containing two cards of equal rank, constituting a pair, such as two 6s, or two aces.

Bet Circle. The circular area in which a player may make an optional bet of twice his original wager after examining his cards.

Bonus Payouts. Payouts made to a player by the dealer if the dealer holds a qualifying hand. These range from even-money for one pair to 100–1 for a royal flush.

Call Bet. The optional wager made by a player if he decides to play his cards rather than folding them. This wager is twice the ante bet.

Drop Slot. The slot that receives the $1 bet for the progressive jackpot.

Flush. A hand containing five cards, all of the same suit, such as five clubs.

Fold. The act whereby the player gets rid of his cards and forfeits his ante bet.

Four of a Kind. A hand containing four cards, all of the same rank, such as four 9s or four kings.

Full House. A hand containing three of a kind and a pair, such as three 4s and two queens.

Meter. The illuminated device above the table which shows the value of the progressive jackpot.

Pair. See *Any Pair*

Pat Hand. An original poker hand before cards are drawn to it. In Caribbean stud poker, all hands are pat hands.

Progressive Jackpot. A separate payout by the casino for a player's hand containing a royal flush.

Progressive Slot. See *Drop Slot*

Push. When both the player and dealer have identical hands there is no payout or loss. This occurs rarely.

Qualifying Hand. The dealer must have an ace–king holding or better to qualify his hand, and in order to permit payoffs to players who have made call wagers.

Rags. Cards of no real value or chance to win.

Royal Flush. The best possible hand in poker, containing an ace–king–queen–jack–10 of the same suit.

Straight. A hand containing five cards of consecutive rank, such as ace–2–3–4–5 or 10–jack–queen–king–ace.

Straight Flush. A hand containing five cards of consecutive rank and of the same suit, such as the 5–6–7–8–9 of hearts.

Three of a Kind. A hand containing three cards of the same rank, such as three 8s. Also called trips.

Two Pair. A hand containing two separate pair, such as two 8s and two 3s.

Upcard. The dealer's exposed card, seen by all the players.

13

Let It Ride®

Let It Ride® is a variation of five-card poker played as a table game. It was originated by the Shuffle Master Corporation, a publicly traded company, and was first introduced to casinos in Nevada in August 1993. It is presently in over one hundred and twenty casinos worldwide, according to the company's literature, and in those casinos over two hundred tables feature the game. In 1995, "Let It Ride,® The Tournament,"™ was introduced after extensive field testing. The tournament offers prizes of at least $2 million, with the possibility of even larger amounts.

I've watched the game being played frequently and have spoken to a number of participants. They like the game because it's an easy one to play, and they feel that the rules minimize their losses. As a couple of players told me, "you can last a long time at this game before losing your money." Of course, that's not the best attitude to have towards a game. You want to play to win, not to endure.

How the Game Is Played

The table used is much like a standard blackjack table, with seven spots for seven participants. In front of each player are three circles, marked 1, 2, and $. Before the cards are dealt, each player must put at least a minimum bet in all three of the circles. In most casinos, the minimum wager is $5, though in some smaller casinos less may be permitted. For the purposes of our discussion, we'll assume a $5 minimum bet.

The dealer uses a Shuffle Master to deal out the cards. This device automatically shuffles and deals three cards to each player. A regular 52-card poker deck is used, without the jokers. The dealer waits till all the players have placed their bets before dealing out the cards. Even though a player has put down $15, or $5 in each circle, he has the option of taking down two of these three bets as the game goes on, as we shall see.

Once the bets are placed, each player receives three cards. In addition, the dealer deals herself two cards, which are known as "community cards." They're called community cards because they can be used by all players to form a hand of five cards, just as would happen in five-card stud. In essence, this is a game of five-card stud, except that each player sees three instead of two cards at the outset of play.

Once each player has looked at his three cards, he must decide whether or not to keep the bet in the circle marked "1." If he feels his hand isn't strong, he scrapes his three cards on the felt surface of the table, just as he would in blackjack when asking for a hit, but here he's signaling to tell the dealer that he wants to remove his chip or chips from the "1" circle.

When the player does this, the dealer will push the chip or chips back to him. A player is not permitted to touch his chips after his bets are made. One other thing—players must keep their cards hidden from everyone else at the table.

Now, let's assume that a player wants to let his bet ride. He puts his cards face down either under or behind his first wager. Even if he has given up his first chip he must still keep his cards hidden from the other players. The dealer now turns over the first of her community cards. Each player now sees four of the possible five cards that form his or her hand. At this point, each player may scrape his or her cards and have the second chip in the circle marked "2" returned by the dealer, or let the bet ride.

A point to note here is that even if a player has let his first bet ride, he can still remove the second chip. Some players don't realize they can do this. If any player has exercised the option to reclaim his first two chips, he or she has no more options left, and must wait for the dealer to turn over her second card.

After all the participants have made their decisions, the dealer shows the final community card. Each player now has a formed hand of five cards. Starting with the player at her right, the dealer now turns over each of the players' cards in turn. She will examine the hands to determine if the players get a payout according to a payout schedule. If a player holds a hand that qualifies for a payout, he or she will be paid according to the payout schedule and the number of chips the player has in the betting circles. If a player doesn't qualify for a payout, that is, has a weaker hand than the minimum required for a payout, the player's chips are removed by the dealer. The player has lost his or her bet or bets.

Object of the Game

This game, unlike Caribbean stud poker or blackjack, doesn't require the player to beat the dealer in order to win. All a player has to do is form a minimum holding or better to get a payout. And his holding is based on his three original cards plus the two community cards. Now let's look at the payout schedule:

Royal Flush	1,000–1
Straight Flush	200–1
Four of a Kind	50–1
Full House	11–1
Flush	8–1
Straight	5–1
Three of a Kind	3–1
Two Pair	2–1
Pair of 10s or Better	1–1

And here are the actual odds of making the above hands:

Royal Flush	649,739–1
Straight Flush	72,192–1
Four of a Kind	4,164–1

Full House	693–1
Flush	508–1
Straight	254–1
Three of a Kind	46–1
Two Pair	20–1
Pair of 10s or Better	5.15–1

Seventy-five percent of the time, the hands will be too weak to receive any type of payout. What this means is that a player may find himself going for a long period without any return on his bets, his bankroll melting away. On the other hand, when he does get paid for good hands, he will be able to receive payments on all of his bets. For example, if a player finds himself with a pair of jacks in the first three cards then gets another jack from the community cards for three of a kind, his payout will be 3–1 on all three bets that he has let ride. If his bets were $10, he would receive $90.

Maximum Payoffs

Practically all casinos have a limit to what they will pay out for any particular round of play. For example, if the maximum payout is $25,000, then a player who has bet $100 on each betting circle and has been dealt a royal flush would only be paid $25,000, instead of the correct $300,000. Even if he had only bet $10 on each circle, a more likely scenario, he would not get $30,000 and so would be $5,000 short of the correct payout. Therefore, it's important to know just what the maximum payout is in any casino where you play Let It Ride®. There should be a sign at the table indicating the maximum payout. If you can't find the information there, ask the dealer or floorman and bet accordingly.

An easy way to calculate the payment you'll receive for a royal flush is simply to divide the maximum payout by 3,000. If the payout is $30,000, that's easy—$10 is the most you should bet for a correct payout. If the maximum payout is the more usual $25,000, then dividing this by 3,000 gives you $8.33. In order to receive a correct royal flush payout you shouldn't wager more than $8 in any betting circle. Don't be shy when asking about the maximum payout—it can even be less than $25,000, all the way down to $10,000. It may also be as high as $100,000 at the Horseshoe in downtown Las Vegas.

What should ·you do if you are about to sit down at a Let It Ride® game and find that the maximum payout is only $10,000 with a required minimum bet of $5. Don't sit down. Find a casino that offers the optimum value for your wagers.

Playing Strategies

As stated earlier, this game resembles five-card stud. But there are differences. First of all, in five-card stud, a player competes against all other competition. Here, the player simply wants to get a hand that qualifies for a payout according to the payout schedule. Then, in five-card stud, certain cards, such as an ace, have enormous value, for an ace-high hand can often win without any improvement. This is not the case in Let It Ride®, where an ace-high hand is a loser. A 10 is just as valuable as an ace, because paired up they are both equal winners. And if they are not paired, they're losers.

At the outset of play in Let It Ride®, a player gets three cards instead of the two he would get in five-card stud. This makes a big difference in strategy, for that extra card gives a player quite a bit more information. In five-card stud, a player stuck with two weak cards at the outset can "fold" his hand, that is, throw away his cards and merely forfeit an "ante," usually about 10 percent of an initial bet, rather than lose a complete bet. In Let It Ride®, no matter how poor the player's hand is, he will have to forfeit one of his three bets.

On the bright side, the Let It Ride® player will win with any hand of 10s or better, and will not have to worry about another player beating him with a superior hand. Plus, he will get a bonus payout for strong hands, and as we shall see later, for really big hands, like straight or royal flushes, he may be eligible to enter a multimillion dollar tournament.

What hands should be played, and what hands should cause a player to remove his bet? This strategy really runs in two parts. First, there is the three-card strategy, and then a four-card strategy. A three-card hand that's worth playing may deteriorate in value so that, after four cards, it is useless. We'll show you how this can happen in a later section.

Three-Card Playing Strategy

Keep the first bet intact if you are dealt the following hands:
1. Three of a kind.
2. A pair of 10s or better.
3. Three to a straight flush, such as 8, 9, and 10 of diamonds.
4. Three to a royal flush, with three high cards, such as king, queen, and 10 of spades. In our strategical discussion, a high card is a 10 or better, since a pair of 10s qualifies for a payout.
5. Three to a flush, with two high cards, and a chance for a straight as well, such as king, jack, and 9. Here, a player would have to hit the 10 and queen for a straight, but there is still the possibility of pairing the king or jack.
6. Three to a flush with one high card, if one card can form an open-ended straight, such as a jack, 9, and 8 of clubs. If the fourth card is a 10, then the player now holds an open-ended straight, with the possibility of pairing two high cards. And if the fourth card is a club, there is a chance for a flush, with a payoff of 8–1.
7. Three to an open-ended straight, with all three cards being high cards but of different suits, such as ♣K, ♦Q, ♠J, or ♠Q, ♠J, ♦10. However, a holding with an ace will not be strong enough, since there is no longer a chance of an open-ended straight. Thus the initial wager is forfeited with a holding of ace, king, queen of different suits. By different suits, I mean that a flush cannot be formed.

Other than these holdings, you should have your first bet removed and returned to you. You still have two bets alive, and there are hands that may surprise you when you see the first community card which is your fourth card. For example, even a weak holding like 10, 3, 2 unsuited can become 10, 10, 3, 2 when the fourth card is revealed, making you a winner. However, what you have to be careful of is this: Don't retain the first bet with a small pair, a pair under 10s. There will be times when you regret it, but in the long run you'll lose a lot of money keeping the bet alive in the hope of improving the small pairs.

I mentioned before that a promising hand, that is, one in which the first bet was retained, can turn sour. Let's look at one of the previous examples. We retain our first bet with a hand consisting of the king, queen, and 10 of spades. But the first community card is a 3 of hearts. We can no longer get a royal flush, a straight flush, a flush, or a straight. All we can hope for now is to pair one of our high cards. In this situation, we remove our second wager. We're always allowed to remove the second bet whether or not we retained the first one.

Four-Card Playing Strategies

With the hands recommended under Three-Card Playing Strategies, you'll still have all your bets riding when you see the fourth card. However, you also will have hands that can possibly be improved with the first bet removed. You should keep the second bet intact with the following hands:

1. Four of a kind
2. Four to a royal flush
3. Four to a straight flush
4. Four to a flush
5. An open-ended straight with at least one high card
6. Three of a kind
7. Two pair
8. A pair of 10s or better

The first four holdings are no brainers. You have a big payout with the four of a kind hand and a shot at some big payouts, especially with the four to a royal or four to a straight flush. At 8–1, the payout for the flush exceeds the odds against getting one, since with four known cards and forty-eight unknown cards, the chances of getting a flush are 9 in 48, or 4.33–1.

With an open-ended straight, you will be paid off at 5–1, while your chances of getting the straight are 8 in 48 or exactly 5–1 against. Since there is no profit involved in this move, you should only hold on to an open-ended straight when there is a possibility of pairing the high card. When going for most open-ended straights, you will have already removed the first chip, since your hand was too weak to play with all three chips. For example, if you started with an unsuited hand of 7, 8, 9, then were dealt a 10, you'd retain the second chip. If the fourth card dealt were a 6 instead of the 10, you'd take back the bet. The 10 makes all the difference here.

The same holds true for holdings of 10s or better. In most cases, you will not start with the pair but may form it when the fourth card shows. In this case, where you started with one or two unpaired high cards, or even a holding of ace, king, queen unsuited, by the time you pair up on the fourth card, you have already removed your first bet.

This can also happen when you get "trips," or three of a kind. You might have started with a pair of deuces and gotten a third deuce with the fourth card, thus already removing one of your three bets. The same holds true for a two-pair hand, which might have begun with 8, 8, 3 then developed into 8, 8, 3, 3.

By the time the last community card is dealt, a player is out of options. If he has removed two of his three initial bets, he can only hope to win the remaining bet if he still has a chance to get a qualifying hand that results in a payout. For example, suppose he started with 8, 4, 3 unsuited (different suits), and as a result of this "garbage hand" has already taken back his first betting chip. The next card is a jack, and with this poor hand, he takes back his second betting chip. Then on the last card he gets another jack, for a pair that pays off at even-money. He has already removed two bets, and now gets one bet back for a gain of a single wager. By getting the jacks, he is paid off at even-money and clears $10. If he had received the jacks in the first three cards and kept all three bets alive, he would have made $30.

By the last card, the player will have one, two, or three bets working for him. With some hands, no matter what comes up, the last community card will not alter his chances of winning. For example, he may have started with three 7s, and kept all his bets working. The fourth card was a 9 and the fifth card was a king. The last community card could have increased his payout if it had been a fourth 7 or another 9 for a full house, but in any event, he was going to get a minimum payout on three of a kind at 3–1.

With other hands, such as a four flush (four cards of the same suit), the last card will determine whether he wins or loses. If it is of the same suit or it pairs a big card in his hand, he has a winner. If it is a card of a different suit and doesn't pair a big card, he has a loser. And he may lose all three bets with this type of hand.

But no matter what he holds, no matter how bad his cards are, the player cannot remove that last bet in the $ circle. He will lose it approximately 75 percent of the time. The wise player will only keep his bets on the table by using our three- and four-card strategies. This way, he will have reduced his possible losses and given himself a chance at winning.

With three initial cards dealt, and with payouts on less than 25 percent of all hands, the player might find himself losing many hands in a row. He can get garbage hand after garbage hand, and there's nothing he can do about it except wisely remove the first two bets. Patience is the keyword in this game. If you get impatient and force the issue, hoping for miracles, you'll find yourself losing a lot of money. Don't play hunches, and don't have delusions that the lone ace in your hand is somehow among the dealer's two community cards.

Playing the way I suggest will give you the chance of winning in the short term but, as I have written, overall the house has the edge in this game. It runs below 4 percent but this is still a formidable advantage. This is not a game to play for serious money, because you can find yourself stuck in long losing streaks. You should always set a loss limit before you sit down. If you reach this limit, leave the table. If you find yourself ahead, leave the table a winner. Don't give it all back. That's my best advice in this game.

If you're ahead, as we mentioned, then get out before all your money goes back to the house. If you get a good run of cards and a few really big hands, leave a winner.

Let It Ride® The Tournament™

In addition to the regular game, with its fixed but relatively small payouts, Shuffle Master Gaming has introduced a tournament limited to players who have received big hands in regular play and have placed a $1 bet on the tournament spot. In order to be eligible for this tournament, this additional bet must be made. It is bet at the same time as the other three wagers, before the cards are dealt out. The tournament spots in front of each player light up when the bets are put down.

By making this extra bet, not only do you have a chance to get into the tournament, which will pay a grand prize of $2–3 million or more, but you will receive "bonus payments" if you are dealt certain big hands. Here is what those payments look like:

Bonus Payments

Royal Flush	$20,000
Straight Flush	$2,000
Four of a Kind	$200
Full House	$100
Flush	$50
Straight	$25

These are set payments, no matter what a player bets. Although they are nice to get, they are far from the correct odds a player should receive for his dollar bet. Again, let's point out that the chances of getting a royal flush are 649,739–1, and of getting a straight flush, 72,192–1. Even the lowly straight payoff of $25 compares rather unfavorably with the chance of getting one dealt as a pat hand, that is, with the five cards the player uses to form his hand, his three plus the dealer's two. The chances of being dealt a straight in this way are 254–1.

The dollars bet on the tournament spot are not all returned to the players in payoffs at the table. Some of this money will go to the casino and Shuffle Master Gaming. In addition, it will be used to fund the tournament playoffs and its prizes. Here's a breakdown as reported by Shuffle Master Gaming.

For each $1 bet, the following money is dispersed:
45 cents to the casino to make payoffs
12 cents as the casino's commission
12 cents as Shuffle Master's commission
30 cents to fund the Tournament playoffs
1 cent for marketing going to Shuffle Master

As far as the basic game is concerned, that is, all bets other than tournament spot bets, the casino keeps all the profits.

Let It Ride® The Tournament™ Playoff Eligibility

In the brochures available from Shuffle Master Gaming, the company states that "if your winning hand is good enough, the casino will ask you to fill out a Tournament Registration form. All the forms are submitted for ranking at the end of the Qualifying Round. The top 100 hands are invited to participate in the Let It Ride® The Tournament™ Playoffs. . . ."

It seems that a "qualifying round" lasts for three months. When you're playing Let It Ride® at a casino during this period of time, you're in the qualifying round if you're placing your dollar on the tournament spot. Will you have a chance to go to the playoffs with a four-of-a-kind hand? Very, very unlikely. Even a small straight flush, such as 6, 5, 4, 3, 2 of hearts probably won't get you there.

In the October 1995 playoff tournament, Shuffle Master picked the top 100 hands plus all ties, and in this case the number of eligible players came to 133. Speaking to a representative from Shuffle Master Gaming about this, I was told that a royal flush will automatically get a player into a tournament playoff. In October 1995, the weakest eligible hands were eight high straight flushes, that is, hands consisting of an 8, 7, 6, 5, and 4 of the same suit.

As the game increases in popularity, the eligible hands will become stronger and stronger, and may eventually be limited to just royal flushes. When you do get a royal flush, however, you will automatically be eligible for the tournament playoffs.

How will you know if you made the tournament playoffs if you didn't get a royal flush? If you have been deemed eligible, you will receive a registered letter and a phone call inviting you to the playoffs. Once you're in the playoffs, as we shall see, you're guaranteed prize money!

The Tournament Playoffs

There are four rounds in all to determine the distribution of the top prizes. According to Shuffle Master Gaming, in October 1995 the prizes were distributed as follows:

Grand prize	$2 million
Second prize	$500,000
Third prize	$250,000
Fourth prize	$100,000
Fifth prize	$50,000

Rounds of Play

As stated before, there are four rounds of play, three semi-finals and a final round. Let's go over each round and show how it is structured.

Round One

All the players eligible for the playoff are entered in this round. Prior to play, each player is given $3,000 as a bonus payment to keep. This money is not at risk during the playoffs.

In addition, each player is given an equal number of non-redeemable chips. These chips have no cash value and are to be used during the first round of play only. They are bet during the first fifty hands of basic Let It Ride®. At the end of the fifty hands, the fifty players with the most chips are eligible to go to the next round.

Round Two

The field has now been winnowed to fifty players. Each player is again given $3,000 to keep, and a new set of nonredeemable chips. The chips from the previous round have been given back and are no longer in play. So, at this point, the fifty players have an equal number of chips. Again, fifty hands are played. The top twenty-five players at the end of these fifty hands are eligible for round three.

Round Three

Prior to round three, each of the twenty-five remaining players is given $3,000 to keep. By this time, they've each accumulated $9,000. They are also each given an equal number of non-redeemable chips to play with. Fifty hands are once more played. At the end of this round, the top five players are eligible for the fourth and final round.

Final Round

At this point, none of the players is given any cash for themselves. They are given equal numbers of non-redeemable chips and are dealt out fifty more hands. At the end of the fifty hands, the player with the most chips wins the grand prize, the player with the second highest total wins second prize, the third highest total wins third prize, and so on to the fourth and fifth prizes.

In October 1995, the grand prize amounted to $2 million. In 1996, the grand prize was raised to $2.5 million, and it is expected to increase again in future playoffs.

These prizes are very enticing. For one thing, unlike lottery wins or even the big Quartermania wins, they are paid in full when they are won, rather than over a twenty-year period. All grand prize winners are given checks for the full amounts, minus IRS deductions! So are all the other prize winners. With such big prizes dangling before them, many more players will be drawn to Let It Ride® and the popularity of the game should increase with time. I expect more and more casinos to feature the game, and more and more casino tables to be devoted to it.

Shuffle Master Gaming expects to have a tournament playoff every three months. For a listing of tournament casinos, dates of current qualifying rounds, and playoff locations, interested readers can call the "hotline" at 1-800-733-4966.

Glossary of Let It Ride® Terms

Basic Game. Let It Ride® played in a casino setting, rather than in the tournament rounds.

Betting Circles. The three circles marked "1," "2" and "$" in which the players' initial bets are placed.

Big Pair. A pair of 10s or better, eligible for a payout.

Community Cards. The two cards the dealer deals to himself, which are used by all players to form their best hands.

Flush. A hand consisting of five cards of the same suit, such as the ace, 9, 8, 4, and 2 of clubs.

Four of a Kind. A poker hand consisting of four cards of the same rank, plus one odd card, such as 5, 5, 5, 5, and Q.

Full House. A poker hand consisting of three of a kind plus a pair, such as 9, 9, 9, 2, and 2.

Garbage Hand. A poor hand consisting of unmatched and unsuited cards, which is not good enough for a payout.

Grand Prize. The first prize given to the winner of the Let It Ride The Tournament.

Non-Redeemable Chips. Chips given to the players in the playoff tournament, which cannot be redeemed for cash.

Pair. A hand in which two cards are of the same rank, such as 10, 10, 6, 5, and 3.

Pat Hand. The five cards that make up an original poker hand, with no cards being drawn to this holding.

Payout Schedule. The table which shows all the payouts in the basic game of Let It Ride®.

Royal Flush. The best possible hand in poker, consisting of an ace, king, queen, jack, and 10 of the same suit.

Small Pair. A pair of 9s or lower, which doesn't qualify for a payout.

Straight. A poker hand of different suits where the cards are in consecutive order of rank, such as Ace 2 3 4 5 or 10 Jack Queen King Ace.

Straight Flush. A holding of a straight where all the cards are of the same suit, such as 8 9 10 Jack Queen of spades.

Three-of-a-Kind. A poker hand that contains three cards of the same rank plus two odd cards, such as 7 7 7 8 10.

Tournament Eligibility. The chance to be invited to the tournament playoffs after holding a very strong hand, such as a straight flush or royal flush.

Tournament Playoffs. That part of the tournament where the hundred best hands and ties in the qualifying rounds play for the grand prize.

Tournament Qualifying Round. A three-month period when players at various casinos vie for the chance to enter the tournament playoffs.

Tournament Spot. The place on the table where bettors put $1 to be eligible for a chance to get into the tournament playoffs.

Trips. See Three of a Kind.

Two Pair. A poker hand consisting of two separate pairs plus an odd card, such as King King 4 4 9.

14

Other Casino Games—
The Side Games

The games discussed in the previous chapters are far and away
the most popular ones offered by the casinos. They get the most
money action and give the house the biggest profits. However,
there are other casino games, sometimes called side games,
which net the casino a steady profit. Not all the games covered
in this section will be found in every casino, but the reader
should know something about them, if for no other reason than
to know that they're all sucker games and should be avoided.

Big Six or Money Wheel

The game is known by either name and is a relic of the old
carnival spin-the-wheel game, in which a wheel is turned by
the operator, and if the correct symbol or number comes up,
the player wins.

Most clubs don't have the big six wheel and those that do
generally have no more than one in operation. However, since
the wheel was a popular attraction for many many years on
the boardwalk in Atlantic City, casinos there have installed
them.

The wheel itself is usually an ornate and elaborate affair
about six feet in diameter. On its pedestal it stands about eight
feet off the floor. The wheel is divided into nine parts, in a
continuous circle, each part holding six pockets, so that there
are fifty-four individual pockets, each holding one of the symbols that can be bet on.

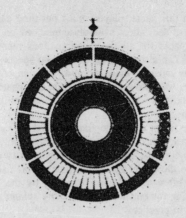

Dividing each pocket are metal nails, and as the wheel is spun, a suspended leather strap hits each pocket in turn, till the machine slows down and finally stops of its own momentum, with the strap then standing clearly in one pocket. Whoever has wagered on the symbol of that pocket wins his or her bet.

The wheels today are marked with American currency symbols. There are $1, $2, $5, $10, and $20 denominations represented, and should the strap stand in a pocket containing any of these symbols, the payoff would be that amount. For example, if the symbol in the pocket were $1, players who bet on the $1 symbol would be paid $1. If the pocket contained a $20 symbol, then bettors would receive $20 for their $1 bet. Of course, there are many more $1 than $20 symbols on the wheel.

In addition to these currency symbols, there are two additional symbols that pay off at $40. One is usually the house logo or symbol, and the other is some kind of ornate symbol, such as the American bald eagle or a joker.

There is also a layout on which players may bet money or chips, and the payouts are either in dollar coins or casino chips. If the payoff is more than $5, the player has the option of receiving dollars or casino chips; below that amount he gets dollars.

To bet on this game, players must put their cash or chips on any one of the wheel symbols duplicated on the layout. There are spaces for all the denominations mentioned, and separate bets can also be made on the two special symbols.

These bets must be made prior to the spin of the wheel; some casinos will allow wagering while the wheel is in spin, but once it starts slowing down, any bets made will be rejected by the dealer.

This game is not a very popular one, but the casino makes a sure and steady income from it nevertheless. Only one dealer is needed to spin the wheel and collect and pay off bets. In most casinos the dealer has much time on his hands; in Las Vegas I've often seen dealers standing by the hour, arms folded, waiting for business, occasionally spinning the wheel just to keep in practice.

Betting often picks up when the casino showroom empties out, for then many young and unsophisticated couples who may have seen these wheels at carnivals stop to play them. The action sometimes gets hot, but never heavy, for the betting is rarely more than a few dollars on any one symbol.

One never sees a high roller at the big six wheel, for the simple reason that any astute gambler knows the wheel is a bad bet. At its best the house edge is 11 percent, and some bets give the casino double that advantage over the player.

The wheel therefore attracts unsophisticated, casual gamblers with some spare dollars in their pockets who want to have a little gambling fun.

There is no single standard wheel, but most big six wheels have the following number of symbols:

> $1: 24
> $2: 15
> $5: 7
> $10: 4
> $20: 2
> house symbol: 1
> joker: 1
> _____
> Total: 54

To calculate the house advantage on each bet, we'll assume a complete cycle of fifty-four spins and a continual $1 bet.

On the $1 symbol wager, the house will win 30 bets and pay out only 24 times for an 11 percent advantage.

With the $2 symbol, the house will win 39 bets and pay out 15 times at $2 each for a 16.67 percent edge.

On the $5 symbol wager, the house will win 47 times and pay out $35 for the seven $5 symbols. This gives the casino an advantage of 25.9 percent.

With the $10 symbol, the house will win 50 bets and pay out $40 on its four $10 symbols for an advantage of 18.5 percent.

With the $20 symbols, the house will win 52 times and will pay out $40 on its two $20 symbols for an edge of 22.2 percent.

On each of the emblem and house symbols, the house will win 53 times and pay out $40. The casino will thus have an advantage over the player of 24 percent.

These house advantages are much too high to make the wheel a good bet, no matter how little the players invest. They would be better off wagering on any of the casino standard table games instead.

In fact, any casino game other than keno gives the player a better chance to win, so my advice is to admire the big six wheel in action, especially if the casino owns one that is antique and ornate, but don't put good money on it.

Chuck-A-Luck

This game, which is played with a device that resembles a bird cage, is sometimes known as bird cage. Three dice are held in a lower wire cage, with another identical wire cage on top. Between the two cages is a small opening, so that the whole thing resembles an hour glass. When the bottom cage is flipped over, the dice bounce through the opening and land at the bottom of the previously empty cage. They are fairly large oversized dice, several inches on each side, and whatever numbers show on top can be seen easily and determine the winners.

Near the cage is the layout. The layout contains only six numbers—1, 2, 3, 4, 5, 6,—which can be bet on, for it's not the total of these dice which the player wagers on, but the numbers that show on each individual die.

If a player bets on number 4, for example, and a 4 shows on any of the three dice, he is paid off at even money. If two 4s show, the payoff is 2–1, and if he should be so fortunate as to get all three 4s, the payoff is 4–1.

It's a game of pure chance, of course, and the house advantage, while not enormous, stands at 7.87 percent. This edge is too high to make the bird cage worthwhile to play. And since so few legitimate American casinos offer this game, you're not likely to see it in action.

Under and Over Seven

Last and certainly least of the side games is this one, sometimes called over and under seven. Like the big six wheel and chuck-a-luck, this is an old carny game often seen at fairs and Las Vegas nights around the country, but rarely found in any casino.

The game is played with two dice, and either the operator rolls the dice out of a cup or they are put into an hourglass device resembling the one used in chuck-a-luck. There is also a layout on which players make their wagers. They can bet on one of three outcomes—under 7, 7, or over 7.

If the dice add up to under 7, the players who have bet on that choice are paid off at even money. If it lands on 7, the players who have made this wager get 4–1, and if it totals over 7, players who have bet in that space on the layout are paid off at even money.

This is a terrible game to play, because no matter what the player wagers on, the house has an advantage of 16.67 percent. Fortunately, even if one were to actively seek out this game (probably from some long ingrained masochistic streak) he or she would be hard-pressed to find it in any legitimate casino.

15

A Winning Approach to Gambling

When most people think of gamblers, they inevitably think of losers. However, it's just as easy to win as to lose, especially in casino gambling, because the casino games recommended for play in this book either give the house a very small percentage as their edge, or in the case of blackjack, the player has the advantage over the casino.

But in order to win players must do the following: They must make only those bets which give the house the lowest possible edge; they must manage their money wisely; they must exercise self-control, and they must play to win, not for the thrill of action. If you follow these sound principles, you can't help but be a winner. And yet the overwhelming majority of gamblers are losers.

Either they are unaware of the principles outlined here or they disregard them. The proof is that casino profits are astronomical, and the casino win-expectation at the basic table games, craps and blackjack, is 20 percent of the drop (money bet at the table).

Recently, I spoke to one of the pit bosses at an Atlantic City casino, and he was complaining that the players were getting too smart at blackjack to give the casino its 20 percent p.c. (winning percentage). The p.c., he informed me, was closer to 17 percent now. He thought that this lower figure resulted from blackjack players having a better grasp of the principles of the game, and the fact that many of them were counting cards, even though the house was taking strong countermeasures to bar card counters.

I didn't leave the man weeping openly about the smaller profits, but he was somewhat concerned. And yet I was dismayed by the figure of 17 percent. In fact, every time casino executives quote that 20 percent profit figure to me, I'm shocked.

With best play at a game like blackjack, with a proper betting strategy and a simple method of counting cards, the player has the advantage in the game, not the house. In craps, with only line and come bets made and odds taken, the house has at best a 0.8 percent edge over the player. Even if a gambler were to play more aggressively and cover the 6 and 8 as place bets, the house edge would never go beyond 1.52 percent.

Despite these figures, one can't find a craps table in a well-run casino that doesn't give the house at least a 20 percent profit margin. And the same holds true for most blackjack tables.

There seems to be no way that the casinos can make so much money. Yet casinos around the country are coining untold millions in profits every month, and the leading casinos in Nevada are getting so rich that they continually expand their operations. What's wrong?

A clue to the situation came from the president of a Strip hotel, who was looking over his computer runs on the daily volume of gambling and win figures one afternoon.

"The figures are sensational," he told me. "Ed, we have to make good money because gamblers are willing to lose much more than they're willing to win."

I stared at him, trying to comprehend his statement, so he explained his concept.

"Sure, gamblers will tell you that they'd love to win a million at the table, but it's not what they win at the table that counts with us, it's what they leave the table with. And for some reason, maybe it's inherent in the gambler's psychology or whatever, they don't want to leave with money. If they beat us out of fifty grand at one session, which is really a big win considering our limit at craps, they'll gamble on till they give it all back. And if they're losing, they'll go on and on, losing and signing markers all night long till they're destroyed, literally destroyed.

"And the strange thing is, no one forces them to play like this. We don't even have to talk up our games. We don't have to drag them to the table with nets. They come willingly, and when they're at the tables, they act like wild men. I don't know why gambling does this to them, but it sure does it, whatever it is. I'm not a psychologist; I'm just in the gambling business, and it's one business that's easy to get customers for—they'll break down the doors to lose their money."

These are sobering words, and yet they're very true, and in my many years as observer, player, and writer on the gambling scene, I've seen it happen over and over again. Gamblers who are behind get frantic, try to get even fast, and go even deeper into the hole.

In other words, these people don't really want to win; all they want is the thrill of the action. So even though the house edge is small, it doesn't matter to these gamblers. They will play till they have no money left, and if they've been winning a fortune, they'll make wild outlandish bets, change the pattern of their play, do anything to prevent themselves from leaving the table as winners.

What the casino president said was true. There is some psychological quirk that prevents many gamblers from being winners. Anyone who's ever been to Las Vegas and Atlantic City undoubtedly has watched some players pull out rolls of $100 bills and bet them on outside place numbers, hardways, and other terrible wagers, and after they'd lost, pull out more rolls of bills. Why are these people at the tables? What do they want to do, just lose their money as fast as possible? It's really difficult to fathom their motives.

And it should be evident to any astute person that most people who play blackjack or craps don't have a true grasp of the odds in the game and the correct strategies for playing these games.

I recently held a seminar for blackjack players, all of whom go regularly to the Nevada casinos on junkets or to Atlantic City for day trips.

There were about forty people in the group, and I handed each of them a paper listing twenty questions on the game. None of these questions were tricky or very difficult. The situations they dealt with come up constantly during play. Not one person in that group could answer all the questions correctly, and only three or four got as many as seventeen or eighteen of them right.

How could these people expect to gamble and win at twenty-one? To make money at blackjack, three steps must be followed: First, players must know the correct play in every situation that arises. Second, they must count cards. Finally, they must alter their bets according to the favorability of the deck.

With the first step, correct strategy, the player is playing even with the house. With the combination of the second and third steps, the player has an advantage over the casino. The people attending were gamblers, some of them, according to their stories, very heavy players, and none of them had mastered the first step. These people didn't want to study the game; what they wanted from me was a magic formula for winning. They thought that, with one hour of my time, I'd transform them into big winners. But it's not that simple. Anything involving skill must be studied and mastered.

To ensure victory, to take home the casino's money, isn't that difficult a task. But to do so, you cannot be impatient. You must first study and learn the games to play, learn the correct bets available in a game such as craps; and in blackjack you must study the basic winning strategies and learn to count cards so that you can alter your bets according to the composition of the remaining deck. This is the first step to winning, and all the information you need can be found in those chapters on the three table games we recommend for serious play: blackjack, craps, and baccarat.

The second step is to manage your money wisely. A section in each chapter on the three recommended games is devoted to money management, and in this chapter we'll repeat the basic principles involved.

Money Management

The first rule is the most important of all rules of gambling. *Don't play with money you can't afford to lose.* This can't be repeated or stressed often enough. No matter how skillful a player you are, no matter how lucky you feel, if you're gambling with money you can't afford to lose, you're asking for trouble. And above all, don't borrow money to gamble with. This leads to disaster. Don't ask for casino credit if you'll have to dig into savings or use essential money to repay the losses.

After you've decided that you can gamble with a certain amount, play according to your gambling bankroll. If you have $1,000, don't start betting $100 chips and risk losing everything before you have a chance to start a winning cycle.

The chapters on blackjack, craps, and baccarat deal fully with the proper total bankroll for the game, the single session bankroll, and the limits of play according to the bankroll. Study these carefully before playing any of these games for real money, for the sections on money management are just as important as those on correct playing strategies.

One rule constantly stressed in these sections is not to play with scared money, that is, money that is insufficient for the game you're playing. If you're at a $25 table in blackjack and have only $200, you're undercapitalized, and you'll either have to forgo higher bets in favorable situations or, worse still, make foolishly high bets in the hope of increasing your bankroll so that you can properly play the game for correct stakes. Either move is bad. Always play with adequate funds, or don't play at all. Be patient. Save up until you can properly bet what you have to in order to take full advantage of the game you're playing.

Self-Control

There is nothing more important than exercising self-control when gambling. Players who don't have this self-control, no matter how skillfully they play, are not going to end up winners.

By self-control, I mean complete control over your emotions at the table. Don't give in to anxiety, to despair, to greed, to weakness and impulse. Always keep your feelings under control through patience and objectivity.

For example, blackjack is a game that can be beaten by an astute player. But that doesn't mean that you can come to the table and steamroll the casino and make a big score. Blackjack is a game of small advantages, of times when the composition of the deck will be favorable to you. It is only those times that must be taken full advantage of in terms of large bets. And even in some of those favorable situations you may not get a winning hand.

In that case, you can't keep making large bets when the deck is neutral and unfavorable in the hopes of making up a previous large loss. That's when you must exercise patience and keep betting according to the composition of the deck. It's very easy to nod and agree, but when at a table, it's quite another thing to follow this precept. But follow it you must, if you're going to win.

The minute you become impatient self-control flies out the window, and strategy gives way to haphazard play. Don't be impatient to make a big score. That can't be done in blackjack. Content yourself with steady, moderate wins at appropriate times. If you think of the long run, then everything is in perspective. If you think only of the moment, then nothing looks right.

If you learn the basic strategies described in this book, learn to count cards and to alter your bets according to the count, study these principles carefully, and practice at home until you feel confident about handling any playing situation, you can beat the blackjack tables at any American casino. You can't expect to win thousands of dollars at one time, for twenty-one isn't that kind of game. You will have to strike when the deck is favorable and only then. Doing that, with a $20 neutral bet, you can expect to win about $200 a day if you devote three hours to the game each day.

You won't always win, and you won't win that exact

amount, of course, but over a period of time you'll be able to average that kind of money. You might think to yourself— what's $200? After all, you've seen players winning thousands at the table (on very rare occasions) and how is $200 going to make any difference in your life?

Here's how. I've had pupils who studied the game under my supervision, and then decided to play it on a professional basis. Winnings of $200 a day, if the game is played 250 days a year, add up to $50,000. And this is a $20 game, not a really big game by casino personnel, and there's little chance of getting barred.

And what's wrong with $50,000 a year for a few hours work five days a week and one hundred days off a year? If you think that way and put the whole picture into perspective, it makes all the difference in the world.

But few are able to do this. They get greedy at the tables, and, when winning, raise their bets to incredible heights, trying to take advantage of one good rush, one winning streak, to empty out the table's trays in one fell swoop—and end up not only losing it all back, but being barred in the process.

If you simply do the opposite of what the casino president stated, you'll be a winner. In other words, if you're winning, don't get greedy, but leave with most of your profits intact. If losing, instead of taking out more money in a vain attempt to get even, limit your losses to the single-session bankroll and walk away from the table. Do those two things when gambling and you'll be smarter than 99 percent of all gamblers.

You must never, and I repeat, *never reach into your pocket for more cash* after you've lost your single session bankroll. That's the time to take a stroll. Do anything else but gamble. Go for a swim, rest in your room, have coffee, but don't keep gambling. In that way you won't get really hurt at any one session of play. This requires self-control, so make certain that you've trained yourself to have this control before you do any serious gambling.

When you're winning, and you will by following the methods outlined in this book, *leave the table a winner.* Always quit a winner, is the old adage of the smart gambler. If you're ahead twenty chips, at that moment tell yourself, I'm going to leave with 10 of them as my profit. Don't ever put them into play or in any way jeopardize them at the table. If they're $5 chips, you've got $50 profit; if $25 chips you've got $250, and if they're $100 chips, you've just made $1,000 for a single session of play. What's wrong with that kind of score?

I've played a lot of blackjack in my life, and how often have I seen players at the table winning thousands while I was sanely winning hundreds. Then, when the tide turned—when the dealer got his share of good cards, when the players' losing streaks began—while I locked up my profit for the night and got up, I sometimes lingered on and watched from a standing position the play of the big winners at the table. Inevitably, they gave back every cent, every single chip they had won. I've seen it happen so often that it's a standard scenario as far as I'm concerned. Leave when you're ahead; lock up most of your profits, and never play with them again. You've got to be a winner, not only at that table, but in the long run.

When playing a fast moving game like craps, self-control often involves going against the mob at the table and believing in your own methods of play. Sometimes, during a hot roll, there's an awful temptation to really sock in the bets on all kinds of outrageous wagers, buying the 4 and 10, for example, or betting heavy money on the 5 and 9 as place numbers, giving the house 4 percent over you. Resist those temptations and stick with the correct come bets, raising them continuously.

The vast majority of craps players, even the really high rollers, the so-called smart players, play a stupid game that dooms them to defeat. They bet pass line, cover all the place numbers, and pray for a hot roll. Don't pray for anything at the table except for patience and self-control, and pray that these two things don't desert you. The hot roll will come along, and by patient play, correct money management, and smart bets, you'll take full advantage of that roll for you'll be one of the few original players still left at the table. The others will long since have been tapped out with their bad bets and inept money management.

Play to Win

This is the final step in our winning approach to gambling. You must come to the table with confidence. By confidence, I don't mean a blind faith in pure luck, for that's the way most players and all losers approach the gaming tables. Confidence is the feeling that your betting and playing strategies are correct, that you thoroughly know the odds and correct plays in the game you're ready to play, whether it be blackjack, craps, or baccarat.

You must make a decision, and that decision is all important in terms of winning or losing. It is the decision to win rather than to play just for the thrill of action. It is true that gambling can be exciting and thrilling. Fine and dandy. It is even better when those thrills are combined with winning money. Thrills paid for with losses are too expensive; the repercussions and the aftermath of defeat at gambling tables are never pleasant. There are few good losers the next morning.

What the casino president (the one who said gamblers didn't want to leave the table with money) didn't understand about gambling is this: that too often the thrill and excitement is not in winning, but in releasing one's anxiety right out in the open. Let me explain it this way. If you're walking by a craps table and watch the action and decide to make an imaginary bet of $1,000 on the next roll of the dice, there's a certain detachment as you stand and watch the roll.

Let's assume you bet against the dice with your mind bet and the roll is a 6. Now you linger and watch the rest of the throws, and a few rolls later, the player sevens out, and you win your mind bet. Slightly pleased, you go on your way, perhaps to the coffee shop for breakfast, where, by the time you've finished your bacon and eggs or lox and bagel, you've forgotten all about it.

But let's assume that, instead of just standing around, you decide to make a bet on the next roll. Let's further assume that you have $1,000 in your pocket for gambling purposes for a couple of days of action and that you never really bet more than $5 or $10 a shot. So you put down $10 on don't

pass and the roll is a 6. You bet $12 as a free odds bet against
the point, and now you're involved in a moderate way. You've
made this kind of bet many times before, but there is a thrill,
an excitement in the air and in your head, because you've
committed money on the layout, and there's no way you can
ever know the result beforehand. Eventually you win, collect
$20 in profits and go on whistling to the coffee shop, your
meal paid for with the $20 in profits.

But let's now move this scenario one step further. Let's
assume that having lingered at the table, you decide, instead
of making a mind bet, to really bet that $1,000 on the next
roll of the dice. Let's assume that there's a $1,000 limit at that
table, so this can be done. Now you don't know what the next
roll of the dice will be. It may not be a 6. It could be anything.

So there's the picture. You put down $1,000 in cash on the
don't pass and say (in a weak voice) "cash plays." The boxman looks you over, and so do the dealer and all the players
around you. You're a really high roller, socking that amount
down in cash suddenly.

The shooter shakes the dice and prepares to roll. At this
point, I can tell you just what's happening inside you. Your
heart is beating so fast that you're dizzy. You imagine that
everyone can see it pounding through your chest. You're tin-
gling, your whole body is alive, and yet you feel weak in the
legs. You've just put yourself into a most thrilling and exciting
situation, because you've allowed yourself to be at the mercy
of your anxieties.

Now I don't have to tell you that this isn't the way to gamble intelligently. But many people do it this way. They bet,
not with their whole cash bankroll at one time, but they wager
way over their heads with money they can't afford to lose so
suddenly, and it does make for thrilling action. It's also thrilling to jump from a cliff with a parachute that you don't quite
know how to operate, and it's superthrilling to go up in a plane
and sky-dive without any lessons.

But is that what gambling should be about—this heart-stopping thrill of anxiety? No way. That's destructiveness, insan-
ity, or whatever you want to call it. Sure, it's thrilling standing

there, with every cent you brought with you resting on the craps layout, waiting for the throw of the dice, but if the next call of the stickman was "7, winner on the pass line, pay the front line," and you watched your $1,000 being snatched away, then the anxiety level will peak with ringing in the ears, the heart pounding even harder, the legs rubbery. What are you going to do now? There's a wan smile on your face as you stagger away from the table, trying to put up a brave front as everyone watches you, wondering who the hell you are, and shaking their heads at your loss. By now the coffee shop won't interest you; the bacon and eggs or lox and bagel are the last things you want. What you need is a tranquilizer. All you can think about is getting out of the casino and out of Vegas and going home.

I point out this extreme example because not many players realize that this same kind of thrill engendered by anxiety is what they're really after at the tables, not winning at all. And in the above scenario it might have been worse if the man won his bet, because then lesser bets wouldn't be thrilling to him and he might spend the rest of his gambling career betting in this frightening manner to keep the thrills going.

Play to win. Bet to win. That should be the only reason you gamble at all. Sure, there is a thrill and excitement to gambling, but that should be enhanced by winning. No one should play just for the thrill, for that is too destructive a motive in the long run. That's what all the losers do.

So remember the four steps we've discussed. Never forget them and never disregard them if you want to be a winner.

1. Make only those bets which give the house its lowest edge, only at those games which give the player the best chance to win. In American casinos these games are, in descending order: blackjack, craps, and baccarat.

2. Manage your money wisely, taking into consideration the total bankroll, the single-session bankroll, losing and winning limits. Never lose more than you take to any one table, and if winning, leave the table a winner.

3. Exercise self-control at all times and never give in to impatience or greed. Never try to win more and more, when

the cards or dice turn against you, for this is greedy and dangerous play. If losing, never make bigger and bigger bets to try to get even.

4. Come to the table confident about yourself and your game. Play to win, not for any other reason, and certainly not just for thrills, excitement, and heightened anxiety.

Follow these principles. They'll make you a winner.

Glossary of Casino Gambling Terms

À Cheval (Roulette): French for *Split Bet*.

Action: The amount of gambling a player does in a casino.

Action Player: A player who loves to gamble; one who gives the casino a great deal of action.

Advantage: See *Casino Advantage*

Agent: A person who works in conjunction with a cheat.

Alembert System: See *D'Alembert System*

American Wheel (Roulette): The wheel used in American casinos, which contains, in addition to the usual numbers 1–36, both 0 and 00.

Anchorman (Blackjack): See *Third Baseman*

Any Craps (Craps): A one-roll bet that the next throw of the dice will come up 2, 3, or 12.

Any Seven (Craps): A one-roll wager that the next roll of the dice will be a 7.

Auction (Chemin de Fer): Bidding for the bank at the outset of play or when a player voluntarily gives up the bank.

Baccarat: 1) The name of the game. 2) A term derived from *baccara*, the Italian word for zero.

Baccarat en Banque: A variation of chemin de fer, where three hands are dealt and there are no set rules governing the bank's play. Also known as *baccarat à deux tableaux*.

Back Line (Craps): A term commonly used for the don't pass line.

Bad Rack: A special file kept by a central credit agency in

Nevada listing those gamblers who have dishonored or refused to pay their gambling debts.

Ball (Roulette): The white plastic ball that is spun counter to the wheel's spin and which, when landing in a pocket, determines the payoffs for that spin of the wheel.

Banco (Chemin de Fer): The term used by a player who decides to cover the entire bank bet.

Banco Prime (Chemin de Fer): The privilege of the player to the bank's right to cover the entire bank bet when there is more than one player calling banco.

Bank, Bank Hand (Baccarat): The hand that is dealt to and acts last.

Bankroll: The stake a player uses to gamble with.

Bar, Bar Card Counters (Blackjack): A countermeasure by a casino prohibiting or removing players who are card counters.

Bar the 12 (Craps): Barring the 12 as a winning bet for wrong bettors, making it merely a standoff. In this way the casino retains its edge over wrong bettors. Some casinos bar the 2 instead of the 12.

Bet: A wager, using cash or casino chips, on any gambling event in a casino.

Betting Right (Craps): Betting that the dice will pass, or win.

Betting Wrong (Craps): Betting against the dice; wagering that they will not pass.

Bettor: See *Player*

Big Bertha (Slots): An oversize specialty machine placed in a casino as a novelty to attract players.

Big 6 and Big 8 (Craps): A bet paying even money that either the 6 or 8 will come up on the dice before a 7 is rolled.

Big Six Wheel: A side game involving a wheel six feet in diameter containing fifty-four slots for symbols, which are bet on by the players.

Bills: An insider's term for $100 bills.

Bird Cage: Another term for chuck-a-luck.

Blackjack: 1) The name of the game. 2) A winning hand consisting of an ace and a ten-value card, dealt as the original two cards of a hand.

Blank, Blank Ticket (Keno): A piece of paper issued by the casino, containing the numbers 1–80, which the player marks to play keno.

Blower (Keno): The device that blows air into the bowl or cage holding the marked and numbered Ping-Pong balls, mixing them and forcing twenty of them into the goose.

Board (Keno): See *Keno Board*

Box Numbers (Craps): See *Place Numbers*

Boxman (Craps): A casino executive who supervises the craps table from a seated position between two standing dealers.

Break the Deck (Blackjack): See *Reshuffle*

Bring Out (Craps): A term used by the stickman exhorting players to make certain bets in order to have the point come up on the dice. Example: "Bet the hard six, bring it out."

Buck (Craps): See *Disk*

Burn a Card (Blackjack): Taking away the top card from the deck by the dealer, who places it unseen either at the bottom of the deck or in a separate plastic case.

Burned Cards (Baccarat): Cards discarded after the decks have been cut and before actual play begins.

Bust, To Bust (Blackjack): To hit a hand so that the total goes over 21, making it a losing hand.

Bust Card (Blackjack): The designation of the 2, 3, 4, 5, or 6 showing as the dealer's upcard.

Bust Hand (Blackjack): A hand totaling from 12 to 16 points, which when hit, might go over 21.

Buy the 4 and 10 (Craps): Paying a 5 percent commission to the house in order to have the place numbers 4 and 10 pay off at correct odds of 2–1.

Cage 1) In keno, a bowl-like device holding the numbered Ping-Pong balls. 2) In chuck-a-luck, the device holding the dice. 3) See *Cashier's Cage*.

Caller (Keno): The casino employee who operates the blower and goose, and who calls out the numbers selected during the game as each is forced into the goose.

Callman (Baccarat): The dealer who runs or calls the game.

Cancellation System: See *D'Alembert System*

Cancel Button (Video Poker): The button that enables a player to cancel a previous decision to hold a particular card before the draw.

Card Counter (Blackjack): A player who keeps track of cards played out so that he can determine if the remainder of the deck or decks is favorable or unfavorable for him.

Caribbean Stud Poker: A form of poker played against the house, where the player's options are either to fold or double their bets.

Carousel (Slots): The area provided by the casino for a group of Bally $1 machines.

Carré (Roulette): The French term for a corner bet.

Cashier's Cage: The place, usually in the rear of a casino, where a player may redeem casino chips for cash or may transact certain credit arrangements, such as cashing checks.

Cash Out Button (Video Poker): By pressing this button, the player will receive all coins previously credited to him by the machine.

Casino: 1) The entire area or space used for gambling. 2) The term for the house, the entity the gambler plays against when making a wager.

Casino Advantage: The edge the house has over the player in any game, usually expressed as a percentage, for example, 5.26 percent.

Casino Checks: The term used by casino personnel to designate their tokens, which are more commonly called chips.

Casino Chips: The common term for tokens issued by the casino in place of money, and having the equivalent value of cash according to their denominations.

Casino Manager: The executive who supervises the entire casino operation.

Catches (Keno): The numbers chosen by the player that correspond to those selected by the operator, and show on the keno board during any particular game.

Center Field (Craps): The stickman's term for the 9, since it is in the center of the field bet area.

Change Color: Changing casino chips into smaller or larger denominations.

Change Girl (Boy) (Person): In slots, the person who aids

players by changing their bills for coins to play the machines with.

Chemin de Fer: The name of the European form of baccarat, derived from the French term for railroad.

Chemmy: The English slang term for chemin de fer.

Chips: See *Casino Chips*

Chuck-A-Luck: A casino side game, rarely played, in which three dice are transferred at random from one cage to another.

Cold Dice (Craps): Dice that aren't passing.

Colonne (Roulette): The French term for a column bet.

Column Bet (Roulette): A wager paying 2–1, whereby a player bets that the next spin of the wheel will come up on any one of twelve numbers in the column he's betting on.

Combination Bet (Roulette): A bet on more than one event or on more than one number, using a single chip.

Combination Ticket (Keno): A versatile ticket that combines unequal groups of selected numbers to form various combinations.

Come Bet (Craps): Betting that the dice will pass after the come-out roll.

Come Box (Craps): The area on the layout where come bets are made.

Come Out, Come-Out Roll (Craps): The initial or first roll of the dice before a point has been established.

Commission: A fee paid to the casino by the player when making certain bets or when being paid off on certain bets in various games.

Comp: The expression, short for complimentary, used in Nevada casinos to designate free services furnished to gamblers.

Conditioning, Conditions (Keno): The ways a bettor chooses to play his ticket, written as a fraction, such as ²⁄₄, which translates to two four-spots.

Corner Bet (Roulette): An inside combination bet with one chip covering four numbers at one time.

Correct Conditioning (Keno): Writing a ticket to correspond with the exact intentions of a player.

Counting Cards (Blackjack): See *Card Counter*.

Cover, Cover the Bank (Chemin de Fer): To wager enough so that the bank bet is entirely faded, or bet against by one or more players.

Craps: 1) The name of the game. 2) The roll of a 2, 3 or 12.

Craps Out (Craps): The roll of a 2, 3 or 12 on the come out.

Credit Button (Video Poker): A button that allows a player to play out coins credited to him without using his own coins.

Credit Line: The amount of credit a player is entitled to at a casino.

Credit Manager: The executive in charge of the credit department of a casino.

Crew (Craps): The four dealers who staff a craps table.

Crossroader: A crook who will cheat on anything he can, or steal whatever he can lay his hands on.

Croupier (Roulette): The house employee in the European game who operates the roulette table with other croupiers; also the European term for the dealer in chemin de fer.

D'Alembert System: A progressive system of betting whereby two numbers are cancelled every time a previous bet is won and one number—the total of the two end numbers—is added whenever a previous bet is lost.

Deal Button (Video Poker): A button, when pressed, that shows the five new cards constituting an original poker hand.

Dealer: The casino employee who staffs and services any of the gambling games the house offers.

Deck: The ordinary pack of fifty-two cards consisting of four suits, each suit containing thirteen cards from the 2 to the ace.

Dernière (Roulette): The French term for last, as in a column or dozen bet.

Dice (Craps): A pair of cubes, each with six sides numbered with from 1 to 6 dots, whose combinations, when thrown, determine the wins and losses.

Die: A single cube, singular of dice.

Disk (Craps): A round plastic object which is black on one side and white on the other. When on the white side and in a place number, it designates that a shoot is in progress and that that number is the point.

Dollars: The insider's term for $100 chips.

Don't Come Bet (Craps): A wager made against the dice after the come-out roll.

Don't Come Box (Craps): The area on the craps layout where a don't come bet is made.

Don't Pass Bet (Craps): A bet made on the come-out roll that the dice will lose or won't pass.

Don't Pass Box (Craps): The area on a craps layout where a don't pass bet is made.

Double Down (Blackjack): A player's option to double his original bet by turning over his first two cards and placing an amount equal to the original bet on the layout.

Double Odds (Craps): A free odds bet made at double the original bet on a line, come, or don't come wager.

Double Zero (Roulette): See *Zero*

Douzaine (Roulette): The French term for the dozen bet.

Dozen Bet (Roulette): A wager on either the first, second, or third dozen on the layout, such as 1–12, 13–24, and 25–36.

Draw: 1) *Keno*—The movement of a numbered Ping-Pong ball into the goose, forced there by hot air from the blower. 2) *Video Poker*—To receive new cards, up to five, after the initial poker hand has been dealt.

Draw A Card: The taking of an additional card by a player in either baccarat or blackjack.

Draw Button (Video Poker): The button, when pressed, that allows the player to draw up to five new cards to his original poker hand.

Draw Ticket (Keno): See *Punch-Outs*

Drop: The casino term for the total money and markers wagered on its table games, from the term "drop box," which is a container where all cash winds up. Drop boxes are located within the interior of the craps, blackjack, and other gaming tables.

Duplicate, Duplicate Ticket (Keno): The ticket marked by the keno writer and returned to the player, duplicating the original ticket.

Easy, Easy Way (Craps): The roll of a 4, 6, 8, or 10 other than as a pair. For example, a 5–1 is an "easy" six.

Edge: See *Casino Advantage*

En Plein (Roulette): The French term for a straight-up bet.

En Prison Rule (Roulette): A rule whereby the player has the option of either surrendering half his wager or allowing it to be imprisoned for another spin of the wheel, in which case, if he wins, the wager will be intact. This rule applies when a zero comes up and the bettor has wagered on the outside even-money choices.

European Wheel (Roulette): See *French Wheel*

Even-Odd Bet (Roulette): An outside straight bet on whether the next spin will be an even or odd number, paid off at even money.

Even-Money: A payoff at 1 to 1.

Face Cards: The jack, queen, and king in a pack of cards.

Fade (Chemin de Fer): See *Cover*

Favorable Deck (Blackjack): A deck whose remaining composition favors the player.

Field Bet (Craps): A bet that the next roll of the dice will come up either 2, 3, 4, 9, 10, 11, or 12.

First Baseman (Blackjack): The player in the first seat; the one who acts first on his hand.

Five Numbers Bet (Roulette): A bet covering the numbers 0, 00, 1, 2, and 3, which gives the house an edge of 7.89 percent.

Floorperson: A casino executive who supervises a limited area of a pit under the supervision of a pit boss.

Fold, Folding: Giving up the cards and player's bets in Caribbean Stud Poker.

Four Flush (Video Poker): Four cards of the same suit, such as four hearts, together with an odd card.

Four of a Kind (Video Poker): A poker hand consisting of four cards of the same rank such as K K K K.

Four Straight (Video Poker): Four cards in sequence, such as 5 6 7 and 8, not of the same suit.

Free Odds (Craps): A bet made in addition to a line, come or don't come wager at correct odds. The house has no advantage on this bet.

French Wheel (Roulette): A wheel containing a single zero, manufactured for European and English casinos.

Front Line (Craps): Another term for the pass line.

Front Money: Cash or bank checks deposited with the casino to establish credit for a player who bets against that money.

Full House (Video Poker): A poker hand consisting of a three of a kind plus a pair, such as 6 6 6 3 3.

Gambler: See *Player*

George: The Las Vegas dealers' term for a good tipper.

Goose (Keno): A transparent tube which holds the numbered Ping-Pong balls after they've been forced there by the blower.

Grand Martingale System: A doubling up system in which a player attempts to gain an additional chip's profit after every previous loss.

Grind: The casino executives' term for a small bettor.

Groups (Keno): A combination of numbers separated from other numbers either by circles or lines.

Gutshot Straight (Video Poker): A four straight that can be made only one way, such as 5 6 8 and 9.

Hand: The cards held by a player to form a complete group or total, such as a 10, 9 to form a 19 total hand in blackjack.

Handle Slammers (Slots): A cheat at slots who probes the weakness of a machine by manipulation and then slams the machine's handle to complete his scam.

Hand Mucker (Blackjack): A cheat who removes small cards from blackjack decks and replaces them with ten-value cards and aces.

Hard Total (Blackjack): Any total without an ace, or where an ace is counted as 1 in the hand. Examples: 10, 7 and 10, 6, ace both are hard 17s.

Hardway (Craps): The term for a 2–2, 3–3, 4–4, and 5–5.

Hardway Bet (Craps): A bet that the number 4, 6, 8, or 10 will be rolled as a hardway before it is rolled easy or before a 7 shows on the dice.

Heat: The pressure a casino puts on a winning player, generally a card counter in blackjack.

High Card (Video Poker): A jack, queen, king, or ace, when paired, which pays the player back his original bet.

High-Low Bet (Roulette): An outside straight wager on whether the next spin will be a high or low number, paid off at even money.

High Pair (Video Poker): A pair of jacks, queens, kings, or aces, which pays the player back his original bet.

High Rollers: The popular term for big bettors.

Hit (Blackjack): To draw an additional card to the original hand. This is usually indicated by the player scraping his cards toward him, or, in casinos where the cards are all dealt face up, pointing a finger at his cards.

Hold: See *P.C.*

Hold Button (Video Poker): The button that, when pressed, will hold a card in the original hand before the draw.

Hole Card (Blackjack): The dealer's unseen card, forming half his original hand.

Hop Bet (Craps): A one-roll wager on any number the player selects, at disadvantageous odds.

Horn Bet (Craps): A combined one-roll wager on the 2, 3, 11, and 12.

Hot, Hot Hand: The gambler's term for a winning hand or series of hands.

Hot Roller (Craps): A shooter who is throwing a great many "numbers" and also making a series of points.

House Advantage: See *Casino Advantage*

Impair (Roulette): French for odd.

Inside Bet (Roulette): A wager on the numbers 1–36, 0, 00, or any combination of these numbers.

Inside Numbers (Craps): The place numbers 5, 6, 8, and 9.

Insurance, Insurance Bet (Blackjack): An optional wager by the player that the dealer has a blackjack when the dealer's upcard is an ace.

Insure a Blackjack (Blackjack): An insurance bet made by a player when he holds a blackjack.

Jackpot (Slots): The grand payout on a machine.

Jokers Wild (Video Poker): A type of video poker machine that has a joker in addition to the normal 52-card pack. The joker is a pure wild card and can be used as any card to enhance or make any hand.

Junket: An organized tour of gamblers to a hotel-casino where they are given free room, food, and beverages plus their air fare, in return for gambling a prescribed minimum amount of money.

Junketmaster: An organizer of a junket.

Junket Member: A player who is part of an organized junket or tour.

Keno: A game in which players purchase tickets on which they mark groups of numbers in the hope that those numbers will be selected.

Keno Blank: See *Blank*

Keno Board (Keno): An electrically controlled board that shows the number of the game and the numbers called by the operator of the keno game.

Keno Lounge (Keno): The area in which a keno game is called and operated.

Keno Runner (Keno): A house employee who collects players' tickets throughout the casino and adjacent areas and presents them to the keno writers as a convenience to the bettors.

Keno Writer (Keno): The casino employee who collects the players' bets, writes the duplicate ticket, and pays off winners.

Kicker (Video Poker): An odd card, usually a high card, held by the player for the draw. Thus, a 3 3 A hand consists of a pair of threes plus the ace kicker.

King, King Number (Keno): Any one number circled on a ticket whose purpose is to combine with other numbers to form various combinations.

King Ticket (Keno): A ticket played with one or more king numbers marked on it, making it a very versatile ticket.

Ladderman: The term for a boxman or floorman who supervises a casino game from a seat on a ladder.

La Grande (Chemin de Fer): The French term for a 9 dealt as a natural.

La Petite (Chemin de Fer): The French term for the 8 dealt as a natural.

Las Vegas Strip: Las Vegas Boulevard South, in Las Vegas, Nevada, running from Sahara Avenue south up to and including Tropicana Avenue, containing a group of world-famous and luxurious hotel-casinos. Also known as the Strip.

Layout: The imprint on the felt surface of a gambling table showing either the betting boxes and rules of the game, or the various bets and payoffs that can be made, with appropriate spaces for those wagers.

Lay the Odds (Craps): An odds bet by a wrong bettor against a point or come number which, if won, will be paid off at less than even money.

Lay Wager (Craps): A place bet against a number repeating by a wrong bettor, who pays a 5 percent commission in order to make this wager.

Let It Ride®: A form of 5-card poker in which players have the option of retaining or giving up their bets.

Liberty Bell (Slots): The name of the original slots machine invented by Charles Fey of San Francisco.

Loose, Loose Slots (Slots): A slot machine that pays off liberally and gives the house only a small advantage over the player.

Low Pair (Video Poker): A pair of 10s or cards of a lower rank, such as 9s, which alone don't constitute a winning hand.

Manque (Roulette): The French term for low.

Markers: Promissory notes or IOUs signed by players who have credit in casinos.

Martingale System: A progressive betting method in which the player doubles his bet after a previous loss.

Mechanic, Slots Mechanic (Slots): The house employee who sets the machines for their payoffs and repairs broken slot machines.

Mills Machines (Slots): The first machines to use fruit symbols and to have a jackpot.

Mini-Baccarat: The game of baccarat played on an ordinary gambling table, with one dealer to service the game.

Mini-Junkets: A junket with different costs depending on how much the player is willing to put up as front money.

Miss, Miss Out: See *Seven-Out*

Money Wheel: Another term for the big six wheel.

Muckers: See *Hand Muckers*

Multiple-Deck Game (Blackjack): The use of two or more decks in the game.

Natural: 1) *Blackjack*—the ace and a ten-value card dealt as an original hand. 2) *Craps*—a 7 or 11 thrown on the come-out roll. 3) *Baccarat*—an 8 or 9 dealt on the first two cards.

Nickel Chips, Nickels: The insider's term for $5 chips.

Noir (Roulette): French for black.

Numbers (Craps): The 4, 5, 6, 8, 9, and 10 rolled during the course of a shoot.

Nut: The overhead costs of running a casino.

Odds Bet: See *Free Odds*

Off (Craps): An oral call that certain of the player's bets will not be working on the next roll of the dice. Also, a term signifying that certain bets on the layout will not be working on a come-out roll, such as place bets and odds bets on come numbers.

On Base (Craps): The term for the standing dealer who is not on the stick.

One-Armed Bandits (Slots): The popular term for slot machines.

One-Roll Bet (Craps): Wagers whose outcome is determined by the next roll of the dice.

On the Stick (Craps): The term indicating that a dealer is now the stickman.

Original Ticket (Keno): The blank filled out by the player and presented to the keno writer, which is the basis for any possible keno payouts.

Outside Numbers (Craps): The place numbers 4, 5, 9, and 10.

Outside Wager (Roulette): A bet on any event at the table other than the numbers 0, 00, 1–36.

Over and Under Seven: See *Under and Over Seven*

Paint: The term for the face cards—jack, queen, and king.

Pair (Roulette): The French term for even.

Pass (Craps): A winning decision for the dice.

Passe (Roulette): The French term for high.

Pass Line (Craps): The area on the layout where a pass-line bet is made.

Pass-Line Bet (Craps): A wager that the dice will pass, or win.

Past Posting: The illegal increase of the original wager by a cheat after he either has seen the result or has seen his cards in a gambling game.

Payoff, Payout: The payment of a winning bet by the casino to the player.

P.C.: The winning percentage a casino has on a particular game or table, based on the profits, divided by the total money bet.

Pit: The area inside a group or cluster of gambling tables.

Pit Boss: The casino executive in charge of a particular pit.

Place Numbers, Place Bets (Craps): A wager on either or all of the following numbers—4, 5, 6, 8, 9, and 10, or any combination of these numbers. The player bets that the numbers wagered on will be repeated before a 7 shows on the dice, other than on the come-out roll.

Player: The term for a gambler or bettor.

Player Hand (Baccarat): The hand opposing the bank hand, which is dealt to first and acts first.

Premiere (Roulette): French for first.

Premium Players: The casino's designation of big bettors, or players with high credit lines.

Press, Press a Bet: To increase a wager after a previous win, usually by doubling the previous bet.

Progressive Machines (Video Poker): Machines tied to a single payoff that increases each time a new coin is inserted and a royal flush is not made. It pays off only on royal flushes.

Progressive Slots (Slots): Slots that increase the potential jackpot each time a new coin is inserted for play.

Proposition Bets (Craps): Wagers that can be made on the center of the layout, such as any seven and hardways.

Punch-Outs (Keno): A ticket, also known as a draw ticket, that has the called numbers for the previous game punched out on a keno blank, so that the keno writer can easily determine if a presented ticket has enough catches for a payoff.

Push: A tie between the player and casino where no money is won or lost.

Qualified Players: The casino's designation of players who bet enough to be invited on junkets.

Quarter Chips, Quarters: The insider's term for $25 casino chips.

Racehorse Keno (Keno): The name by which keno was called prior to 1951, when each number also had the name of a racehorse attached to it.

Rails (Craps): The grooved area at the craps table where players keep their chips when not betting them.

Rail Thief (Craps): A cheat who steals chips from the players' rails.

Rate Card (Keno): The booklet issued by casinos containing the costs and payoffs on tickets having from one to fifteen spots.

Red-Black Bet (Roulette): An outside straight wager on whether the next spin will be a red or black number, paid off at even money.

Reel (Slots): A vertical and continuous holder of the symbols on a slot machine.

Reshuffle (Blackjack): The remixing of the cards by the dealer, sometimes done arbitrarily to harass a player.

Right Bettor (Craps): A player betting with the dice, betting that they'll pass.

Rim Credit: Credit given at the gaming tables.

Roll (Craps): 1) A single throw of the dice. 2) A complete series of rolls until the shooter sevens out.

Rouge (Roulette): French for red.

Roulette: The name of the game involving a wheel, layout and a ball which spins along the rim of the wheel, finally landing in a number, which is the winner for that spin.

Royal Flush (Video Poker): A hand consisting of an A K Q J 10 of the same suit, the best in poker.

Rule Card (Baccarat): The card that shows the printed rules of play for the game.

Runner (Keno): See *Keno Runner*

Rush: The gambler's term for a series of wins, one after the other, forming a winning streak.

Sabot (Chemin de Fer): The French term for the shoe.

Scam: A slang term for a cheating scheme.

Scared Money: Inadequate money used for gambling purposes.

Seven-Out (Craps): The roll of a 7 after a point has been established, ending the shooter's roll with a loss.

Shift Boss: A casino executive who is in charge of the entire casino during one whole shift.

Shifts: The casino personnel's work periods, usually divided into three shifts—day, swing, and graveyard, each of eight hours' duration.

Shill: A house employee who sits at a gaming table to stimulate action and plays with the casino's money, making meaningless bets to create the semblance of action. Also called a starter.

Shimmy: The American slang expression for chemin de fer.

Shoe: A device that holds several decks of cards and enables the dealer to slide out cards easily one at a time.

Shoot (Craps): A complete series of rolls until the thrower of the dice sevens out.

Shooter (Craps): The person throwing the dice at a craps table.

Shuffle Up (Blackjack): See *Reshuffle*

Shylock: A person, usually connected with the underworld, who lends money at exorbitant and illegal rates.

Side Game: A term for games such as big six, chuck-a-luck, and under and over seven, which are rarely played or not available in all casinos.

Single-Deck Game (Blackjack): A game in which only one deck is used.

Single-Session Bankroll: The amount of money a player brings to a gaming table for one session of play.

Sixain (Roulette): The French term for a six numbers bet.

Six Numbers Bet (Roulette): An inside combination bet on six numbers at one time.

Slots, Slot Machines: Metal gambling devices that players activate by inserting one or several coins and pulling the handle. The machines automatically collect and pay off bets.

Snapper (Blackjack): The slang term for a blackjack.

Soft Hand, Soft Total (Blackjack): A hand in which the ace is valued at 11 in figuring the total of the hand. An ace, 7 is a soft 18.

Special Chips: Casino chips not of standard colors, which cannot be redeemed by the player, but must be played out.

Specials, Special Tickets (Keno): Nonstandard keno tickets with special prices and payoffs.

Split Bet (Roulette): An inside combination bet on two numbers at the same time.

Splitting Pairs (Blackjack): The player's option to separate cards of equal rank, such as pairs, and play each hand separately. For splitting purposes 10-value cards are considered pairs.

Split Ticket (Keno): A ticket with which a player can play two or more groups of numbers separately.

Spot (Keno): The term to denote the amount of numbers selected by the player for each individual play or payoff—for example, a four-spot.

Stand Pat (Blackjack): The player's decision not to hit his hand.

Starter: See *Shill*

Stickman (Craps): The dealer who calls the game and handles the stick during the game.

Stiff, Stiff Hand (Blackjack): A hand containing a hard total of 12 or more points, in danger of busting if hit.

Straight (Video Poker): Five consecutive cards, but not of the same suit. For purposes of a straight, the ace can be the lowest or highest card of a straight sequence, such as 5 4 3 2 A or A K Q J 10.

Straight Flush (Video Poker): Five cards in sequence and of the same suit.

Straight Slots (Slots): Machines that pay out in fixed amounts and whose jackpots never vary.

Straight Ticket (Keno): The simplest and most common ticket, in which a player selects from one to fifteen spots or numbers.

Straight Up Bet (Roulette): A wager on a single number, paid off at 35–1.

Strip: See *Las Vegas Strip*

Symbols: Markings on various games, such as slots and big six wheels.

Systems: Progressive betting methods used in an attempt to overcome the house advantage. The most common feature increased bets after each loss.

Table Hopping: Moving from table to table within a casino, which some players do in an attempt to change their luck.

Taken Down (Craps): A bet that is removed and returned to the player, either at his request or as a result of the rules of the game.

Take the Odds (Craps): An odds bet made by a right bettor which, if won, will be paid off at better than even money.

Tapped Out: A slang term for losing an entire bankroll when gambling.

Ten-Value Card (Blackjack): The 10, jack, queen, and king, all valued at ten points.

Third Baseman (Blackjack): The player sitting in the last seat at the blackjack table; the player acting last.

Three Flush (Video Poker): A hand consisting of three cards, all of the same suit, together with two odd cards.

Three of a Kind (Video Poker): A hand that consists of three cards of the same rank or value, such as 8 8 8.

Tight Machine (Slots): A slots that gives the casino a large win percentage by paying out relatively few coins to the players.

Tip: A gratuity given to a casino employee.

Toke: The casino personnel's term for a tip.

Tom: The Las Vegas dealers' term for a poor tipper.

Tough Player: The casino's designation of an astute player who can really hurt a casino with his smart play.

Transversale (Roulette): The French term for a trio bet.

Trio Bet (Roulette): An inside combination bet on three numbers at one time.

Twenty-One: Another name for the game of blackjack.

Two Pair (Video Poker): A hand consisting of two separate pairs, such as 9 9 4 4.

Under and Over Seven: A casino side game played with two dice, rarely seen in any legitimate casino.

Unfavorable Deck (Blackjack): A deck whose remaining composition favors the dealer.

Upcard (Blackjack): One of the dealer's two original cards, dealt face up.

Vigorish, Vig: A gambler's term for the house edge on any bet or game.

Wager: Another term for a bet.

Way (Keno): An individual group of numbers played as a separate entity by the player.

Way Ticket (Keno): A ticket consisting of at least three equal groups of numbers, combining in various ways.

Wise Guy: The slang term for a member of the mob, mafia, or syndicate.

Working (Craps): A designation that bets are on and payoffs will be made or losing bets collected as a result of the next roll of the dice.

Writer (Keno): See *Keno Writer*

Wrong Bettor (Craps): A player who bets against the dice; one who bets that the dice won't pass.

Zero (Roulette): This number, together with the double zero, determines the house advantage in roulette.

Index

461